By the Same Author

Duff Cooper: the Authorized Biography
Lord Lloyd and the Decline of the British Empire
Chamberlain and the Lost Peace
Churchill: the End of Glory
Churchill's Grand Alliance
A History of Conservative Politics 1900–1996
Splendid Isolation? Britain and the Balance of Power 1874–1914

The Princess and the Politicians

Sex, Intrigue and Diplomacy, 1812–40

JOHN CHARMLEY

VIKING

an imprint of

PENGUIN BOOKS

Published by the Penguin Group
Penguin Books Ltd, 80 Strand, London WC2R ORL, England
Penguin Group (USA) Inc., 375 Hudson Street, New York, New York 10014, USA
Penguin Group (Canada), 10 Alcorn Avenue, Toronto, Ontario, Canada M4V 3B2
(a division of Pearson Penguin Canada Inc.)
Penguin Ireland, 25 St Stephen's Green, Dublin 2, Ireland
(a division of Penguin Books Ltd)
Penguin Group (Australia), 250 Camberwell Road, Camberwell, Victoria 3124, Australia
(a division of Pearson Australia Group Pty Ltd)
Penguin Books India Pvt Ltd, 11 Community Centre, Panchsheel Park, New Delhi – 110 017, India
Penguin Group (NZ), cnr Airborne and Rosedale Roads, Albany, Auckland 1310, New Zealand
(a division of Pearson New Zealand Ltd)
Penguin Books (South Africa) (Pty) Ltd, 24 Sturdee Avenue, Rosebank 2196, South Africa

Penguin Books Ltd, Registered Offices: 80 Strand, London WC2R ORL, England

www.penguin.com

First published 2005

1

Copyright © John Charmley, 2005

The moral right of the author has been asserted

Set in 12/14.75 pt Monotype Bembo
Typeset by Rowland Phototypesetting Ltd, Bury St Edmunds, Suffolk
Printed in Great Britain by Clays Ltd, St Ives plc

A CIP catalogue record for this book is available from the British Library

ISBN 0–670–88964–4

To Rachael
as I said I would

Contents

List of Illustrations

Acknowledgements

I am grateful to the copyright holders of the various collections of papers listed in the Bibliography for permission to publish extracts; if I have inadvertently failed to thank any copyright holder, I would be happy to do so if notified.

I am extremely grateful to the National Archives and the British Library, and owe a particular debt to Dr C. Woolgar of the Hartley Library whose electronic version of the Wellington Papers saved hours of my time. I would like to thank Dr Geoff Hicks for his work on my behalf on the Palmerston Papers, and also my old friend Michael John for help on a memorable trip to the British Library. Princess Lieven's handwriting is execrable, and my admiration for those who have edited and translated various collections of her letters is unbounded.

I would like to thank the British Academy for a small research grant, and my own university for assistance with research costs.

I am grateful to my publisher, Kate Barker, of Viking, for her help – and her patience, when other events slowed down the completion of this book. As ever, my agent, Felicity Bryan, was there when I needed her.

On a more personal level, I should like to thank my colleagues and close friends, Professor Carole Rawcliffe and Professor Christopher Harper-Bill, for their unstinting support when I needed it most.

The most personal thanks are due to my family: my sons, Gervase, Gerard and Kit, for tolerating yet another period of abstraction from their father; my step-daughters, Isla and Siobhan, who, with much less experience of it, adapted wonderfully; and last, but certainly never least, my greatest debt is to my wife, Rachael, without whom this would never have been completed.

It is fitting that this book should be, like its author, dedicated to her.

John Charmley
Harleston, 2005

Preface

'I should very much like to come back in sixty years' time to read our letters and to see what posterity thinks of these two intelligent people,' Dorothea Lieven wrote to her lover, Prince Metternich, in March 1822. She was conscious of her role in history, and had she been able to satisfy the curiosity she expressed to Metternich, she would have been a little disappointed, one suspects. She was very much a creature of the world of high diplomacy: her life was spent in the salons of St Petersburg, London and Paris; her chosen companions were those of her own class; her favourite men were ones who exercised power, and for these, and these alone, would she relax the demands of caste. The British Foreign Secretary, George Canning, was one of those exceptions, but not even his brilliance and eloquence could make her quite forget that 'he is a plebeian and has no manners'. She would have agreed with that other outsider in British politics, Disraeli, that 'la haute politique is refreshing: worth living for'. She shared his view that: 'Generally speaking there is no gambling like politics – but when you have to deal only with Emperors and High Chancellors and Empires are [sic] on the main, the excitement, I suppose, a little increases.' Unfortunately for her, the period in which historians shared this view of la haute politique was one in which they also took a dim view of the role of women in politics.

The two classic accounts of British foreign policy under Castlereagh and Canning published between the wars by Sir Charles Webster and Harold Temperley are full of references to Princess Lieven, but both men decline to take her very seriously. The idea that a foreign woman, and one of loose morals at that, could have had an influence upon the foreign policy of Britain was clearly absurd. In what are no doubt more enlightened times, a different view of the importance of women has prevailed, thanks to the work of feminist historians. But these have been, in their own way, as exclusive as Princess Lieven herself; few of them have concerned themselves with the aristocracy, and even fewer with high politics and diplomacy. The result of this concatenation of circumstances is that two centuries after she was born, and a century and a half after she died, Princess Lieven remains, for the most part, a name on the edges of British history.

This is despite the existence of three good biographies of her and a host of edited editions of various portions of her correspondence. Her biographers, H. Montgomery Hyde, Priscilla Zamoyska and Madeline Bingham, bring different strengths to their task, and they have illuminated her life, but they all treat her as an exotic foreigner, and none of them places her in the context she loved most – British high politics and diplomacy. Dorothea Lieven was a copious letter writer, and there is evidence in her papers that in later life she copied out large portions of her more intimate correspondence for possible publication. She knew that she had been important and had seen, at first hand, things that historians would be interested in. She was also conscious of being judged. The Victorian age in which she died was not the Regency period in which she had flourished; its manners and mores were different. The sexual licence of the Regency era had given way to the public prudery of Victorian England, and Dorothea was careful to excise from her letters to Metternich anything that would have revealed the fact that they had been lovers. Fortunately, she was not a good censor, and Metternich was not as expert a master of the tradecraft of spying as he thought. The French *Cabinet Noir*, the secret service of the Bourbons, intercepted and copied some of Metternich's letters to Dorothea, and although he eventually discovered this, there remained several years' worth of them in the French archives; they leave no doubt as to the relationship between him and Dorothea Lieven. There will be those latter-day spiritual descendants of the Victorians who might cavil here: are such subjects not a little below the level of the historian? There is an obvious answer to such a query, and the reader hoping for a salacious rendering of the secrets of the bedroom is best advised to go elsewhere; the assumption that the bedroom holds many secrets is, itself, a prurient one.

There are water stains on some of the volumes of the Lieven Papers, and parts of them have been scorched or damaged in some other way; like the Lieven family itself, they were spirited out of Courland just in front of that great agent of plebeian revenge and philistinism, the Russian Revolution. They contain much of value to the historian, and historians of imperial Russian foreign policy could do worse than spend a great deal of time looking at Dorothea's correspondence with the Russian foreign minister, Nesselrode. Her own letters to her husband of thirty-eight years, Prince Christopher Lieven, give an unparalleled insight into an intimate relationship, but neither they, nor anything else in the archive, throw much direct light on some of the themes a twenty-first-century public might like to know more about. Indeed, there is a bigger problem with the paper trail out of which historians construct their edifices.

This book takes Dorothea Lieven's claim to be what Wellington called a 'female politician' seriously. It does not dismiss her as a gossipy woman who exaggerated her own importance; if Metternich, Castlereagh, Canning, Lord Grey and Palmerston all treated her as one of their number, there is no reason for not following their example. Indeed, in so doing, a whole new aspect of nineteenth-century British politics opens up. Perhaps because our view of that topic was formed by historians writing about men, we have been left with the impression that it was a male world; this tendency has, perhaps, been reinforced by modern prejudice that the only form of political influence is through the exercise of the franchise. Women did not have the vote in national elections before 1918, nor could they stand for parliament; but as any reader of the novels of Trollope or Disraeli knows, an inability to stand for office did not equate to a lack of political influence. In a pioneering study, the historian K. D. Reynolds has written about the concept of the 'incorporated wife', to describe the way in which aristocratic women worked, almost as part of a corporate political entity, with their husbands. This is a useful concept, but at least in the rather earlier period being studied in this book, it does not go far enough.

When Dorothea told Metternich that 'people have no idea to what an extent women influence the elections in England', she touched on the surface of a more important topic. Trollope was not a political insider in the way Disraeli became, but both men had enough experience of the political world to recognize that it could hardly function without aristocratic women. Historians have concentrated upon the male spaces in which politics operated: the hustings, the floor of the Commons, the big platform speeches. This is only natural, since these spaces have left us with written traces of what occurred in them. What we lack is an appreciation of what might be called the female spaces. Yet we know that it was in the salon, at the dinner table, and over the tea cups, that reputations were blasted, damned or boosted; we know that invitations to particular salons or other gatherings were, in themselves, an index of standing in the political world, and were almost a form of political currency. Who sat next to whom, and what was said, or unsaid, mattered as much 200 years ago as it does today. The difficulty is that these 'female spaces' leave little written record. Where it can be picked up here, in Dorothea's letters or the journal of Wellington's confidante, Mrs Arbuthnot, its traces have been incorporated into what follows; but one is left with the consciousness of how much there was that cannot be recovered because it has left so little evidence.

The role of the *grande dame*, of the Lady Glencora Palliser, in British politics awaits its historian. Dorothea Lieven does not quite fit into that category. She was, after all, an outsider. However cosmopolitan the European aristocracy, she was still a foreigner in England, and her understanding of the country remained that of a very well-informed observer. But she could not have operated at all if she had been a unique 'sport'. It takes a modern consciousness, unattuned to the nuances of the past, to believe, by inference, that a male backbench MP for an obscure constituency had more political influence than a woman such as Lady Cowper, who was the sister of one Prime Minister and, eventually, the wife of another. Novelists have understood this in a way historians have not quite grasped. Dorothea's network of correspondents included many women who were as interested in politics as she was herself. They felt the adventure of it, and if they personalized it, so too did their men. It would be interesting to see what British political history in the nineteenth century looked like with the aristocratic women reincorporated.

The editor of her letters to Metternich has described Dorothea Lieven as 'a useful woman, an attractive woman, an unscrupulous woman'; she was all of these things. She loved power – 'an un-amiable trait', according to the same writer, who, as a literary man, assumed too easily that his own prejudices were universal; the politician who lacks that trait may have existed, but has left little trace. Dorothea played the political game with the same gusto as the men who surrounded her; as a woman her object had to be different. She could not aspire to high office in her own right; but that did not mean she could not aspire to its rewards – material and psychological. Her methods were, of necessity, different from those of the men with whom she played the great game. Women are treated differently from men, by men. Although, as the diarist Charles Greville so ungallantly put it, 'without any pretensions to beauty', Dorothea had 'so fine an air and manner, and a counten-ance so pretty and full of intelligence, as to be on the whole a very striking and attractive person, quite enough so to have lovers'; she used what nature had given her as her weapons in the political arena. Pressing as the question is no doubt to some readers, as to whether she really was the 'lover' of so many British politicians, the answer is generally that we cannot know – at least in the physical sense. That she attracted men of power is clear, and that they were attractive to her is equally the case. But one only has to compare her career, or that of Lady Cowper, with that of someone such as the Regent's mistress, Lady Conyngham, to see the differ-ence between Dorothea and a courtesan: the one was interested in material rewards; the other in playing the political game. In his obituary notice, Greville wrote that 'It has been the fashion here, and the habit of the vulgar and ignorant press, to stigmatise Madame de Lieven as a mischievous intriguer, who was constantly occupied in schemes and designs hostile to the interests of our country. I firmly believe such charges to be unfounded.' As the reader of what follows will see, even to the end, Dorothea retained the knack of persuading men that black was white.

1. 'England is not the country of emotions'

On 14 December 1812 the straggling remnants of Napoleon's *Grande Armée* crossed the ice-bound Berezina river into Prussia. Six months earlier, 400,000 strong, it had invaded Russia; now, fewer than 40,000 had returned. It was little wonder that on his birthday, 24 December, the Russian Tsar, Alexander I, should have declared to his generals: 'You have saved not only Russia, you have saved Europe.' His military advisers would have been happy to stop the war once Napoleon had been driven from Holy Mother Russia, but Alexander's vision would not be so constrained. Ever since the reign of Peter the Great a century before, the Romanovs had dreamed of making their backward country a great European power; by chasing the conqueror of Europe to Paris and defeating him, Alexander would establish beyond any doubt that Russia was the greatest power in the world. Alexander knew that Russia would need some help in this enterprise, and it was to that end that he had despatched one of his most loyal courtiers to England as ambassador. When Count Christopher Lieven arrived in London in December 1812, it was British money that he was after. Along with his diplomatic instructions, he brought with him his young wife, Dorothea; for the next quarter of a century he was to be ambassador to Britain, but it would be her presence that would leave a lasting impression on the political world.

Count Lieven, as most of those who advised the Tsar on foreign policy, was not an ethnic Russian. His family, like his wife's, hailed from the Baltic provinces that had been incorporated into the Tsarist Empire by Peter the Great. The Baltic Barons, as their detractors called them, were natural collaborators for any Russian ruler bent on becoming a force in European politics. Cosmopolitan in outlook, steeped in western culture, educated on the German model and fluent in French, the nobility of Latvia, Livonia and Estonia were ideal instruments of diplomacy for tsars, and tsarinas, who wished to dispel the common western stereotype of the Russians as quasi-Asiatic barbarians with manners to match. Some of the native Russian aristocracy grumbled about the way in which their empire's foreign policy was in the hands of 'westerners', but as Alexander I recognized: 'unless I use the help of foreigners who are known and whose talents are proved, the number of capable men, already so small, would diminish further.' The man who acted as foreign minister for most of the period between 1812 and the 1850s, Count Karl von Nesselrode, was a Rhinelander, born in Lisbon and baptized an Anglican. Count Ioannis Capodistrias, who worked with Nesselrode until the early 1820s, was a Corfiote who had sought refuge in Russia. The Russian ambassador in Paris for most of this period, Pozzo di Borgo, was a Corsican opponent of Napoleon who had also found a berth serving his enemy's enemy. By such standards, the Lievens were almost Russian; at least they had both been born as subjects of the Tsar, although their roots were firmly established in the Baltic – Livonia to be exact.

The Lievens had served the Russian crown since the early eighteenth century, usually as soldiers or diplomats, but their opportunity to rise to the top came not via military prowess, but through the personality and influence of the matriarch of the family, Countess Charlotte (Karolovna) Lieven. Recently widowed and living in straitened circumstances in Riga, Charlotte Lieven had been recommended to Catherine the Great as a possible governess for her grandchildren. A forthright and independent-minded woman, she did not mince words when she was interviewed, stating firmly that she feared that the task might be complicated by the dissolute lifestyle of the Empress. Catherine, who had been listening, hidden behind a screen, emerged and told her: 'You will see nothing of that.' The two strong-minded women got on well together. Charlotte Lieven spent forty-five years at court, and was one of the few of Catherine's favourites who prospered under Paul I. But, as one might expect, it was when her charges, first Alexander and then Nicholas, came to the throne that her fortunes flourished. At his coronation, Nicholas I made her an hereditary princess.

'*Corpulente et majestueuse*', Charlotte Lieven was a figure of some austerity, with a reputation, as her upbraiding of Catherine the Great suggests, as a pious moralist. She looked after the fortunes of her family, not least her second son, Christopher Andreevich, who entered the army at the age of nineteen and rose to become Paul I's aide-de-camp and Minister of War by the age of twenty-seven. Seeking a suitable bride for him, the Countess settled upon one of the wards of the Empress, another offspring of the Baltic baronage – the fifteen-year-old Dorothea von Benckendorff.

Dorothea was born on 17 December 1785 in Riga, where her father, General Christopher von Benckendorff, was military governor. General Christopher von Benckendorff had risen to prominence as a favourite of Catherine the Great; indeed, rumour had it that he had been one of her lovers – but since rumour said as much of any handsome young nobleman, this may mean little, and here again, it seems to have been the female connection that brought the proximity to power that meant wealth in imperial Russia. When Catherine sought a bride for her heir, Paul, she looked to the small German courts from which she herself had sprung, and selected Princess Sophia Dorothea of Wurttemberg, who adopted the Orthodox faith, and with it the baptismal names of Marie Feodorovna. The slim young German bride brought a number of gentlewomen with her as attendants; and it was one of these, Charlotte Schilling, whom Baron Benckendorff took as his wife. Bride and groom were Lutherans and Germans who spoke French as their first language, and they profited from their closeness to the sources of all power in Russia. Their first son, Alexander, would follow his father into the military before becoming an aide to Paul's son and successor, Alexander I; under his successor, Nicholas, Alexander would become chief of the Russian secret police and one of the most powerful men in Russia. The next three children all bore names dear to their godmother, Marie Feodorovna: Marie, for herself, Constantine, for her second son and Dorothea, for her own maiden name. But in imperial Russia, royal favour, while the certain path to fortune, was always capricious.

Marie Feodorovna's husband, Paul, was haunted by the fate of his putative father, Peter III, who had been deposed by his mother, Catherine, and later murdered. By rights he knew he should be Tsar, but there was no gainsaying the great Catherine, so he worked off his ill-temper on those around him; in particular, he was a martinet on the parade ground. Dorothea's early life was dominated by the insecurity engendered by the mood swings of the Tsarevich. Her mother, who was known as Lilli to her friends, lost her place at court through her loyalty to her mistress, the Grand Duchess Marie Feodorovna. Marie complained to Catherine about her husband's infidelity, and Lilli Benckendorff took her side against Paul's coarse and ugly mistress, Mme Nedilov. Catherine, it is said, led Marie to a mirror and commented: 'Look at yourself and think of the little monster's face!' But after Catherine's death in 1796, when the 'little monster' became Tsar, Lilli Benckendorff's presence at court was no longer required.

The rigours of fortress life at Riga did not suit her, and already exhausted by the scenes at court that had led to her dismissal, she soon sickened and died, leaving her infant children to the care of their godmother. It was an early lesson in the capriciousness of Russian politics. Paul's wrath did not extend to the children, and he paid for Alexander and Constantine to be educated, the former for the army, the latter for the diplomatic service. Marie and Dorothea were left under the tutelage of Marie, who deposited money for them in the Foundlings' Bank so that they would have dowries when they married; she lamented the loss of Charlotte Benckendorff and did her best for her children. The girls received a good education at the former convent at Smolny, which Catherine had had turned into an educational institute for girls; there they were taught French, Italian and German, to play the piano and to dance. Dorothea was only eleven when she entered the Smolny, but already her mind was fired with thoughts of romance.

Charlotte von Benckendorff had encouraged the suit paid to

Dorothea by Count Elmpt, a rich young nobleman who had fallen in love with her, but the Empress, who had other plans for her ward, forbade the match and sent the young girl back to the Smolny. On the excuse that he had quarrelled with the Grand Duke Constantine, Paul's second son, and a man who combined all the unpleasant qualities of his father with some unique to himself, Elmpt was banished from St Petersburg. In an age when the conventions of romantic love as accepted by society clashed with dynastic interests, Dorothea's position was not unusual, but her reaction to her situation reveals the extent to which the girl was mother to the woman. Revelling in the language of romance, Dorothea later recalled that she 'loved him [Elmpt] with all my heart, I thought of nothing else'. So, at the age of eleven, she promptly embarked upon a secret correspondence with her would-be lover. This, as in all the best romances, was made possible by the tender heart of one of her governesses, who was happy to act as go-between. However, in keeping with the traditions of such novels, the secret was discovered when the Empress paid a sudden visit to her protégée at the Smolny: the governess was banished and Dorothea disciplined. As she later commented: 'in that heroic age of Russian history the love affairs of little girls were treated with military strictness.' Dorothea had learned, at a very early age, that wherever women might love, they had to marry where they were told.

Aged fifteen, Dorothea von Benckendorff finished her formal education and came to the Winter Palace to live with her sister, Marie, who was a lady-in-waiting to the Empress. It was now necessary for Marie Feodorovna to find a husband for her protégée. Dorothea was not considered a great beauty, although this never hindered her romantic career. Even at fifteen she was tall, but despite a little adolescent puppy fat, she was on the thin side and lacked anything much in the way of a bust – a serious disadvantage in an age of low-cut gowns. Her best features were her long, swan-like neck and a 'head of dark chestnut curls'. From adolescence onwards, she relied upon her wit and her skill as a conversationalist to fascinate men – and these seldom failed her. However,

Mlle von Benckendorff's proximity to the royal family guaranteed that, whatever she looked like, there would be no shortage of suitors.

At one stage, after the Elmpt affair, the Empress proposed that she should marry Count Aleksei Arakcheev, a provincial nobleman who was the model of the brutal and ruthless military martinet. A 'man from the furthest reaches of the lesser gentry and a compulsive overachiever', Arakcheev came to Paul 'with his early promising career virtually in ruins and with the ugly stench of scandal clinging to him'. Dorothea avoided marriage to this ogre by that narrowest of margins – the Tsar's whim. Arakcheev fell from favour for a while, and was still in internal exile in 1801 when Paul was murdered. Compared with Arakcheev, Madame de Lieven's son was a safer and kinder catch; however, lively young women rarely have their blood stirred by either of these qualities.

Dorothea was engaged to Count Lieven while she was still at the Smolny, but as the fiancée of such a distinguished figure she was allowed to appear at court. She enjoyed the heady atmosphere and the attentions paid to her by handsome young officers back from the war; a natural flirt, she found it easy to attract men, and her conversation and vivacity soon made her the centre of attention on social occasions. All of this aroused the jealousy of Count Lieven. One evening, stung by the way she was ignoring him in favour of other men, he dragged Dorothea away from them to sit with his mother and her friends. He explained to her that he did not require a society wife. She retorted that she 'could never give up society, it is what I do well and what I enjoy'. Packed off back to the Smolny (yet again), Dorothea unburdened herself of some unkind comments about her beau, which made their way back to him.

Count Lieven wrote to her in anger and sorrow, reproaching her for her 'indelicate conduct towards me'. He accused her of being 'carried away' by the 'false brilliance' of the court. From the moment she had appeared there 'all my happiness has changed into black grief . . . you forgot, and even humiliated a man who was utterly devoted to you . . . It does not surprise me that you found in this society several men you preferred to me, and who suit you better than I do. I have a great many faults, and I should not suit a woman devoted to society; my position and character incline me to a quiet life, and as you have told me you could never renounce a society life, I see that our marriage would only cause unhappiness . . . I therefore promise to rid you of me without doing you the slightest wrong.' With a ponderous pomposity that would grow worse with age, Lieven told her that 'the bad impression that you made on serious people will be only too good a lesson for you. Your wild behaviour will give you cause to repent one day.' He enclosed a note which one of her schoolfellows had sent him as proof that he had reason for his anger. It read: 'Mlle B. has said openly that she no longer loves you, that she will never stop flirting, that she is miserable when there is no one to flirt with, and that she is only marrying you to get away from the convent.'

There was much truth in what the writer of the poison–pen letter wrote. Dorothea had taken to the social life of St Petersburg with the ease and avidity of a woman who had found her natural environment, and there was no doubt that, however grand her future husband's prospects might be, he inspired no passion. However, Count Lieven was Dorothea's passport to the world she craved, and she was shrewd enough to realize that her chances of making a better match would be badly damaged if he broke off their engagement. Illness is often the refuge of those without power, and throughout her life Dorothea would seek it whenever the adverse consequences of her behaviour threatened to over-whelm her. 'I cannot leave my room as my sufferings are still acute,' she told the Count. 'I shall have no peace of mind till I have heard from your own mouth that you pardon me and that you still love me.' A prolonged act of contrition, followed by the promise to 'follow your advice and submit to everything that you exact from me', produced the desired effect of a reconciliation. Count Lieven married Dorothea von Benckendorff on 24 February 1800. As she left the convent for the last time, clad in her wedding finery and wearing diamonds given to her by the Tsar himself, Dorothea was ecstatic: 'I should have liked to get married every day,' she later recalled, 'and I thought about everything, except I was taking a husband.'

Gracious though Paul I had been on her wedding day, Dorothea soon discovered that his eccentricities threatened her future. Paul wanted a nobility of service, and he took away many of the privileges that his mother had extended to the aristocracy. He restored compulsory service and withdrew the rights of personal petition and freedom from corporal punishment that the nobility had previously enjoyed. He imposed severe penalties, including the loss of estates, for any violations of his will. All of this made the nobility chafe uneasily under his rule, and it was only natural that before long, plots were hatched to assassinate him. The focal point of Paul's obsessions and power were his morning parades, where he received reports and announced favours and punishments. In 1800 he issued a law prescribing the precise rules for the command and movement of troops on such parades; those who failed to abide by those rules could expect to suffer. Count Lieven himself fell foul of the Tsar by forgetting to turn up for one of the parades, and an aide was sent from him calling Lieven an 'imbecile'. It was thought wise by the Lievens for Christopher to go down with an illness that prevented his arrival at court in the near future. They were saved from the prospect of severe punishment only by the fact that Paul had alienated so many of his nobility that his days were numbered.

Paul's militarization of government was one sign of a mania for control that expressed itself in many ways, down to trying to ban the waltz and to prescribe and proscribe certain styles of dress, and even particular colours; he issued five times as many orders a month as had Peter the Great, and twice the number of his mother's reign. The overt Prussianization of the army, his reliance on low(ish)-born favourites, all helped mark Paul out as another Tsar who, like Peter III, was in thrall to foreign ways. Dorothea recorded later that by the end of 1800 the Tsar had become 'the object of universal terror and hatred throughout his Empire'. With the fate of his father before his eyes, Paul knew well enough that Russia was an autocracy tempered by assassination, and by 1800 he had begun to suspect that even those closest to him were plotting against him. Count Pahlen, who had temporarily succeeded Lieven at the War Ministry, confided to him that the Emperor was planning to shut his wife up in a convent and his two eldest sons in a fortress. What Pahlen did not tell Lieven was that he was involved in a plot to avert this calamity by disposing of Paul himself. On 11 March 1801 Paul peremptorily removed Lieven from office, declaring that he had been indisposed for too long and that 'business cannot depend on your intestines'. Lieven went to bed 'disturbed in mind', knowing that he had lost Paul's favour and fearing for the consequences. However, the Tsar had an even worse evening – he was murdered in his bedroom.

The first intimation the Lievens had of what had happened came in the early hours of the morning when a messenger arrived from the Tsar. The Lievens, who had feared arrest – or worse – were puzzled to read that Christopher should attend the Tsar at the Winter Palace, when everyone knew that Paul lived at the new Michael Palace. It says much about the atmosphere in St Petersburg that upon being told that the Emperor was the 'Grand Duke Alexander', the Lievens supposed that Paul was putting them to some strange test of loyalty. Dorothea watched from the window of their apartments, having nothing to report to her anxious husband, until, at length, a single carriage drew up and the figure of one of Alexander's aides stepped out of it; at that Christopher decided to go to the Winter Palace. Lieven had been fortunate. Neither Marie Feodorovna nor Alexander showed any thanks to the assassins, who found themselves dismissed from their offices. But as Lieven had not been implicated or in any way involved in the plot, he was reinstated and, thanks to his mother, he sat high in the favour of the new Tsar, Alexander I.

As with all of her generation, Dorothea's early life was dominated by the struggle with Napoleon. She watched her father, her brothers and her husband go off to the wars, while she waited in St Petersburg in the feverish atmosphere portrayed by Tolstoy in his *War and Peace*. It was the one period when she lived the life of an ordinary Russian courtier. She produced four children: the first, a daughter, died in infancy, but three boys born in 1805, 1806 and 1807 attested to the ardour with which the returning Count met his young wife. Naturally, the Empress Marie was godmother to all the boys, who were dutifully named Paul, Alexander and Constantine. The rumours of Dorothea's gallantries attested to the attractions she possessed to others. One of her earliest lovers was Prince Peter Dolgoruky. Dolgoruky was a character straight out of Pushkin, a fiery young aristocrat, whose temper and temperament led him into duels, disgrace and an early death. Metternich, the Austrian Chancellor, who was the great passion of Dorothea's life, had known and not much liked the Prince. He told her that he had thought his besetting sin was presumption, but upon learning that Dorothea had loved him, he added, gallantly, that he understood why.

Another of her lovers was a man of more consequence, the Grand Duke Constantine, heir-presumptive to the imperial crown. Constantine, so named by his grandmother because she wanted him to sit on the throne of a restored Byzantine Empire in a liberated Constantinople, was an unamiable figure, and even Dorothea had to admit that 'the defects of his character effaced any virtues he may have had'. These were such as to drive his wife from Russia in 1801, after which he became 'fantastic, even cruel, and very dissolute in morals'. He shared his father's taste for playing the military martinet, and was, according to Dorothea, 'generally hated and feared in Russia'. The one non-malignant quality people allowed him was that he was a coward – and that was only after he refused the throne in 1825. Constantine told Princess Lieven (as she was by then) that he had told his brother Alexander that he had no wish to be Tsar: 'My father [and] my grandfather died from assassination; I mean to live and die tranquilly.' To Dorothea, however, he showed only his good side: 'Amiable, spiritual, *galant*, he was always that to me, and worthy of confidence.' The fact that Constantine was, at the time of the affair, heir to the throne, may be a sign that even then Dorothea preferred to love where power was to be found; but given the Grand Duke's morals, it may simply have been an affair she was unable to resist. From such dalliances she was snatched away by the demands of Russian foreign policy.

Although Count Lieven has come to be overshadowed by his more famous wife, her career would have been impossible without his. 'Bonsi', as he was known, was a straightforward fellow who did his duty as required. Tsar Alexander I thought well of him and, in 1809, sent him to escort the King and Queen of Prussia to St Petersburg. The beautiful Queen Louise was the great love of Alexander's life, and the fact that she took a liking to the stately Count Lieven meant that, when Alexander was looking for an ambassador to Prussia later in the year, he was the obvious candidate. Young Countess Lieven was not impressed by Berlin, telling her brother that 'the Society here is deadly'. She told her brother that the King 'has little strength of mind, and is as obstinate as a beast. He has been advised not to adopt too friendly an air towards us, and he follows this advice very carefully and even goes beyond it'. The Lievens' task was made no easier by the death, a few months after their arrival, of the radiant Queen Louise, whose role in maintaining Prussian morale in the dark years after 1806 had made her a national heroine. In early 1811 Dorothea noted that the area around the embassy was filling up with Russian troops; war was at hand. At the end of 1810 Alexander had effectively removed Russia from Napoleon's anti-British continental system, and as relations between the two 'allies' became strained, Napoleon had decided to take matters into his own hands in the way he knew best; the French troops were the first part of what was to be a massive invasion force.

At the end of 1811 the Lievens were recalled to Berlin, as Russia broke off diplomatic relations with Prussia. In the spring of 1812 the long-awaited French invasion was launched. The Lievens left Prussia on 30 June 1812, as the *Grande Armée* crossed the Niemen. Having acquitted himself with credit there, Count Lieven was now despatched to London. His initial mission was to secure money and supplies that would enable Russia to carry the war against Napoleon westwards.

The arrival of the Lievens in London made a considerable impact. On the diplomatic front, where Britain had been in virtual isolation for five years, it marked the chance to find an ally against Bonaparte; here, Count Lieven would be agent for his Tsar's diplomacy. Foreign embassies had always played an important role in the social life of the British capital, and for the same five years there had been no embassy balls and no foreign aristocracy to provide an exotic gloss to the social season; here, Countess Lieven would be expected to make her mark. Eventually she would do so with a vengeance, but there was little sign of this in the early days, when she was much overshadowed by her husband and when the impression she made was, to say the least, mixed.

At the first great ball given in their honour, the mistress of the Prince of Wales, Lady Jersey, who was one of the arbiters of society, clambered on to a chair to get a better view of the ambassadress – the 'white bear', as she was called. Lady Jersey was duly impressed by her furs and her diamonds, as well as by her demeanour; this was no uncultivated and boorish Russian. She spoke perfect French and had the manners and breeding of a lady. Equally important from the point of view of Lady Jersey, this vivacious Russian posed no threat to her ascendancy with the Prince Regent. Prince George's taste ran to women like herself – maternal and voluptuous – and Dorothea Lieven was young, tall, skinny and flat-chested.

A consensus emerged that Countess Lieven was 'extremely accomplished' – her playing of the pianoforte was particularly admired; and she certainly had all the attributes of a lady; but people did not warm to her. As one observer noted, she seemed 'equally conscious of her own superiority and the inferiority of other people'; while her attitude towards those she judged un-worthy of her attention gave a new meaning to the word 'super-cilious'. She seemed 'excessively clever, and when she chooses brilliantly agreeable', but it was her haughtiness and her reserve which stood out; and the English do not take kindly to being condescended to by foreign women, however aristocratic their background and exquisite their manners.

Dorothea Lieven's reserve was simply part of her character; acutely conscious of her rank, and used to moving in the etiquette-bound Russian court, she took time to adapt to England and its ways. Her imagination had been firmly captured by the dramatic events in Russia, and as she had witnessed something of the great drama being enacted there, England and the English appeared flat and prosaic by contrast. 'This beautiful England,' she told her eldest brother, Alexander, 'is always the same – an endless chain of perfections which appeal to the reason but leave the imagination untouched.' For her first few months she had been constantly admiring the beauty of the countryside, but after a while it dawned on her that she was becoming bored by perfection: 'England is not the country of emotions.' She should, she acknowledged (with a pardonable boast to an elder brother who had the ear of the Tsar), be 'supremely happy . . . I am everywhere received as no foreigner has been, and I flatter myself that I have been a success, but never would I wish to die in this country.' She did, indeed, flatter herself. Lady Granville, who was one of the first Englishwomen to know her at all well, thought that 'cleverness' was her 'only charm'. She told her sister, Lady Morpeth, that: 'It is everything that makes a person amiable which is wanting in her – gentleness, sweetness, cheerfulness, *abnégation de soi*. There is a great deal of decorum and propriety and I cannot believe any ardent feelings under it.' This verdict, as Harriet Granville was to discover, was only partly accurate. The cool and reserved ambassadress was only one side of Dorothea Lieven's character – and under that polished exterior there were a great many 'ardent feelings'.

It would take Countess Lieven time to adapt to a society and a political system so different from those she had known in Russia. There, everything revolved around the Tsar, who, as an absolute monarch, ruled as he wanted, subject only to his own sense of what was possible. The one resemblance to what she had known lay in the fact that the British King, George III, was mad; but unlike in Russia, this posed no threat either to himself or to those around him. King George was quietly packed away to Windsor Castle, where he grew a patriarchal beard and retreated into a shadow world; in his absence, his eldest son became Prince Regent. Britain was a constitutional monarchy, and the King still possessed considerable powers – if he had the wit and the will to exercise them; Prince George had the former but not the latter. Once one of the handsomest men in Europe, George had degenerated into an indolent corpulence. He divided his time between designing ornate buildings such as the Brighton Pavilion, and designing mistresses whose main interest in him was pecuniary. Always attracted to royalty, Dorothea would come to know him well, but her respect for him was ritual rather than genuine. Although always apt, from her Russian experiences, to overrate the role of the monarch, Dorothea quickly discovered that real power lay elsewhere; in a Europe used to absolute monarchs, whether on the old model of the Tsar of Russia or the new one of the Emperor Napoleon, Britain was a constitutional monarchy where the king shared power with parliament.

Utterly unfamiliar with the very idea of representative institutions, Dorothea regarded the process by which the House of Commons was elected with a mixture of distaste and fascination: 'there is a bustle and a hubbub that would be great fun for little children', she wrote during the 1820 general election. 'Everything is turned to account, women and children too; there is a whole technique of attack, defence and knock-out; there is systematic bribery and, in the midst of it all, a regular saturnalia.' She was simultaneously attracted and repelled by the democratic elements of British elections: 'the proud aristocrat shakes the butcher by the hand, gives sweets to his children, bonnets to his wife, and ribbons to the whole family.' She was also struck by the 'extent women influence the elections in England'. At a by-election in Westminster in 1819, she watched Lady Granville's cousin, Lady Caroline Lamb, campaign for her brother-in-law George, and noted that it was said that she had been worth 2,000 votes: 'there are no two opinions about the price at which the majority of those votes were bought. She made no bones about going into taverns and dancing and drinking with the electors; what else she did is shrouded in obscurity.' Observing the 1820 election in Brighton where she was staying with the Regent, Dorothea noted that everything was 'decorated with blue or pink cockades' – the latter being the colours of the opposition Whigs, the former of the governing Tories. Dorothea discovered that 'everything which displays them is greeted with cheers, everything which does not – with mud and boos. Cheers and insults follow one another and are mingled in the oddest way. What a strange country! What a strange and beautiful thing its Constitution is!'

It was indeed. For all the carnival atmosphere in which elections took place, voting was a privilege generally confined to about a quarter of a million men with property, although because of the organic nature of the political system, there were some seats, such as Westminster, with thousands of electors. Power was concentrated very tightly in the hands of a small aristocratic elite whose wealth was based firmly upon the ownership of land, and government was disputed between Tories and Whigs, who were aristocratic factions rather than political parties on the modern pattern. The Tories, who could be distinguished from their opponents by their support for the powers of the King and for the Church of England, had been in office for most of the previous quarter of a century, ever since George III had made their great hero, William Pitt the Younger, Prime Minister in 1783. Attempts by the Whig champion, Charles James Fox, to wrest power back had failed, and with his decision to come out in favour of the French Revolution splitting the Whigs, Pitt had been able to gather a wide range of supporters behind his patriotic war against the French. Pitt had died in 1806, and Fox a year later, but the two antagonists continued to define party lines a decade later. Those who had stayed true to Fox and the cause of liberty, such as the young aristocrat Charles Grey, despised those who had deserted the purity of opposition for the spoils of office. Those, like Pitt's young disciple, George Canning, who had borne the heat of the day in managing the war against Napoleon and the political problems it caused, had nothing but contempt for those Whigs who had deserted their country when it needed them most. Such entrenched attitudes ensured that party politics were conducted with due acrimony.

By 1812 the Whigs had another deserter to add to their list – the Prince Regent. A boon companion of the hard-drinking, gambling and womanizing Fox, Prince George had espoused Whig principles in his youth, but when he finally came to power with the incapacity of his father, he ignored his old friends and kept the existing Prime Minister, the Tory Lord Liverpool, in office. He repaid the indignation of his old friends by proscribing them from office. As long as he could find a Tory Prime Minister, George would pick one, however incompetent, rather than resort to Grey, the Whig leader. For most of Dorothea Lieven's time in England the Whigs were out of power – but that did not stop her from finding herself generally upon their side. The Whigs were, by some considerable margin, a great deal smarter, in the social sense, than the Tories.

Dorothea, as befitted the wife of the Russian ambassador, socialized with government ministers, but this tended to be on official occasions. She was delighted that the Prime Minister 'takes a very great interest in me', but any reciprocation was down to the fact that she 'quite liked Prime Ministers', rather than to any fellow feeling for him. Liverpool, like most of the Cabinet, was insufficiently grand for Dorothea's taste. What she liked were the Whig magnates with their great palaces at Chatsworth and Castle Howard, and their London mansions such as Devonshire and Holland House; it was here that the smartest society gathered – and towards it Dorothea gravitated by her very nature, although it took time for her to overcome some of the initial coolness towards her.

At first the Lievens lived in the Russian embassy in Harley Street, but it was not commodious enough for a growing family, so they took a large white house which stood in its own grounds between the villages of Streatham and Tooting. Dorothea told her brother Alexander in 1813: 'We are living very quietly, seeing people every day, for the distance from town is so trifling that we are easily reached, and our house is large enough to lodge a number of guests.' Her masters in St Petersburg did not share her sense of self-satisfaction. The foreign minister Nesselrode noted that: 'Lieven continues to succeed as well as his wife continues to fail.' That was, indeed, the case, and the reasons for it are plain enough. Dorothea was left with the task of trying to find a way into an exclusive and cliquish English society that was not altogether sure about her, or her country, whereas Count Lieven was pushing at a door that was only too willing to open.

With the Regent confirming Liverpool in power, foreign policy was placed in the hands of Robert Stewart, Viscount Castlereagh. A tall, handsome, self-contained product of the Anglo-Irish ascendancy, Castlereagh would dominate British foreign policy for the rest of his life; since his father's peerage was an Irish one, he was able to sit in the Commons, which he led for most of the period up to 1822. His job was made simpler by having one overriding aim: winning the war against Napoleon. As he told the British ambassador in St Petersburg, General Lord Cathcart: 'Whatever scheme of policy can most immediately combine the greatest number of powers and the greatest military force against France . . . before she can recruit her armies and recover her ascendancy, is that which we must naturally desire most to promote'; to this object Russia was vital. Castlereagh's greatest fear was that Russia would lend herself to the sort of continental peace being peddled by the Austrian Foreign Minister, Prince Metternich. If Alexander I would give a lead, Castlereagh was convinced that he could bring Prussia and Austria into line to form one final great coalition against Bonaparte while he was still weakened by his Russian adventure.

The main weapon in Castlereagh's armoury was finance. One of the principal purposes of the Lieven mission was to see what subsidies the British would be prepared to offer. Russia was so short of money that as early as April, Count Lieven was warning that she might be driven from the war. Castlereagh successfully pressed the Cabinet and the Commons to agree to a subsidy that allowed Russia to conclude a treaty with Prussia to bring her into the war by paying for her to raise an army of 80,000 men; Russia herself would put 150,000 men into the field. It was little wonder that Nesselrode was happy with Lieven's performance. Satisfaction with the ambassadress would be slower in coming, but with the conclusion of the quadruple alliance between Britain, Russia, Austria and Prussia in March 1814, and the final turning of the tide against Napoleon, who abdicated on 11 April, there emerged conditions more conducive to Dorothea's skills.

2. 'It is not fashionable where I am not'

The quadruple alliance was signed by Tsar Alexander, King Frederick William III of Prussia, the Austrian Emperor, Francis, and Castlereagh. The Prince Regent, piqued at being the only one of the allied sovereigns not to take part in the negotiations personally, invited them all to visit London. The series of formal festivities that would follow saw Dorothea Lieven come into her own as a hostess and as a figure on the English social scene. Those who had been uncertain about her wanted to be seen at grand occasions attended by the famous and mysterious Russian Tsar, and they would suddenly find her charming and personable. For Dorothea, the diplomatic round of the summer of 1815 marked her arrival in London society, but she was able to get some practice in first. Because the Tsar was intimately involved in negotiating the terms of the peace settlement with the French, he told the Regent that he could not come until June, but he offered to send his favourite sister, Catherine, Duchess of Oldenburg, as a harbinger of what was to come.

According to Dorothea, Catherine was seductive in manner and very beautiful; but those under less compulsion to flatter members of the Romanov dynasty thought she had the flat Slavic face and piggy eyes of her father. Castlereagh, mindful of the importance of making a good impression, asked his wife, Emily, to be 'very kind to her and give her all sorts of information and advice about England'. Unfortunately, from its inception to its conclusion, the visit was a disaster. The Grand Duchess was reputed to be on the lookout for another husband, a circumstance that prompted George's younger brother, William, Duke of Clarence, to cross over to Holland to offer her his hand. She dismissed him as 'a mere, vain sailor, who says things to make you die of laughter, and many clumsy things'. Of one thing she was sure: 'I shall not become

Mme Clarence.' If Clarence at least had his amusing side, the Grand Duchess was to find his eldest brother without any redeeming features at all.

As born courtiers of long experience, the Lievens knew how important the Grand Duchess's visit was, and they turned up to meet her at Sheerness with a coach lent by the Regent and a cavalry escort. Catherine told her brother with satisfaction that 'I find the Lievens just exactly as I had left them. The husband seems very well thought of; he tells me they wish to treat me well so as to show their respect for you – even the Opposition.' The Grand Duchess stayed in Piccadilly at the Pulteney Hotel, for which the embassy paid the staggering sum of 210 guineas a week. The Prince Regent announced his intention to call on her, but any expectation he had had of charming her with his exquisite manners went wrong from the start. Forgetting the dilatory habits of autocratic ladies, the Prince turned up at the Pulteney at the prescribed time, only to find that the Grand Duchess was still dressing. The Lievens made their bows and attempted to explain the problem, at which point Catherine, her toilette still incomplete, swept in, unimpressed with the Prince's punctuality. The meeting was not a success. George whispered to Dorothea on the way out: 'Your Grand Duchess is not good-looking', while Catherine told her that: 'Your Prince is ill-bred.'

Things could only get worse, and duly did so at a dinner at Carlton House that evening. The Grand Duchess turned up wearing mourning for her late husband, and spent much of her time lamenting his loss. The Regent responded that she would no doubt soon find consolation elsewhere – a comment which caused the Grand Duchess to respond with a furious glare followed by a stony silence. The Regent had hired an Italian orchestra to provide a musical entertainment, but the Grand Duchess waved it away saying that music made her want to 'vomit'. Little wonder then that Dorothea should have commented: 'we no longer knew what to do.' The end of the evening seemed a long time in coming.

Relations between the Regent and the Grand Duchess never recovered. She went out of her way to offend him. She took care to socialize extensively with the hated Whigs, and spent a good deal of time with the Regent's estranged daughter, Princess Charlotte. She tended to ignore the ministers, and did her best to offend the Regent. At an official dinner at the house of the Prime Minister, Lord Liverpool, Dorothea overheard a heated conversation between Catherine and the Regent, in which the latter was teased about his inability to control his daughter. George thought that he had scored a hit by saying: 'When she is married, Madame, she will do as her husband wishes; for the present she does as I wish.' But the Grand Duchess was equal to this, riposting with a feline comment about George's notoriously bad relations with his wife: 'Your Highness, between husband and wife there can be only one will.' He turned to Dorothea and said loudly: 'This is intolerable.' It was, but the Regent had brought it upon himself.

George's brothers did their best to make up for his attitude by finding the Grand Duchess more than tolerable. She turned down one proposal from the Duke of Sussex and yet another from the Duke of Clarence – requesting in the case of the latter that he should be kept away from any occasion at which she was present. It was only when she threatened to go to visit George's estranged wife, Princess Caroline of Brunswick, that Count Lieven finally put his foot down – announcing that if she did so he would have to resign his post. She retaliated by excusing him from attending upon her, a task that fell exclusively to Dorothea henceforth. The ambassadress thus became the sole link between the embassy and the Tsar's favourite sister, a delicate job, made more so by Catherine's insistence upon compiling lists of dinner guests consisting of the Regent's enemies; fortunately for her sociable instincts, there were enough of these to keep her going for weeks.

This was not the ideal preparation for the Tsar's visit, but it was a useful foretaste of the difficulties it would pose. Alexander was at the height of his power – and popularity. He had finally achieved the old Romanov dream of making Russia a great European power, and with France defeated, there were those who told him that she was now *the* greatest power in Europe. Any ruler with an army of a million men at his back would command respect, but

Alexander's unpredictability made him an object of suspicion to his fellow sovereigns; no one could tell what he would do next. From his youth he had expressed an interest in liberal and constitutional ideas, and there were those who had thought him something of a revolutionary; but the experience of the war against Napoleon had marked him deeply. Mortified by the burning of Moscow, Alexander had turned to religion for consolation. He told the Prussian King that: 'the burning of Moscow at last illuminated my spirit and the judgement of God filled me with a warmth of faith I had never felt before'; he knew himself to be God's instrument for 'the deliverance of Europe from ruin'. An absolute ruler at the head of the largest and most successful army in the world was an object of interest and some fear; one who also thought himself under the direct command of the Almighty inspired considerable suspicion among his allies.

But for the British public, Alexander was the great hero whose armies had defeated 'Boney', and London was *en fête* for all things Russian. Unfortunately for the crowds who had come out to welcome him, Alexander had decided to turn up incognito, and arrived in town without anyone noticing. He had declined the Regent's offer to stay with him at Carlton House, preferring instead the delights of the Pulteney Hotel. Once word got round that the Tsar had arrived, the surrounding streets were thronged with well-wishers and sightseers – which prevented the Regent from paying his respects. When Alexander asked his sister where Prince George was, she simply replied: 'That's what the man's like.' Eventually Count Lieven received a note to say that the Regent had 'been threatened with annoyance in the streets if he shows himself', which allowed the Grand Duchess to tell Alexander that he was so unpopular that he was always hooted in the streets – when he was not having stones and mud thrown at him. In the end the impulsive Alexander commandeered Lieven's carriage and took himself off to Carlton House. He was not impressed with what he found there. His verdict to Count Lieven was that George was 'a poor Prince'.

Alexander was delighted with what he took to be the contrast between the way the English reacted to their own Regent and himself. Dorothea reckoned that throughout the fortnight he spent at the Pulteney, there was a crowd of about 10,000 surrounding it. Everyone wanted to see the Tsar, and many asked to shake him by the hand – which delighted Alexander, who had never tasted the delights of such spontaneous popularity. This did nothing for his relations with the Regent. At a dinner the following evening at Carlton House, Alexander looked 'constrained and bored', while George made unavailing attempts to promote some sort of conversation. When the Regent introduced the Tsar to his new mistress, Lady Hertford, Alexander bowed low but said nothing. George, imagining his guest had not heard, repeated, 'This is Lady Hertford.' Alexander stood there, saying nothing. Lady Hertford made her curtsy and shot him one of her haughtiest glances. 'The fate of the whole visit,' Dorothea recorded, 'seemed to me to be written in that glance.' Dorothea did her best to repair matters, throwing a ball at the embassy a few nights later, when she made an attempt to introduce Lady Hertford. 'There, sire,' she said, 'is someone who awaits and hopes for a word from you.' But Alexander, opining that she looked 'mighty old', declined to go anywhere near her. The result was that the visit fizzled out, with only one more formal dinner and a few receptions. Alexander, chivalrous as ever, expressed a desire to meet the King, but Dorothea explained that it was thought improper to show a foreign monarch a mad king. Dorothea's other success was in persuading the Tsar not to call on the Regent's estranged wife, Princess Caroline of Brunswick.

If the Tsar's visit was a political failure, it marked the beginning of Dorothea's career as a great hostess. Everyone wanted to dine with the Tsar, and invitations to the embassy were eagerly sought – and society finally met the young ambassadress. For her part, Dorothea found her métier. She enjoyed organizing the balls and receptions, and, finding herself at the centre of events and her company sought everywhere, she blossomed. The Tsar, young and handsome in his uniform, was a great social success, making a series of conquests among the British female aristocracy. He was,

Dorothea noted, 'a fine waltzer, and gallant to women, although confining himself to the young ones, and steadily refusing a civil word to those who were not'. The one exception to this was the Regent's former mistress, Lady Jersey, whom he made a point of seeking out. She agreed to throw a ball for him on 15 June, at which point the Regent fixed the previous day as the occasion for giving him an honorary degree at Oxford. The Tsar received his degree, then made his way back to London, where he joined Lady Jersey's party just in time to see the sun rise. It was a gallant gesture, but hardly one calculated to improve relations between the two courts.

The Regent, however, does seem to have appreciated the efforts Dorothea made to smooth matters, and she now became one of those admitted to his intimate society at his exotic Pavilion at Brighton. She and Bonsi were invited down to Brighton in November while the Pavilion was being rebuilt, and they dined with the Regent every day, a mark of condescension for which the courtier in Dorothea was duly grateful. All her life she abhorred late nights, and the Regent, ever the gentleman, let her leave at eleven o'clock, providing his carriage to drive her home. But this, she discovered, had its own perils.

One of those staying in Brighton was the Duke of Clarence. Dorothea thought him 'the least educated of all the English princes. He had no knowledge, vulgar English habits and manners, his conversation was also vulgar.' Clarence had taken it into his head that through Dorothea he might yet find himself with a Russian bride, and had therefore taken something of a fancy to her. He offered her his arm and escorted her to the carriage, and, although unsteady on his legs by that stage of the evening, he got into the carriage with her and ordered the driver to go. Dorothea now began to feel a little uneasy. He asked whether she was cold – 'his conversations,' she later recorded, 'always began like that.' He then asked if he might be permitted to hold her hand, to which she replied: 'It is needless, Monseigneur!' – which did nothing to deter him. 'Fear seized me, for he was evidently very drunk', and with her one free hand she began to lower the carriage window 'as a precautionary measure'. Desperate for a topic to take his mind off her hand – and any other parts of her anatomy to which it might be straying, Dorothea told him that her husband had had a courier from Vienna where the congress that would settle the fate of Europe was meeting. Clarence was not interested in such matters – until she told him that the future of Hanover had been decided. Clarence may have been ignorant, boorish and rather stupid, but 'he had only one fixed idea in politics – Hanover', of which, in due course, he might hope to become Elector. He let go of her hand, and she drove the point home by telling him that the peacemakers had decided to give Hanover to Prussia. He exclaimed, 'God damn! Does my brother know this?' Dorothea told him that no one but himself knew it, as it was a secret straight from the congress. By this time the carriage had reached the door of the house at which the Lievens were staying, and Clarence's passionate nature was wholly concentrated upon a topic which allowed Dorothea to make her escape. When Bonsi got home he was furious when Dorothea told him what she had done, and she was not sure what had upset him the most, the royal attempt on her virtue or the diplomatic difficulty her ingenious excuse had created.

The following day Dorothea explained to the Regent what she had done. He 'laughed like a madman. I had never seen him so diverted'. He joined in the fun by telling Clarence that he would gladly accept Westphalia in compensation for their ancestral home. The whole thing was, of course, a piece of nonsense concocted by Dorothea's need to distract Clarence, but it helped seal a bond between her and the Regent, who always welcomed her company.

Royal favour, added to the Russian visits, helped to transform Dorothea's life in England. She gravitated naturally to the *beau monde*, and of all those whom she had entertained during the Tsar's visit it was the members of the opposition rather than of the government with whom she found she had most in common. Nor was that surprising. Liverpool may have been Prime Minister, but he was a dull fellow in ill-fitting clothes who moved little in society, lacking that most essential of attributes, a fashionable wife.

Much the same was true of the Foreign Secretary, Viscount Castle-reagh, who although a handsome figure in fine clothes, possessed in his Emily a wife whose eccentricities of dress included wearing his garter ribbon in her hair. It was not towards the company of such people that Dorothea felt drawn. Her natural milieu was the smart Whig society that still clustered around Devonshire House and Holland House as it had since the days of Charles James Fox and the immensely glamorous and outrageous Georgiana, Duchess of Devonshire. Although both figures were long dead, something of their aura and style lived on in their descendants, and it was not surprising that Dorothea found herself attracted to the second generation of the Devonshire House set, for it was here that all that was most exquisite, civilized – and scandalous – about Regency England was to be found.

Dorothea's entry into Whig society came through the offices of her first female British friend, Harriet Granville, whose husband, Lord Granville, had spent some time in Russia in 1805 and there-fore had a passing acquaintance with many of the Lievens' Russian friends, and whose brother, the Duke of Devonshire, provided the setting for so much of Whig society at his great London palace, Devonshire House. It was through Harriet that the Lievens were invited to a grand dinner there a few days after the victory at Waterloo. Dorothea had joked with Harriet about her brother's grumpiness: 'I have never seen a man so desolated at having *women* in his house'; but a month later Harriet recorded that he had 'half repented himself of his aversion' to Madame Lieven.

'Harry-O', as she was known, was the daughter of the beautiful Georgiana, Duchess of Devonshire, and perhaps also of the Duke – although in Whig society only maternity was a matter of fact, paternity being one of opinion. According to her mother, Harry-O was a 'very pleasing and sweet girl', but no 'regular beauty'. Another observer described her as being 'plain but remarkably intelligent', which was not the most inspiriting of descriptions for a young woman whose mother was the acknowledged beauty of the day. But she was connected by marriage or descent to all the families that mattered in English society, and she gave Dorothea her entrée into the world in which she felt most at home. Harriet's husband, Lord Granville, may well have met the Lievens during his time in Russia, and given his contacts in St Petersburg, it was not surprising that they should have gravitated towards him and his wife. Granville had been the lover of her aunt, Lady Bessborough, one of whose daughters was the Caroline Lamb whose behaviour at the 1819 Westminster election was so to shock Dorothea. Lady Bessborough had two children by Granville, and though he was the love of her life, she knew that he needed to be married, so suggested and sponsored a match with her young niece, Harry-O; it was one example of the Whig propensity for keeping things within the family. Despite this odd beginning, the marriage was a successful one, and Harriet adored her handsome, if errant, husband. She was an exact contemporary of Dorothea's, and took a liking, if a slightly wary one, to the Russian ambassadress. By the October of 1815 she felt ready to introduce Dorothea to her *monde* – although not without some trepidation, telling her sister Lady Morpeth that she hoped Dorothea would 'not be offensive', as she dreaded 'tiffs'.

In fact, as Harry-O had feared, Dorothea was not an easy visitor. 'As she thinks a good deal of herself,' she told her sister, 'you may conclude that she does not appear to advantage.' Claiming to have a 'fluxion', Dorothea would 'not have a breath of air and frets over her pain and necessary *wraps* from morning to night. My women are good humoured and bear with her I think almost better than I do.' It was, she told Lady Morpeth, difficult to describe accurately just how peevish and sullen Dorothea had been. But this had not stopped her from carrying on a flirtation with Granville's immensely rich brother, Lord Gower. Harriet described it as 'very great, but babyish, not passion'; there was, she commented, 'a great contrast in her very cross dry way and his perpetual titter'. This flirtation continued during their stay at Chatsworth the following week, when, according to Lady Granville, Count Lieven was 'wretched and more jealous than anything I saw'. She thought that Dorothea was 'a mixture of the strangest impudence and most artful contrivance'. She certainly managed to contrive a little longer with her beau, securing an invitation through Harriet to the great ducal palace at Chatsworth, which impressed her as worthy of an emperor. Watching her new friend, Harriet Granville told her sister that she was 'much touched with regard to her. I pity her so profoundly for her education and a thousand things. It is a bad concern but with thousands of excuses – and very unhappy.'

Later, on a visit to Paris, Harriet called on Maréchale Moreau, who knew Dorothea well, and she wondered how their friendship had arisen. They had no common interests or opinions, and they must, she thought, 'differ on every essential point'. Harriet, who was a kind soul, 'talked of my gratitude for her affection, and admiration of her understanding'. Madame Moreau looked at her and said: 'Eh bien Miladi, let us say that as Madame de Lieven is agreeable, you *must* like her' – but if that were not so then she could be censured. There was, when Harriet had pondered these rather sibylline comments, something in them. There was a good deal of boredom in the social life she and her kind led; the glamour and the excitement often went little more than skin deep, and boredom was always only an amusing story or a diverting anecdote away.

It was here that part of the secret for Dorothea's social success lay. Her comments, if a little sharp at times, were never boring, and her background and upbringing made her a reliable source of exoticism which was hard to come by in English society. As Harriet told her other sister, Lady Carlisle, with a little wistful envy, Dorothea could 'keep off bores, because she has the courage to *écraser* [crush] them'. Dorothea, who was herself easily bored, found her English friend a reliable antidote to ennui. As she told Metternich in 1820, 'you run no risk of being bored' with Lady Granville. 'Heavens how witty she is! People think she is malicious; but reputations of that kind are established so quickly, and just as with a woman's frailties, they are always so readily accepted, that I pay no attention to them. How much better the world would be if people were kinder.' Given Dorothea's reputation for malicious gossip, this last comment must have been made with her tongue very firmly in her cheek. Dorothea would visit Harriet early in the morning, then attend the Sunday suppers and soirées which became a regular feature of her social life. So intimate did the two women become that there were times when Harriet simply called on her Russian friend without warning – and at least on one occasion she found her with Lord Gower, 'which embarrassed me', she told Lady Morpeth, 'but not them'.

Dorothea's wit was of the sharp kind, and did not always spare her friends. It was a mark of Harriet Granville's tolerance that she should have told her brother, without any hostile comment, of Dorothea's greeting to her on one occasion: 'How well you look dear. I am so happy to have a friend *qui a de l'embonpointment.*' It might, of course, have been the case that a woman in possession of the more voluptuous *décolletage* that was the fashion of the day, did not much mind being called fat by a woman who had a 'bust like a skeleton's'. Dorothea's figure would have been more fashionable two centuries later, but in her own era she would always be at a disadvantage to those, such as Harriet Granville, or her other great friend, Emily, Lady Cowper, whose figures were set off so well by current fashions in women's clothing. The question of whether Dorothea compensated for her want of the more obvious female charms by other physical qualities was one on which opinions were divided – but not evenly. Lady Bessborough, Lord Granville's long-time lover and Harriet's aunt, told Granville in 1813 that Dorothea had looked 'very pretty and gracious the other night', but such encomiums are few. More frequently encountered are comments such as those of the one-time French foreign minister, the Vicomte de Chateaubriand, who said that she had a sharp, angular face and a reddish nose. When one acquaintance told her this at Aix-la-Chapelle in 1818, she replied, rather splendidly: 'I know it only too well, but these are things which are *not* said.' The editor of her letters to Metternich commented that 'Physically, Madame de Lieven was never a true beauty', and thought that the famous Lawrence painting of her showed that she had 'a rather too prominent nose, large ears and too long a neck' with a mouth that was 'disgracieuse' [ungainly]. Perhaps only a Frenchman could, after this, rescue the day with the comment that despite all of this 'what comes out of her physiognomy, beneath her beautiful fair hair is real charm: her eyes are deep and tender' and 'l'ensemble est fin et spirituel'. Harriet Granville described her as appearing to walk almost 'independent of her body', and thought she possessed considerable grace and charm. Others were less impressed, with one Regency dandy commenting ungallantly that he admired her 'in spite of her teeth', before adding that 'I have never known her intimately enough to object to the effects said to be produced from her economy of clean linen.' And yet, even as the balance of comment shifts towards the conclusion that Dorothea was no great beauty, the fact that she held an enduring fascination for men of power comes as a reminder not only of the cliché about beauty and the eye of the beholder, but of the difficulty of fixing on paper the transient but powerful forces of personality which make an individual attractive. Perhaps the best verdict on her was that 'she was never of remarkable beauty, but she produced all the effect of being so.'

It was not, therefore, surprising that Dorothea's relations with other women often had a competitive edge to them. Harriet Granville was amiable enough, but even she thought it worthwhile noting, because of its uniqueness, the occasion in 1822 when 'Madame de Lieven was for a whole week invariably gay and brilliantly agreeable.' Dorothea disliked those whom she saw as a threat to her position – most notably the wives of other ambassadors, particularly when, like the Austrian Princess Esterhazy, they were younger, prettier and of more ancient lineage than herself. She dismissed the Austrian as a 'mediocre person' with 'pretensions to airs and graces . . . the kind of woman who always wants to be the centre of social interest'. She told Metternich that Princess Esterhazy had legs like 'solid pillars all the way down!' Dorothea was scandalized at the willingness of the Princess to expose those legs when asked to by the Marchioness of Worcester: 'These Englishwomen are quite incredible. As for my colleague, it is quite simple; that is just her way.' It was perhaps unsurprising that Princess Esterhazy was, according to Dorothea, at the centre of any malicious gossip about her. The French ambassadress, the

Comtesse de Boigne, noted Dorothea's 'treacherous and hostile politeness' towards Princess Esterhazy and put it down to the fact that the Austrian was 'younger and prettier' and possessed a rounded figure, which 'seemed to emphasise the hopeless thinness of her rival'. When someone described Madame Apponyi, the wife of the Austrian ambassador in Paris, as a 'giraffe' and said that she and Princess Lieven were animals of the same kind, one of Dorothea's acquaintances countered that they were nothing of the sort, 'one would eat the other and have nothing but a poor meal of it', which led Harriet Granville to comment that she had no doubt which would do the eating: 'One sees Lieven crunching the meek Apponyi's bones.'

Perhaps because Englishwomen provided the frame within which the picture of her social dominance was set and therefore posed no challenge to it, Dorothea was more tolerant of them – although some of her comments were no less barbed. Writing in 1820, she confessed that despite her long experience of them, 'Englishwomen always astonish me.' The occasion for her comment was a party at Castlereagh's house at which 'those members of the party who had some sentimental preoccupation went for a stroll' into the bushes and promptly vanished from the scene, leaving the ballroom occupied only by 'little girls, dancers of the calibre of my husband and the master of the house, a few old women and myself'. She would, she said, 'like to take their indiscretion for the height of naiveté; but, after all, they have husbands, and I confess myself baffled'. 'What strange beings these Englishwomen are!' she told Metternich a few years later, commenting on their propensity to elope. Still, she said, 'Englishmen cannot resist hairy arms', which no doubt explained everything. Nevertheless to those Englishwomen who enjoyed her favour, Dorothea was a welcome companion. Writing to her brother, Frederick Lamb, in March 1821, Emily Cowper confessed how sorry she would be to see Dorothea leave: 'she is so clever and agreeable.'

Emily Cowper was another member of the great Whig network, connected with Harry-O through her brother George Lamb, who was married to Harriet's half-sister, Caroline St Jules, known as

'Caro George'. This was to distinguish her from the wife of Emily's older brother, William – 'Caro William', Lady Caroline Lamb, the daughter of Lady Bessborough. The matriarch of the Lamb family, Elizabeth, Lady Melbourne, was, according to taste, one of the wickedest women in England, or one of the most attractive – not, of course, that the two are mutually exclusive. She was notorious for her advice to young brides 'that they had one duty towards their husbands – they must provide them with *one* legitimate male heir', after which they might take their pleasures where they found them. This was advice she had herself acted upon; as her son William, the second Lord Melbourne, was heard to say when admiring a picture of her: 'a remarkable woman, a devoted mother, an excellent wife – but not chaste, not chaste'. Lord Byron once said of her that 'after all, Lady Melbourne is a good woman. There are *some* things she will stop at.' These did not include, according to the gossips, seducing Byron, who was also sleeping with her daughter-in-law, Lady Caroline Lamb.

Emily Lamb had all her mother's ambition and worldliness, but far greater charm and flexibility. She was the only surviving daughter, and was adored by her brothers William and Frederick: 'pretty in a neat, trim style, animated, witty, devoted to her family, but fundamentally hard and worldly', was the view of one unfriendly commentator. These last traits made her a suitable sparring partner for Dorothea, but to describe her as 'hard' without commenting on her feminine, caressing qualities is to miss what made her irresistibly attractive to so many men. Dorothea described her to that connoisseur of women, Metternich, as 'charming, subtle, amusing and kind'. She possessed, in abundance, the dynamism, ambition and organizational gifts necessary to preside over a political salon, as did Dorothea, so it is not surprising that they became friends – or that that friendship was tinged with rivalry and spiced with a little feline malice. In later, unhappier times, Dorothea looked back with fond nostalgia to the days when she and Emily had 'laughed heartily' when 'we met in our rooms after dinner to exchange confidences. Those were good days.'

At the centre of the 'good days' was Almack's. Almack's Club

was 'the seventh heaven of the fashionable world', and admission
to it was controlled by the seven 'Lady Patronesses' who exercised
a 'pure female despotism', from which even the greatest were not
immune. Dorothea and Princess Esterhazy were the only two
foreigners; the other patronesses were Lady Castlereagh, Lady
Jersey, Lady Sefton, Mrs Drummond-Burrell and Emily Cowper.
Every Wednesday evening in King Street the patronesses would
meet in the 'Blue Chamber' to decide who could, and could not,
be admitted to their society. There was, of course, a good deal of
caprice about this, as about all other despotisms. Emily, despite her
dislike of her sister-in-law, Lady Caroline Lamb, insisted, against
Lady Jersey's wishes, that she should be admitted to Almack's,
commenting (in a superb line which encapsulates the spirit of the
time) that: 'I think it hard to exclude a person from a ball where
six hundred people go if they really are received everywhere.' It
was at Almack's in the spring of 1816 that Dorothea is said to have
introduced the waltz to English society, setting off with Lord
Palmerston on to the dance floor, and scandalizing those who
thought it improper that a man and woman should be so intimately
connected in public. As Byron, whose lameness prevented him
from waltzing, wrote:

> From where the garb just leaves the bosom free,
> That spot where hearts were once supposed to be,
>   Round all the confines of the yielded waist,
>   The stranger's hand may wander undisplaced.
>   The breast thus publicly resign'd to man
>   In private may resist him – if it can.

Such antics, and her social contacts, did nothing to recommend
Dorothea to those who disapproved of the second generation of
the Devonshire House set, but they established her place at the
heart of fashionable society. As she moved, butterfly-like, from the
Pavilion at Brighton, where she flattered the Regent, to Lady
Jersey's salon, and then on to Emily Cowper's home at Panshanger,
before setting off for Hatfield House, she could justifiably boast to

her brother Alexander in faraway St Petersburg that: 'It is not fashionable where I am not. My life,' she told him, 'is now very different from what you knew it.' Harriet Granville noted of her that she was 'become famous for civility and *empressements* to everybody. Her manner is much softened, and, as far as the most perfect propriety in all one sees and the most amicable terms with her husband and the greatest *égard* for him go, a great change has taken place.'

It was essential to appear to be on good terms with one's husband, whatever the reality of the situation might be – appearances mattered, not least when what lay beneath them was often a seething mass of adultery. There was little doubt, however, that it was the Countess and not the Count who mattered. Harriet Granville noted that sitting next to Bonsi at dinner, 'I was never so comfortably bored and I can conceive the connoisseurs thinking it a sort of little Paradise.' The Comtesse de Boigne, the French ambassadress, noted the curious contrast between the vivid impression left by Dorothea, whom she described at this time (1816) as being 'little loved but greatly feared', and Bonsi: 'I do not know what he was. Certainly he was a man of breeding, and grand manners; speaking little, but to the point, cold, but polite . . . He was completely eclipsed by the incontestable superiority of his wife, who *affected* to be very attached and submissive towards him.'

Returning from what she called her 'round of all the country seats in the kingdom', in February 1816, Dorothea told Alexander that 'I have never enjoyed England as much as during the past twelve months. I see and know a number of people, and really enjoy myself. You would be satisfied now with my habits of life; to begin with, no more walks, the same hours as the rest of the world, plenty of society, and, finally, I live like the rest of my fellow-creatures.' She even managed the remarkable feat of being on good terms with the Regent and his daughter, Princess Charlotte. She delighted in Charlotte's marriage to Prince Leopold of Saxe-Coburg, and saw her frequently afterwards. As she exulted to Alexander: 'London Society is very gay and brilliant this season. I amuse myself like the rest; I keep late hours, I dance but I do not walk, and I find the exchange excellent for my pleasure and not even bad for my health . . . I may say that my soirees and those of Lady Jersey are the most agreeable and the most brilliant.' She had reason enough to be pleased. In so far as it had one, London society had taken her to its heart, where she would remain for the following twenty-five years.

3. 'Are you in truth myself?'

The period between the defeat of Napoleon and the Congress of Aix-la-Chapelle in 1818 saw Countess Lieven at the height of her social success. On her arrival in London in 1816 the Comtesse de Boigne noted that Dorothea 'held the leading position' and 'enjoyed an undisputed importance and political influence of a wholly personal character'. But this came at a price. The Comtesse remarked that the Russian ambassadress was much feared but little loved.

In many ways life was sweet. Dorothea's sons were 'growing apace', with young Paul proving to be 'the leader of all the disturbances' at his school, where he had learned to box and to make 'as much noise as a regular John Bull'. The visit of the Tsar's younger brother, Grand Duke Nicholas, in the autumn of 1816, was, in sharp contrast to Alexander's own, a great success. The tall, handsome Russian Grand Duke cut a fine figure at Almack's, where he was noted for 'whirling our English beauties round the circle to a quicker movement than they had previously learned to practice'. Among her new friends was the victor of Waterloo, the Duke of Wellington, whom she pronounced 'very agreeable'. Time would intertwine their fates, but at this juncture she simply rejoiced in the company of the most famous man in Europe. According to the Comtesse de Boigne, there were many 'rumours concerning her personal conduct', and Wellington, who himself enjoyed a well-deserved reputation for gallantry, was among those with whom Dorothea was supposed to have had an affair. The number of her putative lovers no doubt expanded in the rumour-mill, and at various points most British foreign secretaries and prime ministers would be added to it.

Whatever might have been the virtues of the aristocratic circles within which Dorothea moved, marital fidelity was not among them. The Grand Whiggery in whose company she so delighted were notorious for their dissolute ways. Their interconnectedness was not confined to intermarriage. Harry-O seems to have been faithful enough to her beloved Granville, who may even have reciprocated after the death of her aunt, Lady Bessborough, in 1821. Emily Cowper, though, followed in her mother's footsteps by refusing to confine her favours to her dull husband, Lord Cowper. Chief among her favourites was the young Secretary at War, Lord Palmerston, known as 'Lord Cupid', who had whirled Dorothea around with such gusto at Almack's. Her sister-in-law, Lady Caroline Lamb, the wife of her brother William, who became notorious because of the passion with which she pursued the poet Lord Byron, drew a devastating picture of the milieu in which she moved in her autobiographical novel, *Glenarvon*. She described how her heroine, Calanatha, found her simple and honest opinions effectively debauched by the society to which her new husband introduced her. Among his friends and family: 'overefinement [of virtue] was the constant topic of ridicule. Every thought was there uttered and every feeling expressed: there was neither shyness, nor reserve, nor affectation . . . Opinions were there liberally discussed; characters stripped of their pretences . . . the refinement, the romance, and the sentiment which she had imbibed, appeared in their eyes assumed and unnatural'. When her mother-in-law, the promiscuous Lady Melbourne, complained about her morals, Lady Caroline defended herself by saying that it was the fault of her husband, William, who 'amused himself with instructing me in things I need never have heard or known'.

This was the world of *Les Liaisons Dangereuses*, and provided one kept up appearances, what individuals did behind closed doors was no one else's concern. Lady Caroline Lamb found herself ostracized not because of her affair with the poet Byron, but because of the unguarded way she pursued him, and then because of her temerity in publishing a novel about it in which she satirized her husband and his family. As one of Dorothea's correspondents told her: 'It is natural that women are deceived more often than men, and the reasons are simple. Most men search only for what they are sure they will find, whilst women are looking for what they experience, and a profound knowledge of the human heart often leaves them unable to decide.' The correspondent was Prince Metternich, who, earlier in the letter, had asked Dorothea to tell him the story of her life and love affairs; he was, he said, deeply in love with her. Whatever the truth of that, by the time she received his letter, she had fallen deeply for him.

There was something frenetic about Dorothea's immersion in the social scene. In part it kept at bay her constant enemy, boredom: 'I find boredom so frightful,' she wrote on one occasion, 'that I prefer any other form of suffering.' Her frequent complaints of illness were often, she recognized, the consequence of boredom. In 1823 she wondered whether 'I am going into a decline; or is it that I am merely bored? All the same,' she reflected, 'it would be stupid to die of boredom.' Beneath the glitter and the glamour of the life she was leading ennui lurked, and there are signs that by the summer of 1818 it was beginning to take its toll. So depressed was she that 'my mind was so vacant that I could think of no reason for going on living.' To occupy her time, she decided to translate Byron's *Childe Harold*. Sitting on a rocky point on Brighton beach she came across the lines from the fourth canto of the poem, which 'says terrible and sublime things about death by drowning'. As she sat on the rocks, which were only visible at low tide, she 'felt that nothing could be simpler than to stay on the point until the sea had covered it'. She later wondered whether 'we all have a certain tendency to madness, which only the right circumstances are needed to bring out.' Looking back, she concluded: 'Evidently my hour of madness had come. I experienced no distress of any kind, nothing but a great unconcern in my heart and in my head. I waited on the rock a good half hour, my mind made up; but the tide did not rise. When at last it did, my madness ebbed as the water advanced.' It was perhaps not surprising that Count Lieven decided not to leave his wife behind when he was summoned to attend the Congress of Aix-la-Chapelle in the autumn.

The congress had been summoned under the terms of the Vienna settlement that had ended the Napoleonic wars. In 1815 it had been agreed that the allied armies should remain in France to provide the restored Bourbon King, Louis XVIII, with the support that might be necessary to guard against any Napoleonic attempt to overthrow him; by 1818, with the new regime firmly established, the question of whether to withdraw allied forces had to be answered – as did that of France's status; should she be admitted to a wider, quintuple alliance? It was precisely for this purpose that Article VI of the second Peace of Paris (20 November 1815) had provided for periodic meetings of the allied sovereigns. Having missed the social excitements of the famous Congress of Vienna in 1814–15, the so-called 'dancing Congress', Dorothea could look forward to at least a simulacrum of them while her husband dealt with the dry detail of diplomacy; that was not quite how it worked out. This owed everything to her meeting with the Austrian Chancellor, Prince Clemens von Metternich.

Metternich's enemies accused him of smugness and pomposity, and while there was something in this, it must be said in his defence that he had much to be self-satisfied with. Metternich was the scion of a minor Rhineland aristocrat, and his charm and abilities had seen him appointed as Austrian foreign minister in October 1809 at the age of thirty-six. He had cautiously guided his Empire through the rapids of Napoleon's Europe before switching sides in 1814 to become one of the architects of the peace settlement. The Emperor Francis had rewarded him generously, and by 1818 he was one of the richest men in Europe – as well as one of the most famous. Since fame and money had been two of his main pursuits in life, Metternich's air of self-satisfaction is easily explained. There were those who doubted whether he was as wise as his aphoristic oratorical style suggested. Lord Clancarty, one of Castlereagh's closest collaborators at Vienna, had dismissed Metternich as 'a mere hand to mouth politician, adopting measures without foreseeing their most natural consequences, & leaving these at the entire mercy of chance & destiny'.

The accusation that Metternich sacrificed strategic principles for tactical advantages had much to be said for it, and Clancarty's analysis was a shrewd one:

Brought into public life during the period of the French Revolution & versed in the pernicious system of diplomacy of that period – tho' usually acting upon the impulse of the moment, when professing to adopt any measure or principle, this is sought for and drawn from the only source with which he is acquainted. Eaten up with vanity, surrounded by flatterers, & with a quickness of apprehension which might perhaps have been better bestowed, he is led to conceive himself as a finished states-man, when, in point of fact, he is far removed from even comprehending the first rudiments of the part in which he believes himself so perfect an adept. Mistaking intrigue for diplomacy, & preferring chicane to plain dealing – not withstanding the most inveterate habits of idleness, he invariably selects the narrow & intricate path instead of the strait and direct route to his object. In short he stands as an example of what in my opinion is one of the greatest curses of modern times – viz. – the existence & frequency of considerable talents, without common sense to guide them.

Viewed as a whole, Metternich's career tends to confirm this harsh verdict, but in 1818 he was at the height of his fame and power, and at Aix he saw himself as one of the arbiters of Europe. 'I have never seen,' wrote Metternich, as the meetings started, 'a prettier little Congress, it will not cause me any unpleasantness'; nor did it.

Metternich would have agreed with his later admirer, the states-man and academic Henry Kissinger, that power was a great aphrodisiac although, unlike the American, he had some natural advantages in the pursuit of carnal pleasures. According to one contemporary account: 'His features were perfectly regular and handsome, his smile was full of graciousness, his face expressed both benevolence and the most delicate gentleness.' Among his many lovers had been the beautiful Princess Bagration, whose flimsy low-cut dresses had won for her the sobriquet of the '*bel ange nu*' at Vienna. But, to his disappointment, there were no beautiful Russian princesses when he arrived at Aix. It would be in the spirit of what was to follow if it could be said that the arrival of Dorothea Lieven, three weeks into the congress, transformed this situation, but the truth, as so often, was more prosaic.

The fact was that compared with its glamorous predecessor at Vienna, the Congress at Aix was something of a bore. Writing to Harriet Granville on 11 October, Dorothea lamented the 'total absence of pleasure' in what she described as a rather 'dirty little town'. Instead of being surrounded by statesmen deciding the fate of Europe, the great ones of the earth were either ill, like her own Tsar, or too busy for pleasure. This left the women to amuse themselves with gatherings at Lady Castlereagh's or Countess Nesselrode's, where the only entertainment on offer seemed to be the singing of Metternich's favourite opera singer, Madame de Catalani, who, in Dorothea's opinion, could not sing a note in key. Attempts to liven things up scarcely helped. Lady Castlereagh threw a ball, but it was, according to Dorothea, 'as good as a ball could be where there were too few women'. A blossoming affair between the 'inseparable' Wellington and Lady Caroline Greville provided a little distraction, but Dorothea was thrown back for amusement on her old lover, the Grand Duke Constantine, with whom she 'renewed my *tendresse*'. A more potent antidote to boredom awaited her in the form of the Austrian Chancellor.

Dorothea had met Metternich in passing during the festivities in London in 1814, but he had made no great impression on her. She noted to Harriet Granville that he had aged – and that he seemed to be having little amorous success, although she admitted that that might be put down to the paucity of pretty women. Dorothea was in no doubt about Metternich's reputation. Conscious of it himself, he went to some lengths to explain it away when he got to know her better. 'The woman I love,' he told her, 'is the only woman in the world for me', and he went on to claim that he had 'never been unfaithful' ['Je n'ai jamais été infidèle']. He admitted to only two 'liaisons' and said that for the rest, when he was not in love, he found a 'pretty woman who wants everything but love'. It was not surprising, in the light of this, that

Dorothea's first reaction to meeting him at Aix should have been unfavourable. By 22 October she was reporting to Harriet Granville that 'you will have a good deal of work to do to put me on my legs again.' However, things had improved as far as Metternich was concerned. He was, Dorothea wrote, a little livelier – if only in retelling his memories; but there was more to this than she revealed to Harriet Granville.

Nesselrode, who rather favoured the conservative statesmanship of Metternich, and who had noted Dorothea's attitude towards him, suggested to him that he should try to win her over. The old charmer needed no further encouragement, and at a dinner party at Nesselrode's took the opportunity to single her out for attention. As he later recalled, it was Napoleon who had broken the ice between them. He regaled her with his memories of the heady days of Napoleon's downfall, and she sat there enraptured. 'I will swear,' he later told her, 'that I never realised he could be so useful – more useful on top of his rock than he ever was on his throne.' It was then, Metternich told her, that he knew that whatever judgement the world had made of her, 'you proved that you were attentive to those things which illuminate the essential woman.' He knew, at that moment, that he had misjudged her. At least that was what he wrote in the first flush of his passion for Dorothea, although an alternative reading might be that it was only then that he decided that there might be someone at the congress worth seducing.

On 25 October Metternich organized an excursion to Spa, taking the Lievens and the Nesselrodes along with some of his Austrian colleagues. He later told his wife that it had been a successful trip: 'we stayed the night at Spa and in the morning we amused ourselves by driving around the neighbourhood.' If he omitted the most interesting details of how he amused himself, that was wise of him. On the outward journey he had had to give up the pleasure of sitting with Dorothea because someone else wanted to sit with him, but on the way back he proposed that she swap carriages to be with him. It was then that he realized that those who had described her as 'a woman of great charm' had been correct. On 28 October he paid his first 'albeit formal' visit to her: 'the hours which I passed seated at your feet proved to me that it was the right place to be. It seemed to me when I went back to my own house as if I had known you for many years.' The one thing he did not detail in this letter was 'the day when you came to my house; *you* had the fever – my friend, you belonged to me! Do not ask me what I have felt since, I have felt it – if you do not know: if you have not felt it you will not be mine!' These few incidents, he told her, had become the object of his life and, he believed, of hers. 'You feel an inner emptiness,' he told her, 'which needs to be filled; your husband is good and loyal, but he is not what a husband should be; the arbiter of the fate of his wife.' He told his 'bonne Dorothée' that she had a charm that he had never before encountered in any woman; 'can you believe that I could love you more than I have ever loved before?'

If Dorothea did believe this smooth and well-practised routine, it was because she wanted to; the experienced old seducer had it right with his comments about the virtues and shortcomings of Count Lieven. He was, indeed, a good and loyal husband, but he had never made Dorothea's heart beat faster – and now she had found someone who did. Unfortunately for the lovers, the next two arrivals at Aix were Dorothea's godmother, the Dowager Empress Marie Feodorovna, and her formidable mother-in-law, Countess Lieven, and it was necessary for both Dorothea and the Count to accompany them to Brussels. Metternich wrote her a series of hasty notes: 'I have found you,' he complained, 'only to lose you . . . the day you return will be the best of my life.' Then, waxing lyrical, he went on to say that 'I have experienced a whole period in my life in less than eight days. It would seem like a dream to me, if I did not understand myself. A person is all or nothing for me. My soul is not capable of feeling – or thinking – in half measures.' Dorothea was, he proclaimed, 'a part of my very existence. Those objects that lure the majority of men are without any effect on me . . . Perhaps,' he concluded the hastily written note, 'we shall find each other again another day. I shall be what I am today. So few friendships please me, but when they do they do not end. Vow to keep a beautiful memory and do not have any regrets.' The cynic might be apt to respond that Metternich was after precisely what the majority of men in his situation want from women, but Dorothea was not a cynic, and to be written to in this vein by one of the most powerful men in Europe was just the sort of intoxication that would save her from any more gloomy thoughts on Brighton beach.

When Dorothea returned to Aix on 13 November she was greeted by an ardent letter from the new apostle of romantic love: 'I have passed,' he wrote, 'a most wretched yet comforting night. Wretched because I did not close my eyes, and comforting because I thought so much about the object which is the sole centre of my thoughts. The object of my thoughts has become me, the whole of me. Everything which is outside her has become nothing.' There was a 'reserve' side of him where he carried on the business of politics and diplomacy, dictating memoranda, answering despatches and such like, but his true treasure, that which created his inner happiness, was something quite apart from this quotidian existence. He would not, he declared, offer her such a bad bargain as to tell her the cares of his official life, but that part of his existence that was occupied by love he would share with her. 'I told you yesterday that of all the certainties that which I have found difficult to grasp, the most difficult is the certainty of believing myself to be loved. Why do you inspire me with a security that I have known so little of during my life? Why have I no fear of indulging myself towards you with that feeling of security which I have never experienced before? Are you in truth myself? In fact I believe this, as one believes in something one does not understand.' In this, at least, there was perhaps a germ of self-knowledge. Metternich was in love with the idea of being in love, and he clearly took a great deal of pleasure in the role of the ardent suitor; but what he loved was the reflection of himself in the mirror of his own self-regard.

Metternich managed to see Dorothea that evening. He wrote to her immediately afterwards, heading his letter 'midnight', and thanking her for a beautiful day. 'You have given alms to a beggar . . . I have seen you, I have been able to say what I feel, I have heard you say the one thing I needed – I know it and I wish to teach it to you every hour of my life! Am I quite cold, my dear friend? Am I the man you took me for in those days before you knew me . . . you will come to know who I am better than I can tell you today! Begin by believing in me and finish by loving me, love me with all your heart from this moment, tomorrow and ever, and do not fear regrets: I, who am *you*, will never betray you.' He needed, he said, to know what name she liked to be called by and the date of her birthday. Then he bade her goodnight, telling her that he knew whom he would be sleeping with, and who would be in his thoughts when he awoke. It would have taken a heart made of sterner stuff and a marriage made of more durable stuff than Dorothea's to have resisted such a torrent of emotion. Those romantic dreams which had been stirred in the eleven-year-old Dorothea by her passion for Count Elmpt, and which her marriage had done nothing to satisfy, had once again been given wing.

The Lievens left Aix finally on the morning of 18 November 1818, travelling first back to Brussels and then on to London. Metternich lamented their separation, but he told her that he knew that she too felt its pain. He apologized if he had seemed rather cool when saying farewell, but with others around he had dared not say what he felt. As lovers will, Metternich finished his long day's labours by turning his mind to thoughts of his 'bonne Dorothée', writing to her as midnight struck. After dinner he had talked with the Russian minister to Turin, Prince Kozlovski, who had told him that he loved only voluptuous women with plump cheeks and plenty of flesh on them; Metternich replied that he loved only women whose figures were not so ripe, and what he loved was the soul of the woman, not her physical attributes. Kozlovski accused him of being 'sentimental', which Metternich denied. 'I either love, or I do not love, that is all,' he told Dorothea. He wondered wistfully whether she felt, as he did, that there was a great void in the world? He would give anything to see her. With the clock that they had both heard the previous night striking now only for him, he bade her farewell and asked her not to forget him and their time in Aix.

By the morning Metternich had decided that he could not bear
to be without her, and under the excuse that he needed to go to
Paris to discuss the future of the Spanish colonies with the French
government and Wellington, he decided to depart for Brussels on
21 November in time to see his love. He penned a quick letter to
Dorothea to tell her the good news: 'Mon amie, je t'aime *beaucoup.*'
He adjured her to be 'kind and gentle with your husband. No
quarrels, they do more harm than good, and I do not care for
them. If you wish to be angry, think of your lover and say to
yourself that he would blame you for it.' How many friends, he
wondered, would give her such advice?

At this juncture in the relationship, Dorothea seems to have
taken Metternich's words in the way he wanted, as a sign that he
cared for her. It would not be long before she would begin to
wonder whether he had other motives, but for the moment it was
enough to wait in Brussels for his arrival, which was a day later
than he had wished. They had four days together, or as together
as they could contrive, surrounded as they were with monarchs
and diplomats. As the hour of her departure approached, Metternich again poured out his feelings of loss and desolation: 'you sense
what I sense, feel what I feel . . . be my friend for ever – for life.'
He spent 27 November in a daze, wandering around Brussels
before ending up at the Hotel Wellington where he saw Castlereagh and his wife, happily sitting together. Lady Castlereagh
seemed to him to know what he was feeling, and she took his
hand as though to tell him so: 'I pity myself so much,' he lamented,
'that nothing my friends say can diminish my pain.' Back he went,
sorrowing (or so he wrote) to Aix, where the memory of what
had passed there with Dorothea was almost too much for him:
'My dear friend, nothing in me is the same as it was six weeks ago.
I feel cut in twain; I am here, and yet I am not. It is right that I do
not stay at my lodgings, but I am in that dear room where I was
with you for one moment – and what a moment!'

Dorothea arrived back in London to Metternich's passionate
outpourings – and promptly broke down. She had been feeling
sick towards the end of her stay at Brussels, and by the time she

reached London she was 'in great danger from an inflammation of the throat and lungs'. It was not until early January that she was well enough to catch up on her correspondence. Reflecting on the past few months she told Alexander that 'we have come back well satisfied with our journey – my husband much pleased by the favour and confidence displayed by the Emperor, and I by the interest of the scene passing under my eyes.' She added that 'for my own part I made some interesting acquaintances of whom I shall always retain a pleasant remembrance'; which was one way of putting it. She was, however, able to keep up her correspondence with Metternich. He told her that she was the last thing he thought of before he slept, and the first on his mind when he awoke; 'the great misfortune of our position is that we have so little contact.'

Dorothea hoped that Bonsi might be transferred to another embassy – Paris or Vienna would have done nicely, particularly the latter; but the Tsar was not moving his ambassadors about, and so the Lievens stayed in London, and the lovers stayed hundreds of miles apart. Metternich was, however, a most assiduous correspondent, writing to Dorothea most days, telling her of his life, asking her about her own and generally descanting on the world as he saw it. 'Do you know,' he asked her in January, 'what the real difference between men and women is? For a woman love is everything, for a man it is just part of his life.' Such musing made her doubt the sincerity of his protestations of fidelity, but he was not daunted, hinting that he knew something of her own past: 'Tell me everything. I know when you have been happy and when you have not. I know, for the rest, all that concerns you; you do not need to give me the *names*, I believe that I could supply them. You have made your choices and you have been betrayed – what young woman has not?'

Metternich was not blind to the charge of hypocrisy that his enemies might have levelled at him for his affair. He was, after all, renowned as a champion of the old order and the most conservative values. He was always mindful of Dorothea's status as a married woman, and thanked her for heeding his advice to be sweet and nice to her husband: 'I do not have his rights – nor he mine,' he told Dorothea. 'I have never broken up a marriage, I respect *the law*, which I observe – but that does not apply to loving, because loving is beyond the will of the individual.' But, as a man of the world, Metternich took a wider view of such liaisons. It was, he told her, rare in their sort of lives to be able to combine real love with marriages arranged for more worldly reasons. 'You were a mere child when you were married,' he told her on 2 February 1819, 'and you were placed in a position that does not correspond to the natural development of a woman's character. A young girl needs only love. To her, love seems something spiritual; she does not know its material, bodily aspects. She does not know that it is this which drives her, and which awakens in her a strange, but charming emotion. The girl is then thrown into the arms of a man who begins at this point which ought to be the end. Thenceforth the very course of nature has been inverted – which it never can with impunity.' Because, for men, the act of taking a woman was an ending, whereas for the woman it was a beginning, marriage, which ought for the woman to have been a reward, became something distasteful, and thus was 'victory turned into defeat'. Under this 'regime', which was 'unconstitutional', the spirit sank; in this at least, he joked, he was a 'liberal' and a believer in those constitutions which in the political world he so detested. 'The spirit remained repressed until, finally, it broke forth. At that point, family life often seemed nothing but a grim burden, a duty, an insupportable weight – it seemed nothing more than an obstacle to happiness. The spirit was, in short, in revolt, and snapped those chains which now seemed insupportable, and took its stand on a vigorous declaration of *the rights of man*.'

In the political world, Metternich was the sworn enemy of the doctrine of the rights of man, and he was not much fonder of it in social relations. The natural result of such freethinking was that the individual looked to find 'happiness everywhere but in the servitude of duty'. But to live in such a way was to see life 'lived outside of the constraints, in desire, longings, vain hope, error and regret'. And then came old age: 'romance is done, and once more

facts are visible in all their simplicity. Happy are those who, when
that distant day comes, cannot reproach themselves for laying up
a store of bitter, and enduring, regrets!' In what respects, he asked,
had she done wrong, and what had she to reproach herself with?
For not finding in her marriage what she could never have found
there, and for searching for what she could not find in her husband?
Did her conscience reproach her for looking for love outside of
her marriage? If it did, Metternich would not say that it was wrong:
'I respect the law before everything,' but he recognized that at
times he was too weak to keep it: 'Mon amie, pardonne-moi cette
faiblesse,' he begged; she shared his weakness; they had both done
wrong, they knew, and there was no other excuse than the one
he had already made – which was that marriage was not where
one usually found love. Marriage was an institution sanctioned by
the Church and by society for the rearing of children, 'not to
satisfy the wishes of the heart' – but in the end the heart would
have its way. 'I am convinced that happy marriages will not be
very frequent until they take place between men of forty and
women of thirty. Each partner would then know whom to choose.'
The world, he told her, moved in step with the demands of society,
which the heart often finds it difficult to meet. 'But do not look
outside yourself for the cause. When I told you, long since, that I
wanted you to be nice to your husband, I realised I was giving
you a piece of advice which few men know how to give. But you
ought, my dear, to love me for this, for you, the real you, would
never love, in the man you thought worthy to be your lover,
anything that was not right, or at least wise, in some particular
circumstances. Are we wise to love each other as we do? I cannot
tell. But it is certain that I could not do otherwise.'

With its quasi-philosophical romantic musings, its egocentrism
and its air of worldly-wise superiority, this letter was, while more
revealing than most, typical of the letters that Metternich was
to despatch to Dorothea over the years. That she doubted his
protestations is clear enough from some of Metternich's responses
to her letters. Just after writing the long missive about 'love' and
'the rights of man', he asked, indignantly, if she could give him

the names of the two Englishwomen with whom she supposed him to be in love: 'I have no recollection of any.' Englishwomen, he claimed, were 'singulières', and not at all to his taste, with their strange manners; he had not been in England since he was eighteen, in 1794. Dorothea's reaction to his special pleading can only be inferred from that portion of his letters which was copied by the French secret service. She returned all his letters, which have been lost, and in her old age she carefully edited her own side of the correspondence to remove most of the evidence of its real nature. Had French agents not opened and copied the letters Metternich sent to her in the period immediately after Aix, we should know even less of their relationship than we do, and in this case it would be a shame, not because of any lubricious interest, but because knowing what we do about the relationship helps us to understand the effect Metternich had upon her.

Although Dorothea threw off the pulmonary illnesses which had dogged her since her return to London, she could not seem to regain her health fully – and by early February she knew why; she had evidently taken literally Metternich's advice to be nice to her husband, and she now discovered she was pregnant. 'You have profited from my lessons,' Metternich told her when he heard the news. 'I told you that I wanted things to go well in your *ménage*. I don't know whether your pregnancy is the result of my advice, or whether no such advice was needed, but in any event you are going to have a child; what would you have me say about it? Certainly not what you fear – that it would prevent me coming to see you at the earliest possible moment. No, my dear friend, you don't know me well enough if you could think such a thing for even an instant. I love you no less whether you are *one* or *two*. Pregnancy in marriage doubles its bonds, but not its delights. The children themselves bring happiness. My dear, how could I be annoyed with you for being happier?' He hoped that she would have the daughter she was longing for. 'Your pregnancy will perhaps make you well, but take care of yourself. I already love your little daughter – but never as much as her mother.' It was all eminently civilized and, as such, very much in Metternich's style;

whether Dorothea was quite as pleased with his reaction as he expected her to be might be doubted; if his view of women and love was correct, then it would seem improbable.

As Dorothea prepared for her *accouchement* by spending some time resting at Lady Jersey's house at Middleton in early September, she thought fondly of her lover: 'If only you had been here this summer what wonderful opportunities we should have had of seeing each other at our leisure!' She had, she said, often been left alone for four or five days by her husband's need to be back in London. She had, she told him, dreamed about him: 'I could see you, my dear, and we talked and talked; and, in case anyone should overhear us, you took me on your knee, so that we might speak lower, my dear Clement. I could hear your heart beating, beating beneath my hand, so hard that it woke me up. It was my heart answering yours. *Bon Dieu, mon ami*, how it beats as I write this! Will my dreams ever come true? My Clement, have you ever time for dreams?' Six weeks later, on 15 October 1819, Dorothea was delivered of yet another son, her fourth. The boy was christened George, in honour of the Prince Regent, but there were, of course, those wits who called him '*l'enfant du Congrès*', and thought that 'Clement' might have been a more appropriate Christian name; but even making allowance for Melbourne's comment about paternity being a matter for speculation, there seems little reason to doubt that of young George. Dorothea had not seen Metternich since November, and such was her love for him that at some point during their correspondence she would have let it slip had her lover been the father. The real father wrote to his brother: 'In spite of the serious fears with which she had approached the birth, she had never had a happier confinement than this one.' It would be hard to disagree with that verdict; Dorothea had indeed been very happy – but not for the reasons her husband supposed.

4. 'Europe's safety anchor'

On 4 February 1819 Metternich wrote: 'My dear, you love me well, for you now love that Austria which you used not to love'; for him the relationship was not just an opportunity to indulge his amorous propensities. The liaison between Metternich and Countess Lieven happened just as a *rapprochement* occurred between Austria and Russia; this may have been mere coincidence, but the fact that it would end as relations between the two powers broke down, suggests there may have been an element of calculation buried among the romantic outpourings. Dorothea was certainly in an excellent position to provide Metternich with something he needed quite as much as the knowledge that he was loved – and that was a window on to Russian and British policy. The Congress of Vienna may have succeeded in producing a settlement of Europe that was to last until the middle of the nineteenth century, but that it did so owed as much to the diplomacy of the powers afterwards as it did to the virtues of the peace treaty itself; it also revealed the extent to which Russian military power worried her allies. The British ambassador at The Hague, Lord Clancarty, caught the mood in Vienna and London when he wrote of his fear that 'the Emperor of Russia is desirous of ending matters as he began, by dictating his will as the sovereign law of all Europe.'

Metternich wanted to create a stable international order, and it had been to this end that he had participated in the defeat of Napoleon. Much though he admired Bonaparte's ability to control the social forces unleashed by the French Revolution, he feared that he wanted to use the international anarchy they had created to secure French hegemony in Europe. He would look around, ultimately in vain, for a way of equalling Napoleon's domestic achievement, but Metternich abhorred his influence in international affairs, and had certainly not fought to replace the hegemony of France with that of Russia. In Henry Kissinger's words: 'the dispute between the Tsar and Metternich . . . [was] in substance a contest over the nature of a stable international system.' Alexander 'sought to identify the new international order with his will' and to create a system 'safeguarded solely by the purity of his maxims'. Metternich, having less faith in the perfectibility of human nature in general, and that of the Tsar of All the Russias in particular, 'strove for a balance of forces which would not place too great a premium on self-restraint'. In this he found a fellow spirit in the British Foreign Secretary, Castlereagh.

Unlike most of his fellow countrymen, Lord Castlereagh did not regard the defeat of Napoleon as signalling the end of Britain's connection with the continent. Towards the end of the Vienna Congress he had suggested to the Tsar that the 'sovereigns were solemnly to pledge themselves in the face of the world, to preserve to their people the Peace they had conquered, and to treat as a common Enemy whatever Power should violate it'. He was disturbed when the Tsar took this idea and transformed it into the 'novel proceeding' of the Holy Alliance. He put it down to the 'deeply religious tinge' which the Tsar's thinking had taken under the influence of Madame de Krudener, 'an old Fanatick, who has a considerable Reputation among the few High Flyers in Religion that are to be found at Paris'. Metternich told him that the Austrian Emperor 'felt great Repugnance to be a party to such an act, and yet was more apprehensive of refusing himself to the Emperor's application [and] that it was quite clear that his mind was affected'.

What both Metternich and Castlereagh had wanted was a defensive alliance to protect the peace settlement, and provision for meetings of the allies to review the international situation periodically; what Alexander had come up with was a proposal, the Holy Alliance, which bound all 'Christian Sovereigns' to recognize their common brotherhood and to adopt as their 'sole guide' Christian principles, 'namely, the precepts of justice, Christian charity and peace, which far from being applicable only to private concerns, must have an immediate influence on the council of princes and guide all their steps'. Metternich told Castlereagh that it was clear that 'Peace and Good Will was at present the Idea which engrossed' the Tsar's thoughts, and as a result, Alexander was being 'reasonable on all points', which made Metternich 'unwilling to thwart him in a conception which, however wild, might save him and the rest of the world much trouble, so long as it should last'.

The British declined to sign the Holy Alliance on the ground that, as a constitutional monarch, the Regent was in a different position from his continental counterparts, but Castlereagh, like Metternich, recognized the importance of staying on good terms with Russia. When, in December 1815, he noticed 'some little distrust in Count Lieven's manner, not so much founded upon a doubt of the substantial Politicks of this Gov[ernmen]t, as of the personal cordiality prevailing between the August Personages themselves', Castlereagh went to some pains to try to reassure the Russians. As well as talking matters over with Count Lieven, he told the British ambassador in St Petersburg, the earl Cathcart, that 'I will personally pledge myself for the desire of my court to act upon the most liberal principles with that of St Petersburgh to maintain the true spirit of the alliance, the Peace of Europe & the settlement we have concluded.' But there was the rub – what was the 'true spirit of the alliance'?

Made anxious by Alexander's eccentricities and the power at his disposal, Metternich sought to conciliate him while trying to persuade the British that they ought to be wary of Russian ambitions and do more to counter them. Castlereagh was wise to Metternich's motives, but far from averse to cooperating with him to ensure that the Russians did not gain an undue preponderance of influence on the continent. At Aix the Tsar had suggested a new alliance which would have guaranteed not only the existing international order as set up at Vienna, but also its domestic counterpart. This implied a commitment to interference on the continent that was at odds with British traditions, and so Castlereagh could not give his assent. Metternich, who had no objection to preserving the existing order, none the less feared that such an alliance could become a vehicle for Russian interference all over

Europe, and so turned aside Alexander with the excuse that the
Holy Alliance provided for all that was necessary. The Congress
of Aix ended with all the powers in agreement to continue the
alliance – but the fact that there was now clearly a difference
between how the British and the Austrians might interpret it
meant that Metternich needed to keep a close watch on both his
allies; his liaison with Dorothea gave him a perfect vantage point
from which to supplement the information he could obtain
through more usual diplomatic channels.

Dorothea could, and did, provide him with a medium through
which he could strive to influence Russian policy; but at the same
time the unique position which she had created for herself in
English society presented him with an invaluable insight into its
workings. Metternich noted with delight that she was frequently
invited to the Regent's Pavilion at Brighton: 'if I were the seigneur
of Brighton,' he told Dorothea, 'you would be there all the time,
even as I would myself; in that case London would see me
infrequently.' When the Regent's long-time mistress, that Lady
Hertford whom the Tsar had so studiously ignored, was replaced
in January 1820 by Lady Conyngham, Dorothea was able to report
that 'although we no longer live in the times when Madame de
Pompadour directed the politics of Europe, I do not regard this
London revolution as entirely without significance.' Castlereagh,
she explained, was 'a relative of the ex-favourite, and their connection put him on a more intimate footing with his master and gave
him an added power. He is sulking now, and his sulks will strain
their relations.' In fact, as things turned out, Castlereagh's relations
with the new 'favourite' would have more significance than Dorothea had supposed. Her attention was now drawn towards politics,
knowing that this was what would interest her lover. The French
ambassadress, the Comtesse de Boigne, was close to the mark when
she commented acidly that for Dorothea 'every question could be
reduced to one of personalities.' Indeed, there were times when
Dorothea felt intimidated by Metternich's letters. 'I like you to
realise sometimes that I am stupider than you,' she wrote in 1823.

Her pleasures, Dorothea had once told him, 'are those of a

rather limited intelligence; but that is because, whatever you may say, great intelligence is not really my strong point'. Metternich, however, was adept at soothing such fears. 'I believe you,' she replied to one missive in 1822, 'when you tell me that I do not bore you – for if it is true, as you say, that I am sometimes witty, sometimes stupid, and strong and weak and a number of dissimilar things, it must be very entertaining.'

But it was not simply for the entertainment they offered that Dorothea's letters were valued by her lover; Metternich needed no one to tell him that knowledge was power, and she offered him an insight into English life that was not readily available elsewhere. Dorothea jealously guarded this role, even to the extent of seeing herself in some sort of rivalry with the Austrian ambassador, Prince Paul Esterhazy. It is a mark of her changing role that having at first regarded the beautiful Princess Esterhazy as competition to be seen off, Dorothea should have switched her barbs to the ambassador himself as her own role became more political. 'Your Paul,' she told Metternich, 'amuses me a great deal. He has just the sort of silliness that is very effective . . . I don't deny him intelligence, for he has good judgement; but what he does lack is will power; and, rich as he is, it seems a pity he cannot employ somebody to tell him what he wants or to make him want something. It is the absence of this faculty that hampers him and gives him such an air of vagueness. The same drawback extends to his opinions. He continually hesitates to form any'; this, at least, no one could have said of Countess Lieven. When she discovered that Metternich had used her letters in an official report, she went into rhapsodies: 'I am overwhelmed by the honour you do them. Did I give you any news? I never know what I write to you; I tell you everything at random.' It prompted her to wonder what people in the future would make of their correspondence: 'people will wonder what we were about – whether it was love or politics.' She confessed that 'I really do not know what we are at. I see no great danger in continuing our romance, for we shall remain five hundred leagues apart; and, since we have enough intelligence for this kind of amusement, let us go on.'

Metternich was not the only statesman who showed an interest in Dorothea's opinions. Her letters to her brother Alexander came to the attention of the Russian foreign minister, Count Karl von Nesselrode, who wrote to her in June 1819 suggesting that she might like to keep up an occasional correspondence with him; this she did, for the next fifteen years. Nesselrode was, like the Lievens and the Benckendorffs, another of those 'westerners' whom Alexander I used to direct his foreign policy. A conservative and bureaucratic figure, Nesselrode became State Secretary for Foreign Affairs in 1814. This did not mean that he occupied a role analogous to that of Castlereagh or Metternich. As Lord Walpole told Castlereagh upon his appointment: 'it would seem . . . to be a temporary measure . . . there appears little chance of any man of talents or reputation being appointed to the office of Minister for Foreign Affairs: the present, as a permanent appointment, would be highly disapproved of. Count Nesselrode enjoys no consideration whatsoever, but is merely considered as the Emperor's *Secretary*.' Castlereagh told Lord Liverpool in 1814 that it was Alexander's 'habit to be his own minister and to select as the instrument of his immediate purpose the person who may happen to fall in most with his views.'

'I abstain from all personal reflection,' Nesselrode told Count Lieven in 1813. 'His Majesty is acquainted with me well enough to know that the first aim of my actions is the good of his service and that if he does not agree with my opinions, I am not in a position to say anything.' Nesselrode proved a past master of this courtier's art, and it did him no harm to be on good terms with the sister of one of Alexander's most influential advisers, or to have her take on British affairs. Dorothea was also a useful conduit to the man whose views on European matters most resembled his own – Metternich. Although in private Metternich was not impressed with either Nesselrode's abilities or his strength of character, in public he took care to flatter someone who was very useful to him. Those who later accused Nesselrode of having 'sold out to the Austrians' were not wholly inaccurate; unlike the Tsar's other advisers, Nesselrode favoured a cautious, conservative policy, and in this he and Metternich were natural allies. Nesselrode's conservative alignment with Austria had lost him the Tsar's favour for a while in 1815, but as Alexander began to lose faith in his old liberal views and looked towards a diplomatic alignment that would preserve the peace of Europe, then Nesselrode, with his contacts with Metternich, once more became useful.

From this point of view, Dorothea, by providing a link between Nesselrode and Metternich, formed an invaluable part of a troika that began to move Russian diplomacy in a more conservative direction. Metternich watched developments in Russia with great interest, aware that Nesselrode's partial restoration to favour in early 1820 was a sign that things there were moving in a direction favourable to his own policy. Nesselrode, like Metternich, was a reactionary conservative who 'favoured strict repression of progressive elements, preservation of legitimate monarchical authority, and the dynastic and territorial integrity of the great powers'; in short, if not a man with whom Metternich could do business, he was a conduit through which it could be done.

The gradual *rapprochement* between Russia and Austria that took place between 1818 and 1820 was bad news for the British. Metternich had objected to Alexander's desire to intervene everywhere when he had feared that it would be the Trojan horse for Russian aggrandizement, but as the Russian Tsar became increasingly receptive to his message about the dangers of revolution in Europe, his apprehension lessened. Metternich's success in August 1819 in getting the German Confederation to agree to the Carlsbad decrees, which allowed governments to control the press and the universities and to take special action against suspected revolutionaries, was matched on the international stage by the progress made in convincing Alexander that his old enthusiasm for constitutions and liberal thought should be abandoned. In early 1820 revolutions in Spain and then Naples lent credence to Metternich's many sermons about the dangers of revolution. The Russians responded by suggesting that since these revolts posed a danger to the peace of Europe it was necessary to convene a congress to decide what action should be taken against them. This raised in stark form the question of what the quadruple and quintuple alliances were for.

From Dorothea's letters, Metternich was well aware, even before the blow fell, that he was unlikely to get any help from the British. Castlereagh's backing for the alliance had never been a passport to popularity for him, and the weakness of the Liverpool administration during 1820 made it impossible for the Foreign Secretary to risk his credit any further. The death of George III in January 1820 brought the Regent to the throne in his own right as George IV, but this carried with it the considerable embarrassment of what to do about his estranged wife, Caroline of Brunswick, who now became Queen. The new King demanded that his ministers should procure a divorce for him, but Liverpool refused, and if George could have found an administration willing to give him what he wanted, Liverpool would have been out there and then; since he could not, the Prime Minister remained, but the King was most unhappy, not least with Castlereagh. It had fallen to Castlereagh's lot to tell the King that 'all the powers of Europe were strongly impressed with the impolicy of his attempting a divorce, which c[oul]d only serve to bring forward all the old stories of his treatment of the Princess in the first years of her marriage'; Metternich had told him in 1818 that he would be willing to come to England in person to dissuade the King from taking such a step. Since George IV had no alternative to keeping his ministers, he kept them, but he liked neither them, nor their advice; he did, however, secure a promise that if Queen Caroline returned to England to claim her rights, they would agree to bring in a divorce bill.

Nor was the King's displeasure the only thing the ministers had to worry about. While Metternich was busy trying to put down revolution on the continent, in Cato Street, London, a band of plotters was discovered planning to assassinate the whole Cabinet; there had been, it transpired, particular competition over who would have the honour of cutting Castlereagh's throat. When Dorothea dined with him in late February 1820, he had constables guarding his house and 'two loaded pistols in the pockets of his breeches. He showed them to me at table. I was nervous every time he made a movement to offer me anything; I sat sideways on in my chair; I edged away from the left and got so near to my right-hand neighbour that he could put nothing in his mouth without elbowing me.' Wellington, in sharp contrast, took no precautions at all, although 'everybody knows that he is always followed.' It was with a little relief that Castlereagh left London in early March to stand for re-election in his Irish constituency – although that was another distraction the ministers could have done without.

Although Liverpool continued to command a majority after the general election, his administration still lacked the firm foundations from which Castlereagh could have conducted a more active foreign policy. 'The King,' Dorothea told Metternich, 'is a dangerous madman . . . Can one imagine anything more absurd than an amorous and inconstant sexagenarian who, at the beginning of his reign, gives up all his time to a love affair? It is pitiable.' Besotted with his new mistress, Lady Conyngham, whose links were with the opposition, George harassed Liverpool and showed his distrust to such an extent that Dorothea was convinced that it would not be long before there was a new government.

The arrival of Queen Caroline in England in June provided a total distraction from other business. Liverpool had to fulfil his promise to bring in a bill that would allow divorce, but that meant that all the royal dirty linen would be washed in public. George may have been indignant with the wayward behaviour of his wife, but his own had not been of the best, and with the mob firmly on her side, ministers found themselves supporting a most unpopular cause. It was, Dorothea thought, singular that a ministry which had 'put up a glorious fight against a hostile Europe' and which had 'triumphed over the greatest difficulties, foreign and domestic, ever to have confronted a government' was going to be 'defeated by a woman'. George Canning, perhaps the greatest orator on the government side of the House, decided to resign, claiming that his former relations with the Queen necessitated such a step; since rumour had it that he had been among Caroline's many *amours*, this was not a surprise – although it did greatly weaken the government just when it needed his debating ability most.

The summer was dominated by the question of the Queen's divorce, with ministers steadily on the defensive, and with their overthrow being constantly predicted. Dorothea told Wellington that it would be disastrous if England acquired a new administration at such a moment in the affairs of Europe, to which the Duke responded: 'Do you suppose that any other consideration holds us back? We should have thrown up the whole thing twenty times over if Castlereagh and I had not represented to our colleagues what the general consequences would be if we resigned. We shall be firm; we must hold out.' Delighted as she was to hear this, Dorothea remained doubtful of their capacity to do it. Wellington was, however, correct in his prediction, although the divorce dominated politics until the autumn.

Dorothea, like Metternich himself, recognized that no alternative government was likely to follow the foreign policy pursued by Castlereagh; unfortunately for them, as Wellington's comments suggested, only he and Castlereagh were really committed to it. They had been asked by the distracted Cabinet to draw up a policy for dealing with the consequences of the revolution in Spain. Wellington's view, based upon long experience of Spain, was that 'there is no country in Europe in the affairs of which foreigners can interfere with less advantage', and he counselled staying well clear of any calls to do so. Castlereagh had to consider the wider international repercussions of non-intervention – but took the view that the domestic consequences of doing so would be even worse. He would have been happy for Metternich to have intervened in Spain, but this was not, in his view, an area where the alliance could operate – not, at least, his conception of it: 'it never was . . . intended as an Union for the Government of the World, or for the Superintendence of the Internal Affairs of other States.' Castlereagh was in 'no doubt of the general danger which menaces more or less the stability of all existing Governments from the principles which are afloat', but he doubted whether foreign intervention would do anything to avert it. 'The Principle of one State interfering by force in the internal affairs of another in order to enforce obedience to the governing authority, is always a question of the greatest moral, as well as political delicacy,' Castlereagh thought, and he could not see British public opinion being content to watch their country intervening to put down a constitutional regime, however unstable; that, he believed, would do more to destroy the alliance than anything else. As Esterhazy warned Metternich before Castlereagh sent him a copy of his memorandum: 'The British Cabinet wish, as the Duke of Wellington has often said to me, that the Alliance sleeps.'

Count Lieven passed Castlereagh's comments to his master – who refuted them strongly; this was not his idea of the alliance. He wanted the five powers to make a joint remonstrance at Madrid, recommending a 'wise constitutional regime'. Metternich, never happier than when he could mediate between two allies who could not agree on the best course of action, was not displeased by this turn of events: he disagreed with Castlereagh, but understood the limitations to which he was subject; he agreed with Alexander, but feared the consequences of letting a Russian army cross Europe. He was in the happy position of being able to tell the Tsar that he agreed that they ought to stand firm against revolution, but that it would be unwise to reject the advice of the Duke of Wellington if he thought military intervention in Spain undesirable. From this happy position he was jolted by the news in July that there had been a revolution in the kingdom of Naples. Revolution in Spain was bad enough, but could be contemplated with more equanimity than in Naples, which was the largest of the Italian kingdoms and which was bound by treaties of alliance to Austria; this was a direct threat to Austria's vital interests.

Dorothea told Metternich that the British were 'dumbfounded by the news. You will not be; you will act'; and she congratulated him on the foresight he had shown when, a few months earlier, he had said that 'the year 20 will witness many unexpected events.' She thought that the news would complete Alexander I's disillusion with constitutionalism: 'My Emperor is full of qualities, of fine and good intentions, of rectitude. Nevertheless if one investigates the source of all the troubles which are at present convulsing the world, does one not come back to him? Is it not his liberalism that has strengthened the democratic party in Europe? This is a painful admission. But must he not make it himself at the bottom of his heart? That he has recovered, I firmly believe; but the seed he has sown is still sprouting.' This was, indeed, a bold declaration on the part of a Russian, and is some indication of the influence which Metternich had had upon Dorothea; it also reveals what bound her to Nesselrode, whose conservative instincts the Tsar was coming increasingly to share. She was correct in her prediction of the Tsar's reaction; henceforth he would listen to the siren voice from Vienna, and he demanded the convening of a European congress to concert action. This request put Castlereagh in a difficult position. He shared Wellington's view that since this was a problem that fell squarely within the Austrian sphere of influence then 'Devil take me, Prince Metternich must march.' If he warned his allies what he was going to do, they would give their consent and Austria would crush the revolution; his only caveat was that Austria 'must come out of it with clean hands'.

Castlereagh told Metternich through Esterhazy that as far as Britain was concerned, the situation in Naples was far more serious than that in Spain, and that while he stood by his State Paper of 5 May, because this revolution was a threat to neighbouring states, Britain would support Austrian action – although, of course, she could take none herself. Metternich was now in a dilemma. Fearful of a Europe-wide revolution, he doubted Austria's ability to combat it by herself, and he was happy to work with Russia; but he did not want to end up playing the part of Sancho Panza to Alexander's Don Quixote, and he was worried by the Tsar's insistence that France should take part in the congress. In a long and impassioned letter to Castlereagh on 8 August he outlined his predicament. It was, he said, the greatest crisis of his career, and he needed more than tacit British backing if he was going to be able to resist whatever demands Alexander would make at Troppau.

The moment could not have been less propitious from Castlereagh's point of view. The hearings in the Lords about the Queen's divorce were about to take place, and as Dorothea described it, London was in ferment: 'the Opposition believes there will be a revolution; the Ministry perhaps fears it.' The London mob came out in force to support the 'wronged Queen', but, as Dorothea told Metternich: 'Few men have Lord Castlereagh's intrepid coolness, and more than once nothing but his unruffled appearance has overawed the mob.' But with the Queen taking the house next door to him, he was obliged to move: 'he was told that however courageous it might be to brave the danger, his presence became criminal when it provoked a disturbance'; he was reduced to having his bed installed in the Foreign Office. These were not propitious circumstances in which to support publicly the forces of counter-revolution on the continent.

In an effort to prevent a breach with Britain, which would have meant wholly committing himself to Russia, Metternich suggested that Castlereagh might want to send an observer to the Troppau Congress; this would not commit Britain to any action, but would signify moral support for the alliance. From Count Lieven, however, Castlereagh was getting a quite different story about the congress. Where Metternich suggested that it would not be on the model of Aix, and thus not a full-scale meeting of the alliance, it became clear that this was exactly what Alexander wanted.

Castlereagh urged him to take unilateral action, which, he averred, all the other powers would be bound to sanction: 'All we ask of our Allies is not to annoy and cripple us when it can be avoided, by phrases and forms, which in fact lead to nothing more substantial than to indulge the Russian Emperor and his Minister, the latter in composing and the former in promulgating high-sounding declarations which, be assured, do not fall in with the sentiments which are to be found on either side of the House of Commons.' With the opposition emboldened by the government's discomfiture over the 'Queen's business', where the case eventually had to be dropped because of the amount of damage it was doing to the King, the Whigs felt able to press it on its reaction to events in Naples. Liverpool was forced to answer that Britain was in no

way committed to Austria. It was little wonder that Harriet Granville should have reported that Dorothea was '*outrée* with England
for refusing to take a part in this new dish of Continental troubles'.

Britain did send an observer to the Troppau Congress, but
Castlereagh had been wise not to go further, since it culminated
in a Protocol, which provided for the allies to intervene to restore
legitimate regimes that faced a threat from revolution. It was
decided to invite King Ferdinand of Naples to a further congress
at Laibach to discuss the future of his kingdom. Castlereagh told
Metternich that the decisions that had been reached 'were so
directly opposed to the political and constitutional system of Great
Britain that the latter must disavow and even protest against them';
and, knowing that Esterhazy had been attempting to win over
George IV, he warned that 'if the King were to sanction them he
would be on the road to abdication.' He told Count Lieven
wistfully that: 'I have never before so much regretted as now not
being with the Emperor and able to submit my thoughts to him.'
He was sure that, face to face, he could have convinced Alexander
that turning the alliance into something like an international police
force was not the best way forward for its unity. 'The Emperor,'
he reminded Lieven, 'has repeated on every occasion his unshaken
determination not to contract new engagements, not to form new
ties outside those existing, not to seek new guarantees outside the
General Alliance. This determination is, in fact, Europe's safety
anchor. Why change it now?' It was an excellent question, to
which the next two years would provide the answer.

5. 'He listens to me'

'Troppau' became shorthand for a policy of intervention by the Holy Alliance. Castlereagh's opponents had always accused him of truckling to the reactionary instincts of Metternich and his Carlsbad decrees passed by the Frankfurt parliament in 1819, curbing freedom of speech and the press. Now they could go the whole hog and charge him with being in league with a newly reactionary Tsar to keep Europe in chains. Knowing that this would be the case, Castlereagh had moved quickly to distance himself publicly from what his allies had done. He wrote a despatch on 16 December 1820, reiterating most of the points made in his paper of 5 May, but this time in a form designed for parliamentary consumption. This did not, however, mean that he had decided to part company with the men with whom he had worked since 1814, as he assured Count Lieven in late December 1820. He told him that his heart bled at having to send such a despatch. Castlereagh remained attached to the alliance, he told Lieven; he too hated revolutions, and recognized that they might be dangerous to Britain. His problem, he reiterated, was not with the aims and intentions of the allies, but with the issuing of a proclamation; if it was published, he would have to issue his counterblast, but that did not mean that he wished to separate himself from the alliance. Castlereagh's difficulty, as he told his half-brother, Sir Charles Stewart, was that the allies were basing themselves on something that looked very like the divine right of kings, which was hardly something that the House of Hanover could maintain: 'we cannot adhere to their doctrine, and if they will be theorists we must act in separation upon matters not specifically provided for by Treaty, which seems an odd option for them to make in the present state of Europe.'

Castlereagh's ambivalence about the turn events were taking

was increased by the results of the congress at Laibach in January 1821, where it was agreed to send Austrian troops to Naples. Much though Castlereagh approved of what had been done, the insistence of his allies that the Austrians were acting in the name of the whole alliance meant that Britain had to enter a protest. Whatever he thought privately, in public Castlereagh could not be seen to support the reactionary powers. In a circular to all British embassies on 19 January 1821, he made it plain that Britain was not in any way associated with the actions of the other powers.

The task of trying to alienate neither his own public opinion nor his continental allies was one that imposed a great strain upon an already overworked politician; and as he began to feel it, Castlereagh found in Dorothea a sympathetic outlet for his anxieties. For him she became the unofficial conduit through which Metternich could be assured that whatever needed to be said for public consumption, Castlereagh would not desert his old allies. Castlereagh was the sort of politician appreciated best by his peers. Sir Robert Peel, writing in 1839, doubted

whether any public man (with the exception of the Duke of Wellington) who has appeared within the last half century possessed that combination of qualities, intellectual and moral, which would have enabled him to effect under the same circumstances what Lord Londonderry did effect in regard to the Union with Ireland and the great political transactions of 1813, 1814 and 1815 . . . To do these things required a rare union of high and generous feelings, courteous and most prepossessing manners, a warm heart, and a cool head, great temper, great industry, great fortitude, great Courage, moral and personal, that Command and Influence which makes other men willing instruments.

This was a well-deserved tribute to one of Britain's greatest foreign secretaries, but Castlereagh was neither a gregarious nor a popular figure. As Dorothea told Metternich in early 1822, 'he knows very few people in society, which consists mostly of members of the other camp and of women who, like my friend [Harriet Granville], do not know him well enough to find him amusing.' Dorothea herself found him sympathetic, and during 1821 she drew him closer to herself – so close that she felt obliged to reassure Metternich: 'If you hear any remarks about my intimacy with him, please do not think there is any harm in it. When he meets me he fastens on to me; we spend whole evenings together and he never leaves me.' The reasons for their burgeoning friendship were partly personal, but it is hard to avoid the conclusion that, as usual with Dorothea's friendships with men of power, there was a good deal of political calculation involved. As she wrote to Metternich after Castlereagh's death: he was 'perhaps the only man in England who understood European politics, and whose principles as well as his inclinations urged him towards friendship with Austria'.

Dorothea was encouraged to draw closer to Castlereagh by Metternich when she finally saw her lover again in October 1821. It had been nine years since the Lievens had left Russia, and the Count applied for leave to attend to his own affairs. He and Dorothea agreed that since his journeying would be expensive, she should stay behind. But rather than incur the costs involved in acting as ambassadress, she should go to Spa in Germany to await his return; this offered the chance for her to see Metternich again. She and Bonsi went as far as Rochester together before parting. Dorothea surprised herself by how bitterly she wept at his departure: 'I found myself isolated, lost and very sad,' she told Lady Granville, writing from Calais on 3 June 1821. 'The force of habit is strong,' she told Metternich, 'and now that I am deprived of his presence and his protection, I forget that differences of character and disposition now and then cause me unpleasant moments.' She soon discovered that 'there is nothing more exhausting than being without a husband. You have to think, you have to devote all your intelligence to arranging where to sleep and where to dine.'

In Brussels Dorothea spent most of her time with the Prince and Princess of Orange, whom she found both stupid and boring: 'ah mon dieu que c'est bête d'avoir de l'Esprit.' It was not until she arrived at Spa that she realized how good Brussels had been. It was, she told Harriet Granville, 'the coldest, ugliest and emptiest place it is possible to imagine'; there was neither society, letters, nor even sunshine, and because she had been there three years earlier with Metternich, the local commandant thought that she was there incognito and had her put under surveillance. She had actually had to spend three days with no one of any intelligence to speak to: 'I need distractions,' she complained to Harriet, 'and I am wasting away through boredom.' Her one consolation was the correspondence she received from Harriet, but that was scant compensation for the other oppressions of life in Spa, which lifted only when the kings of Prussia, Wurttemberg and the Netherlands arrived there in July.

One of the things that occupied her mind during this season in social hell was the news of the revolt in Greece. In March 1821 there was an uprising in what is now Romania, against Turkish rule, which was followed by similar events in the Peloponnese. Fortunately for Metternich, the Tsar was still with him at Laibach when the revolt happened, and he was able to counsel Alexander against doing anything to support a rebellion against lawful rulers. This was advice which was urgently needed, at least from the Austrian point of view. The Ottoman Empire had lost its last two wars against Russia, and at the end of them it had had to cede territory. Austria did not wish to see Russia profit further from Turkish weakness, but the temptations for Alexander to intervene were immense. The Greeks were fellow Orthodox Christians over whom, since the 1774 treaty of Kutchuk-Kainardji, the Russians had claimed rights of protection. Had Alexander moved to assert those rights, he could also have furthered the dynastic aims of his grandmother, Catherine the Great, who had not given his younger brother the name Constantine by chance. Aware of these temptations, Metternich moved to convince the Tsar that what mattered about the Greeks was not that they were Christian but the fact that they were rebels; it would be inconsistent to suppress rebellions in Spain and Naples and then to support them in Athens. From Spa, Dorothea observed what the British newspapers were saying about the Russian Tsar not helping the Greeks and pronounced it 'une bêtise'; if Russia were to try to do so, she would be criticized and her motives would be suspect. In this, as events would show, she was right.

By August Dorothea had migrated to a little watering-place near Wiesbaden called Schlangenbad, which she found a good deal more agreeable: 'You have no idea how pleasant the baths here are,' she wrote, 'you come out quite white and with your skin as soft as satin, whilst the warmth is delicious.' One of the reasons her spirits had risen was that Schlangenbad was near Metternich's Rhineland castle at Johannisberg, but the Greek revolt and the revival of the Eastern Question kept him in Vienna for the whole summer. However, just when Dorothea thought that she would have no relief from the boredom that had dogged her since she left England, she received a summons from George IV inviting her to visit him in Hanover. The invitation came, in reality, from Castlereagh, who had asked Metternich to Hanover to discuss the Eastern Question, and he thought that Dorothea's presence might ease matters; Count Lieven had also been invited, but he would not be able to get there until after his wife. Dorothea arrived at the same time as Metternich, which gave the lovers a week together before the Count arrived; there was much catching up to be done.

No letters survive from this reunion, but this time, unlike three years previously, *l'amour* was not the only item on the menu. Metternich was pleased that he had prevented Alexander from doing anything rash about the Greek revolt, but he was not arrogant enough to think that a few words of warning would suffice for ever; it was necessary to formulate a policy, and to that end he needed to talk to the man who had helped him restrain Alexander for so long – Castlereagh. He was received by George IV with a degree of flattery which proved excessive even to one of his nearly insatiable appetite for it: the King compared him to Cato, Caesar, Gustavus Adophus, the Younger Pitt and Wellington: 'I do not remember ever having been embraced with such tenderness, and I have never in all my life heard so many pretty things said about me.' This was in sharp contrast to what George had to say about his ministers. Metternich knew, from Dorothea's accounts, just how bad the King's relations with Liverpool and the Cabinet had become. Wellington had told her in June that he was 'certain that if we give the slightest occasion we shall be dismissed the same day'. Passing this on to Metternich, she told him that 'if the King is mad, his Ministers are very feeble.'

One of the things that Dorothea and Metternich could do was to try to help restore relations between Castlereagh and the King. George was angry with all his ministers for, as he saw it, failing to rid him of Queen Caroline, and the fact that she had conveniently died in August did not make him any more forgiving where Liverpool and his colleagues were concerned; Castlereagh was in particular disfavour because of his wife's behaviour. Emily Castlereagh had incurred the wrath of the King's new mistress, Lady Conyngham, by not inviting her to supper. She took it as a deliberate slight and complained to the King, who would not have been mollified had he heard Castlereagh's explanation that his wife 'was much too high-minded to pay court to *any one*, much less to a woman whose only notoriety arose from so shameful a cause'. Dorothea and Metternich both worked on George IV to persuade him to take Castlereagh back into favour; indeed, so successful were they that there was some talk about whether he should succeed Liverpool as premier. From Metternich's point of view, it would have been a 'real benefit' had Liverpool given way to Castlereagh: 'our political standpoint would certainly gain by England's taking a more vigorous grasp in the world's affairs.' Liverpool had told Castlereagh in the spring that if he did retire then he 'was the person he looked to be his successor at the head of the Government'; but the problem with that was that it was likely to bring Canning to the Foreign Office.

The reasons why Canning's appointment to the Foreign Office aroused fear in both Castlereagh and Metternich will be more fully considered in the next chapter, but suffice it to say at this point that, in the words of the Duke of Wellington's confidante, Harriet Arbuthnot, 'Mr Canning was a man whose public character was so tainted that he had never been of the use to us which, from his great talents, he ought to have been.' Dorothea did not know Canning well since 'he does not go into society. He is very domestic, his wife is ugly and jealous, and he never lives in London, so that it is very difficult to see him.' She was aware of his reputation as a great wit, but thought that it was merely 'designed to impress'. She told Metternich not to worry about him: 'Mr Canning is not well thought of; he made a compromise with his principles, and that is never forgiven in England.' Time would show that while Dorothea was right to think he would never be trusted, she was wrong to draw from this the conclusion that Metternich should not worry about him.

Thus it was that the meeting at Hanover brought Castlereagh and Dorothea closer, as she was delighted by the rapport between him and her lover. As she later told Metternich: 'you gave me a taste for his conversation.' No great orator, Castlereagh was rather inclined to let his sentences drift on at the expense of sense and his listener's patience, but 'his phrases are always unexpected.' Dorothea particularly treasured his comments about England's attitude towards Austria: 'We regard her as the pivot of Europe and our shoulder is always ready to support her. We are like a lover whom she will always find waiting for her; and we like her to help her other lover, Russia, who is perhaps not always so faithful, but who must be treated all the better for that very reason.' Inelegant though this formulation was, it expressed the truth of Castlereagh's Austrian policy. He knew that it was essential for British interests that Austria should not find herself with no alternative but to cooperate with Russia; his difficulty was avoiding such a policy appearing as though it involved cooperating with autocratic regimes to suppress the liberties of Europe.

Castlereagh returned to England in advance of the King and the Lievens, but rather than trying to take advantage of this situation, he used it to prepare Liverpool and his colleagues for the King's return by persuading the Prime Minister that a position at court should be found for Lord Conyngham as a means of effecting a reconciliation. Castlereagh could have been Prime Minister had he wanted the post, but he preferred to help reconstruct the administration and to bring George IV and Liverpool together again. 'All the merit for this reconciliation,' Count Lieven told

Nesselrode on 9 December, 'is due to Lord Londonderry, who has been able cleverly to accommodate the interests and *amour propre* of the two sides.' At a banquet at which Esterhazy was present, George IV declared: 'I regard Prince Metternich as the first statesman in Europe, and after him Lord Londonderry; these two Ministers understand one another so perfectly, and their agreement is so important in the present state of Europe, that this circumstance alone ought to outweigh all other considerations.' Lieven reported, correctly, that the Hanover visit had appreciably fortified the existing intimacy between Metternich and Castlereagh; he ought to have known, since his wife was the most active agent in maintaining it.

Dorothea told Metternich that 'you cannot imagine how pleased Lord Castlereagh was to see me again. He came in with open arms; I simply had to open mine half way, so that we gave each other a kind of semi-tender embrace.' Castlereagh asked her whether she thought that Metternich really liked him, and she took the opportunity of reassuring him that he did. He told her: 'It is extraordinary how much at ease I feel when I can talk to Prince Metternich: it is the same with you; my ideas are all fluid'; when she replied that 'fluid was charming', Castlereagh 'gave a loud Ha, ha'. Indeed, so close did the ambassadress and the Foreign Secretary become that when George IV, as a gesture of peace, invited all his ministers to Brighton, he specifically told Castlereagh that Dorothea would be there: 'that means,' she told Metternich, 'that he thinks there is something between us.' At dinner 'he told Londonderry to come and sit by me. He has a passion for encouraging the affairs he suspects.' But having done that, the King monopolized Dorothea for most of the evening.

To the modern mind, the question of whether George IV was correct to think that there was 'something' between Dorothea and Castlereagh is bound to loom large; but in this, as in so many other instances, it is doomed to have its prurience frustrated by want of evidence. When, in old age, Dorothea edited her letters to Metternich, she pruned them of passages which would have revealed the true nature of their relationship, which is a reminder that the mid-Victorian period was a good deal less open than the Regency era had been, and that those who survived into it adapted to its mores; were it not for the accident of the French secret service intercepting some of Metternich's letters to Dorothea, we should even lack evidence that the two of them were lovers, although everyone assumed they were. We know that Dorothea was not faithful to her husband, and we know that Castlereagh was, in Harriet Arbuthnot's words, 'a great flirt & very fond of ladies', and that he occasionally resorted to prostitutes for relaxation from his labours, but while suggestive, these things prove nothing. Dorothea liked to tease Metternich with the idea that there might be some intimacy between her and Castlereagh, but this signifies only that she was as big a flirt as Castlereagh himself. What brought the two of them together was Metternich, who also kept them together; whether anything else cemented that relationship is something that posterity cannot know.

Dorothea formed the essential link in the troika between the back-in-favour Nesselrode, Metternich and Castlereagh; all three of them had a common interest in restraining Alexander I from going to war over the Eastern Question, because they feared that, to quote Castlereagh's message to the Tsar, such a war 'would assist the game of the revolutionists in Europe, to whom, and to whom alone the late events are to be attributed'. That Metternich and Castlereagh had other reasons for wishing to restrain the Russians was not, perhaps, something either of them chose to share with the Russian ambassadress to London.

Like Metternich, Castlereagh was not blind to the moral impulses that might impel the Tsar to intervene on behalf of the Greeks, but, as he showed in a letter to Alexander on 28 October, he was at one with his Austrian friend in doubting the application of morality to foreign policy: 'It will naturally occur to every virtuous and generous mind, and to none more probably than to the Emperor of Russia's own – indeed it is the first impression which presents itself to every reflecting observer when he contemplates the internal state of European Turkey – viz: Is it fit that such a state of things should continue to exist? Ought the Turkish yoke to be forever riveted upon the necks of their suffering and Christian subjects . . . It is impossible not to feel the appeal; and if a statesman were permitted to regulate his conduct by the counsels of his heart instead of the dictates of his understanding, I really see no limits to the impulse, which might be given to his conduct, upon a case so stated. But we must always recollect that his is the grave task of providing for the peace and security of those interests immediately committed to his care . . . I cannot, therefore, reconcile it to my sense of duty to embark in a scheme for new modelling [*sic*] the position of the Greek population at the hazard of all the destructive confusion and disunion which such an attempt may lead to, not only within Turkey, but in Europe.' It was this shared sense of the importance of what a later generation of politicians would call *realpolitik* that brought Castlereagh and Metternich together; they both knew that Alexander lacked it, and hoped, through the Lieven embassy, Nesselrode, and their own efforts, to supply what nature had neglected to – a curb on the Tsar's enthusiasms. The under-standing with Castlereagh also gave Metternich 'the advantage of being able to prove to Russia how far one can go with England when one understands how to speak her language'.

The Tsar was now fast retreating from the support he had tended to offer to liberalism and constitutionalism, and as he did so his distrust of Metternich ebbed, and as this happened, Nesselrode's star rose. At Laibach it had been Nesselrode, not the more liberal Capodistrias, who had edited the final declaration in which the powers pledged themselves to combat the forces of revolution. Over the winter of 1821 to 1822 Castlereagh and Metternich waited to see who would prevail: if Alexander decided to go to war in the spring, then Capodistrias and those who wanted a more 'Russian' policy would have won; if he did not, then Nesselrode, with his cautious, reactionary conservative diplomacy, would have carried the day – and it was the aim of Castlereagh, Metternich and Countess Lieven to ensure that this would happen.

During this period, Dorothea was at the heart of British politics, and a more or less permanent resident at the King's Brighton Pavilion, where she watched the ministers come and go, delighting in the fact that whenever Londonderry or Wellington were summoned, George would tell her that he had done so for her sake: 'I should like to know,' she teased Metternich, 'which he thinks I prefer. I let him do it, for it is all to the good.' Wellington, who came to the Pavilion for the first time in early January 1822, was 'astonished by it'. As Dorothea told Metternich: 'I do not believe that, since the days of Heliogabalus, there have been such magnificence and such luxury. There is something effeminate in it which is disgusting. One spends the evening half-lying on cushions; the lights are dazzling: there are perfumes, music, liqueurs' – and the Duke's reaction to it all was characteristic: 'Devil take me, I think I must have got into bad company.'

Meanwhile, the battle for the soul of Alexander and of Russian foreign policy reached its crisis. From St Petersburg the British ambassador, Sir Charles Bagot, reported that 'the labour and intrigues of Count Capo d'Istria to bring on the war are inconceivable', and no one could be sure of the Tsar's decision until he announced it himself. By late February Alexander had decided: instead of sending an army across the Pruth into Moldavia, he sent a diplomat to Vienna; although he thought his allies had misunderstood him and failed to give him the necessary support, he could not take the responsibility for declaring war when he was 'well aware that the smallest spark which falls upon such combustible materials may kindle a flame which all our efforts may perhaps hereafter be insufficient to extinguish.' Although Capodistrias would later complain that Alexander had sacrificed Russian interests for those of Europe, it would not be until the summer that Alexander would definitively pronounce against going to war over the Eastern Question. In the meantime, Castlereagh spent much time in negotiation with Lieven and Metternich to exert a pacifying influence upon the Tsar. Much was thought to depend upon the sequel to the meeting at Hanover, which would take place in the summer.

Castlereagh's other contribution to better Anglo-Russian relations was to grow closer to Dorothea. She recorded how, in late February when she was taking her morning walk alone,

Castlereagh dismounted from his horse and walked with her: 'The fact is that, being so accustomed to tell one another everything, we no longer have anything to say, except *tête-à-tête*; and then we never stop. I really believe that he loves me with all his heart.' They talked about the meeting in the summer, which was due to take place in Florence, and Castlereagh said that he wished to be there, 'holding himself aloof, but at the same time prepared to take part in any discussions that may occur'. She assured him that Metternich wanted him to be there. 'He does not,' she told Metternich, 'speak quite frankly with me yet, because he thinks I am more intimate with the heir presumptive than I am. All the same, I am often surprised at what he says to me; he must trust me, and he is right.' Just how struck with Dorothea Castlereagh actually was may be a matter for speculation, but of her utility to him as a channel of communication to Metternich, there can be no doubt.

Castlereagh was well aware of the worries his correspondence with Metternich and the Tsar caused to his colleagues, and he was equally alert to the fact that there were things he would like to say to them that would not create a good impression if they came to the attention of the House of Commons; for such communications, Dorothea was ideal. Writing to him on 4 March, she told Metternich that 'I feel obliged to pass on to you what Lord Londonderry confided to me yesterday. He does not know if he will write to you himself on account of his colleagues, who would think it too official a step. But he wants the point made clear to you.' The 'point' was that 'we are in perfect agreement, Prince Metternich and I, on the fundamentals of every question; but in the application of our views on the Eastern Question, I find a shade of difference which makes me anxious to bring him around to my point of view.' Metternich wanted discussions with the Turks about meeting Russia's demands entrusted to a set of commissioners, but Castlereagh thought that the issue of those talks was so important that it would be better if more senior and skilled negotiators were entrusted with the task.

The traffic between Dorothea and Castlereagh was not all one way; she offered herself as a mediator in the almost equally difficult task of brokering a settlement between Lady Conyngham and Lady Castlereagh. She made a great effort to get on good terms with the favourite, although privately she found her an object of contempt. 'Love which allows nothing to interfere with it is all very fine; but how extraordinary when its object is Lady Conyngham! Not an idea in her head; not a word to say for herself; nothing but a hand to accept pearls and diamonds with, and an enormous balcony to wear them on. Is it really possible to be in love with a woman who accepts diamonds and pearls?' But with Lady Castlereagh unwilling to try to curry favour with Lady Conyngham, even Dorothea's diplomatic skills were of no avail. 'I see no means of bringing about a reconciliation,' she lamented to Metternich in January 1822. Even when Dorothea arranged to take Lady Castlereagh to see the favourite in late April, 'she gave me the slip, and I am furious. She is the most changeable person in the world.'

Matters came to a head in May when Lady Conyngham told the King that she would not attend a state banquet if Lady Castlereagh were invited. At the King's request, Dorothea interceded and managed, eventually, to persuade Lady Conyngham that it would be 'in the worst possible taste' not to invite the Foreign Secretary to a dinner for the Crown Prince of Denmark, while it would be 'a personal insult' to invite him but not his wife. 'I can think of no more difficult job,' she confided to Metternich, 'than getting round a woman's vanity, when one can appeal neither to her reason nor her decent feelings.' Dorothea was, however, taken aback by Castlereagh's reaction when he wormed out of her the truth of the matter: 'he suddenly flew into a positive rage. "You have shown me my position, our position, clearly. Things cannot go on like this. We cannot put up with a Lady Conyngham who is powerful enough to offer us such affronts."' This seemed to Dorothea 'singularly ill-judged'; after all, she counselled him, Lady Conyngham was the King's mistress and 'could not be opposed', which meant simply putting up with the inconvenience of her opinions. But Castlereagh would not be mollified and threatened to resign if things got any worse: 'I have done enough for my country and my master to be independent in that respect; and nothing can stop me.' His 'wild appearance' and confused talk disturbed her – as did his parting shot: he looked her full in the face and asked, 'And you – you are also a traitor.' It all struck her as very odd, and when she talked to his brother, Sir Charles Stewart, about his 'singular frame of mind', he explained that 'Londonderry is disgusted with everything. One more reason for disgust – this woman's quarrel – and the cup overflowed.' Dorothea was so upset by Castlereagh's strange behaviour that she left the reception without saying anything. In the carriage on the way back to Harley Street she told her husband what had happened. His response was: 'Either I am mad or he is!'

Sir Charles Stewart explained that his brother was suffering from the effects of overwork. He felt that he was bearing the whole burden of the government and getting no support, and now he saw younger men, such as Robert Peel, being brought in who might challenge his position in the Commons. He knew, Stewart told Dorothea, 'that he has enemies' but 'he does not know who they are, and thus suspects them all.' This suspicion extended even to Wellington, which amazed Dorothea, who said that he might as well suspect her, as she was even friendlier with the King and his mistress than Wellington. Stewart 'burst into tears. He told me that Lord Londonderry was broken hearted, and that he had never seen a man in such a state.'

When Dorothea saw Castlereagh a few days later she was, she told Metternich, horrified: 'Londonderry looks ghastly. He has aged five years in the last week; one can see that he is a broken man.' He feared, she said, that they were intriguing to have Wellington put in his place as Foreign Secretary. 'All this,' she admitted, 'has its plausible side; and if one were distrustful to start with, one might credit it; however, you know that it lacks foundation. Politically, I should be exchanging one evil for another.' She wondered why Castlereagh had 'contracted these suspicions? It seems to me that I have an honest face. Why cannot he see what is in my heart? Well, I shall leave him to calm down a little; he will soon come to his senses.' Dorothea worked hard to help bring this about. She persuaded Lady Conyngham that the

King's prestige depended upon the forthcoming visit to Florence and that it was essential for this that Castlereagh should be there. She agreed, and the King told Castlereagh that he wanted him to go with him later in the summer. 'He was,' Dorothea reported to Metternich, 'radiant, and I began to brighten.' Castlereagh was much more like his old self. Metternich had written him a letter on 6 June in which he said that he was looking forward to their meeting soon: 'it is the beginning of a new era and I have great hopes for the future.' He told Castlereagh that it was essential that they should stick together, and if he should fail him: 'I will stand alone and the struggle will be unequal.' He asked Dorothea to tell Metternich that he looked forward to seeing him soon. After dinner, Sir Charles Stewart, who seemed rather unhappy at the fact that the quarrel had been sorted out, came up to Dorothea and said: 'I congratulate you; you must be proud of yourself; you have made the King obey you . . . everything you wish is done, and we must all run at your bidding.' However, a few days later, the King changed his mind and decided to go to Scotland instead of to Florence. Dorothea reported that a general gloom had descended upon the court: 'They do not know what to do with their summer; they all look as though they were on the point of committing suicide.' As it transpired, this was, in one case, closer to the truth than Dorothea could have realized. On 12 August Castlereagh killed himself by cutting his left carotid artery.

'Ah, what a frightful tragedy – I am shaking from head to foot – Londonderry! What an end!' Dorothea wrote to Metternich as soon as she heard the news from Lady Conyngham. Castlereagh had been confined to his home at North Cray suffering from a breakdown, and while alone, he had seized the opportunity to kill himself. As Dorothea learned the grisly details, she passed them on to her lover: 'I can imagine only too well,' she wrote, 'how sad you must be.'

6. 'All my Ministers are fools'

Castlereagh's suicide stunned the political world, and nowhere were its effects likely to be more acutely felt than the Russian embassy. His attachment to the system of diplomacy established at Vienna was unquestioned, and despite the growing difficulties caused by the issue of whether or not to intervene in the internal affairs of other states, both Metternich and the Tsar had been able to rely upon Castlereagh's goodwill; the same could not be said of his successor, George Canning. Canning, a protégé of the Younger Pitt's, was the most brilliant, and therefore the most controversial, political figure in England. Canning's political ascent had been rapid, and by 1807 he was Foreign Secretary. He was the most talented orator in the Commons in an era where that talent was more highly prized than it has been in more recent times, and it would have seemed incredible to him that it would take him until 1827 to ascend to the premiership.

Canning was, however, the Winston Churchill of his day – even down to the rapidly receding red hair. The British are always apt to mistrust talent that blazes too brightly, and Dorothea Lieven summed this up when she described him as 'restless and ambitious. His colleagues are not at all like that.' Politicians bred to West-minster as one of the responsibilities inherited wealth carried, found something distasteful in the sight of naked ambition, and sought to find reasons for it. In Churchill's case much would be blamed on his American mother; in Canning's it would be attrib-uted to the fact that his mother had spent time as an actress – then often a euphemism for something even less reputable.

As with many ambitious men, Canning's sharp wit was accom-panied by a thin skin, and he found the aspersions cast on his background hurtful, and he reacted by developing a personal style that was often taken for arrogance. In 1808, as Foreign Secretary in the Portland government, he had been involved in manoeuvres designed to remove Castlereagh from the War Office. When Castlereagh found out about this he challenged him to a duel, in which Canning was wounded in the thigh. Although Canning resigned, his talents were too great to be excluded from office for long, and in 1812 Liverpool offered him the Foreign Office, but he insisted on leading the Commons as well, so the job went to Castlereagh; now, a decade later, the opportunity had returned to him. But his ascent to the Foreign Office was not unproblematic, despite Wellington's comment that 'a Foreign Secretary must be able to talk French, Canning could talk French and nobody else could, therefore he must be Foreign Secretary.'

Castlereagh's position had been buttressed by the cordiality of his relations with the troika that dominated British foreign policy, the monarchy, the Cabinet and the Commons. Canning, as Dorothea told Metternich on 10 September 1822, occupied precisely the opposite position: 'The Opposition hates him; the King loathes him; the Ministers distrust him; those who want him do not like him. His personal following is a mere drop in the Ocean.' But in case this gave Metternich any hope that he would not be appointed, she added: 'In spite of all these reasons for keeping him out, public opinion demands him; and he will receive the most important post in the Government.' There was a brief ray of hope when Canning took objection at the extremely grudging attitude of George IV's letter offering him the Foreign Office: 'He declares that it is exactly the same as being given a ticket for Almack's and finding written on the back: "Admit the rogue."'

The King hated Canning because of his connections with Queen Caroline. Canning had certainly been her 'intimate adviser', and George IV put his own construction on what that had meant, and told Liverpool that he did not want him in the government. This was consistent with the line he had taken since 1820, but the difference between then and now was Castlereagh's death. In Liverpool's view Canning's presence at the Foreign Office and in the Commons was essential to the survival of his government, and so the King's reluctance was overcome – and 'the rogue' was admitted. Mrs Arbuthnot, like many of Castlereagh's friends, found it offensive that his old post should be occupied by such a man: 'I cannot now see without feelings of the utmost bitterness his place so unworthily filled'; she took what comfort she could from Castlereagh's comment to her that 'he did not think Canning an upright and honourable man, but he still thought he might be made a useful person.' In comparison with the views of Canning entertained elsewhere, Harriet Arbuthnot's were positively charitable.

Dorothea had hoped that Wellington would become Foreign Secretary – and not only because she regarded him as a personal friend. Wellington assured her that British policy would not change just because of Castlereagh's death: 'that policy is already marked out, and the Cabinet cannot turn aside from it.' He tried to reassure her by saying that he had told Liverpool the same: 'I say it again on every possible occasion. Let England abandon that policy, and you plunge Europe, and consequently yourselves, into chaos.' But, as she told Metternich, Dorothea was not at all reassured. Her view was that the Foreign Secretary had a very great influence upon the direction of policy and that 'if his opinions were not absolutely identical with those of the Cabinet, it would be easy for him, by a thousand means at his disposition, insensibly to alter the Cabinet's policy.' As for the Duke's assurances that his presence in the Cabinet would be a sufficient guard against this, Dorothea told him 'that man will cheat you!' Canning, she told Metternich, may have had the 'most brilliant talents' but he had 'no stability in his principles'. The reasons for her anxiety were obvious. As she later recorded: 'the Holy Alliance had been the constant object of the sarcasms of Mr Canning; the Grand Alliance that of his strong antipathy; it bridled England, and for that reason was repugnant to her insular pride.' She thought that the alliance 'was supported by no Englishmen except by the Ministers. The invariable aim of Mr Canning from the moment he succeeded to Lord Castlereagh was to resume the liberty of action which suited the temperament of his nation.'

Historians have taken issue with Dorothea's verdict, arguing that it was the Holy Alliance and not the Grand Alliance which was the object of Canning's aversion; but given that Russia's interpretation of the Grand Alliance was identical to Alexander's Holy Alliance, this would have been a distinction without a difference to Dorothea. That England should work with the other great powers was the 'policy' she favoured, and she had every reason to anticipate that Canning would disturb it.

As far back as Aix-la-Chapelle, Canning had made plain his objection to the 'system' of congresses. He had no difficulty accepting the need for a specific meeting to discuss the future of France, but thought 'the system of periodic meetings of the four great Powers, with a view to the general concerns of Europe, new, and of very questionable policy.' He feared Britain becoming involved 'deeply in all the politics of the Continent, whereas our true policy has always been not to interfere except in great emergencies, and then with a commanding force'. He thought that the British people would be likely 'to look with great jealousy for their liberties, if our Court is engaged . . . with great despotic monarchs, deliberating upon what degree of revolutionary spirit may endanger the public security, and therefore require the interference of the Alliance'. Castlereagh's response to the Troppau Congress was sufficient proof that he too had no desire to become unduly involved in interfering with the domestic concerns of other states, but he did not, and could not, share Canning's disdain for the 'despotic monarchs'. His entire system, as we have seen, was predicated on the assumption that wherever possible Britain would work with her allies; she could not, of course, intervene in places like Naples in the way the Austrians did, and it might be necessary to remind Metternich of this, but nothing must be allowed to obscure the fact that Britain, as one of the great powers, was part of the Concert of Europe, not a second-rate nation. Had Canning come to office a few months earlier, it is likely that there would have been no British representation at Verona – but since that had already been agreed upon, Wellington was despatched.

For Dorothea the congress promised to answer the pressing question of 'what to do this autumn'. Her mood after Castlereagh's death was sombre; as she wrote to Metternich on 29 August from Brighton: 'What a gloomy year, and what a gloomy life I am leading!' She wondered about the way she was living her life. 'Is this really the way I ought to use my intelligence? I find that people stupider than I am have a hundred times more sense. Real intelligence consists of being happy, and I am not happy . . . I must find some way of distracting myself.' A congress was the perfect distraction – not least because it gave an opportunity for fresh intimacy with Metternich himself. The initial intention had been to hold the congress in Vienna, which would have suited Dorothea splendidly, but when she and her husband arrived in Salzburg, they discovered that the Tsar had asked for it to be moved to Verona. Still, she was able to spend a few days in 'picturesque' Salzburg, amid the first snows of winter. The society was very much to her taste, as she spent most of the time with the Austrian Emperor and Empress, the Russian ambassador, Pozzo di Borgo – and Metternich. Her spirits soared accordingly. She spent every morning in 'promenades superbes' and every evening in soirées, she told Harriet Granville – a 'boring life' indeed.

Once at Verona, Dorothea was in her element. 'Every evening,' she told her brother, 'the Congress meets at my house, so that I enjoy the daily society of the most interesting people in Europe.' Her one complaint was that because Wellington and Metternich spent so much time in her drawing room, she saw everyone at Verona apart from her own countrymen. Although she claimed that Nesselrode and Metternich had 'urged me to allow this as a resource for them', and stressed the advantages to be gained for Russian policy from such an arrangement, she noted with some acerbity that 'those who should be on the best of terms with me are precisely those who keep me at a distance as they would an enemy. Because I have spent ten years in England they look upon me as an Englishwoman, and because I see Prince Metternich daily, they think me an Austrian.' She was affronted by the 'cabal against me', but took comfort from the fact that the Tsar 'disapproved' of it. If there were those who thought Mme de Lieven 'Austrian', the reason was not far to seek. Her affair with

Metternich was common knowledge, and no one could be sure how the Tsar might regard such a liaison.

Dorothea did not let such suspicions ruin her *'félicité Véronaise'*, as she slipped into the sort of diplomatic routine that suited her best. She rose at ten every morning, but never retired before two the following day, and thanks to her arrangement with Nesselrode and Metternich, she managed to do all that needed doing without ever leaving her own house. Every morning she received Wellington, Nesselrode and Metternich, lesser fry being barred during this period. Unsurprisingly, Metternich was the most assiduous of her visitors, seeing her every morning for an hour or two. Every evening the congress assembled in her drawing room. She divided the diplomats into three categories: 'five or six very spiritual'; a few who were 'agreeable'; and the rest as 'mutes and bores'; needless to say it was only the first category who stayed with Dorothea and Metternich until the early hours of the morning. The 'feminine element' at the congress was, she told Alexander, 'weak', *'les Hurons'* excepted, which left her 'the sole representative of my species'. The comment about the 'Hurons' was a catty reference to the only other woman of note at the congress, the beautiful Juliette Récamier, the mistress of the French representative, the Vicomte de Chateaubriand; he had recently returned from America and delighted in retailing stories of the natives he had seen there. He fitted very firmly into Dorothea's third category of diplomat – a 'bore'.

Chateaubriand reciprocated Dorothea's dislike. In his memoirs he described her as a 'commonplace woman, tiring and arid, who had only one form of conversation – everyday politics'. She was, he wrote, the 'dowager' of Verona, whose only claim to fame was that she had the 'honour of seeing Prince Metternich at those hours when being tired from the weight of great matters, he amused himself in *effiloquer la soie*' [silken dalliance]. She had first come across Chateaubriand in April, and saved herself some time by deciding on sight that she 'did not care' for him. She told Metternich that the Frenchman had 'thousands' of affectations. He had told her that he was bored in society, to which she had said she would introduce him to some clever women whose conversation 'would be certain to give him pleasure'. He had responded that he did not like clever women and preferred stupid ones, to which Dorothea had responded: 'In that case I am surprised that you are bored, for you have so much chance of finding what you need.' She found him 'rude' and 'disagreeable . . . He displays a complete lack of taste and courtesy.' She told Metternich that he 'goes about with a sentimental, dreamy air and a heart for sale – but nobody wants it'. He was, she thought, like a 'hunchback without the hump'. In her opinion, his warped character distorted whatever qualities he might have possessed. He was 'the least interesting and least sentimental of men'; even his *amours* lacked elevation. His mistress in London was the wife of the French actor Lafont: 'He spends his evenings with her and talks for three hours on end about glory, enthusiasm, and, I fancy, also about virtue.' As she commented to Metternich: 'I can forgive him his mistress; but I cannot forgive a clever man for wasting enthusiasm, glory and virtue on such an audience. A clever man who does that must be a fool.' She thought him ill bred, he believed her superficial and supercilious; they both had a point. But Chateaubriand was not the most tiresome feature of the congress from Dorothea's point of view; the fear that Canning's advent to the Foreign Office would mean a change in British diplomacy became a reality in her own drawing room as Nesselrode and Metternich found themselves on the other side from Wellington.

The Duke had been seriously ill before leaving for Vienna, and the extra journey to Verona had not helped matters; but the old soldier recovered his physical vitality quickly. As Dorothea wrote to Harriet Granville on 9 November, 'the Duke is in a better state of health, but not in a good humour; he is bored, they vex him and I am truly pained that things go so little as I had hoped . . . He sighs for the moment of departure, and I love him so much that I would sigh also if that would give him pleasure, but it would not, in any way.'

The question that vexed both Wellington and Dorothea was that of allied intervention in Spain. The French were anxious to send an army across the Pyrenees, but they knew that any attempt to do so in their own right would be opposed by the other powers, so they hoped to be able to act as mandatories of Europe – a line greatly favoured by Tsar Alexander, who was anxious to send his own troops there. Metternich, as usual, torn between fear of revolution and Russian aggrandizement, preferred to wait and see what happened. Canning did not care what happened as long as there was no intervention by the alliance: 'I am to instruct your Grace at once frankly and peremptorily, to declare that to any such interference, come what may, His Majesty will not be a party.' This came as an unpleasant shock to Metternich when Wellington broke the news on 30 October. The following week was, Wellington told Canning on 5 November, a 'stormy' one. Metternich was anxious to keep the alliance together and used every argument he could to persuade Wellington of the need for Britain to agree to intervention in Spain: 'it was obvious that they are all very much embarrassed [and] little at their ease on this question.' Wellington reported the general view that 'England separated herself from the allies during the affair of Naples very unnecessarily.' As Wellington was not authorized to move from the position staked out by Canning, there was nothing to be done. It was little wonder that the Duke was sighing to get back to London.

The separation of Britain from the alliance, although the most vexing political result of the congress, was not the only disappointment suffered by Countess Lieven. As at Aix, Dorothea used the opportunity of her proximity to Nesselrode to lobby him for a transfer – preferably to Vienna, although she was prepared to go to Paris. She urged her brother Alexander to press her case with the Tsar – ten years, she reminded him, was 'a long time'. Nesselrode was no more willing to accommodate her wishes than he had been at Aix. It was unlikely that he could have persuaded the Tsar to move the Lievens to Vienna – Dorothea's intimacy with Metternich was a useful source of information for the Russians, but information in that situation passed both ways, and there were limits to how much trust could be placed in either the ambassadress or the Austrian Chancellor. Dorothea's intrigues failed, and she and the Count travelled back to a cold and wet London – to face the aftermath of Verona.

One of the benefits of being in high favour with the King was that Dorothea did not have to linger long in town; no sooner was she back than she was summoned down to Brighton – to be immersed in George IV's increasingly bizarre fantasy world. Having spent a fortune building the Pavilion, George spent increasing amounts of time there with his latest favourite, Lady Conyngham, and he liked to gather around him those who would amuse and inform him; Dorothea came into both categories. The King seemed to have two obsessions: the paternity of Dorothea's youngest son, George, and the fracturing of the alliance at Verona. The King was godfather to young George Lieven, '*l'enfant du Congrès*', but now fancied that his relationship was somewhat closer than that. He had noticed, he told his courtiers, a likeness between himself and his young namesake. Dorothea, who knew how the King's propensity for imaginative recreation worked, described to Metternich what would happen next: 'Up to the present he says it as a joke; in a few days he will be saying it meaningly; later he will let it be understood that he had good reason for saying it; and still later he will persuade himself that he really can take the credit'; the fact that young George looked 'very like his father, but even more like old Madame de Lieven', would not concern the King – although Dorothea discerned no likeness between him and her mother-in-law. It was, of course, her métier to suffer the idiosyncrasies of deluded monarchs, but worth it for the information she could collect when George had exhausted his flights of fancy – and the influence she could try to exercise.

The King was much distressed at the gap that had opened up at Verona between himself and his old allies, and he wondered whether there would be a war. The odds on one breaking out were rather good, he thought. Although Canning would boast in April 1823 that Britain had broken up the congress system and thereby frustrated the ambitions of the continental powers, there were other ways of regarding the events at Verona. One of the senses in which Canning may be considered one of the progenitors

of 'modern' politics is in his predilection for 'spin'; his rhetorical
triumphs often seemed in inverse proportion to his real ones. As a
result of Verona, the Holy Alliance powers had decided to withdraw their ambassadors from Spain; the French, while associating
themselves with this policy, had not, but made it plain that they
were ready to send troops across the border into Spain. Castlereagh's policy of aligning Britain with the other great powers in
order to prevent any one of them gaining a unilateral advantage
from any crisis, was not Canning's – and there were those, most
particularly the King, who were displeased by the results. He told
Dorothea that 'All my Ministers are fools.' Dorothea, guided, no
doubt, by her instinct to flatter royalty, could not but agree. Then,
laying on the flattery with a silver-plated spade, she told the King
how much he had been missed at Verona, and 'how much his new
Minister was distrusted' and 'how useful it would be if he took a
hand himself, seeing that since the death of Lord Castlereagh, the
Allied cabinets no longer had a real friend in the English Cabinet
except the King.'

George lapped this up. He told Dorothea: 'That is true, but we
have to be careful of our situation. I look on Prince Metternich as
the first statesman of Europe; but he has one fault – that of relying
too much on his own abilities, with the result that he is not afraid
of putting himself and other people in false positions.' Dorothea's
lover must have disliked the last comment as much as he would
have appreciated the great compliment. The King, however,
thought himself well situated as he was: 'My Government no
longer includes anyone who is not second-rate; Mr Canning has
to make up to me to retain his post, for his colleagues loathe him;
I am aware of all this.' Whatever the King's fantasies about paternity
– or Waterloo if it came to that – he was not a poltroon when it
came to politics, as he showed with his comment that they must
'keep an eye on the House of Commons', where Canning's ability
'makes him powerful. The House is more Liberal than you care
for: that's the trouble.' Warming to Dorothea's flattery, the King
moved back into the more comfortable realm of fantasy politics,
telling her not to worry about the House of Commons: 'I pursue

my own policy, and if I am compelled to make apparent sacrifices, you will see that essentially I do not change.' He thought Canning was a 'clever man. He is trying to win me over and shows every readiness to follow me in politics as well as in personal affairs . . . For the rest he is plebeian and has no manners.' Dorothea was delighted when, at dinner that evening, the King boasted that 'I have never had a more interesting conversation in my life than I had this morning with Madame de Lieven.' Both sides of the King's character – the shrewdness and the folly – were shown in his comment to her that 'if you are writing to Metternich, tell him that between ourselves we call him "OR" [Oesterreiches Reich – Austria]; he is real gold, the purest and most precious.' The seeds for a future coup against Canning had been sown.

Dorothea's tactics – appealing to male vanity and the dislike felt for Canning by his colleagues – could be used with advantage elsewhere – particularly with Wellington, whose resentment at the part he had played in Verona had turned to mortification. Dorothea reported Wellington's complaints to Metternich as proof that 'there is no longer very great unity' between him and Canning. She took the opportunity of a prolonged visit to his house at Strathfield-Saye to try to win him over to her cause – and found herself in a situation that tempted her 'virtue'. Referring to the separation between England and the allies that had taken place at Verona, Wellington said he regretted it, but could not quite explain it. Dorothea pretended to understand that it was 'natural' for England to act differently from the other powers because 'she had not the same moral imperatives', but she wondered whether, in these revolutionary times, it would not turn out to be a mistake. The Duke's temper, always easily fired, flared up: 'Do you take us for Jacobins? Damme, I'll show you what I wrote about Spain, and you will see if M. de Metternich ever said anything stronger.'

When, the following morning, he was as good as his word, Dorothea told him that she was sorry that others could not see his despatches because 'it would greatly change the idea that had been formed of the behaviour of his Cabinet.' Wellington told her that she could give an account of them to her husband and to

Metternich – to which she responded that he could do so himself. The Duke explained that he could not show secret documents to foreign diplomats without the Cabinet's permission. Leaving aside the curious fact that this remark was addressed to the wife of a foreign diplomat and the lover of the Austrian Chancellor, Dorothea asked him whether he approved 'of your Cabinet making itself out worse than it is? Frankly no one places any confidence in Mr Canning.' Even when foreign powers had confidence in Castlereagh, 'personal relations' with the Duke had been valuable: 'how much more precious these relations must be now, with a Minister who inspires mistrust!'

Dorothea tried to persuade him that he would do much good, and no harm, if he let Count Lieven and the Austrian ambassador, Paul Esterhazy, see British despatches on Spain. She joked to Metternich that: 'You may suppose this conversation was rather a strain on my virtue.' This was not a reference to the Duke's propensity for gallantry, but rather a slight piece of self-mockery: 'You will realise that a lesser woman would have been very happy to have had the Duke of Wellington's confidences. You can imagine that. For a moment, I smiled to myself at the thought of being the direct channel of information interesting to my Court and to you. But when I reflected what good it might do, I immediately sacrificed my vanity, and finally persuaded Wellington to show Esterhazy and my husband what he had read to me.' She thought Wellington was 'feeling some slight remorse for what happened at Verona' and wondering whether, had he shown more 'diplomacy and flexibility . . . things might have turned out differently'. She suggested to Metternich that Wellington's desire to 'make reparation' might 'be turned to good account'. The main problem, she thought, remained Canning's 'insatiable ambition'. Dorothea told the Duke that Canning was 'without the confidence of anyone' and that 'all his colleagues looked on him with distrust.' When Wellington expressed his surprise at Dorothea's being so well-informed, she told him that 'he must be aware that she knew England & our state of parties as well as he did, & that the eyes of everybody, English & Foreign, were turned upon him as the only chance we had of being saved from confusion.' In full flattery mode, Dorothea added that 'it was well known how discontented he was with the state of things & from what honourable motives he remained quiet; but that everybody hoped he would keep a sharp look out on Mr Canning.'

Dorothea's poor opinion of Canning remained constant, despite the efforts of Harriet Granville to convince her otherwise. Lord Granville was one of Canning's closest friends, and when Dorothea returned from Verona, Harriet had invited her along to dine with the great man. She was, Dorothea told Metternich, 'extraordinarily arch about it – it is as if she wanted to confer him on me as a lover. I shan't take him.' Dorothea, pleased at the assiduity with which Canning paid her court at dinner, told Metternich: 'I believe he can be managed.' While Harriet tried to persuade Dorothea that Canning was not the devil incarnate, she performed the same office for Metternich. 'She knows you very well,' Harriet told the Prince; 'she must be cleverer than I am, for she understands you from hearsay, as I understand you from acquaintance . . . She sees you both as god and devil; I can understand her perplexity; for I have not a very clear idea of you myself.'

But all Harriet's protestations about Canning's virtues did not prevent a disastrous dinner party at the Duke's on 30 January 1823. Dorothea sat on the right hand of the great man, and spent most of the evening talking with him about the main guest – Canning himself. Count Lieven later reproached her for not speaking to Canning very much, but her comment to Metternich spoke volumes about her views on that subject: 'I don't see the necessity of going to any great trouble. We hardly know one another, and I have a feeling that our enforced relations will not last long.' She thought that even Harriet, 'in spite of her infatuation' with the man, was embarrassed by Canning's 'plebeian' manner. But she did take enough note of her husband's strictures about the need for discretion to exercise some of it the following morning when Harriet asked what Wellington had said about Canning. 'Nothing but good,' was her tactful, but entirely untruthful response. Harriet was not deceived: 'Well, Mr Canning speaks of the Duke with

great admiration. It is very strange, but nobody tells me the truth
these days.' Harriet, although the friend whose company she
enjoyed the most, was, Dorothea grumbled to Metternich, 'no
use' since 'she is too fond of her husband and her husband is too
fond of Mr Canning.'

Dorothea was delighted to find that familiarity with his new
Foreign Secretary did not make the King like him any the more.
From Brighton in early March, she reported to Metternich that
George had said about Canning: 'I do not like him any better than
I did. I recognise his talent, and I believe we need him in the
Commons; but he is no more capable of conducting foreign affairs
than your baby. He doesn't know the first thing about his job: no
tact, no judgement, no idea of decorum. But what is to be done?'
If he changed his minister he would, he thought, 'only get someone
worse . . . The best is bad; but the worst would be hateful, and
there is nothing in between.' As long as George's hatred of the
Whigs made him refuse to entertain the idea of changing his
ministers, and as long as Liverpool told him that Canning was
essential in the Commons, he would have to tolerate Canning –
or so it seemed; Dorothea, it transpired, thought differently.

7. 'What is to be done?'

When George IV asked 'what is to be done?' about Canning, he was reiterating a question being asked in all the chancelleries of Europe. Diplomacy is about tone as well as policy. Countess Lieven was making a serious point when she told Wellington that it was only natural that 'no one places any faith in Mr Canning' because 'we do not know him well enough.' Where she turned out to be too optimistic by far was in the assumption that if only her own government and that of Metternich could see the inwardness of British foreign policy, even through the medium of Wellington's indiscretions, they would be reassured. Indeed, two things swiftly became plain: the first was that there was no need of secret channels to discern the nature of Canning's policy; the second was that it was what Canning claimed it to be – which made it extremely worrying. Such a lack of finesse would have been, in itself, distressing to those who, like Dorothea, delighted in the elite nature of *la haute politique* and in its esoteric and arcane rituals; the content of that diplomacy made matters even worse.

The first sign of the storm to come was the response of the British Foreign Secretary to a speech made by Louis XVIII of France on 28 January 1823. The gargantuan, gout-ridden old Bourbon was dragged in state to the opening of the French parliament, where he delivered the speech from the throne. The French had handled the aftermath of Verona with some suppleness. They had associated themselves with the actions of the Holy Alliance, but had not withdrawn their ambassador from Spain. At the same time they had refused a British offer to mediate between themselves and the Spanish, while not declining a further recourse to London's 'good offices' at some future date. It was difficult not to conclude that the French were looking to intervene in Spain militarily, but in a way that protected them from Britain's wrath by securing the goodwill of the Holy Alliance.

Louis XVIII's speech did nothing to dispel such suspicions. The proclamation that a 'hundred thousand French' were ready to march into Spain was bad enough, although by this stage hardly unexpected, but what followed created uproar in the British press. Referring to his fellow Bourbon, the King of Spain, Louis declared: 'Let Ferdinand be free to give to his people the institutions they cannot hold but from him.' This assertion of the absolutist doctrines of legitimacy in such a pure form attracted huge criticism in Britain. Canning told Count Lieven on 31 January that Louis's speech was unacceptable: 'How do you expect us to support, or even tolerate, such a doctrine, when our form of government is rooted in the very opposite principle?' The tone was unmistakable, but just to make sure that he was being understood, Canning added: 'Listen to the opinions of the whole of England, and you will see if we can do anything to help people with such ideas.'

He made the same point in a despatch to France on 3 February, which, to the horror of adepts of the old diplomacy, he had published. Mrs Arbuthnot thought it 'most ill-judged'. In it Canning 'completely identified himself with the revolutionists, & in his arguments used their language . . . I cannot think Mr Canning will go on long.' But that was exactly what Canning proceeded to do, following up these formal protests with a speech at Harwich on 11 February in which he said that: 'If unhappily a state of hostilities should be eventually unavoidable, the country was fully prepared to meet the emergency. If it were assumed that exhaustion had succeeded to our gigantic efforts in the late war, that was certainly a most erroneous conclusion.' The public response, to judge by reaction in the press and the Commons, was hugely favourable. The Holy Alliance courts were going to have to get used to a new diplomatic style.

The frequency with which Canning's rhetorical triumphs were succeeded by diplomatic setbacks might seem to invite more questions about his diplomacy than historians have been used to ask.

Undeterred by Canning's speeches, the French armies continued with their preparations for the invasion of Spain. Canning's response was characteristic. On 31 March he delivered a stern warning to the French, outlining the terms on which Britain would allow their intervention: there must be no permanent military occupation of Spain; there must be no attempt to acquire any of Spain's Latin American colonies; and there must be no incursions into Portugal. This amounted to an ultimatum, and in what was becoming his usual style, Canning had it published in the press a mere five days after it had been delivered in Paris. On 6 April the French marched into Spain.

On 14 April Canning came to the bar of the House and laid before the Commons all the diplomatic papers relating to what had happened. His speech was uncompromising. He ridiculed French attempts to claim to be acting in the name of Europe – exposing the part they had played at Verona and accusing them of breaking up the alliance. He denounced the French King's speech: 'no Member of the House thought of it with more disgust and abhorrence than he did.' He proclaimed himself a 'Liberal, yea, a Radical Minister', and expressed the hope that Spanish liberalism might come 'triumphantly' out of the struggle with France. In the debates that followed, as much praise was heaped upon Canning as odium was bestowed upon his continental opponents; in the final vote on 30 April the government's majority was 372 to 20. It was a great personal triumph.

Canning's popularity in the country at large was not replicated in the close air of the Brighton Pavilion. When Dorothea dined there with the King and his mistress on 27 March, she was told that 'I and my Ministers are of the opinion that your Emperor is behaving magnificently in this Spanish affair. You may repeat this.' She promptly did so – to Metternich. George proclaimed that: 'I am a Royalist to the core, and . . . hold all the new doctrines in abomination.' To his complaints that British policy had not been understood by the statesmen at Verona, Dorothea replied that they understood that the King would not 'consent to a resolution that would actually constitute your Government the patron of the

Radicals'. Stung by the implication, he asked Dorothea what she meant, and she replied that if Britain let herself be drawn into the war in Spain 'it would be none the less obvious that you were at the head of all the Jacobins in Europe. Surely, that would not be an ignoble part for a power such as England.' George turned to the one Cabinet minister present, Lord Bathurst, and exclaimed loudly: '*There you have it. Have I not repeatedly told you the very same words?*'

There was only one answer to this – and Bathurst loyally agreed that the King had, indeed, always said as much. George declared that England was following a policy of neutrality because it was the policy he wanted; Dorothea imitated Bathurst. In full flow, and encouraged by the universal acknowledgement of his sagacity and foresight, George declared: 'We have an abominable Constitution. I would rather be a shoe-black than a member of that odious parliament.' At this, Bathurst shifted in his seat uneasily, and presumably did much the same when the King and Dorothea deprecated the way in which Lord Liverpool had backed up Canning in his denunciation of Louis XVIII's speech. Dorothea soothed him by assuring him that everybody knew that 'the great majority' of the Cabinet actually agreed with him. 'My dear,' George concluded, 'after all there is only one man in the world.' Dorothea, daringly, indicated her dissent: 'No, Sir, there are two.' The King said that he meant Metternich, to which she responded prettily: 'Yes, and I mean Your Majesty' – at which the delighted monarch squeezed her hand. As she left he grabbed her arm: 'Well, what do you think of this conversation? I wanted to show you how I treat my Ministers; and I wanted to show my Minister the footing I am on with you, eh?' Adept, as always with royalty, Dorothea replied with more feeling than sense: 'Sir, I think I should like you to be King and Minister both at once.' In fact, Dorothea had been, as she told Wellington, rather disgusted by such an 'unseemly' scene. She hoped, she said, that Bathurst knew her and her knowledge of British politics well enough to understand that 'I had taken what the King said in the right spirit and for what it was worth.'

Dorothea's boast to Bathurst about her understanding of British politics was not far wide of the mark. Her social contacts gave her an unrivalled insight into the political situation at Westminster. She was on terms of intimacy with the King and his mistress, and knew well what the court was thinking; Wellington told her everything that went on in the Cabinet; she had just started up what was to be a long and significant correspondence with the leader of the opposition, Lord Grey; and, of course, Harriet Granville gave her access to what might be considered the 'enemy' camp. It was little wonder that it was at this juncture that Nesselrode should have asked her to write to him regularly about events in England – no British politician had a foot in as many camps as the Russian ambassadress. But if Dorothea gave both her own court, and Nesselrode, an insider's view of high politics, her contacts gave her no access to power.

Wellington and the King were both furious with Canning over his handling of the debates in the Commons. Wellington told Dorothea that 'his colleagues declare in a body that they cannot work with Mr Canning.' The King refused to see the offending minister and wrote to rebuke him. Even Lady Granville wondered whether it might not be better if Canning were to go. His position was, as Dorothea told Metternich, 'curious. He is on bad terms with all the foreign Cabinets, with all his colleagues, with the Tory party, and, worst of all, with the Opposition, whom he imprudently boasted of having mastered.' Considering the small amount of time he had been in office, Canning had notched up an impressive tally of enemies. The King complained vociferously that 'My Ministers want to start a revolution in England.' Dorothea reassured Metternich that 'you can rely on it, they are working to get rid of Canning.' 'They' were the King, the heir-presumptive (the Duke of York), 'all the Ministers and all their supporters, who, in fact, comprise the majority of the two Houses'. But, to adapt one of Canning's most famous phrases, he called in the new political world to redress the balance of the old. By his forceful speeches, in and most significantly *out* of the Commons, he appealed over the heads of the traditional political nation to that wider, newer Britain brought into existence by what historians used to call the industrial revolution. As MP for the bustling and expanding port of Liverpool, Canning was in touch with the new mercantile and industrial sources of wealth, and his appeal to their national pride did not go unanswered. However, those over whose heads Canning's appeals passed would not lightly yield the game to him.

It was a mark of the position that Dorothea was taking in British political life that she should have found herself at the centre of the one serious attempt to clip Canning's wings. After a decade in England, she was beginning to feel almost at home there. Initially she had been inclined to laugh at the British preoccupation with the weather and for 'attributing to the wind so much influence on their temper', but she had now 'completely given way to that influence. If the wind is in the east, I am ill-natured and cross.' But there were still many occasions on which she was reminded of her foreignness in the eyes of the British.

Dorothea sent her letters to Metternich via the Austrian embassy in London. When she was in Brighton in April 1823, she decided, on a whim, to take the letter to the post office herself. When she found that the usual office had been closed, she asked a passer-by where the new one was. Over her simple white walking dress she wore a surcoat, corded at the waist, as was the English fashion, but her smart striped turban, with a little turned-up brim, marked her as a woman of quality, and she attracted attention as she wandered hither and yon asking for directions in her broken, heavily accented English. Initially she thought 'they were making fun of me, especially as several passers-by began to laugh; but, after a moment's reflection, I was satisfied that it was my foreign accent that amused them.'

Nor was it simply the lower orders who made Dorothea feel uneasy. One of the few escapes from the King's presence in Brighton was dinner with Emily Cowper, who acted as hostess to Lord Grey and other members of the opposition who liked to assemble there; but such occasions could be quite as boring as being with George IV. There was a dinner on 6 April with thirteen members of the opposition 'half of whom I scarcely knew. Only English was spoken, and I aired my entire English vocabulary.' As she complained to Metternich: 'Really, the English are a strange people; and how clumsy! I did not know my neighbour at table. He is a nobleman, who never leaves his country house. He did not dare look at me when I spoke to him, though I could see from the movement of his eyelids that he was longing to see what kind of strange animal I was.' After dinner he stared at her from behind a screen, but 'apparently what he saw did not make him want to resume the conversation; for he took his hat and went.' Another nobleman 'stretched himself out at full length on a sofa' and 'in less than half a minute I heard him snoring. Can you,' she asked Metternich, 'imagine me in the middle of all of this?'

It is from this period that Dorothea began to become involved in British politics in a way that would characterize the rest of her stay in England. Canning's advent to power upset the smooth running of the alliance that had, despite the strains of his last two years, been the norm under Castlereagh. In these new circumstances both Nesselrode and Metternich found Dorothea's access to the widest circles of British politics invaluable. She was flattered by their interest in what she had to say, but clearly unsettled by it: she was conscious, as she told Metternich during this period, of her intellectual inferiority. 'I am,' she said, 'made up of all the most contradictory qualities. I am active and lazy; cheerful and melancholy; brave and cowardly. I change with the wind.'

Her health, always a good indicator of her spirits, was constantly bad throughout the whole of 1823, and her letters are peppered with complaints about it. In August it was bad enough for her to decline an invitation to stay with the King in the 'Cottage' he was occupying at Windsor while the castle was being refurbished. In the end, however, she gave in to his pleas, but doubted whether it would be, as he claimed, 'good for me'. She complained to her brother Alexander that 'late dinners and long evenings do not suit me' but that she had to endure them lest she should be 'preventing my husband from being brought into closer contact with the King. You don't believe me when I say I have had enough of this life of an Ambassadress in England . . . what is the good of getting people to like you, when etiquette forbids you forming intimacies.' She had enough self-knowledge to realize that this might appear somewhat disingenuous, and she begged Alexander to keep her complaints to himself 'for those who do not understand my feelings will think me vain, and God knows I am not that – but only sick and sad-hearted.' Her melancholia was only increased by the death of her father in July.

It was a sign of Dorothea's state of mind that even politics failed to distract and absorb her. Canning's rhetorical triumphs had firmly established his position as Foreign Secretary, while the French army's victories in Spain succeeded in restoring Ferdinand, who then provided ample proof of Wellington's dictum that there was no country in whose internal affairs one could interfere to less profit than Spain; the viciousness of the restored King's revenge on his enemies revolted even those who had restored him.

The long parliamentary recess meant prolonged trips to the King's 'Cottage' at Windsor, where she was more than ever the victim of ennui. She lunched with the King at eleven o'clock, went for a drive with him from two until four, then dined in the evening before playing cards or the piano. 'Occasionally,' she lamented to Metternich, 'the conversation is interesting; but, usually, it is so stupid that one begins to doubt one's own intelligence. I look into my mind and, honestly, I find nothing in it; if you were to beat me you would not get a sensible idea out of me.' A little mordant relief might be gained from such sights as the corpulent monarch gazing at his equally large mistress 'with an expression in which somnolence battled with love', while she looked at her true love – 'a beautiful emerald on her arm' – but, Dorothea thought wistfully, 'there were better ways of spending an evening, and I remembered Verona.' With that in mind, when her doctors suggested that she should travel south for her health, Dorothea decided to visit Milan.

The official story was that the Countess Lieven was travelling abroad to recover her health; but the truth was that her malaise was the result of her passion for Metternich, as was the reason for her journey; he had promised he would meet her in Milan. Dorothea was now sailing rather close to the wind. A discreet *affaire* amid the bustle of a diplomatic congress was one thing, but travelling to Milan, unaccompanied, to meet her lover, came very close to the kind of behaviour that society might be unable to condone. Discretion was all. Despite the fact that he knew otherwise, she always told Wellington that she was not Metternich's mistress: 'Je ne suis pas la maîtresse du Prince Metternich, et je ne le serois [*sic*] jamais' ['I am not Metternich's mistress and never shall be']. The fact that she complained about the inconveniences of travelling alone on the poor roads through Geneva to Milan is less surprising than the fact that she was willing to endure these things at all. Dorothea loved her comforts, and these included important and amusing company. All these she was willing to forgo in order to see Metternich. Not even the editorial excisions that she made on her letters to Metternich in later life can disguise the nature of her feelings towards him at this time. Some of her female friends, worried about her health, advised her 'that I should be better if I were to indulge in some perfectly innocent little affair of the heart. The motion was passed unanimously.' It is perhaps significant that she should have passed this on to Metternich, as she had already complained that 'you have never done me the honour of treating me as a pretty woman.'

In case Metternich failed to pick up the heavy hint being dropped, Dorothea resorted to another tactic to provoke her lover – the spectre of competition from another man. It was at this time that she began to make frequent references to a new beau, the leader of the Whig opposition, Charles, the second earl Grey. If Dorothea was seeking to create a spark of jealousy in her lover, Charles Grey was an ideal source. Born in 1764, Grey had been the lover of the infamous and glamorous Georgiana, Duchess of Devonshire, by whom he had had an illegitimate daughter who was brought up as his sister. He married Georgiana's niece, Mary Ponsonby, in 1794, and had fifteen more children by her. One of the greatest orators of the day, Grey was to play a notable part in Dorothea's life after 1830, as we shall see, but their relationship seems to have begun during this disturbed period of her life in 1823.

In early February Dorothea told Metternich she had had a 'furious letter' from Grey about Wellington's conduct at Verona and the government's foreign policy, and by April they were close enough for him to give her the credit for the 'moderation' he had shown in the debates over Spain. 'Lord Grey,' she informed Metternich on 9 May, 'is very attentive to me.' He invited Dorothea to the Lords on 12 May, accepting her condition that he must say nothing that 'might be unsuitable for me to hear'. Grey was as good as his word, and during a two-hour speech uttered nothing critical of the absolutist powers. He was, Dorothea noted, 'coquettish towards me', and as a result did not, she thought, speak as well as usual: 'Everyone remarked his embarrassment, and he admitted it to me himself.' Dorothea admired Grey's style, telling Metternich that he had 'the most beautiful diction in the world' and 'the noblest pose', but not his politics: 'He does not like our principles, etc., and that is all twaddle. I did not dine until six in the evening and slept badly as a result. That is what comes of letting oneself be ruled by Lord Grey.'

The political differences between them would always remain, but at this early stage Grey was content simply to question why it should be so when he believed 'our characters to be so well suited to one another in all other respects'. He wondered whether 'you will laugh at this vanity which has thus escaped me? Or will you regret, as I do, that so many years were lost before I found out how much I was formed to love and esteem you?' Grey's most authoritative biographer concluded that he 'almost certainly at some time in the later 1820s became her lover' – and although the grounds for this would appear to be little more than gossip and deduction from the available sources, there seems no reason to question the verdict; although 1823 would be a better bet as the date for the start of the affair, when Dorothea's mood was so volatile, and when she was seeking to provoke Metternich's jealousy. She told Metternich on 5 July 1823 that the opposition Whigs looked 'askance' at her because they supposed that she had 'some kind of influence' over Grey; acknowledging that ever since they had known each other well he had 'retired from affairs' and was now openly saying that 'the Spanish affair is over', she did not 'know whether I deserve the credit; but I know I have not taken much trouble. I am too bored and cross and ill to take trouble over anything.'

As the time for her departure drew nearer, Dorothea's ills increased, and from her own description it would seem as though her nerves were getting the better of her. She told Metternich in one of the last letters written before she departed that 'all worries, excitements and annoyances go to my knees.' Harriet Granville, knowing one of the attractions of Milan, commented slyly: 'I have never heard of sentimental knees before.' Dorothea hated travelling alone, and had doubts about whether or not she should be going at all; but the lure of Metternich was too great. She wrote to him from the boredom that was Geneva imploring him to keep sending her news of the great world: 'My mind is accustomed to it and I should be sorry to get out of the habit. My husband is the soul of prudence . . . It is the same with the letters the Duke of Wellington will write me. So, without you, I run the risk of relapsing into the conventional feminine role; and it seems to me that would be a pity' – she asked him to 'treat me as I deserve'. In writing thus, Dorothea was relapsing into another conventional feminine role, and Metternich responded by playing that most conventional of male roles – the heartless cad.

Dorothea arrived in Milan only to learn that despite his promises, there would be no quiet evening tête-à-têtes with her lover. 'Why did you ask me to come?' she complained bitterly. She had, she protested, 'left all my comforts, all the interests of my life, all my intellectual habits, for the sake of an alien sky which warms my body but leaves my mind utterly vacant'. She decided to travel on to Florence, hating 'having to arrange everything and think for myself. I should like someone else to take all the responsibilities, and I should like that someone to be my husband. I always prefer what is natural; and I find my position here unnatural'; it saddened her to think that 'all I care for' was either beyond the Alps or the

Apennines. She would, she told her errant lover, 'go back to our habits of five years past – weekly letters. Will that suit you?' She told him that her husband wanted her to return, and 'it would not take much to make him implore me to come back, just as, at the slightest encouragement, I should take the road for England. Indeed, I am only staying as a matter of form.' Neither her pleas nor her threats disturbed the imperturbable Metternich, who was clearly happy to keep their relationship on the epistolary plane of the past few years. Hurtful though it was, Dorothea caught glimpses of this truth when she wrote: 'You are hurting me; while I am only sparing you boredom.'

The truth was that Dorothea was in an uncomfortable dilemma. She longed to return to the comforts of England, but was caught by her own excuse for leaving it. Having departed because the English winter would be bad for her health, she could hardly return in December, so she had no choice save to winter in Italy. Her eldest son, Paul, came to join her, and she settled down to enjoy such society as was to be encountered in Florence and Milan. She continued to write to Metternich, although less frequently, and her letters were full of local gossip. However unhappy, she stuck to her own rule that 'at no age should a woman dispense with reserve about her relations with a man.'

During this period the tone of her letters to Metternich changed perceptibly, and when his missives were few, or tardy, she threatened to look elsewhere for amusement – and more. When there was no courier from him on 12 February 1824, she wrote: 'To punish you, I am going to dine with your friend Lord Dudley. If he abuses you I shall tell him he is right. I shall be very hostile to Austria today . . . In short I am going to change from an extremely good ally to the worst possible. It is very bad policy not to write to me.' Nor was this 'woman scorned' threat entirely in jest. As she contemplated her return to London, she wrote of the King's satisfaction that parliament had allowed him £300,000 for the restoration of Windsor Castle: 'English finances are magnificent. There has not been such internal prosperity for thirty years. You can see that you will not be able to overthrow Mr Canning.' But someone with more access to the inner workings of British politics might do what her faithless Metternich could not do.

Dorothea did not return to England until May 1824, and she hardly wrote to Metternich – the passion was, if not spent, then at least dissipated – henceforth the two of them would drift apart. Nor was this entirely for personal reasons. Back in October, as she passed through Geneva, she recorded a conversation she had had with the former Russian foreign minister, Pozzo di Borgo, who believed that the liberal cause would win, not just in Spain, but everywhere. He thought that Tsar Alexander would recover from what he called the 'self-important delusion' of the previous two years: 'He will feel, as his people wish him to feel, the ignominy of being ruled by an Austrian Minister. But the awakening must not come too late – he might pay too dearly for it.' At this, she told Metternich, she 'secretly applauded'.

Dorothea was reunited with her husband at Dover, whither he had come to meet her, and they travelled slowly back to London. Their reunion was clearly a tender one, although this did not, in the first instance, stop her from thinking that she ought to go back to Russia. George IV offered her the use of his yacht, but she was tempted by the land route which, although more tiring, offered the chance of a reunion with Metternich at one of his estates. However, her return home got her only as far as Dover, where her husband called a halt to it; it was not any jealous instinct that prompted this sudden change of plan. Some time before her departure, Dorothea had been suffering from sickness in the morning – and by the time she got to Dover she was convinced that she was pregnant. She was nearly forty, and this would be her sixth child, so it was not surprising that the Count was not keen on the idea of her travelling all the way across Europe. Instead she settled down to await the inevitable – and to catch up with the question of what was to be done about Canning, who had gone from strength to strength in the eight months she had been absent.

8. 'To rule the foreign policy of England'

Lord Grey told Dorothea that she would be 'very much surprised by the changes I should find' now that she was back. In fact little had changed – except the degree of resentment felt against Canning. The loathing came from every side: Metternich, who maintained the clandestine correspondence with the Duke initiated by Dorothea, complained loudly of the 'isolation' of Britain from her former allies; the ambassadors grumbled that Canning was so changeable that they had no sooner sent off a despatch than they had to write another contradicting it; Wellington resented the ascendancy that Canning had over Liverpool, and felt that the two of them were deciding foreign policy without consulting him; and then there was the King, who could hardly contain himself, so many were his grievances against the Foreign Secretary. He told Dorothea in June that he 'hated him as much as ever'.

Canning's decision to attend a dinner in the City hosted by those who had abused the King during the crisis over his divorce particularly irritated him. Declaring loudly that he would 'never forgive' him, George wrote Canning a letter so insulting that it was designed to force him to resign. Wellington, realizing the damage that would be done to the monarchy if the King tried to force Canning out on this question, persuaded him to tone down the letter – but this did nothing to improve the King's temper. He declared to the Duke that Canning was 'the damnedest fellow in the world & that he could not bear him'. Canning's decision to invite the King and Queen of the Sandwich Islands to London provoked further outbursts from the King, who declared to Dorothea: 'Think of that damned fellow wanting me to have dinner with the King & Queen of the Sandwich Islands, as if I would sit at the table with such a pair of damned cannibals.'

If Canning's opponents were to be found mainly in the ranks

of the Holy Alliance and its sympathizers, the reason was obvious; his foreign policy, like his style of diplomacy, was anathema to conservatives. He seemed to be aligning England with every revolutionary movement he could find. The worst part of it was that there was every chance that he might become Prime Minister in the near future. Liverpool's health seemed to be failing, and it was obvious from what his doctors said that he could not remain Prime Minister for much longer. In such a situation the politicians were doing what their kind always do – trying to find the rising sun so they could genuflect in its direction. If Canning's pre-eminence marked him out as Liverpool's natural successor, his unpopularity with his colleagues suggested that he would have to look elsewhere to find a Cabinet. Grey and the Whigs would be willing to help out – at a price. This was one point of view.

As might be imagined, when Dorothea put it to Wellington, he had other ideas. Although no longer on intimate terms with Liverpool – the two men had quarrelled over Canning – Wellington saw himself as the natural successor. The heir-presumptive, the Duke of York, and the more conservative members of the Cabinet, had urged Wellington to take the premiership, but the Duke declined to move against Liverpool; only if the King decided to appoint Canning would Wellington and his supporters act – and when they did their strength would be sufficient to keep Canning out. The fact that the King detested Canning made it unlikely that Wellington would have to act in this way. To Dorothea's query about whether his lack of debating experience in parliament might not tell against him, the Duke replied breezily in the negative: 'To begin with, I can learn; if I want it, it will come back to me. And, even if I can't, the Duke of Portland had no more idea of speaking than I have; and yet he was head of the administration.' While true, the example was not encouraging, since it had been during Portland's incumbency that Canning and Castlereagh had fought their duel.

Canning may have been unable to stop the French from intervening in Spain, but he was determined that they should not do so in Spain's Latin American colonies. In the so-called Polignac

Memorandum which he circulated after a meeting with the French ambassador, Polignac, in October 1823, Canning made it clear that the French should not try to interfere in Latin America, and that if they attempted to do so, Britain would not allow it; and he threatened to recognize the independence of those colonies if there was any French move to try to gain control over them. He also refused to take part in any European conference on the question of the Spanish colonies. It was, even Metternich admitted, a masterstroke, isolating France from the Holy Alliance powers and establishing British primacy. His action in working with the Americans to help them promulgate what became known as the Monroe Doctrine further established him as a dangerous revolutionary. The Holy Alliance powers were now unable to act against those colonies which had revolted against Spanish rule, and Canning wanted to follow this up by granting diplomatic recognition to the successor-states; this involved him in a major argument with his colleagues, most of whom did not want to go that far – it also gave his enemies a chance to try to unseat him.

Wellington, who objected to what he called Canning's 'tricking & shuffling' way of doing business, thought that his ultimate object was to 'break up the Quintuple Alliance', which would lead, in his view, 'to war directly'. Wellington agreed with Metternich when he said that since no power gained more from peace than Britain, he could not understand why Canning wished to destroy a system of cooperation which had maintained peace in Europe for nearly a decade. Wellington declared that 'his whole life has been spent in fighting against the Liberals . . . that the Treaties he had made had promised a long & prosperous peace, & now the work of his life is undone from Mr Canning's mere *love of undoing*, from his dislike to a settlement not made by himself, & to gratify his own spleen.' The question of what could be done about this state of affairs was one in which Countess Lieven, Esterhazy and the King all took a hand – along with a little help from Wellington.

It is in the nature of clandestine diplomacy that its details should be occluded, but Canning had little doubt that there was a conspiracy against him, led by Metternich, whom he called the 'greatest rogue & liar on the Continent, perhaps in the Civilized world'. As he told Granville in March 1825, 'I have evidence, which I certainly believe, of his having been for a twelvemonth at least, perhaps longer, at the bottom of an intrigue with the Court here – of which Mad[am]. Lieven was the organ – to change the politics of this Government by changing *me*.' As usual with Canning, there was an element of hyperbole in this allegation, and he was always apt to see the hand of Metternich or Russia in anything that threatened to disrupt his plans, but he was not completely wrong in supposing that the Holy Alliance would have liked to see the back of him.

If Canning's dating of the 'intrigue' is correct, then Dorothea must have been a latecomer to it, since she was not in the country in March 1824, and she did not go to the 'Cottage' again until June 1825. But then the earliest discernible signs of any concerted attempt to outflank Canning came only in late May and June 1824 when George IV approved a scheme to get Metternich to intervene in the dispute over recognizing the Spanish colonies by proposing a conference of the powers. But Canning, suspecting the source of the proposal, rejected it and continued to argue that it made no sense not to recognize states with whom Britain had important trading interests.

Canning's sensitivity to anything coming from the 'Cottage', and to Russian intrigue, was shown starkly in a fiery exchange of letters with Wellington in early October over the question of whether he should go to Paris, ostensibly to congratulate the new King, Charles X, on his accession, but actually, as he told Liverpool, to urge him to 'break with the Alliance & league himself with England to oppose the views of Russia'. Wellington, who believed that the consequence of France leaving the alliance 'must be war in Europe at no very distant period', thought this an extremely bad idea and wrote to Canning to dissuade him. Canning replied testily denying that he had intended to visit Paris: 'I do not expect indeed that any Russian agent would approve of anything that had or might be supposed to have a tendency to bring the Governments of England & France into habits of confidence. I know that Russia governs Continental Europe thro' Pozzo [di Borgo] . . . but I hope it is not to be understood as our settled policy that *we* are to square our most indifferent actions by the same rule of obedience.' Canning complained bitterly that while he was not supposed to go to Paris, Lord Westmorland, who just happened to hold different views on the question of recognizing the Latin American republics, had been allowed to linger there on his way to Florence, before returning and immediately going down to the 'Cottage' at Windsor – and now, coincidentally, Wellington was wanting Canning not to go to Paris. Wellington's response was to say that if Canning thought that he could 'defeat the influence of Pozzo di Borgo, not only in France but throughout the S. of Europe', he did not see how it was to be done: 'situated as we are in relation to other questions, acting as we do in direct opposition to what those Courts consider their vital interests'. Canning wondered 'whence you draw your information', adding that, while defeating the influence of Pozzo was 'a most admirable & praiseworthy object', he had 'never stated it as mine'. He accused Wellington of having had his information from Lieven and implied that he was acting on his behalf – an insinuation that Wellington denied but which showed who Canning believed his enemies were. He was certainly correct if he thought that Dorothea had had a hand in the affair – she it had been who had discovered Canning's intention of going to Paris, and she it was who had stirred him up to oppose it. Battle was now joined in earnest.

Dorothea, who was shown both sides of this extraordinary correspondence by Wellington, thought that 'Canning must feel himself in a very strong position to have the audacity to write it, and, alas! Wellington must be in a weak position to have swallowed it'; she told Metternich on 2 November that 'things cannot go on like this.' In this, at least, she and Canning were in agreement.

Historians have tended to follow Canning's version of events and have written about the 'Cottage Coterie' as a foreign intrigue designed to defeat a patriotic British Foreign Secretary. The most authoritative historian of Canning's foreign policy, Harold Temperley, wrote that 'Wellington cannot fairly be called a member of the "Coterie", though he occasionally attended their meetings'; although true, this creates a seriously misleading impression. Without Wellington there would have been no 'Coterie'. As Dorothea told Metternich, Wellington was 'the only check we have on Mr Canning's follies'. One could reverse the usual version of events and come nearer the truth: the 'Coterie' was a useful instrument for Wellington against Canning. Dorothea could meet with the King and with the Austrian ambassador, Esterhazy, at the 'Cottage' for the weekends, they could bitterly complain about Canning and his many iniquities, and they could write to Metternich, but none of this amounted to effective opposition to Canning; that came from Wellington, and without him the 'Coterie' would have had as much influence as any other group of hyper-critical diplomats.

Dorothea was at the centre of the web because she was the link between Metternich, Wellington and the King. She spent an increasing amount of time at the 'Cottage' in the late summer and early autumn − not all of it very comfortably. As her pregnancy developed and her figure lost its habitual thinness, she found herself, as she told Metternich, 'developing quite to his [the King's] taste', and thus became the object of his amorous attentions − much to the irritation of George's mistress, Lady Conyngham. As the summer heat grew, so did the tensions at Windsor − and, for Dorothea, even escaping to the river for a boat-trip brought no relief. She found herself seated between the King and the Duke of York, 'wedged betwixt their perspiring royal thighs; and heat and disgust made me feel really ill'. She resorted to speaking Russian to her husband to get him to extricate her from 'my torrid situation'. 'Heaven preserve you from the knees of the King and the Duke of York, especially in 25 degrees of heat.' It would not be by such means that Canning's policy would be overthrown.

Once Wellington's role is appreciated, it can be seen that the 'Coterie' had a serious point about the direction of British foreign policy. Historians have tended to elide the differences between Castlereagh and Canning as being ones of tone, rather than substance, but the older version of events seems to have something to commend it. This represented Castlereagh as a more 'European' figure and Canning as a more insular one — which was exactly Dorothea's view up to about 1825. She, and Wellington, saw him in this way because that was how he appeared to them. While it is true that Castlereagh had not been able to go along with the decisions taken at Troppau, he had none the less remained sympathetic to the reasoning employed by Metternich, and the tone he had adopted towards his allies had always been one that invited them to have confidence in him. Wellington thought that this confidence was an essential tool for keeping the alliance together. Canning's wanton squandering of it, from Wellington's point of view, through self-dramatizing gestures in the House, ill-timed public speeches, and the revelation of confidential despatches by tabling them in the Commons, all seemed calculated to destroy the alliance on which the peace of Europe depended. It may be that, like his self-appointed successor, Palmerston, Canning expected to be able to have the benefits of the alliance when it suited Britain, without paying any of the price necessary when it was inconvenient, but to expect other statesmen to appreciate this and comply accordingly was to indulge in the sort of insular arrogance that was bound to leave Britain isolated. Across the range of issues facing the alliance during his first two years in office, Canning seemed to be taking up positions which were unhelpful at best and, at worst, positively harmful to the stability of Europe.

Canning's touchy insistence upon dealing with every issue himself, and in his own way, meant something like a complete reversal of Castlereagh's diplomatic methods. Where Castlereagh had tried to work with his allies through the medium of congresses and conferences, Canning's aversion to them amounted almost to a phobia. He would allow no congress on Spain, nor on Spain's Latin American colonies, nor yet on the Greek question; the fact that in all these cases, especially the latter, the result was a needless loss of life, concerned Canning far less than the effect on his own prestige. In January 1824 the Tsar suggested that the great powers should unite in a congress that would force the Turks to accept a solution which provided for the creation of three independent

Greek principalities. Although Metternich did not like the details of the Tsar's scheme, which looked rather like what it was, an attempt to set up three client states for Russia, he was happy to have a congress, relying upon his diplomatic skills to wean Alexander away from his plans; but Canning dragged his heels throughout the year.

In November 1824 Dorothea urged Metternich, and her own government, to put aside the secrecy in which their bilateral negotiations were being conducted, and to allow her to tell other members of the British Cabinet so that they could oppose Canning. A British refusal, she argued, would break 'the last bond uniting England to the policy of the Continent'. It would mean a 'complete revolution in the political system of Europe'. Dorothea was correct in perceiving that it was only in the Cabinet that Canning could be challenged, but that was not easily done, given his own flair for the dramatic. With his Cabinet opponents still divided over where and when it was best to challenge him, Canning threw down the gauntlet to them in December by proposing that Britain should recognize the independence of the Latin American republics – and take a very firm line with France over her occupation of Spain.

The Duke of Wellington thought that Canning's proposed despatch to France was couched 'in a most menacing warlike tone'. When Canning found that even Liverpool was inclined to agree, he used his quick wits to devise an alternative version, in which he wrote that although Britain was worried by France's actions in Spain, she 'must submit' to the fact of the occupation. Having, as he saw it, exposed the folly of the opposing view, he tore up the paper and went back to his original despatch. Mrs Arbuthnot's account of Wellington's reaction spoke volumes for the way Canning's opponents saw such gestures: 'As the Duke justly says, is this a man to rule the foreign policy of England, who in the solemn deliberations of the Cabinet carries such childish frivolity & ridiculous sarcasm?' Wellington's criticism was that Canning was needlessly offending the French. No one could accuse the Duke of being a Francophile, but he thought that throughout the French had been acting with the support of the Spanish King, so it was difficult to object to what they were doing. In Castlereagh's day, he lamented, Britain would have found out from Lieven and Esterhazy what the French were up to and would have acted in concert with them if it had been decided that they were up to no good. But now 'the art of diplomacy is at an end' and Canning, 'in total ignorance of the opinions of every court in Europe, sends a menacing question to France, which if she declines to answer, must be insisted upon with the sword . . . & we may have, for anything he knows to the contrary, all Europe against us!'

On the subject of recognition of the former Spanish colonies, Wellington also found himself at odds with Canning and the Prime Minister. He accepted that there were good commercial reasons to recognize the independence of the republics, but he feared that it might lead to war with Spain, and while Britain would easily win such a conflict, she might find herself at war with other powers as a consequence. In addition, the measure had little support in the Cabinet and would encounter the sincere opposition of a King whose support for the principle of legitimacy was well known. Wellington offered to resign over the issue. He complained to Dorothea that Canning was 'on the point of burning his fingers in thirty different ways', but when she said, 'Well, let him burn them in one and throw him out', the Duke replied: 'It is easy to talk, but the fire would spread to the whole of England, and we should be the first to burn'; he saw no way open other than resignation. However, the Duke thought better of this and decided that he could do more good by staying in the Cabinet where he could try to moderate Canning's policy.

It soon became clear that Canning was playing a clever game. He knew, via the French ambassador, that the French were willing to offer assurances about the nature of their occupation of Spain, but preferred, for reasons of his own, to resort to despatches warning the French about their behaviour. By thus implying that the French could not be trusted in Spain, Canning was able to argue that the best security against France taking over the Latin American colonies was to recognize their independence; it was a totally spurious argument – but no Foreign Secretary has ever appealed in vain to British Francophobia. It was the sort of trickery that maddened his opponents, who saw in it nothing more than Canning's love of shaking things up. As one experienced diplomat put it, comparing Canning to his predecessor, it was strange to reflect that 'formerly, we had a minister who could neither write nor speak & who exercised an unbounded influence in every Court in Europe. Now we have one who is a master of both arts, & we know nothing & are consulted about nothing.'

In the end, Canning moderated his language to the French, but insisted upon the recognition of the republics, threatening to resign, as did Liverpool, if he were gainsaid. Under such a threat, the Cabinet gave in, but the King refused to agree when he learned that Wellington was unhappy with the decision; he also wanted to consult the other great powers before finally making up his mind. The Duke told him that the only alternative was to dismiss his ministers and find another government – which would not be a simple matter: 'therefore the best thing to do was to yield but to watch Mr Canning narrowly and keep him as straight as possible.' Dorothea was disgusted with such pusillanimity: 'So the outcome of all these Cabinet meetings is that they have ended as [Canning] wished them to end. What weakness!'

Canning was sanguine enough about the reaction of the other powers to his diplomatic style. He told Granville, with evident amusement, that when the Tsar had heard that Britain would not take part in a congress devoted to the affairs of Greece, he had 'flown into a passion' and declared that 'he will be damned if he ever talks Greek to us again'; what, he wondered, 'will he say and do when he receives Pozzo's account of the South American treaties? Will he publish a manifesto?' The fact that Canning had managed to drag his refusal out across the course of 1824 was a clever piece of diplomatic manoeuvring, but it left him open to the charge most often levelled at him by his opponents – that he had no fixed principles. During that period the crisis deepened: the Greeks lost further ground militarily, and the Turks turned to the Pasha of Egypt, Mehmet Ali, to solve the problem for them by using his highly professional army against the Greek rebels. The fact that Canning had recognized the 'belligerent' status of the Greek rebels marked, as did his moves in the same direction with the Latin American republics, the width of the chasm opening up between Britain and her old allies. As even Temperley admitted, Canning 'had now reached a definite separation from the Neo-Holy Alliance over Greece, as over everything else, and isolation is dangerous in diplomacy'.

The news of Canning's triumph on the question of a congress officially reached the courts of Europe on 11 January, but thanks to Dorothea's sources of information, both the Tsar and Metternich knew about it in advance. In early March Canning received what he called the 'high & mighty displeasures of their Courts' with some disdain. When Count Lieven began to read out the Tsar's despatch, Canning interrupted him, asked him whether he was authorized to deliver a copy of it, and upon receiving a negative answer, 'I declined hearing it unless he could give me his word that no copy would be sent to any other Court.' He complained that the process suggested by the Russians would make him responsible before parliament for responding to a despatch the full import of which he would not be able to judge properly unless he saw it. When Count Lieven asked what he was to do, Canning said he could 'do what he pleased – but that I took exception now before I heard a word of his despatch, because I would not have it thought that the contents of that despatch, whatever they might be, had anything to do with that exception'. He explained that he was really refusing to hear it because he knew that St Petersburg had instructed Lieven not to give him copies of recent despatches on the Turkish question, but had gone on to tell the other Courts that their sense had been 'communicated' to him '& acquiesced by my silence'; he would not, he declared, be tricked in that way again. Canning allowed Lieven to speak in the sense of the despatch, but insisted on taking his own record and sending it to the Russian embassy so that if the papers needed to be published, it would be clear that he had dissented strongly. He played the same game with Esterhazy.

When Maltzahn, the Prussian ambassador, tried simply to deliver a lecture to him, Canning, 'provoked' by his tone, decided to 'pay off his reserve' with him, 'and accordingly said a few as disagreeable things as I could'. He was determined, he told Granville on 4 March 1825, 'to teach the Holy Alliance'. When Granville asked him what he should say to Metternich who had claimed to be 'indignant', Canning let rip with the comment quoted above that he should tell him that 'he is the greatest rogue & liar' in Christendom. Now that he had won his victory, he was determined to savour it – and to let Metternich know that he knew what he had been up to. He knew, for example, that the King, through some 'incredibly ill-advised expressions', had told Metternich that the intrigue against Canning might still succeed, and that Metternich had urged Esterhazy 'to keep himself safe – but let Madame Lieven do all; to watch the impression upon the King; but not to commit himself or his government'. He told Granville that if the intrigue had continued he would have resigned on the South American question 'and I would have declared openly in the H[ouse] of C[ommons] – taking care to keep safe my source of intelligence – that I was driven from office by the Holy Alliance'; he would also have told the House that the 'system . . . of personal communications between the Sovereign and the Foreign Ministers, was one under which no English Minister could do his duty'. As he said to Granville: 'If, after such a denunciation and the debates which would have followed it, the L[ieven]s and Esterhazy did not find London too hot for them, I know nothing of the present temper of the English nation.'

What had made Canning 'indignant' was not the assumption by his opponents that 'the Jacobin Minister & his Politicks [*sic*] would be thrown overboard', that was part of the political game, but rather their presumption in thinking that he would 'only keep his seat by consenting to throw overboard his Politicks'. What amazed him was that Metternich's 'correspondents in this country, should have supposed it possible that, with a view even to objects of interest & ambition, one could have hesitated what choice to make if the alternatives had been presented'. Canning resented Metternich's tendency to attribute his own motives to Canning.

Dorothea was correct when she told Wellington that 'Canning's popularity makes him master in the Cabinet', although the Duke, stubborn to the end, denied it and maintained that 'it is a false glitter which will not take in any sensible person; that it will all vanish in smoke', and that if he really ended up isolating Britain 'it would be the end of his political career, for such a system had all English opinion against it.' But, as time would show, the Duke's interpretation of what the country would and would not allow, was not often very accurate.

Canning's overactive imagination had, to some extent, created the 'intrigue', and it says much about the way his mind worked that he should have regarded in such a light the opposition his attitude provoked. Canning was socially insecure. He knew that his background aroused condescension from those whose inferior talents led them to take refuge from his triumphs in snobbish disdain – but that did not stop it hurting. During a dinner given for the King by the Duke back in June, George 'never stopped making jokes' about Canning to Dorothea: 'he remarked, very rightly, that Canning is too gushing, that he hates me and over-whelms me with attentions.' The 'natural result of embarrassing someone', Dorothea told Metternich, 'is to be perfectly at ease oneself', and she found her relations with Canning 'amusing'. 'All the time he is hating me and feeling embarrassed he tries to be witty and makes clever remarks. But he is one of those men who always kill any conversation. You have continually to begin again; and I get bored.' She noted that Canning 'hardly ever goes into society', and that when she met him at a reception at the Marchioness of Hertford's 'he came up to me with his usual alacrity and then stood rooted to the ground at my side, looking wretchedly awkward, as he always does.' After a short interval of watching his discomfort, Dorothea invited him to sit down: 'he accepted this favour with a humility and gratitude that were really quite funny.' She thought that Canning had 'a kind of fear of me which makes him unable to keep away from me. The truth is that there is a sort of attraction about the people one hates.' Dorothea hated Canning all the more when she discovered that Metternich had put off his journey to Paris because of him. She reported that ever and anon there were continued rumblings of discontent from Canning's opponents in the Cabinet, but she assessed these at their correct value: 'they did not daunt him when they were courageous. Are they likely to overthrow him now they are afraid?' Dorothea was correct when she told Metternich that 'we must put up with this plague until he takes it into his head to break his own neck.'

Dorothea's fifth son was born in late February 1825, just in time to coincide with Canning's triumph; she named the boy Arthur, after the Duke of Wellington. Deprived by Canning's animosity of a visit to London by Metternich, Dorothea looked forward to his trip to Paris, although not the reason he was making it; Princess Metternich was seriously ill. She died in early March, and Dorothea poured out her sympathy to the stricken Chancellor – who acknowledged the excellent qualities of his late wife – before remarking on how the press were commenting on his visit to Paris, which he thought would have a good effect politically; truly, for a politician, in death we are in the midst of life. As Canning put it in a slightly different context: 'Metternich . . . is quite incorrigible.' The asperity of political conflict was not tempered by private tragedy. Canning told Granville that since he was sure that Metternich would 'recommence his intrigues', he should 'know how well I am apprised of all the good that he intended me. And I should like him to understand that a renewal of similar attempts may lead to some publick [*sic*] manifestation of what is past, as may let the House of Commons, & the Publick into the secret.' He kept a weather eye on visits by Dorothea and Esterhazy to the 'Cottage', but the King had learned his lesson. He sent his doctor and confidant, Sir William Knighton, to see Canning, who was laid up with gout, on 27 April, ostensibly to ask after his health, but in fact to make overtures of peace.

Henceforth there would be only one master of British foreign policy – and the King ceased his practice of private correspondence with Metternich. However, this did not, as things turned out, mean the end of the influence of Countess Lieven – quite the opposite.

9. 'The Emperor took me for a man'

The first impact of Tsar Alexander I's refusal to 'speak Greek' to Canning fell upon his cousin, the diplomat Stratford Canning, who was on a special mission to St Petersburg, and who wrote that he had been met with great coolness. The Foreign Secretary was unperturbed, telling Stratford in February: 'I trust that the Emperor of Russia will recover from his pet, and that we shall again be on terms of good understanding with Russia.' Canning had declined to take part in any congress mainly because he thought Metternich was trying to bring Britain 'once more into Conference on the principles of European jurisdiction . . . He saw as clearly as I could do, that a second circular like that of Laybach [*sic*], or a second dissent & separation like that of Verona would have made us supremely ridiculous.'

That it was Metternich and not the Russians to whom Canning had taken objection was shown by his determination to cultivate the Lievens. He told Stratford Canning on 23 February 1825 that he did not want the Lievens replaced: 'In the present state of our relations and in the ticklish temper of the world, a great, rough, staring, whiskered *owski* on the one hand or a fine intriguing *ozzo* on the other (of which species the Russian diplomacy is generally composed) might easily snap the thread, which is quite strong enough to hold if it is not strained too hard.' Dorothea noticed that 'Canning has become friendly, at least to my husband.' Nor was that the only change in the air. Her own epistles to the apostle of legitimacy lessened in their frequency; political infidelity was in the offing.

Unable to 'speak Greek' with the British, the Tsar had turned to Metternich – but the results had not been what he had expected. Canning, despite his crippling gout, could not suppress a considerable smile when he heard that the discussions in St Petersburg between the Russians and the Austrians had revealed 'a wide difference of opinion between the two Imperial Courts, upon the first principle of the proposed intervention'. 'Nothing,' he told Granville, 'could be better calculated . . . to satisfy me with the position which we occupy.' Canning suspected that Metternich had hoped that 'if he had had us in the mess, the still wider differences between (what he supposed to be) our opinions & those of both Austria and Russia, would have brought them comparatively nearer each other, by rendering us the mark of their common attack – a clever scheme!' Cynical interpretations of Metternich's motives were seldom wide of the mark, and Canning had, in this instance, penetrated to the heart of the matter. Alexander I had wanted a congress to sanction the use of force by Russia against Mehmet Ali's men in the Morea, and to this Metternich had many objections – most of which he did not dare mention since they were to do with his fear of Russian ambitions. Thanks to Canning, the option that he had had in Castlereagh's day, that of cooperating with Britain against the Tsar, did not exist, and he was reduced to the expedient of suggesting that the Holy Alliance powers might recognize the independence of Greece. The idea of the apostle of legitimacy proposing in the case of Greece what he had protested against in that of Latin America caused Canning no little amusement.

As Alexander I began to object to Metternich posing as the arbiter of Europe, he found himself sharing at least one of Canning's opinions. There was, in fact, no bar to Anglo-Russian bilateral cooperation, at least on Canning's part; what he objected to was multilateral diplomacy on behalf of the alliance. There remained the barrier of Alexander's bar on 'talking Greek', but as early as March, although Nesselrode was maintaining it, Stratford Canning thought he 'could perceive from his tone that the manner in which that sentiment had been indulged in was now itself become a subject of regret to this Government'. Nesselrode was also at pains to stress that whatever form Russian intervention in Greece might take 'it would not only be commenced in the spirit of Peace, but accompanied throughout with zealous efforts to effect the restoration of order by means of persuasion alone'; that, in itself, was a sign of Russia's willingness to at least leave open the option of talking separately to the British. Stratford was able to get the Russians to listen to the British point of view because of what Nesselrode called the 'earnest desire entertained by His Imperial Majesty to cherish a cordial understanding with the British Government', but there was still a gulf between the two powers. The Russians increasingly saw the need to intervene swiftly to 'guard against the evils to be apprehended . . . from the triumphant establishment of Greek Independence'; the British still wished to avoid the use of force. In these circumstances there was nothing more to be done – and unless some shift in position took place, the Tsar would free himself from dependence upon Metternich only to act unilaterally.

The shift in the Tsar's attitude towards Metternich was not simply the result of a difference of opinion on the Greek question. The Austrian Chancellor, renowned for his vanity, had been in-discreet enough, while in Paris, to boast of his influence over Alexander I, talking freely of how he was working with him in Greece only in order to keep Russia confined. All of this was relayed to Dorothea, and to the Tsar himself, through the energetic Russian ambassador in Paris, Pozzo di Borgo; the Tsar did not forgive his old ally. Potentially, Dorothea was in a difficult position. As she was known to be Metternich's lover and confidante, sus-picions might have been directed towards her; but she was more than equal to the occasion. She had noted Canning's willingness to keep on good terms with Russia, and she knew enough about British politics to understand where Canning's real animosity was directed. Dorothea also knew more than almost anyone else about how Metternich worked. The personal coolness that had been growing between them had begun to take on a political dimension once the extent of Metternich's manipulation became clear. The journey to Russia that had had to be postponed because of her pregnancy was rescheduled for June, and although she had no clear scheme worked out in her mind, she resolved, she recorded, to 'tell the Emperor the truth, if he did me the honour to speak to me of his affairs'.

It was more than a decade since Dorothea had spent any time in Russia, and she 'found there with joy after thirteen years the customs of my youth, the maternal goodness of the Empress, with joy even the unwonted etiquette of the Court'. Having grown used to the informal, even lax, ways of George IV at the Pavilion, she found it difficult to adapt herself to the mores of her own country, in particular the 'abdication of dignity by each person in order to incarnate it in the sovereign' which 'contrasted greatly with the country from which I came'. She watched the old women chaperone the young 'to give to young people the example of respect to old women', and reflected that at the age of forty 'I had got to midsummer'. The old Russian habit of 'hurrying too much in order to wait a long time' was just one of the ways in which the autocrat made his presence felt. And yet, at the heart of the court there was an absence – the autocrat was not there.

Alexander's unpredictability had been a fact of European diplomacy from the start of his reign, and the internal struggle between his liberal views and conservative instincts had not ceased to trouble him. His conservative alliance with Metternich over the Eastern Question had run counter to dynastic and Russian interests – at least as others saw them. The spectacle of fellow Orthodox Christians being massacred by Muslims was one that provoked the anger of Russian Christians. A war against the Grand Turk might lead to that great event so long and devoutly wished for – the return of Constantinople to the Orthodox – when carpets in the Hagia Sofia could be rolled up and the whitewash be removed from the famous icons; after a gap of nearly 400 years the Orthodox liturgy could once again be said in the Church of the Divine Wisdom. The dreams of the great Catherine for her dynasty could be fulfilled, and the name of the Romanovs would be for ever linked with the most glorious moment in the history of the Faithful.

From all of these great and glorious consummations Alexander had turned his face. Russia was a western great power, part of the Concert of Europe that he had helped create in 1815. Russia was also the champion of legitimacy and conservatism; no monarch need fear his people as long as Russia's sword was ready to spring from its scabbard; the 'gendarme of Europe' – or was it the Don Quixote? Metternich had murmured words of caution into Alexander's ear ever since the Greek revolt of 1821, and the Tsar had acted upon them: he had been the champion of European conservatism rather than of Russian Orthodoxy; of the Concert of Europe rather than of Russian nationalism; and of monarchical solidarity rather than of Romanov dynastic interests.

His reward for this self-abnegation was to hear that Metternich was telling the French that he had managed the Tsar wonderfully well and had prevented him from acting in Russian interests. What seems to have vexed Alexander the most was Metternich's comment that: 'I found the Emperor a Jacobin; I have made him an Ultra; it only remains to make a tyrant of him.' Alexander, like so many of his predecessors, was sensitive about Russia's position in the world, and unlike some of them, he had worked hard to make her a truly 'European' power; now it seemed that despite his sacrifices, Russia was still not accepted as such. It was little wonder that the Tsar isolated himself at the magnificent palace at Tsarskoi Selo, seeing his ministers only at set hours, and spending the rest of his time meditating on works of piety. All of this Dorothea heard, but for the whole time she spent with the Empress Elizabeth, she saw nothing of her reclusive husband. Then, finally, she was sent for, and she waited alone in his richly furnished apartment until, fifteen minutes after the time of their appointment, the Tsar emerged.

The only account we have of the meeting is Dorothea's own, and it was written in the awed manner with which she was wont to recount the doings of the Tsars: 'The Emperor received me with the familiar good humour that I always had from him. He was so isolated from all contacts with man, his habits had become so monastic, his mind so suspicious that the sight even of a person like me seemed to embarrass him. I do not know why, but this embarrassment gave me courage.' After they had discussed the various chancelleries of Europe, with particular mention being made of the weaknesses of Metternich, Dorothea's 'courage' emboldened her enough to say: 'Put your foot down, Sire, and you will make the whole world tremble.' That, Dorothea recorded, 'was precisely what the Emperor did not think he could dare to do'. After an hour and a half they parted. Dorothea purred with pride when her brother Alexander told her that the Tsar had said: 'I left your sister a young woman; I have found her a stateswoman.' She played her hand carefully, avoiding getting involved in court factions, but telling Nesselrode what she had said to the Tsar. 'He was a little frightened at the boldness of my talk with the Emperor . . . but seeing my good courage and the reserve of all my behaviour, he communicated to me from his side what might help me in the vague idea which I had formed'; this was 'to detach ourselves from Austria and re-approach England, for everything could be done by this double relation'. Here, the fact that both the Tsar and Nesselrode knew about the intimate nature of Dorothea's connection with Metternich gave her critique of the Austrian Chancellor particular resonance; she was very critical of Austrian policy and the limitations it imposed on Russia. The timing of this move was highly significant.

In May the conference being held in St Petersburg on the Greek question had broken up in bitter disagreement; Nesselrode had told the Austrian ambassador, Lebzeltern, that he could not trust himself to speak on the matter. Lebzeltern, worried by this turn of events, naturally sought out Countess Lieven as a friendly face at an increasingly hostile court. Dorothea asked him to tell Metternich that 'if he did not bestir himself to arrange our affairs with Turkey, conveniently, he could be sure that we should take up the matter ourselves, and that we should declare war on Turkey.' Lebzeltern replied: 'You dare not make war. The Tsar has more to fear from his army than from his enemies.' This comment came back to her in December when there was an attempted coup, one of whose leaders was Lebzeltern's brother-in-law, Count Trubetzkoi.

Towards the end of her stay in Russia, Dorothea had another interview with the Tsar; this time she learned his views on Metternich and Canning. Of the former, Alexander declared: 'I am discontented with him. His method is not straight'; on the

latter, his comment was to inquire: 'Canning is a Jacobin, is that
not true?' It would have taken someone with less political nous
than Dorothea not to have given the response that Alexander was
looking for: 'You will pardon me, Sire, Canning is not a Jacobin.'
Since that was exactly how she had described him in a letter to her
brother on 27 April 1823, she showed her usual sang-froid in
ignoring past comments that no longer corresponded with what
was politically convenient. Canning, she told the Tsar, 'was the
enemy of Prince Metternich'. Given Alexander's feeling about
Metternich's portrayal of him as an Austrian dupe, Dorothea's
switch of allegiance was politically and personally sensible.
Although she left no record of it, she must have been mindful of
the difficulties that her relationship with Metternich would have
posed given the direction in which the Tsar's mind was moving;
as his lover, she would naturally have been suspect; offering her
insight into his thoughts as a further reason why Russian policy
should change, put Dorothea on the right side of the Tsar. On
18 August Alexander told his ambassadors that since Russia had
not been supported at the conference, they were to tell their
various courts that any questions of future cooperation with them
on diplomatic matters would be decided *ad referendum* by the Tsar
himself; as to the Eastern Question, they were told that Russia was
not satisfied by the behaviour of the Ottoman Porte and that war
could not be ruled out.

The following morning, 19 August, Nesselrode saw Dorothea
before she left Russia to return to London. He reported, verbatim,
what the Tsar had said to him the previous evening about her: 'I
have found her sensible on all questions. She judges fairly and
without prejudices. An idea has come to me which I have been
working out for some days. Could we not profit by her return to
England to re-approach that Cabinet? She knows the influential
persons in that country, she enjoys great consideration, she well
knows the means to use her position to render the service I ask of
her.' Alexander had grasped the fact that as long as he held to the
Metternichean policy on Greece only Austria profited by it. Under
pressure from his military and diplomatic advisers to act in Greece,

he had decided to do so, but realized that if he acted alone he was liable to unite the Concert of Europe – but this time against himself. If England would work with him, Alexander told Nesselrode, 'we are sure of controlling events and of establishing in the East an order of things conformable to the laws of religion and humanity.' The Tsar's difficulty was that it would not 'suit my dignity' to begin to 'talk Greek' with the British – at least on his own initiative. Nesselrode explained to Dorothea that she was to be the instrument for the change of Russian policy precisely because the Tsar could not be seen to retreat from the position he had taken up the previous winter. She was to 'make the Cabinet of England under-stand that, if it takes a step, it will not be repulsed, and that we shall always be ready to welcome its ideas'.

By her own account Dorothea was 'disturbed' and 'remained a moment nonplussed'; but she was clearly delighted at the turn events had taken. Here 'was the most cautious and discreet of ministers compelled to entrust the most confidential, most intimate and most bold political projects to a woman. It was new and something to laugh at.' She explained the problems that might lie in her way: Canning's isolation in the Cabinet; his unpopularity with the King; England's Turcophil tendencies; and finally, the government's horror of supporting revolutionaries. Then, of course, came the real difficulty: 'how were we to begin when we had shut our mouths to England?' Nesselrode's response spoke volumes: 'A woman knows how to make people speak, and that is why the Emperor considers you are a unique opportunity, and your presence here has been for him like a revelation.' When Dorothea expressed the 'incredible idea' in her own words – that what was being proposed was a total diplomatic revolution that would result in the Turks being driven from Europe and a Christian power being erected in their stead, 'Nesselrode seized himself by the head and looked fearfully at the door. "My God! If the Emperor heard you!" Then, very low, "Ah, well, it is possible that is what he dreams of", and moving his spectacles up over his forehead, he gave way to a movement of lassitude and despair.'

Her conversation with Nesselrode was 'gay and serious by turns, the conclusion was that I should obey and be very diligent'. She wrote down her understanding of her instructions, then Nesselrode pulled his spectacles down from his forehead and read the note: 'That,' he said, 'is the true wish of the Emperor, he is going to be attached to that idea, don't forget it for an instant!' In order to safeguard the '*paix du ménage*' it was agreed that Dorothea would 'instruct my husband in everything, that he should take the question in hand, if I succeeded in putting it *au monde*, and that the Count de Nesselrode should furnish me with a letter of credence to that effect'. This last point was crucial, since it was hardly to be expected that Count Lieven would take his wife's word that Russian foreign policy had changed so dramatically. Ever the cautious bureaucrat, Nesselrode wrote a brief note which said baldly: 'Believe all the bearer tells you.' That was, indeed, a flourish worthy of Alexandre Dumas, and with it, the conversation ended and Dorothea set off for London.

Dorothea liked to claim that she reached London with the same speed as a diplomatic courier, but that was an example of her love of hyperbole and her sense of the dramatic, since she arrived back in England on 28 September, two weeks after a courier would have; still, some licence must be allowed for the poetic imagination. On her way she had written to warn Metternich that 'there is a certain coldness towards you. I beg you to give the matter real thought. It will take very little to cause real trouble. It seems to me that you ought to adopt conciliatory measures.' She asked him to 'accept what I tell you at its proper value' and to 'trust in my tact and in my zeal. Do not reply that I am wrong, and that it is you who are right. Even if you are, be quick, waste no time in arguing; but try to make your peace.' It was good advice, but Metternich could not take it, even had he wanted to. If Russian policy began to shift towards action in Turkey then he could not support it. But neither could he have conceived that the Tsar would be able to 'speak Greek' to Canning – hence his assumption that little notice needed to be taken of Dorothea's vatic warnings. Piqued, Dorothea told him: 'The Emperor took me for a man; he treated me as one as regards confidences, and as a woman as regards

attentions and consideration'; since this was the exact opposite
of the way she felt Metternich was treating her, the Austrian
Chancellor would have done well to have pondered the reason
for her change of tone — but such was his armour-plated
self-confidence that he did not.

Canning was well aware of the divisions between the Holy
Alliance powers over Greece, but was none the less surprised when
the Lievens called on him on 24 October 1825. Count Lieven,
claiming to be acting 'in entire personal confidence' and 'without
the orders of his Court', gave Canning a copy of the Tsar's circular
despatch of 18 August, along with a résumé of the points at issue
between Russia and her allies over the Greek question. Canning
noted with great satisfaction that: 'It is impossible for ill humour
to be expressed more strongly than in the tenour [*sic*] of these two
documents.' Lieven told Nesselrode that 'my conduct will prove
to you that I have understood the sense of the "living despatch"
that you have sent me.' Canning told Liverpool on 25 October
that none of the other powers had imparted such 'confidences', and
that Russia's 'wrath against Austria, or rather Count Metternich, is
great; and I must own not undeserved.' The real question now,
he thought, was when Britain should intervene: 'I am quite clear
that there is no honesty in Metternich; and that we cannot enter
into joint counsel with him without the certainty of being
betrayed.' It was not without a great deal of self-satisfaction that
Canning imparted the great and good news to his friend Granville:
'The King . . . begins to apprehend that I have not, as he was
taught "to apprehend", lost to him his station among the "Powers
of the Continent" but only changed it from the tail of Europe to
the head. What is to be done is a different thing, but nothing just
yet. Things are not ripe for our interference, for we must not,
(like our good Allies) interfere in vain. *If* we act we must finish
what is to be done.'

What Canning firmly believed was that if there was to be any
action with regard to Turkey, Britain must act '*alone*' because
'combined operation is nonsense in a case in which the principles
on which we and our allies act, are as different as the objects at

which we respectively aim'. Canning did not believe that the Holy Alliance was at an end, and he thought that any idea of 'combined intervention' would lead the Tsar to Constantinople 'quite as directly as the leaving him alone' because 'the *principle* upon which Russia calls upon her Allies is that of the Holy Alliance.' He told the French ambassador, Polignac, as much, adding that 'we who protested against the decisions of Verona, and in some sort those of Laybach, are at liberty to protest against the Emperor of Russia's march to Constantinople in a representative capacity as well as in his personal one'; – something the French could not do. Great, then, was Canning's fury when he discovered that his new ambassador to Russia, Lord Strangford, had actually suggested joint intervention at the Porte. When Count Lieven read the account of Strangford's initiative to him on 17 December, Canning had to have the offending phrase reread three or four times. He wrote to Strangford on 31 December: 'I want words to express the astonishment which I felt.' He issued a blistering rebuke, and despite Strangford's attempts to extricate himself, it was clear that he would have to go. But by this time a fresh problem had arisen.

When Dorothea had left St Petersburg, the Tsar had departed for Taganrog with a few attendants; his object had been to seek solitude. On 18 December the news reached England that the Emperor Alexander had died on 1 December. For once the purple prose of Countess Lieven was justified when she recorded that 'This event echoed through Europe like a thunderclap.' Rumour had an open field in which to play, and it was soon being said that Alexander had met the same fate as his father; the uncertainty increased when it became clear that there was some dispute over the identity of his successor – and even whether he had died at all. Dorothea was devastated, on political and personal grounds. She told Metternich: 'I can think of nothing but our misfortune. I cannot sleep; I can only weep; I weep from the bottom of my heart.' She was 'astonished' to 'realise to what an extent he confided in me'. The Tsar had, she wrote, given her 'a new interest in life. I had great political influence upon him and I should soon have had more. He was the kind of man liable to become infatuated;

and it was a new experience to him to have political relations with
a woman . . . As long as the secret of my influence went no further
than ourselves, I should have kept my position. It would have been
unique. I believe I should have done good.' Metternich may have
taken leave to doubt her last comment, but could not dissent from
what she had said. Her anxieties increased with the news that the
throne had gone not to her old lover, the Grand Duke Constantine,
but to the youngest brother, Nicholas – and that he had had to
deal with a revolt by young aristocrats – the Decembrists – among
whom was the Austrian ambassador's brother-in-law. This raised
a clamour in Russia against Austria to such an extent that Lebzeltern was 'compelled to withdraw himself from Society' and to
ask to be recalled to Vienna.

Where 'old people hesitated at the first moment' to put much
trust in a new Tsar who might not last very long, 'it was not the
same with Canning' – so Dorothea wrote. She was correct in
discerning that 'It was just the novelty of the person and the
situation which nerved his mind and made him imagine the hope
of a revival of a policy more conformable to his view.' Canning
decided to send the Duke of Wellington on a special mission to
St Petersburg to congratulate the new Tsar – a gesture which,
according to Canning, was received by Count Lieven 'with astonishment, & then *literally* with tears of pleasure at having to
announce to his Court such a proof of my resolution to carry into
effect the system of renewed confidence which I had opened to
him in October'. It was a sign of the way his mind was moving
that Canning should have felt able to expand on the motives for
what he thought might seem a surprising plan to Granville. He
admitted that 'the D of W would not have done for any purpose
of mine a twelvemonth ago – no more would confidence with
Russia', but now, 'the Ultra System being dissolved', some of its
'elements become useable for good purposes'. What Canning
hoped to do was to 'save Greece through the agency of the Russian
name upon the fears of Turkey, without a war, which the D of W
is the fittest man to deprecate'; he sent the Duke 'to the autocrat
without any apprehension that he will dream in his own head, or

put into the autocrat's any chimera for a new Holy Alliance'; moreover, after the ambassador's gaffe, Wellington was 'the only agent by whom I could suppress & extinguish Strangford'.

The news that Dorothea had brought back from St Petersburg, while satisfying, was hardly enough to quell Canning's anxieties. He knew that before his death Alexander had decided that Russia would have to go to war with Turkey, so when Nicholas said that he would continue his late brother's policies, this was not very 'cheering' from the British point of view. Canning's instructions were firm on this point: 'Our object is, if possible, to prevent Russia from going to war.' What he hoped was that by proposing either British or joint Anglo-Russian mediation with the Porte and with the Greeks, a diplomatic solution could be found to the Greek problem; but any such solution would have to be bilateral and not multilateral, and in view of Strangford's mistake, Canning emphasized at length to Wellington that there should be no talk of a Concert of Europe. The problem, however, was what to do if diplomacy failed? But, at least in February, Canning's confidence in his own ability to conjure up a solution remained strong. Wellington was less optimistic, confiding to Bathurst on 17 February that: 'Excepting in the way of conciliation, which is certainly very desirable at the commencement of a new reign, I don't expect to do much good in my mission . . . if war is on any account desirable to them, I don't think I can prevent it.' Dorothea was even more sceptical. In her view Canning intended to 'compromise him [the Duke] and mock him at the same time – a double pleasure'. By making Wellington the instrument of his policy, Canning would commit him to a line on Greek independence that ran counter to the one he had taken on Latin America – with the incidental advantage that during the time the Duke would be out of the country he would be master of the Cabinet.

From Dorothea's point of view the early months of 1826 were ones of great uncertainty. She would have been aware of the rumours that Nicholas intended to replace Nesselrode, and the recall of her husband in March prompted speculation as to whether or not the Lievens would be removed. It is some indication of how much the diplomatic situation had changed in a year that Canning now wrote to Wellington urging him to emphasize the importance of keeping the Lievens in London: 'You cannot say more than is true, of our desire to keep him here.' Much as Canning would have deprecated the replacement of Nesselrode, he was more worried by the prospect of losing Lieven who 'could not be replaced here with advantage'. In fact, as things worked out, it might have been better for Canning if Lieven had stayed in London, since his presence in St Petersburg led to the signing of an agreement which did not altogether please the Foreign Secretary.

Canning had, in fact, been too clever by half in sending Wellington with a complicated and nuanced set of instructions. The Duke and nuance consorted badly together, and it was Count Lieven who helped to bring matters to what was, from the Russian point of view, a successful conclusion. The Duke had been surprised when Nesselrode first disclaimed any intention of wanting to patronize the Greek rebels, and then said that Russia's aim was to 'establish in Greece the conservation of order'. He was alarmed to hear that the Russians were about to present the Turks with an ultimatum on other points at issue between the two countries and spent most of his time trying to prevent a Russo-Turkish war rather than, as Canning wanted, emphasizing the importance of the Greek question. On 4 April 1826 the Duke signed what became known as the Protocol of St Petersburg. This provided for British and Russian mediation with the Porte on the Greek question, and implicitly recognized that an independent Greek state would be created, the boundaries of which would be fixed by Britain and Russia. Thus far, so good, but Canning was not best pleased with the sixth article, which stipulated that the other great powers would be asked to accede to the protocol and would join with Russia in guaranteeing the settlement – something that Britain would not do.

According to Dorothea, Canning was 'not quite sure whether to congratulate himself on a success or to complain of a snare – for it had gone much beyond his wishes, England found herself

irrevocably engaged. He witnessed to me simply enough his hesita-
tion and even his regret.' Still, according to her, Canning found
some consolations: 'thinking of the dislike Prince Metternich was
going to conceive and of the mystification practised on the Duke
of Wellington'. He told the Countess, with some regret, that 'If
the Duke had been more acute [*fin*] he would have played his
cards better on his side, so as not to be the only one mystified.'
Dorothea recorded that she and her husband 'were too prudent
to laugh'.

10. 'I have become sensible'

The realignment of Britain and Russia had been intended by Canning to disrupt the Holy Alliance – and in doing so it also helped to deliver a final blow to one somewhat less sacred, that between Dorothea and Metternich. As we have seen, she had reacted frostily to his selfishness in not responding to her overtures in the winter of 1823, and their relationship had never recovered its former warmth; from the time of her visit to Russia in 1825, she became increasingly distant. Dorothea knew better than to stay involved with a man who was now the object of Russian suspicions, but she had a more personal reason for finally severing contact with him in 1826.

The Duke of Wellington's sister-in-law, Lady Georgiana Wellesley, visited her father, the ambassador in Vienna, in the spring of 1826, and the gossip she brought back displeased Dorothea. Metternich, she reported, was often to be seen at the house of a Mademoiselle Leykam. Was she, Dorothea asked pointedly, his 'mistress' or his 'new wife', as rumour suggested? 'So much for the constancy of men,' she told Metternich in a letter written on 16 May. Lest he should think that she was upset by this development, she asked, 'Don't you think my reproaches are rather lukewarm?' But she rather spoiled any effect this might have by adding: 'If I were to take my revenge – Heavens no, I shan't take revenge. So much for the folly of women.' She adjured him to 'love me as you have always done', despite the Greek crisis and 'in spite of young ladies'. But her true feelings showed when she could not resist reverting to the topic that had upset her most: 'What a strange man you are! Taking notice of a little girl! I should look funny, if I were to bother myself with a little boy! This is not a threat; I would rather kill myself.' She did not do anything so melodramatic, but she felt all the pain of a woman in her forties who hears that her lover has taken up with a younger and more attractive woman. Her feelings still bound her to the silken dalliance and the memories of Aix-la-Chapelle, but her duty pulled her away from these things; this she could bear; what she could not, was the fact that Metternich was so indifferent to her own pain. As her husband negotiated with Wellington in St Petersburg, and the diplomatic revolution took effect in the great world, Dorothea felt her world shift along with it.

While Metternich was courting the future Madame Metternich, Dorothea herself was being pursued – but not by a 'young boy'. For some time in the spring of 1826, Dorothea had found herself being summoned down to Brighton or over to Windsor to see the King. Now that Canning had mastered George IV, and Dorothea was on the same side, she was no longer so assiduous in her duties to him, so in the end he resorted to issuing a 'royal command' through Wellington for her to attend on him.

The King's ostensible reason was that he wished to discuss political matters with her, but after a few moments' conversation on such matters, he revealed his true purpose. He was, he told Dorothea, bored by his current mistress who was, he said, a fool. She agreed with this verdict, but thought it dull-witted of him to maintain such a mistress. Her superciliousness was tested to its limit when she discovered that she was the chosen replacement. The King confessed that he had 'been in love with me for thirteen years', but had 'never dared to tell me; he hoped I should find it out for myself', but since she had not, he had to tell her. An 'inner voice' had told him that she 'alone could guide him. Our minds are alike; our views agree; my tastes will be his.' Or, as he put it passionately: 'In a word, Heaven made us for one another.' This declaration, accompanied as it was by 'would-be amorous glances', embarrassed Dorothea, but she was courtier and flirt enough to deal with it. She responded by saying that she too thought that they were 'so close to one another', and their ideas 'so much the same that I felt that he must at least be my cousin'. That was not enough to checkmate the corpulent old lecher who protested that he could not be satisfied with just the 'spiritual side', since he was 'really and truly in love with you, very much in love'. All that remained was for Dorothea to decline regretfully to fill the proffered vacancy, protesting that she did not want to 'destroy' their 'old friendship'. George asked her to look in his bedroom before she left. Calculating, perhaps, that she could outrun the King if the worst happened, Dorothea glanced inside, where she saw the portrait of herself by Sir Thomas Lawrence hanging on the wall; he declared that he would never part with it. She made her excuses and left. But that was not the end of his pursuit.

Dorothea spent a week at the 'Cottage' in Windsor in early June, and she was persuaded to take a turn in the garden after lunch, only to find herself, once again, the object of the King's amorous intentions. While she was preparing for the walk the King presented himself at her window and begged to be allowed to enter her room. So passionate and exaggerated were his gestures that it was almost more than she could do not to give way to laughter – so she called her maid instead, at which point the King 'fled so hurriedly that he almost fell'; it was, she told Metternich, 'a scene that was sufficiently ridiculous at his age'.

The only infidelity indulged in by Dorothea was of the political variety – as Canning's star rose in her firmament. Formerly socially maladroit and insufferably egotistical, he now became an 'extraordinary character', whose vivacity, charisma, intelligence and 'dogged persistence' marked him out as exceptional; of course there were still those social solecisms which showed his origins, but these simply allowed Dorothea to indulge in her favourite pastime of patronizing her social inferiors. It also gave her a chance to use her influence with the King to persuade him to give Canning 'thousands of opportunities for showing his Minister a politeness which is not due to his rank in society'. Canning visited Dorothea every Sunday afternoon at the new Russian embassy at Ashburnham House where she revelled in her new appreciation of his genius – losing no opportunity of telling Metternich of their intimacy: 'In everything he will always get what he wants.' Her courting of Canning occasioned some amusement to those such as Harriet Arbuthnot who remembered how recently her attitude towards him had been otherwise: 'She quite pursued him about the room, to the great amusement of the whole party.'

With Count Lieven still absent in St Petersburg engaged, along with Nesselrode, in discussions about policy towards Turkey and Greece, Dorothea effectively played the part of Russian ambassador throughout the middle of 1826, passing messages on to Canning from her own government and reporting back on his responses. Dorothea's political affections were an invariable indicator of the state of the political weather, and more than most she found it always possible to look towards the rising sun – a talent which now produced its due rewards from the hand of a grateful Tsar.

The accession of Nicholas I brought the Benckendorffs and the Lievens to new heights of fortune. Dorothea's favourite brother, Alexander von Benckendorff, became head of the Russian secret police and a key adviser to the new Emperor; her eldest son, Alexander, was appointed to the Russian mission to the United States, while she was elevated to the rank of Princess when her husband was made a Prince in the honours Nicholas bestowed at his coronation. 'We are the only persons,' Dorothea proudly boasted to Lord Grey, 'on whom this title has been conferred.' This may have impressed Grey, but it did nothing for her fellow ambassadress, Princess Esterhazy, wife of the Austrian ambassador, who, freed from the constraints imposed by Dorothea's old relationship with Metternich, now gave vent to her dislike. The two women were known to 'hate each other like poison', and Dorothea lost no opportunity of criticizing the conduct of Prince Esterhazy, telling Metternich himself that 'he has covered himself with ridicule.' Princess Esterhazy was thought to have won a point against her rival when, at a party at Wellington's home, she commented, apropos of Dorothea's insistence on being addressed as 'Altesse', 'Do you want to know where the power of the Autocrat of all the Russias ends? He cannot make an *Altesse*'; this expression of the contempt of the Habsburg court for the semi-barbarous Russians was calculated to wound the new Princess at her weakest point: like all Russians she was sensitive to any insinuation about how 'European' Russia was. Since Princess Esterhazy was regarded

in English society as 'gay, lively' and 'good-humoured', while
Dorothea, for all her 'talents and cleverness', was 'not popular'
because 'she has no heart and is always acting a part', there was
general approbation for her put-down. Dorothea's response was
to work on Canning's dislike of Esterhazy's part in the 'Cottage
Coterie' so that he inquired whether it might be possible to move
him to Paris.

Her Serene Highness, the Princess Lieven, found that her new
rank did not preserve her from the social consequences of her
friendship with Canning. Harriet Arbuthnot recorded that 'she
certainly has shewn wonderful want of tact and good sense in her
mode of effecting her political change, for she has disgusted all her
old allies . . . She courts the whole Canning family to the total
forgetfulness of her own high rank and station.' When Wellington
paid the Princess a visit on 16 July, she complained bitterly 'of
the state of *abandon* in which she found herself. She said she
was neglected by everybody, that she lived absolutely alone, that
nobody went near her, and she cried about it'. As Mrs Arbuthnot
noted, not without satisfaction: 'I suppose she begins to find that
her Canning connection does not answer, at least not as far as
Society goes.' But Dorothea was unrepentant, telling Lady
Georgiana Wellesley that if Metternich asked about her change
of allegiance she should tell him: 'I have become sensible.'
Metternich, already 'greatly alarmed' at the prospect of a new
young Tsar over whom he would have no influence, and who
might be 'led by the prevailing feeling in Russia to engage in war
with Turkey', was losing his last insight into the heart of Russian
policy. Dorothea now took Canning's side in everything – and
great delight in taunting Metternich with his comments.

When the new King of Portugal, Dom Pedro, abdicated in
favour of his infant daughter, Dona Maria, and issued a constitution, Dorothea told her husband that it had made Esterhazy
'choke' because of 'the effect it will have on his chief'. Metternich
had, after all, 'established the dogma that there is nothing legal save
what emanates from the Sovereign', so how could he object to a
monarch granting a constitution – 'And how could Metternich

ever swallow a constitution? I think people are much amused at that. In truth it is the only thing that makes me laugh at this moment.' In one of her last letters to him, she asked Metternich to 'enlighten me on the point; for I do not understand it in the least'.

Yet, even as the moment of separation loomed – or perhaps because it did – Princess Lieven found herself in the grip of nostalgia for the past and what it had contained. It was in such a mood that she wrote to Metternich in early August when she confessed that 'we have long had the habit of trusting one another. It seems so natural to me to let my thoughts run on when I am writing to you, that I feel quite lost when I cannot tell you everything. Times have changed; let us not change. Affection should not be inconstant like circumstances.' The past and the future began to separate out, even if, for the moment, they swirled around her at the same time. It was reminiscent of the scene she had witnessed at Windsor at the beginning of August when the King had played host to the little Princess Victoria. Dorothea had noticed that for all the caresses he had lavished on her 'I could see he did not like dandling on his sixty-four-year-old knee this little bit of the future aged 7.'

Nostalgia pulled one way, but Dorothea was inexorably bound to the diplomacy of her own country. Russian policy was to woo Canning, and she went in that direction willingly, captivated by his charisma. But even as she separated from Metternich politically and personally, she was mindful of the longer-term future. She made a will in the autumn of 1826 in which she provided for Metternich's letters to her to be returned to him after her death, and she asked him to do the same: 'It seems to me that our correspondence should be of the greatest value to an historian of our times . . . It strikes me that the truth will emerge more clearly from this exchange of letters than from any memoir which may be published.' In one of her final notes to Metternich, written on 22 November 1826, Dorothea suggested that they should 'start again from the beginning'. She missed his letters, and she assumed that the same was true for him. 'We should be hard put to it, you and I, to find in the whole world people of our own calibre. Our hearts are well matched, our minds too; and our letters are very pleasant . . . I repeat: you will find no one better than me. If you meet your like, show him to me. Good-bye.' It was, perhaps, significant that she sent her very last letter to her former lover on 12 December – the day on which Canning gave one of his most famous speeches in the Commons. A few months later she heard that Metternich had married his beautiful young blonde. It was, she commented icily, a shame that the 'Chevalier of the Holy Alliance had ended by concluding a *mésalliance*'. It was, of course, unreasonable of her to be jealous, but reason plays little part in the desires of the heart.

It was not only with the sharp edge of her tongue that Dorothea could draw comfort as she observed Metternich; she knew enough about his attachment to his diplomatic system to know how much pain Canning's triumphs would give him. Ever since 1815, the Austrian Chancellor had endeavoured to 'prevent the separation of the Continental Powers upon great political questions', but having failed to do this on the Greek issue, his failure was now compounded by events in Portugal. His response to these was twofold: in the first place, in the old manner, he sought to convene a European congress to secure a consensus on how to act against Dom Pedro; in the second, he professed his willingness to support any steps which the Spanish might take to prevent the contagion of constitutionalism. But the Russians refused to participate in any congress, lent no support to any intrigues in Spain, and generally supported Canning's line.

In November the Portuguese government appealed to Canning for help against aggression from insurgents who were based in Spain, and on 12 December 1826 he invited Dorothea to witness him speak in the Commons on the subject. To a packed House he announced that the order had been given for British troops to embark for Portugal 'by whomsoever attacked'. Britain, he declared, did not go to 'rule' or to 'dictate' but 'to preserve the independence of an Ally. We go to plant the Standard of England on the well-known heights of Lisbon. Where that Standard is planted, foreign dominion shall not come!' To those who taunted him with having done nothing comparably dramatic to prevent the French invasion of Spain in 1823, Canning responded with another of his magnificent flights of rhetoric: 'I resolved that if France had Spain, it should not be Spain with the Indies. I called the New World into existence to redress the balance of the old.' The House was filled with cheering, and Canning was the hero of the hour. As he wrote to Granville on 14 December: 'If I know anything of the House of Commons from thirty-three years' experience, or if I may trust to what reaches me in report of feelings out of doors, the declaration of the obvious but unexpected truth that "I called the New World into existence to redress the balance of the old" has been more grateful to English ears and English feelings ten thousand times, than would have been the most satisfactory announcement of the intention of the French Government to withdraw its army from Spain.'

Dorothea's satisfaction at witnessing this moment of high drama was lessened by the fact that in the excitement of the moment Canning's secretary, Stapleton, forgot that she was immured in what was called 'the Ventilator', and remembered her only when the debate was over. When he opened the door she exclaimed that she had to leave at once because she was late for a dinner, complaining that 'mon mari me battra' ['my husband will beat me'].

Whether or not the Prince beat her, he certainly found Canning's speech difficult to explain away in St Petersburg. Across Europe the chancelleries were horrified by what their inhabitants took to be a declaration of solidarity with revolutionaries everywhere. From Paris, Pozzo di Borgo spoke for many when he commented that 'we must avow a sad and terrible truth, that is, that there is a revolution in England in the minds opposed to the tranquillity of the monarchs of the Continent, and that if any struggle were to break out between England and any other Power, the man who presides over the Cabinet of London and the nation as a whole, would have recourse to the blackest means to accomplish their aim, that is to satisfy their pride and their insatiable rapacity.' Nor was it only across the Channel that indignation was rife. For those Tories who had long resented Canning's liberal ways, the speeches were 'the most abominable ever heard'. Wellington fumed that 'we pass in Europe for a Jacobin club.' Even Dorothea, who had called the oration 'masterly', found herself obliged to tell Wellington that 'it was not possible to say what a bad effect Mr Canning's speech had had all over Europe & all over England' – a reversion that prompted Harriet Arbuthnot to complain that Dorothea was 'so abominably false I hate the Duke to talk to her'. On this score, at least, she need not have worried, for the Duke and the Princess were soon to be on the very worst of terms.

The cause of the breach between Princess Lieven and her old admirer was to be found in her new political allegiance to Canning. The foundation of this new alignment was the need to keep Britain and Russia together on the Greek question; the protocol of 4 April, while a beginning, was very far from being anything like a conclusion. For a start, both sides thought that they had won an important point and mistook it for the whole game. Canning was happy enough to have broken up the Holy Alliance, but as Metternich pointed out to the British ambassador in Vienna, Sir Henry Wellesley, he had potentially paid a high price for this prize. If the protocol did not positively 'sanction' war, it 'at least in no way opposed an attack on the Porte' by the Russians, nor did it 'contain any guarantee such as in the event of an attack on the Turkish provinces would be necessary to tranquillise the apprehension of Europe'. This, of course, was why Princess Lieven had been so delighted at the signing of the protocol.

At first it appeared as though Metternich's fears were groundless. The separate Russo-Turkish dispute over matters unconnected with Greece was brought to a peaceful settlement in October at the Convention of Akkerman. The Russians took care to maintain solidarity with Britain, refusing to let their other allies have copies of the 4 April protocol, and telling London that 'when two Empires, like Russia and Great Britain, agree on essential issues, it would be rash to reveal it.' But those Tories such as Wellington, who had supposed that the protocol would lead to a settlement that would leave the Porte's sovereignty over Greece intact, soon found themselves undeceived by Canning's interpretation of it. Wellington told his colleague Lord Bathurst that the Foreign Secretary was 'certainly a most extraordinary man. Either his mind does not seize a case accurately, or he forgets the impressions which ought to be received from what he reads or is stated to him; or knowing or remembering the accurate state of the case, he distorts and misrepresents facts in his instructions to his ministers with a view to entrap the consent of the cabinet to some principle on which he would found a new-fangled system.'

Wellington had spotted that in a despatch to Stratford Canning, who was negotiating with the Turks over implementing the demands contained in the protocol, Canning had talked of the independence of the Greek state as a given fact – which in his view it was most certainly not. Bathurst wondered whether Lieven's 'zeal' for the Greek cause 'came from the Foreign Office'; he, like Wellington, wondered whether there was not an informal agreement between Canning and the Russians. Canning's view of where the protocol had left him on the Greek question was summed up in a remark which Bathurst overheard him make to Liverpool in September 1826: 'We may do what we please about it.' In this, as in so much else, Canning boasted more than he could deliver.

The major problem with Canning's policy was what would happen if the mediation provided for in the first article of the protocol should fail to obtain the desired result? Britain and Russia could work well together while the answer to that question was unresolved. By article six of the protocol the other great powers were to be asked to accede to it and to join with Russia in guaranteeing the final settlement, when it was reached; this kept Canning and Prince Lieven busy over the winter of 1826–7. The Austrians gave a lukewarm acceptance to the protocol but declined to give any guarantees since the British themselves were unwilling to offer any. As Wellesley told Canning on 3 November: 'I can see enough to lead me to apprehend that our negotiations at Constantinople are not likely to experience any cordial support from this Government.' He also reported that in Metternich's view it was unlikely that the Russians would negotiate in good faith since they actually wished to provoke a war with the Turks. There, as Metternich had spotted, was the nub of Canning's potential problem. Nesselrode had told Alexander I that an alliance with Britain would make him the 'arbiter' of the Greek question, a line which explains much about the zeal with which the Princess espoused the cause of Canning; no other British politician would have gone so far – but no one else had Canning's invincible self-belief.

Wellington spoke for most of the Cabinet when he told Canning on 8 November that in negotiating with the Russians over how the protocol should be implemented he thought 'your refusal to go to war cannot be too peremptory.' But Canning *was* prepared to countenance the possibility of a Russo-Turkish war if that was what it took to keep in step with the Russians. He believed, and was no doubt encouraged by Dorothea to believe, that his personal genius could square this particular diplomatic circle; after all, the Turks were unlikely to yield except to the threat of Russian force, so there could be little harm in letting the Russians rattle their sabres. Since the Cabinet were not happy with such a line, Canning circumvented them. He went to Paris in mid-September and stayed there for six weeks. Finding the French eager to join with Britain and Russia in a formal treaty of alliance, Canning effectively went ahead with his own policy. He told Prince Lieven on 20 November that even if the other great powers would not cooperate with them, 'we are prepared in this case to pursue with Russia alone this work of conciliation and peace.' It was not until late November, however, that the Lievens were able to report that they were confident of Canning's good faith. During this time Prince Lieven tried to keep Nesselrode's anxieties at bay by reminding him that allowances had to be made for Canning's difficulties with the Cabinet – and for his anxiety to include France before moving forward.

While Prince Lieven was busy securing Canning's consent to a policy whose thrust was opposed by a majority of the Cabinet, his wife was busy trying to find a government that would be more amenable. Tumultuous times seemed to be in the offing. Liverpool, who had been Prime Minister for as long as the Lievens had been in London, was clearly ailing. In November 1826 he fell sick, and even when he felt fit enough to return to office, he confided to Mrs Arbuthnot that he felt 'wholly unfit for these troublesome times'; he said that although his relations with Canning were 'cordial & friendly', he had 'not strength & nerves to bear Mr Canning's perpetual notes'. Even Liverpool's famed emollience was hardly sufficient to keep Wellington and Canning in the same Cabinet. The Duke found Canning's deceitfulness well nigh intolerable, stigmatizing his style as amounting to 'mean & revolting trickery'.

Looking back a year or so later, Wellington recalled that he had done his best to prevent Canning negotiating a triple alliance with France and Russia, and that he had been the only member of the Cabinet who was actually aware of what Canning was doing. Canning himself could have been under no illusion as to his fate should Liverpool leave office – there was no conceivable possibility of the old Tory Party holding together. Canning's enemies would coalesce around someone like Wellington; although the question of whether the Duke could carry enough parliamentary support to form an administration was a moot one. But, as Princess Lieven knew well enough, there were other materials available for the construction of an administration which had Canning as its chief – although they were not Tory ones. It was here that Dorothea could be of most use to her country – and her new hero.

The fall of Canning would have been a great blow to Russian designs in the Eastern Question. Wellington's caution, his suspicion of Russia's intentions, and his unwillingness to contemplate any treaty that would have allowed Russia to go to war with Turkey, made his accession to power an object to be dreaded; but Dorothea's political contacts suggested there were ways of avoiding this. Wellington and the Tories may have held Turcophil views, but elsewhere there were voices to be found upholding the cause of the Greeks. Writing to Dorothea on 12 November 1826, her friend Lord Grey, the leading Whig politician, congratulated her on the success of the recent Russian campaign against the Persians and the peace concluded with the Turks at Akkerman, adding: 'I had rather it had been the other way, that you had accommodated matters with Persia, and were engaged in a laudable endeavour to drive these miscreants out of Europe.' Although Grey himself might have been too partisan a figure, at least where his relations with Canning were concerned, to join a Canningite administration, there were other, more moderate figures, such as Lord Lansdowne and Emily Cowper's brother, William Lamb, who might be so persuaded. Then, in February 1827, what had been a matter for the soothsayers became the most vital issue at Westminster when Liverpool suffered a major stroke. It was not immediately apparent that he would not, as he had in December, recover enough to remain as premier, but within a few weeks it was plain that he would be fortunate to survive, and that it was hopeless to expect him to play his old role. This led to a prolonged political crisis that was not resolved until early April.

Princess Lieven's instinct for backing the rising man had never been more accurate than in her support for Canning. For all the mistrust he aroused, George Canning was the key figure in any political realignment. His sympathy for the cause of Catholic emancipation, along with his liberal foreign policy, aroused as much Whig admiration as it did Tory disgust; but the Whigs were an exclusive body, and while their leader would have happily bedded an actress, he was not inclined to be led by the son of one. Grey had grandly stigmatized the great speech of December as 'imprudent in the highest degree; and the whole tone and character of it those of a man who thinks only of the success of the moment, and has no proper feeling either for what belongs to his own station, or what is required by the interests of his country'. It was hardly surprising that Grey did not want Canning to be Prime Minister; but his views were not as important as he thought they were. Canning had already discounted Grey, and as far back as the previous May had opened secret talks with the more moderate Lord Lansdowne with a view to making him Prime Minister; but Liverpool's stroke threw the political world into turmoil.

It was a mark of Canning's unique position in British politics that the prospect of his succeeding Liverpool should have occasioned a full-scale crisis. There were many who shared the view of Castlereagh's brother and successor as Lord Londonderry that Canning was a 'charlatan parvenu' under whom no gentleman should consent to serve; others saw him as the only possible man. In the forefront of this latter group was Princess Lieven, who used her influence with the King to lobby for Canning – knowing, as she did so, that Esterhazy was advocating Wellington. But she had the better candidate – and a better way with the King.

Dorothea spent much time talking to Canning, who was down in Brighton trying to recover from an illness he had picked up at the Duke of York's funeral in January. During their carriage rides, he explained to her how his use of the press and the Commons had allowed him to outmanoeuvre the old 'Tory aristocracy', and how he would not allow them to keep him from the first place that was his due. She watched with some admiration as he survived the assault of those High Tories who wanted to keep him from office, and she twitted Wellington on the subject when he came down to talk with George IV on 28 March. She asked whether he had been named as Prime Minister, and when he said that the difficulty 'lies with one man', she suggested that he must have decided whether to 'remain with him, or to have him against you'. This cruelly highlighted Wellington's dilemma. He admitted that 'the whole Cabinet would not remain a week if he left it', but claimed he could not accept him as leader. Dorothea's response was 'Then it is really very difficult for he wants to be it.' Canning later asked her whether she knew what the King had decided, but she disclaimed any inside knowledge; she doubted, however, whether George would yield to the bullying tactics of Canning's High Tory enemies. In this she was right, although Canning would have done well to have listened to her warnings about the paucity of support for him in the Cabinet.

When George IV asked Canning to form a government on 12 April, many of his old colleagues resigned, and he was able to do so only by taking in some Whigs – but here too Grey's enmity meant that he could not rely upon the Whigs as a group. With her keen eye for such things, Dorothea accurately diagnosed the problem: 'the truth was that Canning, indispensable as a member of the Cabinet, was antipathetic to everybody in his quality as head. English aristocratic pride revolted at obeying a parvenu and a bourgeois . . . and all the talent and incontestable superiority of Canning were insufficient to conceal the inferiority of his origins.'

11. 'We ought to love Canning'

On 12 April 1827 Canning achieved his great ambition and became Prime Minister. Such was the controversy he aroused that he split both the main political parties by doing so. Moderate Whigs such as Lansdowne and Emily Cowper's brother, William Lamb (who was about to become the second Viscount Melbourne), joined him, but Grey stood aloof, while true Tories followed Wellington and Peel into opposition. There was something at once magnificent and tragic about Canning's triumph. His 'incontestable superiority' had allowed him to defy the social prejudices of his age, and without his triumph the careers of Peel, Gladstone and even Disraeli would have been unimaginable; but the cost was enormous. The illness that had dogged him since the Duke of York's funeral refused to go away, and the strenuous effort of Cabinet-making did not help the process of recuperation. While he was out riding in carriages with the Princess discussing his political problems, he was not getting the rest he so badly needed; nor was it much better once a government had been formed. The key question, not least from the Russian point of view, was who would succeed Canning at the Foreign Office. He was the only minister who knew what was going on in the tripartite negotiations between France and Russia; indeed, when Prince Lieven pressed him for a quick response to the draft treaty from Russia, Canning asked for a further delay on the ground that he was having to instruct the Cabinet in its business. In the end it was not until 22 May that an Anglo-Russian draft was sent to Paris for approval.

Part of the problem was finding a Foreign Secretary. The obvious choice was Lord Granville, a long-standing confidant of Canning's, whose Whiggish connections and experience as British ambassador in Paris made him uniquely qualified to help the new administration. But no sooner was it made than Harriet Granville descended on Dorothea, begging her to use her influence with Canning to persuade him to withdraw the offer. She descanted eloquently upon Granville's incomparable virtues, but protested that his idleness and incapacity for speech-making in the Lords made him unsuitable for the post: 'in short, her husband was a marvel, but she much preferred that he should not be called upon to prove it.' Dorothea did as Harriet asked, but it left Canning still wondering where to find 'a minister who was, in reality, only the docile executor of his instructions'. Canning was not the first, nor would he be the last, Prime Minister to want such an object, but he did not hit on the one foolproof solution adopted by Salisbury in 1885 – that of taking on both posts. He suggested Lansdowne as a way of enticing the leader of the more moderate Whigs to lend his support, but Dorothea 'opposed this choice on the sole ground that he was a Whig. In the eyes of all foreign diplomacy this title then was more than equal to a radical today.'

Canning suggested his friend, Lord Dudley, as a possibility. He was not a figure of any weight in the political world, although Dorothea knew him well from the salons, where he had a reputation for being 'very bizarre, very peevish, hypochondriacal, slanderous, pushing absent-mindedness to the verge of rudeness'; but he did have one recommendation for the post: Metternich could not stand him. Canning did not know this, so Dorothea was able to explain that the two men 'had *une querelle de salon* at Vienna which makes them irreconcilable'. In this way, for the first but not the last time, Dorothea had a say in the appointment of a British Foreign Secretary. Lord Grey told her confidentially, and with the assurance that she could 'depend upon this', that Granville would be going to the Foreign Office, so she enjoyed Canning's *coup de théâtre* on St George's Day when, at the grand banquet for foreign ambassadors, he announced Dudley's appointment. The look on Esterhazy's face was reward enough for Dorothea; Metternich's displeasure was her delight.

Dudley's appointment signalled what everyone could have guessed, namely that Canning intended to keep foreign affairs in his own hands. This meant that the tripartite treaty over Greece was safe, although it was not until 6 July 1827 that it was finally signed. The Treaty of London was the final triumph of the Lieven mission. Canning pledged Britain to join in demanding an immediate armistice from the Greeks and the Turks, and agreed that force might be used if either side refused the demand. This gave Canning some say in where and when force might be used; and it gave the Russians the assurance that they would not face a European coalition if they did go to war with the Ottomans. Canning was happy enough, telling Granville on 13 July: 'Greece thus disposed of – we shall come next to the peninsula.' He concluded by adding: 'But I must take a few days' rest . . . for I am quite knocked up.' Things were a great deal worse than that. Canning had never recovered from the illness he had picked up at the Duke of York's funeral, and despite (or perhaps because of) the best efforts of his doctors, he died on 8 August. Grey, who had never liked him, nevertheless expressed everyone's feelings best when he wrote that there was 'something awful and striking in the premature extinction of great talents in the very moment of their successful ambition'.

Canning's death was a mortal blow to Dorothea's hopes. Back in January, when his health had first deteriorated and there had been fears that he might die, she had opened her heart to her brother Alexander on the subject of her new hero. She acknowledged the imprudence of his speeches, and thought that a man 'whom vanity and success carry away to the extent of giving his words a meaning at variance with his intentions is not a statesman'; but she still believed that Russia had 'cause to love Canning'. He was 'not a Jacobin, and he is the only member of the English Cabinet who is well-disposed, entirely well-disposed, towards Russia'. She saw clearly that with Austria and Britain on bad terms with each other, Russia was 'respected' and 'feared'. For Dorothea, 'As between the two Ministers, who hate one another, Canning is not the greater rogue – that is absolute truth. To sum up, may I be whipped for it, but I assert we ought to love Canning.' She had counselled patience when the Russian court had been irritated by the slowness of the negotiations for the treaty, arguing that 'one must swallow many disagreeable things . . . so long as one attains one's object.' She told Alexander that Canning's death was a 'catastrophe' for Russia, since he was 'the sincere friend and ally of Russia. After him – well! We shall see.' With a little, if pardonable, exaggeration, Dorothea wrote that 'everybody who is not Metternich is in despair.' The 'Apostolics', she told Grey, 'will sing a paean of victory'.

With Canning gone, British politics lost its dynamic force and fragmented. The King, in search of a quiet life, asked the former Chancellor of the Exchequer, Frederick Robinson, now Lord Goderich, to take on the premiership, which, after much pressure, he agreed to. The government was Canning's – without Canning – that is to say without its life force; it was, indeed, the simulacrum of an administration. At the Foreign Office Dudley went through the motions of trying to fill Canning's place, but his diffidence was such that 'he is capable of asking his colleagues if he dare say "perhaps"; an honourable man of much talent, immensely wealthy, but he is an amateur Minister.' The one thing to be said for the new Cabinet was that its members 'have grown old in their distrust of Austria'. The one exception was Wellington, newly restored as Commander-in-Chief. He looked 'very coldly' on Dorothea: 'he cannot forgive me for having preferred the Minister friendly to the Greeks to the Minister friendly to the Turks'; it was, she averred with startlingly inaccurate complacency, 'of no consequence'. From the point of view of Russian foreign policy, the Goderich administration was a pale imitation of its predecessor. Committed to the triple alliance, the new ministers fell headlong into the trap that Metternich had always predicted awaited the British – that of cooperating with the Russians in coercing the Turks. The Greeks, who were losing the war, readily agreed to the demand for an armistice; equally understandably, the Turks refused it. The allied fleet was ordered to prevent fresh supplies from reaching the armies of Ibrahim Pasha. On 20 October the allies opened fire on the Turco-Egyptian fleet, destroying it at the battle of Navarino. For Dorothea it was a great naval triumph, and one in the eye for Metternich; but the victory had fatal effects on her diplomacy.

The danger of becoming involved in a Russian war against Turkey had always existed, and it is hard to see how even Canning could have avoided Navarino; however, he would most certainly not have reacted to it as Goderich and company did if only because he could never have been accused of timidity and over-caution, which were the hallmarks of their reaction. Dudley did not want to commit Britain to anything, which was the one sure way of bringing on a Russo-Turkish war. Had the British joined the Russians in their proposed naval blockade in September, perhaps the Turks would have given way then, but they did not because they wanted to avoid conflict. The conflict having happened, Dudley then sought refuge in appealing to Metternich to use his good offices with the Porte, which disgusted the Russians without producing any good effect; whatever Canning would have done, it would not have been this. Goderich and company were paralysed by the enormity of the action for which they had unwittingly become responsible. Wellington and other opponents of Canning's policy were saying: 'we are playing the game of Russia, she alone will profit by this business; our Ministers are incapables, who allow themselves to be duped by Russia.' Grey, who was a supporter of the Greek cause, was not alone in being 'thrown into consternation', and he told Dorothea he could find no justification for what had happened.

Ever the armchair warrior, Dorothea had been roused from her sickbed by the joyful news and could only say 'rejoice'. Navarino was, she declared, 'a fine moral fact, and a fine military action'. That the news of the action should have reached Metternich on his wedding day was a nice bonus for Dorothea – whose Christian virtues did not extend to forgiveness. Her job, as she saw it, was to provide the Goderich administration with the spinal column, which had been omitted at its birth: 'they need to be taken by the shoulders daily to shake up their courage.' She was sure that if war came, the British would join it.

Metternich described Navarino as a 'catastrophe', although he

did not let it ruin his nuptials. He had always feared Canning's
policy would lead in this direction; it was but melancholy satisfaction to be proved right. For a decade and a half his aim had been
to ensure that Russian power would not be used for purely Russian
purposes; that it would, in effect, be put into commission. Until
1820 he had worked intimately with Castlereagh to this end, and
those, such as Nesselrode, who wanted a western orientation for
Russian policy, had been happy to play his game; indeed, Dorothea
herself had been a major player in it. Had the British stuck to
Canning's line after Navarino and lived up to Dorothea's hopes,
then Russia would have been constrained by the need to keep her
allies on board, but with the Turks responding by repudiating the
Treaty of Akkerman, and the British refusing to declare war on
the Porte, a Russo-Turkish war loomed into view.

To assuage British anxieties, the Russians assured them on
12 December that any such war would not be one of conquest or
annexation. The British Cabinet practised conjugating the verb 'to
tremble' (to adopt Dorothea's cruelly accurate phrase): on one
side, Huskisson and Lansdowne pressed for action; on the other,
Dudley and Goderich argued that while something should be
done, they could not be sure what it should be. Dorothea described
Goderich with disdain as 'as cowardly as the most timid woman',
and remarked with contempt on his excuse that 'his nerves will
no longer stand the strain.' Her own nerves only ever gave way
to ennui, and in the thick of the political action she was like
Wellington at Waterloo, calmly surveying the battlefield and seeking to provide reinforcements where they might be necessary.

For Dorothea the essential thing was to keep Canning's policy of
the Russian alliance intact. Here she looked to the self-proclaimed
Canningites for support. Dudley, Grant, William Lamb and Lord
Palmerston had all agreed to join Goderich on the condition
that he would continue Canning's liberal policies at home and
abroad. Palmerston, the most vocal of these in foreign affairs, had
been in every government since 1808, but saw himself as the
upholder of the Canningite flame abroad; he was full of suspicion
of Metternich, whom he thought had acted 'a shabby and a foolish

part', and was anxious to cooperate with Russia. Dorothea knew
Palmerston through her friendship with Lady Cowper, who had
long been his mistress, and over the next two years she would
come to know him much better; but their long and eventually
troubled relationship began to grow as she looked around her for
some vertebrate English ministers who would maintain her version
of Canning's policy. The fact that the Whigs and the Canningites
seemed disposed to allow the Russians to occupy the principalities
of Wallachia and Moldavia, traditionally the measure taken by
the Russians to put extreme pressure on the Porte, made them
Dorothea's natural allies – just as Wellington's hostility to such a
measure increased the gulf between her and her old admirer.

As she cultivated the Canningites and sought to impart firmness
to Dudley's diplomacy, Dorothea also used her charms on Grey.
George IV would not have Grey at any price, and however much
the great Whig earl bore this as a mark of distinction, he resented
his exclusion. His refusal to support Canning's administration had
done as much harm as his parliamentary attacks on the great man,
and, as we have seen, he reacted coolly to Navarino. Dorothea did
'everything possible to rally him to our side', using the characteristically self-interested argument that 'you cannot hinder us from
being powerful, attach yourselves to us by complete confidence in
the Emperor's straightforwardness; that is a chord you can always
touch with effect, and therefore there is no ground for apprehension.' She assured him of her fondness, and disarmed him enough
for him to admit that 'success . . . covers everything'. Grey told
her that he could 'answer for his own feelings' towards her, and
would be 'only too happy if I could be assured that it existed in
anything approaching the same degree' on her side. She assiduously
fed him details of Russian policy, reiterating, as her husband did,
that if the Russians did cross the Pruth, it would be for no selfish
ends. What had to be guarded against was Metternich's attempt to
'direct' Turkish policy to revenge himself on Britain and Russia
for daring to act without him. She assured him that 'we Russians
have the most sincere desire to avoid war', but that Turkish insolence in repudiating the Treaty of Akkerman and in demanding

reparation for Navarino was likely to bring one about all the same.

Dorothea spared no effort in massaging the tremendous ego that was Grey's. When he announced that he would return from his Northumberland fastness, she responded playfully that she knew he was really coming to harass the ministers rather than to pay court to her, but that she looked forward to seeing him again: 'We will have long talks together, and providing you promise not to raise your voice and talk louder than I do, we shall end by understanding one another. Only, if it is to be a strife of lung-power, I decline the contest.' She knew, she flattered, that he could upset the administration were he so minded, but she was sure that he was not 'going to displace those who have ever been your personal and political friends to replace them by men whom you have always professed to regard as your political adversaries. It would be absurd to suppose it; and I for one do not suppose it, since I have no doubts concerning either your head or your heart. Let us, however,' she concluded, 'leave all this for our *tête-à-têtes*.'

For the rest, all Dorothea could do was watch the farce that proceeded to engulf the government of '*Lady* Goderich', as she called the premier. On 14 December 1827 the tearful Goderich wrote to the King advocating the addition of Lord Holland to the government (something Dorothea had been urging since October), but in a postscript he said that because of his wife's health he felt unable to continue as Prime Minister. The King cast around for another first minister, and ignored the suggestion that the Whiggish Holland should join the government; but it proved difficult to find a successor. George tried Canning's old friend Lord Harrowby, but neither the Whigs nor the Tories wanted him, so on 19 December, Goderich was offered his old job back. Then, on 21 December, following a quarrel between two of his ministers, Goderich told the King he did not know what to do. In response, George told him to 'go home and *take care of himself*; and keep himself quiet'.

At this point Dorothea succumbed to illness – as usual when the going got tough – and took to her bed. The situation was now extremely perilous. At Constantinople the ambassadors of France, Russia and England withdrew, and the Sultan issued a *Hatti Sharif* calling upon 'the Faithful' to take up arms against the Infidel. With the Porte repudiating Akkerman, the Russians called upon Britain and France to carry out the Treaty of London, making it clear that they would do so themselves come what might. In the midst of this, in early January 1828, the King sent for Wellington; nothing could have been less welcome to Dorothea. The good news was that in order to form an administration Wellington needed the support of the Canningites, who insisted that Dudley should stay at the Foreign Office in order to signal the continuity with Canning's foreign policy; the bad news was that Wellington did not agree with that policy. When Dorothea heard of Wellington's appointment she declared to Emily Cowper that it was a dreadful catastrophe. She asked him to call on her, but was mortified that when he did so he talked about nothing more serious than the weather. According to Mrs Arbuthnot's self-satisfied account, Dorothea '*cried* about it to Bulow, the Prussian Minister, and was *outrée* at the idea of being treated with such contempt'.

For the past decade she had been accorded increasing respect by senior politicians: first Metternich, then Canning, had come, she thought, to rely upon her; she was on the most affectionate terms with Lord Grey and with all the Canningites, and it was an affront to this sense of her own importance that Wellington should treat her as of no consequence. She told Alexander, in an attempt to reassure herself, that 'England . . . is no longer suited to an apostolic regime, and Wellington knows this, so he is negotiating with Canning's friends.' She made it plain to her friends that the Russians would implement the Treaty of London whether or not the British followed. Worst of all was the knowledge that Esterhazy, the Austrian ambassador, was well in with the Duke: 'these insolent Austrians talk about making Russia tremble, at which I simply shrug my shoulders.' It was Esterhazy's view that if there was a war its real cause 'was to be found in her [Dorothea's] jealousy of Metternich'. Little wonder that Harriet Arbuthnot should have commented: 'It is curious enough that the loves and intrigues of *une femme galante* shd have such influence over the affairs of Europe.'

Dorothea's main problem was that having so identified herself with Canning, she had no influence with Wellington; this hurt both her self-esteem and her influence. During his re-election campaign in Liverpool, the leading Canningite, William Huskisson, had declared that Wellington 'had assented to a continuance of the system of free trade and of Canning's foreign policy'. Wellington used a speech in the Lords to deny the existence 'of any such corrupt bargain'; but for the moment the necessity of parliamentary arithmetic kept the Canningites and the Duke together. Wellington had been reluctant to keep Dudley at the Foreign Office, but had done so in order to keep the Canningites; the two men had agreed that the government should abide by the Treaty of London – which left room for differing interpretations of its meaning. The problem was that without a common interpretation of what the treaty meant, Wellington and Dudley were forced into the worst of all worlds. Had they accepted Russian demands for Greek independence in generous terms, they might yet have won the day, helping to force the Turks to yield without further bloodshed; but this they would not do.

In the Lords, on 29 January, the King's speech referred to Navarino as 'this untoward event' against the forces of 'an ancient ally', and only Holland defended it. The previous day Lieven had handed Dudley a proposal from Nesselrode which provided for a series of offensive measures: the occupation of the principalities in the name of the allies; a blockade of the Greek coast and of the Bosphorus and Dardanelles; and for the allies to 'penetrate even to Constantinople, there to dictate peace under the walls of the Seraglio'. It took the British nearly two months before they answered Nesselrode, and then their only response was that any military action should stop short of a general war.

Wellington was absent from a crucial Cabinet meeting on 4 March, but sent his views to Dudley by letter, in which he argued the case for accepting severe limitations not only upon the degree of independence granted to Greece, but also on her frontiers. When the Cabinet discussed his views on 9 March, the Canningites opposed such a niggardly settlement for the Greeks, and found themselves joined by Peel, much to the Duke's displeasure. The result was further negotiations with Lieven and the French. Dorothea continued to rely upon the Canningites, in particular Palmerston, but her impatience with Wellington grew apace. When Mrs Arbuthnot expressed the hope that war with Turkey might yet be avoided, Dorothea 'got into a passion directly' and said that after what the Turks had done that was hardly likely. 'There never was,' Harriet Arbuthnot noted with satisfaction, 'any person in such a *fausse position* as she is in'. According to the Wellington camp, Dorothea had 'disgusted all parties by her uncalled for interference in our internal concerns' and was now 'furious' because the Duke had 'put her back into her proper place'. There was much in this, as in the observation that Wellington 'neither considers her as a friend nor as a politician, & that she cannot brook'. The idea that she would accept being 'put back in her place' was, however, too optimistic by half.

If Dorothea found Wellington increasingly irritating, her husband complained of Dudley's uselessness as Foreign Secretary: 'he said that it was impossible to do anything with him' and that he 'came to the conferences predetermined to say nothing & to settle nothing.' At the conference called after the Cabinet on 9 March, Lieven had given the British another note from Nesselrode which set out the Russian grievances against the Turks and her determination to seek redress through war. The Russians took their ground not on the Treaty of London but on the way the Turks had denounced Akkerman, but Nesselrode pointed out that the London agreement allowed the Russians to take such action; Nicholas was still anxious to work with his allies if they would accept his terms for Greek independence, but if not he would execute the Treaty of London consulting only 'his own interests and convenience'. The Duke wanted to withdraw from the treaty or at least to declare Russia excluded from it, but the Canningites, true to Dorothea's wishes, would not hear a word of this and advocated cooperation with Russia. Palmerston, who was foremost among those resisting the Duke, thought that Wellington 'is evidently very anxious to break with Russia. He has a strong personal dislike to Russia. He has had violent quarrels with the Lievens'; in fact, it was only with Dorothea, and there Palmerston thought Lady Jersey and Mrs Arbuthnot, who 'both hate Madame de Lieven', were influencing him. Dorothea, delighted by Palmerston's stout resistance, called him '*our* Minister', and reported his view that the British should 'trust' Nicholas and act with Russia. But Wellington would not act in that spirit, and on 26 April 1828 the Russians declared war on Turkey.

Now were Dorothea's ambitions curbed, although she did not see it, nor, as we shall see in the next chapter, did she accept it. She had played a skilful game since the death of Alexander I. Through her contacts with Canning she had been able to help bring about a diplomatic revolution, even if Canning's motives had not been those of Russia. It had suited Canning and the Tsar to teach Metternich a lesson, even as it had suited Dorothea to pay her faithless lover back in his own coin and beat him at his own game; in these things she had taken a great delight. But too much of her triumph depended upon Canning. The policy of the triple alliance was his alone, and as it turned out, no one else knew what to do with it. The Canningites were willing to advocate a policy of working with Russia, but they were not able to make their voice count against that of Wellington, and here the personal diplomacy of Princess Lieven had made a fatal error.

Wellington remained the conservative figure he had been when Dorothea had looked for his help against the liberal Canning, but once the latter had shown his willingness to work with Russia, the former had been abandoned; Russian diplomacy had been a great deal more pragmatic than its liberal detractors imagined. Dorothea, as we have seen, imagined that Wellington was a busted flush, which was true as long as Canning dominated the scene, but she continued to believe that he could be manipulated through her contacts with the Canningites. 'The Duke of Wellington has been obliged to make himself a Liberal,' she told Alexander on 19 May, but he was, she complained, 'as obstinate as a mule'; still, she predicted happily, 'he will give way rather than give up his place.'

In this, Dorothea underrated Wellington, yet again. The tension between him and the Canningites may have paralysed British foreign policy, but his resources for dealing with the latter were not exhausted. In late May their touchy leader, Huskisson, threatened to resign over the question of what to do with two parliamentary seats that would need to be redistributed from constituencies disenfranchised for corruption. He may, as his friends thought, only have been hinting at going in order to put pressure on Wellington, but if so he miscalculated badly; Wellington accepted his resignation. Dudley, who had become attached to the Foreign Office, was loath to resign with him, but in the end the Canningites took the view that having come in as a group, they should go out in the same way. Lord Aberdeen replaced Dudley at the Foreign Office, and the policy of the triple alliance was now effectively dead.

When Aberdeen paid a courtesy call at the Russian embassy Dorothea was at her most forthright: 'I am always glad to see you, but I am sorry to see you Minister for Foreign Affairs, because I consider you an Austrian, and an enemy of Russia.' Aberdeen explained that he had called on her precisely because he had heard that 'she had expressed strong opinions on him, which were entirely mistaken.' He was not 'Austrian' or 'anti-Russian', he was, he explained patiently, 'an English' minister. Dorothea very politely and formally told him that if he denied being anti-Russian she would believe 'his word of honour'; she could not, however, believe the same of Wellington: 'she knew well the Duke's sentiments about Russia.' Only a few days earlier, she told him, one of her fellow countrymen had met Esterhazy in the street, and the latter had exclaimed happily that every dog had its day – in place of the 'Russian' Canning, they now had the 'Austrian' Wellington. Princess Lieven had effectively declared war on the victor of Waterloo; what Palmerston and the Canningites had been unable to do, she would have to do herself. The scene was set for the remarkable spectacle of a Russian ambassadress trying to frustrate the foreign policy of the British government.

Harriet Arbuthnot's strictures about the 'loves' of a *femme galante* are a warning against accepting gossipy titbits at face value. Both Wellington and Aberdeen were, at different times, Dorothea's lovers, but then so too was Metternich, and from the summer of 1828 she was at war with all three men; this was not because of any 'woman scorned' complex (although in Metternich's case such feelings probably added spice to her campaign), it was because her *amours* were subordinated to the interests of her country. When Alexander I had aligned Russian policy with that of Austria after 1818, Dorothea's romantic involvement with Metternich had been a useful extra source of information; but as soon as he and his successor shifted in a more 'Russian' direction, Metternich became part of Dorothea's past, and her allegiances moved on.

Dorothea's conversion to the cause of Canning continued after his death. Because she took the credit for the change of policy in 1826 that had brought Britain and Russia into cooperation on the Eastern Question, she identified herself so completely with Canning's policy that she took exception to any attempt to change it. She had two objections to Wellington: in the first place, now that she was a Canningite she thought him too 'apostolic' – that is too reactionary; in the second place, she thought him too 'Austrian'. Wise diplomacy would have suggested giving the Duke a chance before condemning him, but Dorothea was beyond the reach of discretion, and before long her hostility to Wellington was common knowledge. From Paris, Lady Granville asked her sister, Lady Carlisle, whether it was true that 'Mme De Lieven and Lady Cowper are very personally bitter and angry with the Duke?' The Arbuthnots were 'ready to laugh in her face' when the Princess went out of her way to be civil to them; they knew her view of the Duke and took her attempts at friendship at their true value –

which was nothing. Policy and personal preference aligned Princess Lieven with Wellington's opponents at home and abroad, and her attempts to frustrate British policy were so blatant that the Duke soon began to wonder whether he should not either demand her recall or, if that step was too serious as it might imply that Anglo-Russian relations had broken down, whether he should not try to find some more devious way of ridding himself of a woman whose machinations were tiresomely persistent.

Canning had become acceptable to Dorothea when his policy had coincided with Russian interests. The thrust of Russian grand strategy had not changed since the days of Nicholas's grandmother, Catherine the Great; only the means to that end varied. The Grand Turk was visibly weakening and, as we have seen, the Philhellenism of British public opinion proved a valuable tool in helping push Canning's government towards a position where supporting the Greeks had become a policy indistinguishable from an anti-Ottoman one. Metternich remained more worried about the cause of legitimism in Europe than the plight of the Balkan Christians. What did it profit the Habsburg Empire if the Greeks should once again be free, if that also meant that the two forces Metternich feared most – nationalism and the Russians – should gain by it? Since Wellington cared equally little for these foes, it was natural that his government should be identified with Metternich's policy.

As Russia moved towards war with the Ottoman Empire, both London and Vienna had good cause to fear the result. Thanks to the Treaty of London and to Navarino, Wellington and Metternich could not actually oppose Russia moving to implement the terms of the former by force; but that did not mean that they liked it. If Russia won – and everyone assumed she would – then what terms would be imposed on the Ottomans? If the Russians sponsored the creation of a Greek Christian state they would become its patron, and there seemed no reason to suppose that they could not repeat this trick with other Balkan nationalities such as the Serbs or the Wallachians; the prospect of a Russian-dominated Balkans was not one to be welcomed by the other great powers. The British had an additional reason to be wary of Russian gains at the

expense of the Ottomans. While Metternich did not care what
happened on the Asiatic side of the Bosphorus, Wellington did. If
the Russians gained territory from the Turks in the east, they
might threaten the overland route to India through the Red Sea
and the Persian Gulf; visions of what became known as the 'Great
Game' appeared to Wellington as the Russo-Turkish war broke
out in May 1828.

The Princess had courted the Arbuthnots because she hoped
that they would help her to persuade the Duke to support the
Russian demands on the Turks. With her usual faith in the infalli-
bility of her own logic, Dorothea really could not see what the
problem might be. It was, she told her brother Alexander, 'easy'
to be the representative of a Tsar like Nicholas I – 'firm and
haughty'. In Dorothea, the latter quality manifested itself in an
arrogance that was all but insupportable. For her, the reason the
English had turned Turcophil after Navarino was that the 'Eastern
Question has never been clearly explained' to them. It did not,
however, signify, since from where she stood Wellington had
no alternative but to comply with the execution of the Treaty
of London. When the Duke refused to oblige her, she decided
to make him. The effect on the already delicate state of Anglo-
Russian relations was serious.

Ever the partisan, Dorothea acted as she did for her usual mixture
of emotional and political reasons. In the first place, she disbelieved
in the omnipotence of the Great Duke. The fact that Wellington's
government existed only because, as the Duke of Devonshire put
it, 'Mr Canning's friends have joined Mr Canning's enemies', gave
the Princess grounds for believing that through her Canningite
connections, she could bring the government down. In the longer
term she was correct, and she did indeed bring Palmerston closer
to Grey, thereby helping to create the axis that would dominate
British foreign policy in the post-Tory era; but the price she paid
personally was heavier than she realized. In the short term she
alienated Wellington to the extent that he resolved never to forgive
what he called her 'cold-heartedness & ingratitude'. But there was
a longer-term consequence attaching to her behaviour.

Dorothea in full bloom – just as the Regent liked her

Cool and collected
– Castlereagh as
Dorothea first
knew him

Aberdeen, whose attitude to Dorothea so
shocked Earl Grey

Alexander I, the Tsar who took Dorothea
for a man

Wellington's friend Harriet Arbuthnot, who was scandalized by Dorothea

'The woman I love is the only woman for me,' Metternich told Dorothea – and all the others

'Can you imagine me as Madame Guizot?' The Frenchman who was her last, and greatest, love

Lord Liverpool, the 'archmediocrity' who governed for fifteen years

Earl Grey, the very image of the English grandee, who perfumed his letters to Dorothea with musk

Lord Granville, the husband of one of Dorothea's greatest friends and the ambassador in Paris for much of her career

William Lamb, the brother of Emily Cowper and husband of the scandalous Lady Caroline

Old corruption himself.
Talleyrand's niece set up a rival salon to Dorothea's

George Canning's 'plebeian origins' did not prevent Dorothea from cultivating him – when it suited Russian interests

Wellington, the greatest Englishman of his day – and the particular object of Dorothea's intrigues

The Prince Regent, who found Dorothea much to his
taste when she was pregnant

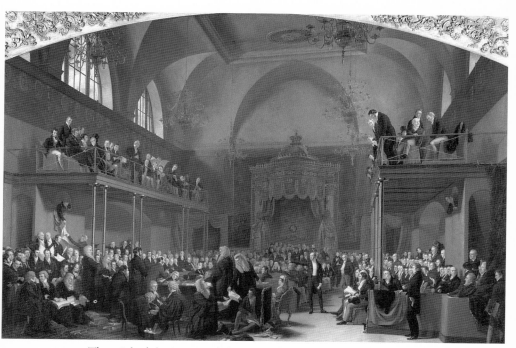

The trial of the 'wronged Queen', which so intrigued Dorothea

Palmerston – Lord
'Cupid', who was
Dorothea's protégé
and nemesis

Dorothea in
serene old age

Harriet Arbuthnot was obviously a partisan witness, but when she noted that Dorothea 'disgusted all parties by her uncalled for interference in our internal affairs', she was not wide of the mark. Palmerston and Grey both paid her court and thanked her for her help, but they were not the men to be pawns in her game. It was most useful to them, as Wellington's opponents, to have information on Russia, and for the Russian embassy to be so clearly opposed to the Duke. But having seen at close quarters how keen the Princess was to involve herself in British politics for the good of her country, they were both forewarned and forearmed about her and her *modus operandi*, to the extent that when she tried to repeat her successes during their term of office, they acted with the utmost ruthlessness to cut her off. But in 1828 it suited Grey – and Palmerston – to court the Princess.

Although, as ever, Dorothea over-personalized her politics, her instincts were acute. With Wellington now in charge of a purely Tory administration after June 1828, he would be vulnerable to a parliamentary junction of the Canningites with the Whigs, and given her contacts, there was no one in a better position to play marriage-broker between these two parties than the Princess. Dorothea could see lying around her the materials from which a new coalition could be formed: if the Canningites could be brought together with those Whigs who had joined the Canning government, then there was the nucleus of a government waiting to be formed – and, never short of confidence in herself – she even had its Prime Minister: Grey himself.

Grey, now best remembered for the 1832 Reform Act that bears his name, bore quite a different reputation in the second decade of the nineteenth century. A formidable roué, even by the standards of the era, he had been the lover of the notorious and beautiful Georgiana, Duchess of Devonshire, who bore him an illegitimate daughter he refused to support. Tall, 'commanding' and dignified, Grey was one of the greatest parliamentary orators of the age, a man whose attack on Canning in early 1827 had been credited with bringing on his early death. He was wealthy, handsome and endowed with a formidable political talent, and his career ought to have been one of unbroken success, but with the brief exception of 1806–7 he had never served in a government.

In part this was to be explained by his politics; very Whig of very Whig – even if he had been made and not begotten – he was *persona non grata* to the King, who suspected that Queen Caroline had been among his conquests; nor had the part Grey had played in supporting the Queen in 1821 been forgotten. But there was more to it than a simple royal veto (although that should not be discounted too lightly). Grey's temperamental faults nearly cancelled out his considerable gifts. He was touchy to the point of almost being unable to work with anyone else. It was not just that he resented criticism; he could not abide it and would not bear it. He was aware that others had opinions, but did not see why he should concern himself with them unless they happened to coincide with his own. He was impatient of those with a slower understanding than himself, and generous in attributing this quality to others, and his doubts about his own fitness to lead a party were well-founded. By 1828 he was nearly sixty-five and along with infirmities imposed by advancing age he also felt a 'diminution of energy and ambition' which left him more than ever prey to his old demon of depression; he was, he told the Princess in February 1829, in a 'sort of neuter position'.

Hypersensitive as he was, Grey was none the less flattered by Dorothea's constant urgings that he should take the leading position in British politics for which he was, in her view, so well fitted. It may be that there are politicians who lack the vanity to succumb to such lavish praise, but they have left no trace on history. Dorothea, whose correspondence with Grey had begun in the early 1820s, stepped up its intensity after 1828 as she sensed his utility in a volatile political scene. The question of whether they were lovers is not one that is susceptible of a definitive answer, although given Grey's reputation with women, it would not be outrageous to suppose that they may have been; he certainly perfumed his letters to her with musk, which may be taken to signify what the reader wants. But however the prurient might think this the obvious question to dwell upon, others have a more pressing claim on the historian.

It was Dorothea's instinct for men of power that prompted her correspondence, and if marital infidelity occurred, it was as a means to an end rather than an end in itself. Wellington's government was 'contemptible and cannot last', she told Alexander in late February. It was only 'there for want of a better'; and if she could help to create a successor to it, then she would be serving both her own interests and those of her country – or so she believed. This line of thought illustrates both her strengths and weaknesses as a female politician. By cultivating Grey, she was keeping in touch with a man who was seen by others as a likely leader, but she was also acting as a conduit between him and the Palmerston group. Her letters to Grey, teasing and political, constantly pressed him to act by implying that in not doing so he was effectively supporting the Duke; on a man of Grey's vanity, such insinuations could have only one effect. However, if the role she played in bringing Grey together with Palmerston and company illustrated the acuity of her instincts, her easy assumption that an administration headed by her friend Grey would be more to Russia's taste shows her limitations. The Whigs may have been opposed to Wellington's eastern policy, but her reasons for supposing that they would be more Russophile are not easy to grasp.

The Whigs were traditionally Francophile, which might not have mattered in the reign of the autocratic Charles X, were it not for the fact that the France that men such as Holland and Lansdowne admired was that of the revolution. They were also inclined to look with sympathy on the plight of Poland, something that was unlikely to lead to them sympathizing with the Tsar. The sight of these straws in the windy rhetoric of Whiggery should have given even the Princess pause for thought, but there were whole bales of hay that she ignored. The Whigs stood for curbing the power of the crown and were on the side of liberalism everywhere; this was hardly likely to lead them to support Russia. For her to assume that Palmerston was 'our Minister' was to make a general assumption from a specific case with inadequate supporting evidence. She seems to have had occasional glimpses of the truth; for example, complaining to Grey in early 1829 that: 'I feel again and again that in your eyes I have the defect of not being an Englishwoman.' But she drew away from following such comments to their logical conclusion. Even when Grey annoyed her by suggesting that England might mediate in the Russo-Turkish war, she responded that: 'I still regard you too much as my friend to be vexed with you'; there would be a heavy price to pay for her myopia.

At the time, however, it was Prince Lieven who began to feel that he was paying a considerable price for indulging his wife's caprices. Anxious to return home to attend to his affairs following the sudden death of his mother, the Prince applied for leave, to the very considerable annoyance of his wife, who believed passionately that they both needed to be in London at such a critical moment. Prince Lieven's patience with his self-willed wife began to fray. So bad did their relationship become that although they were in the same house, they began to communicate with each other by note, which is why we can follow the progress of their mutual irritation. 'What,' he asked her, 'is the underlying cause of these deplorable relations that exist between us?' He thought that they were disturbing their rest and undermining their constitutions. In a phrase familiar to many couples whose marriage is in a dark and dangerous place, he wrote despairingly that: 'If we could find out the real reason perhaps we could cure it?' This was unlikely to happen given his own explanation for their plight – which amounted to blaming Dorothea: her intransigence, her lack of pliancy, her love of her own opinion, had, he thought, created unfortunate scenes in public which had cut them off from society since people blamed him for not controlling her.

Dorothea reacted as she always did when Christopher went into his resentful moods. She protested her love and devotion to him, told him how much his accusations hurt her and ended by writing: 'I beg you on my knees to come to me and forgive me. God knows what has been my fault; my only fault is to love too much.'

When he ignored this, she became more dramatic, protesting at the 'rudeness with which you treat me', and threatening to leave him unless his behaviour improved. What, if anything, Christopher said in response to all of this is unknown – but instead of her leaving him 'forever', he departed on a tour of Birmingham. Yet again he had screwed up the courage to protest, but in the end he failed to act. It was little wonder that the view of the Austrian ambassador – and others – was that he was a 'good kind of man, well-intentioned &, if let alone, would be peaceably inclined, but that he was driven on by his wife'.

It was not only Prince Lieven and Wellington who were beginning to find Dorothea too much. The resignation of Palmerston, Lamb and Dudley in May brought the earl of Aberdeen to the Foreign Office. Dorothea's attitude to Aberdeen had been established in their first official conversation when she had called him an 'enemy to Russia' and an 'Austrian sympathizer'; this was both impolite and impolitic, although it hardly compared to her later comment to him when she accused him in so many words of lying. For his part, Aberdeen regretted only that the Princess's comments could not be repeated in the House of Lords, as that would give him a chance to prove that he was 'neither knave nor fool'. Her opinion of him did not change, at least until the 1830s. Aberdeen was, she thought, 'a wretched Minister!' The freeness with which Dorothea expressed her views ensured that they were no secret, while her flirting with Grey, Palmerston and any other opponents of Wellington, opened her to the justified charge that she was interfering in domestic politics.

'English domestic politics,' she told Grey in October 1828, 'excite my curiosity and interest to the utmost.' The problem was that her interest seemed confined to damaging Wellington, whether by supporting his parliamentary opponents over the Eastern Question, paying court to those who opposed his bill to emancipate British Catholics from the restrictions that barred them from public life, or by seeking to influence the new British ambassador in St Petersburg, Lord Heytesbury, against his own government. In the face of her cavalier disregard for even the ordinary civilities of diplomatic intercourse, Wellington cast around for expedients. His first recourse was to fall back on their long relationship and to revert to what Dorothea called 'some of his former coquetries'. When they met at Windsor in August 1828 the Duke was 'more conciliatory and more urbane', complaining that 'I had treated him badly' and that 'I did not invite him to come to see me as I did formerly.' The 'Beau' did not find his old flirting partner in a mood to respond, but he made another attempt in the same vein in October, expressing sympathy for Russia's losses in the Turkish campaign and offering his advice. Since Dorothea's brother Constantine had just died on the Turkish front, Wellington's attempt to improve relations was both well timed and well aimed; but again it was to no avail. He was, she thought, 'trying to deceive me by the calm and conciliatory tone in which he discussed our affairs – I am convinced of his ill will towards us. His change of language can only be deceit.' This was unfair in as far as the Duke was making a genuine effort to get back on to something like decent terms with the woman responsible for interpreting British behaviour to Nesselrode and the Tsar. The problem he faced was that the more he sought to appease her, the more outrageously Dorothea behaved.

However much modern politicians may claim that issues are more important than personalities, few commentators act as though they believe it, and in the early nineteenth century personal relations certainly did matter. In early 1829 Heytesbury warned Aberdeen that Tsar Nicholas believed that Wellington was person-ally responsible for much of the British hostility to Russia during the period since the outbreak of the war with Turkey. This was the prelude to a long debate over whether or not to press for the removal of the Lievens. Wellington's view was that ever since 1826 the Princess had 'taken pains to represent my conduct whether in or out of Government in the most unfavourable manner' to the Tsar. He alleged, not without justice, that the Lievens had 'been what is called in regular opposition to the Government. They have misrepresented to their Court all that we have done, and particularly that I have done.' He had made no complaint against them, but was clearly tempted to do so, although at this juncture he was 'vain enough to think that I am too strong for Prince and Princess Lieven' and preferred to suffer their machinations a little longer rather than take them as seriously as they took themselves.

It was typical of Dorothea that she should have personalized her dispute with Wellington's government – and that she should have been so free in her comments about its chief. She told Lady Cowper: 'How mistaken we have been about Wellington, after all he is no more than an Irish adventurer.' Dorothea backed the Duke of Cumberland and those Ultra Tories who opposed Wellington's decision to grant Catholic emancipation, and she plotted against him wherever she could. The French ambassador, Polignac, thought that she exercised great influence on the King himself, repeating his phrase that she was 'la tête plus forte en politique de ce pays ci'. Aberdeen, who was rather more susceptible to the charms of the Princess than Wellington, wondered whether, at least on the domestic front, they did not give Dorothea 'credit for more activity than she deserves. That she would do us all the mischief in her power is most certain, but the knowledge of this makes us apt to fancy her at the bottom of every intrigue.'

Wellington was less easily duped. He knew that Dorothea had been stirring up the reactionary Cumberland in an attempt to get George IV to refuse to countenance Catholic emancipation: 'she and M. de Lieven have knocked at every door . . . and every description of faction and party in order to break down the existing administration. To attain this object all is fish that comes into her net.' He attributed her opposition to political rather than personal motives: 'the fall of this administration if only for a day would give them [the Russians] time to do much which they cannot do at present, and she would drown us for that day if she had the power.' He well knew that she had selected Grey as his preferred successor: 'Why? Because Lord Grey entertains some old opposition opinions of Mr Fox's that the Turks ought to be driven out of Europe.' The result of this was that by August, Aberdeen was telling Heytesbury that 'we cannot consider their presence in England as likely to contribute to the good understanding of the two governments.' Even by Aberdeen's exalted standards, this was a considerable understatement; there could not have been a worse moment for Anglo-Russian relations to be in such hands.

The Russian war on the Ottomans had aroused deep suspicion in Britain, and the fault lines that developed were to become familiar throughout most of the nineteenth century. On one side were those like Grey, who held to the view that the Turks should be cleared out of Europe because their empire was rotten to the core. This view was to be shared, at least until 1833, by Palmerston, who would subsequently change his mind. This suggested a line of policy that looked forward to some extent to the full-blown polemic of Gladstone in 1876, when he urged the expulsion of the Turk 'bag and baggage' from Europe. On the other side of the question were those who preferred to take their geopolitics straight, without any dose of liberal uplift.

Wellington's main concern throughout the war was that Russia would crown her victory with territorial gains that would destroy the Ottoman Empire. The Tsar may have consistently declared his intention to take no Turkish territory, but his word was given little credence. As to the Russian claim that their peace settlement at Adrianople was a moderate one, the British begged to differ, taking the view that it 'was certainly not in conformity with the expectations held out by the preceding declarations', because it 'appears vitally to affect the interests, the strength, the dignity, the present safety, & future independence of the Ottoman Empire'. When Aberdeen told Princess Lieven in October 1829 that he felt he had been 'duped' by the Tsar, he was really expressing Wellington's views. True to form, he hastened to tell Heytesbury to communicate the British stance to Nesselrode 'with all the caution and explanations which may be necessary to prevent it producing an unpleasant effect'. The problem for Aberdeen was that Nicholas's 'falsehood and ambition' had produced the worst possible impression on British public opinion and left him looking like a Russian dupe. In these circumstances it was essential to 'avoid any misunderstandings' – which was not likely to happen as long as Princess Lieven gave vent to her spleen.

Although it would be an exaggeration to assume that Anglo-Russian relations revolved around the Lievens, it would not be very much of one. As Aberdeen wrote to Heytesbury on 22 December 1829: 'With a view to the improvement of our friendly relations, I cannot help mentioning the Lievens. It seems quite impossible that anything like cordiality should exist between the two Governments, when the Representatives of Russia in this country are engaged in every intrigue which can possibly be set on foot to shake the King's Ministers.' Wellington, characteristically, went a good deal further, telling Aberdeen that 'they are the only cause of estrangement between our two countries', adding that he was not going to demand their recall only because 'this would do more harm than good.' Aberdeen tried a less formal approach to prevent the Lievens from doing further damage. In his carefully worded letter to Heytesbury of 22 December, he outlined the extent of the damage he thought was being done: 'Their hostility is open and avowed, and there is no Party so discordant, with which they are not allied, in the hope of promoting this object.' This meant that official communications had become 'inconvenient', while 'Confidence is impossible.' The result was that 'absolute silence is frequently necessary, when we know what would be the immediate consequence of anything like freedom of intercourse.' Aberdeen was under the illusion that Wellington was their chief target and that 'their language regarding me is different.' In so far as there was any substance to this belief, it was not in a way that would have brought Aberdeen much joy. To Dorothea he was simply 'a poor diplomatist . . . He is merely Wellington's chief secretary'; whereas Wellington was 'the most obstinate mule I have ever known'.

By this stage, as Aberdeen's letter indicated, relations between the Princess and the two leading figures in the government had effectively broken down – and it is hard not to indict Dorothea as the cause. Her delight in the Russian victory was understandable, but expressed with characteristic lack of tact. Visiting Chatsworth in early autumn 1829, she went about saying that she could now speak her mind about 'le grand homme', as she called Wellington, adding that she took additional pleasure in Russia's successes because they would embarrass him. Mrs Arbuthnot was sickened by the reports that a charade on the word Constantinople had been acted out, ending with a laurel wreath being laid at Princess Lieven's feet: 'her insolence is beyond all bearing,' she noted, before telling the Duke, who was 'much nettled'. Even Grey found her reports of her conversation with Aberdeen in early October 1829 too much for his patriotism. However much he disagreed with Aberdeen's policy, he found it distasteful to read Dorothea's description of him complaining that he and Wellington had been Russia's dupes: 'Your account . . . would have amused me very much if I had not felt mortified that an English Minister should have exposed himself to a rebuke at once so severe and so just.' If Aberdeen and Wellington were on the verge of demanding the recall of Princess Lieven and her husband, it was not without cause.

Deciding that it would be too risky to ask for the Lievens to be recalled, Aberdeen and Wellington proceeded by other means. In the spring of 1829 the Tsar had sent Count Matuscewitz to 'overhaul' the Lievens, and the rumour was that the Prince would be made Minister for Foreign Affairs, being replaced by the Count. When this failed to happen and the Count stayed in London, Aberdeen took advantage of his presence to let him know how much damage the Princess was doing to Anglo-Russian relations. Matuscewitz was, Aberdeen told Heytesbury, 'fully aware of the prejudicial effect which their position must have upon the business of the Emperor'. Heytesbury was told to use every opportunity short of an official complaint to make it plain that 'their removal from this country would unquestionably be a great advantage under present circumstances.'

Aberdeen admitted that Heytesbury's instructions were not easy to carry out; Heytesbury thought that they were impossible. He told Aberdeen that 'it was useless' to think that Matuscewitz would be any help: 'You can have no idea of the *managements* that are necessary towards a powerful man in this country from those who are not his equals in rank so long as his favour continues.' Prince Lieven was in high favour because of his long family connection

with the Tsar, while Dorothea enjoyed the patronage of her influential brother, Alexander, so it was unlikely that any social inferior
would wish to be caught criticizing them. Heytesbury decided to
speak unofficially to an unnamed figure who was 'much nearer the
fountain-head', and he was confident that his words would be
'repeated *verbatim* to the Emperor'.

By March 1830 Aberdeen was hinting that the results of this
indirect approach seemed a little long in coming, since the connection of the Lievens with the opposition 'is certainly inconvenient
and is quite new in the history of this country'. He was also
concerned that the Lievens had managed to learn about the contents of his previous letter through the offices of the figure to
whom Heytesbury had spoken: 'Your experience must have shown
you,' Aberdeen complained with wonderful insularity, 'that it is
impossible to be too cautious with foreigners of any nation.' For
his part, Heytesbury expressed incredulity that Aberdeen could
ever have believed that 'what was going on here could be kept
a secret from the Lievens.' Heytesbury was incredulous that
Aberdeen should think that the Tsar would accept that no complaint was being levelled against the Lievens just because his
comments about their role were prefaced with a statement to
that effect. Given that Alexander Benckendorff was Dorothea's
brother and the Tsar's most 'intimate counsellor', the most probable source of the Lievens' knowledge of Aberdeen's letter was
easily identified.

This effectively ended Wellington's attempts to deal with the
Princess, who was quite indignant when Grey asked her whether
she had been aware 'of the attempt to get you removed'. She
put it down to her espousal of Prince Leopold for the Greek
throne, which was either a remarkably barefaced piece of cheek,
or simply an example of her ability to convince herself of what she
wanted. But by this stage she was not worried about Wellington's
hostility. Wellington's government was already badly weakened
by his decision to proceed with Catholic emancipation despite his
previous opposition to it. Although he had perfectly good pruden-
tial reasons for so doing (such as the probability of severe trouble

in Ireland if he did not), Wellington had come to office pledged to oppose Catholic emancipation, and those who had helped destroy Canning on the issue were not willing to forgive their former hero his volte-face. The last real anchor keeping Wellington in place was George IV's hatred of Grey and the Whigs, but by May 1830 the corpulent old rake was visibly failing. 'I think,' Dorothea wrote triumphantly to her brother, 'that with the King's death we shall see a notable change. If this should happen all our friends will be in power.'

13. 'If she catches me I'll be damned'

Wellington's virtues did not include a propensity to forgive his enemies, and by the end of 1829 the Princess was very high on any list of them he might have kept. The depth of his resentment against her can be gauged from his comment to Aberdeen in August that the Lievens had 'behaved very ill. They have played an English party game instead of doing the business of their sovereign since I have been in office. I have the best authority for asserting that both have been engaged (as principals) in intrigues to deprive my colleagues and me of power since January 1828.' In Wellington's eyes they were 'the sole cause of the coolness which exists between the two governments at the moment'; an exaggeration that throws as much light on the Duke's mental processes as it did on the role of the Lievens. As the Duke himself was well aware, the reasons for tension between London and St Petersburg were numerous. The Turkish war had simply brought to a head the festering sores caused by friction between two ambitious empires, and Wellington was nearer the mark in terms of explaining the Anglo-Russian antagonism when he told Aberdeen that: 'I don't believe one word of the desire for peace of a young Emperor at the head of a million men, who has never drawn his sword.' Wellington disliked the fact that he was having to pick up the broken shards of Canning's policy; and he extended that feeling to Dorothea, as one of its principal architects.

By aligning Britain with France and Russia, Canning had hoped to gain some influence over Russian policy, and to push the Turks by diplomatic pressure in the direction of making concessions to the Greeks; his premature death deprived historians of the pleasure of seeing how even that master of presentation would have dealt with the consequences of the battle of Navarino. As things transpired, Canning's policy left Russia as Europe's mandatory

to implement the policy of the Treaty of London by force. If
Wellington's eastern policy was open to criticism with regard to
Russia, then the fault was Canning's poisoned legacy. Where the
Wellington government came in for extra criticism was over the
question of the frontiers of a possible Greek state. Even before
the end of the Russo-Turkish war, it was accepted that there
would be a Greek polity, but Wellington and Aberdeen had two
motives for keeping it as small as possible: the fear that it might
become a Russian client state; and the anxiety that taking too
much territory from the Ottoman Empire would precipitate its
decline.

Those who supported the Greeks from the liberal side naturally
criticized the Tories for such a policy, and the Princess, who
desired a larger Greece for exactly the same reasons as Wellington
did not, was happy to supply the Philhellenes with all the assurances
they could want about the disinterested nature of Russian intentions. She was correspondingly jubilant with the terms of the
Treaty of Adrianople. 'It is,' she told Grey on 12 October 1829, 'a
peace that is glorious for Russia and proves her generous, if it be
remembered how completely the Ottoman Empire lay at her
mercy. We have at least shown that we do not seek to destroy this
Empire.' That was not how it looked to Wellington and Aberdeen.

'We are certainly in a bad way,' Wellington wrote to Aberdeen
on 25 August, before the ending of the war between Russia and
Turkey, 'and nobody can see a creditable road out of our difficulties. We have made the greatest sacrifices of opinions, principles
and national pride and prejudice to our allies. In return they have
not performed their promise.' Unless they did so, Wellington
warned, 'we can make no concession. We can talk of nothing
excepting in the tone and quality of a power that is degraded.'
Bound as they were to put to the Porte the suggestion for an
independent Greece, all they could hope for, Wellington thought,
was that the Turks would reject it, or that it would be so small in
size as to be in effect a Turkish appendage. Adrianople did not
strike them in the way it did the Princess: Harriet Arbuthnot's
comment that 'the Emperor of Russia has behaved precisely like a

second Bonaparte' summed up their response. In a formal despatch to Heytesbury on 31 October, Aberdeen stated that the consequences of Adrianople were 'so various & important, & influence so powerfully the future happiness and tranquillity of all nations', that it would be 'inconsistent with the station which His Majesty fills among the Sovereigns of Europe, as well as with that frankness which he is desirous should characterise all his relations with the Cabinet of St Petersburg' not to let the Russians know how Britain regarded the peace treaty. Not even the diplomatic language into which Aberdeen compressed the substance of the British complaints could disguise the bitterness caused by Russian conduct.

Aberdeen took his stance on the fact that while, as good allies should, Britain had relied upon Russian good faith in declaring war on the Turks, and had therefore made no comment when the war had broken out, London had always stressed that even the 'most complete success in the justest cause would not entitle the stronger party to demand from the weaker, sacrifices which would affect its political existence'. This did not just mean that the Turks should not lose too much territory, since the British had made clear their fear that 'the demands for indemnity and compensation might be carried to an extent as to render compliance scarcely practicable, without reducing the Ottoman Porte to a degree of weakness which would deprive it of the character of an independent state.' This was precisely what Wellington feared had now happened. Of course, as the Princess had pointed out, the scale of the Russian victory was such that the Tsar could have exacted whatever terms he had wanted, but since throughout the war he had professed that 'far from desiring the destruction of the Turkish Empire, he was most anxious for its preservation', it was rather rich of him to expect any great reward for keeping to the letter of his words – at least that was how the British saw matters. The problem for London was that in observing the letter of his promises, the spirit of them had not been honoured. 'Modes of domination,' Aberdeen observed, 'may be various', but they were all equally irresistible. Although Russia received only small accretions of territory, these were strategically important ones. In particular,

now that Russia had 'uninterrupted occupation of the Eastern
Coast of the Black Sea' she not only controlled the sea itself, but
found herself 'in a situation so commanding as to controul [*sic*] at
pleasure the destiny of Asia Minor'.

For all the criticisms levelled by their opponents at their diplomacy, Wellington and Aberdeen had spotted what would be the
crucial axis of Russian expansion over the next quarter of a century:
'Russia holds the keys, both of the Persian & the Turkish provinces'
and 'no serious obstacle can arrest her progress' eastwards. To the
west, with Wallachia and Moldavia 'rendered virtually independent
of the Porte', and with Serbia now an 'independent and powerful
state', the 'circle' of hostile powers would be 'completed' by the
creation of an independent Greece, 'the recognition of which, by
the Powers of Europe is scarcely compatible with the security,
perhaps not with the existence of the Turkish Empire'. The commercial parts of the treaty were equally injurious to Turkish sovereignty, giving rights to Russian traders and forcing the Turks to
pay a huge indemnity, but most objectionable of all to London
was the Russian stipulation that merchant vessels of all nations
should be allowed through the Straits without conceding any right
of inspection to the Turks; there seemed no way of ensuring that
Russian warships did not pass through in the guise of merchant
ships.

At the heart of the British complaint, and thus of the rising
Anglo-Russian antagonism, was the change in the balance of power
in the Near East caused not only by the Treaty of Adrianople, but
also by the Treaty of Turkmanchi which ended the Russo-Persian
war in 1828. It was not just that as an Asiatic power herself, Britain
disliked seeing another European power muscle into her sphere of
influence (although she did). The president of the Board of Control
of the India Board, Lord Ellenborough, enshrined British fears
neatly when he told Wellington on 15 October 1829: 'limited
indeed would be the views of that statesman who could think that
her acquisitions in Asia did not affect the relations of Russia with
the Powers of Europe.' After all: 'whatever enables Russia to
produce the same effect upon the Asiatick [*sic*] frontier with fewer

troops and at a diminished cost, enables her without increased exertion to devote a larger portion of her forces and of her revenue to intervention in the affairs of Europe.'

It is in this context that the Duke's quarrel with Princess Lieven should be seen. At a time when it was important that St Petersburg should have a clear view of the policy of the British government, they were getting instead the biased opinion of the Princess. According to Wellington, Prince Lieven, 'by delays, misrepresentations, etc., etc. defeats the objects of all our requisitions, and forces us to the point of concession or guard upon every trifling point'; the result of this was that no business could be conducted through the Russian embassy in London. 'We may,' Wellington concluded, 'rely upon it that the object of Prince Lieven is not to keep this country on good terms with the Emperor excepting by the humiliation of this country.' What Anglo-Russian relations needed at this point was careful handling – but what they got was the continuing vendetta between the Princess and the Duke. Wellington took the opportunity of a meeting with Lieven and Matuscewitz on 4 and 5 September to make clear to the latter the degree to which the former was impeding the achievement of a good understanding between Russia and Britain. Responding to complaints made by the Tsar through Heytesbury about the Duke himself, Wellington protested his desire to have the 'best understanding' with Russia, and professed himself baffled to understand how anyone could think that he had acted in any sense hostile towards her.

Wellington's meaning was made clearer in his letter a few days later to Heytesbury, which formed the opening shot in his attack on the Lievens: 'They have misrepresented to their Court all that we have done, and particularly that I have done.' Even Grey, who enjoyed Dorothea's feline malice against his opponents, thought it wise to warn her 'of the necessity of your not interfering in our domestic politics' because the 'charge of doing so not only does you harm personally, but throws obstacles and difficulties in the way of the business with which you are entrusted'. But she did not condescend even to reply to such good advice – let alone take it, and she continued to delight in working with Wellington's opponents to undermine him.

The only reaction in St Petersburg to the Duke's complaints was the appointment of Prince Lieven as temporary foreign minister in early 1830 when Nesselrode went on leave. For the moment, at least, the Princess was impregnable. Aberdeen's rather feeble attempt to curb the Lievens by securing support at St Petersburg was a dismal failure. If it did anything, it underscored how poor communication between the two courts had been. The Princess took great pleasure in telling stories that reflected badly upon Wellington and Aberdeen, and she seized every opportunity to crow over anything that discomforted them.

One of Dorothea's stratagems can be glimpsed from Aberdeen's comment to Heytesbury that he believed that her main venom was directed at the Duke while she used quite different language about him. There seems little doubt that the widowed Aberdeen found Dorothea attractive enough to allow her liberties that even Grey found surprising. Her flirtatious manner pulled him into the admission that he felt duped by the Russians, and when she gave him the direct lie, he simply accepted her censure, claiming that he had been willing to put up even with 'dishonour' in order to preserve the peace. Her response: 'Come, come my dear Lord, I am more English than you are, for I am ashamed of what you are saying to me', was very much to the point, but said much about the fascination she had for him. Grey was mortified: 'it is new in the history of diplomacy, and still more in that of Scotchmen, to meet with such an avowal as that you describe Aberdeen to have made, and for what purpose but to expose himself?'

But perhaps Grey protested too much? He had enough experience to know that clever men can make fools of themselves given encouragement from the right woman. At the same time as she was making fun of him in this way, and describing in melodramatic terms how she triumphed over him in the contest to find a ruler for the new Greek state, she was using all her charm on Aberdeen, telling him that he was the King's favourite minister, and that Wellington was nothing compared to him. Although Aberdeen

claimed to 'see through' these 'cajoleries', the Duke was right to
suspect that 'he is a little caught'. He certainly continued to give
the Princess good copy to pass on to her Whig admirers. When
the new, and very absolutist, Polignac ministry was appointed
in November, Dorothea, after criticizing its members *seriatim*,
exclaimed: 'they are all a pack of fools', to which Aberdeen replied:
'Of which Government are you speaking – of ours, or of the
French?' Grey, who was something of an authority on such matters,
caught the truth of it when he commented to Dorothea: 'You
surely must have fascinated Aberdeen to make him talk in such a
manner.' Despite the growing evidence of the damage being done
by the Princess to Anglo-Russian relations, Wellington's pride
would not let him insist on her recall, which meant that things
continued to deteriorate.

When Dorothea made overtures, such as inviting Wellington
to dinner at the Russian embassy, that seemed designed to lead to
the passing of olive branches, it transpired that the other guests
were leading members of the opposition, and that he had to put
up with petty insults such as Harriet Granville refusing to bow to
him, and saying that she was amused to see how it put him out of
countenance. Meanwhile, the Princess let it be known that she
had advised George IV to change his administration and make
Palmerston Prime Minister; given that he was the 'most bitter of the
Opposition', this added fuel to the flames. Wellington's response,
which was not to attend the next ball at the Russian embassy, fell
some way short of dealing with the problem.

Dorothea saw matters in a different light. She had a profound
contempt for both Wellington and Aberdeen. This was founded
in part on the conviction, imbibed from her close contacts with
Grey and Palmerston, that the ministry could not long endure. As
the date for the autumn session of parliament approached in
October 1829, Grey reported with amusement the new whisper
circulating, which was that the Princess was supposed to be
securing his support for a 'systematic opposition' that would
include Huskisson, Lord Melbourne and Lord Holland. Such
rumours were now constant and reflected the extreme weakness

of Wellington's position. Russia's perceived triumph in the Eastern Question had been an additional blow to an administration rocked by the Catholic emancipation crisis; relations between 'King Arthur' and George IV were so bad that the only thing that kept the Duke in office was the King's reluctance to turn to the Whigs. But the King was dying, and his likely successor, the Duke of Clarence, had no such bias. Insulting a weakened and tottering ministry with a limited lifespan must have seemed a risk-free option to Princess Lieven. Even had it not been, Dorothea was hardly averse to risk. The second reason for her behaviour was the triumphalism she felt following Adrianople.

'Never was Russia so great as at this moment,' she boasted. In this mood she saw nothing to gain from being either tactful or diplomatic. 'There is no longer,' she told her brother Alexander, 'any idea of conciliating the good-will [of the English]; Russia will never be able to gain from them.' She thought that Russia 'must adopt a firm attitude and enforce it by polite but cold language'. When Grey was less appreciative of the great treaty than she liked, she told him bluntly that: 'It was not to please England, or anyone else, that we signed it.' It was only 'in deference to Europe, and to what I may call its prejudices' that 'we have maintained the Ottoman Empire, for in point of fact, it lay with us to destroy it had we so chosen'. Even if true, perhaps especially because it was true, such comments should hardly have been made, and she would have cause to rue them. For the Russian ambassadress, whose husband was going to take charge of the Foreign Ministry and whose brother was one of the senior counsellors to the Tsar, to write in such a vein was not calculated to do anything save make British fears about Russia's ultimate intentions worse. Grey and Palmerston were happy enough to rejoice in the discomfiture of Wellington, but they did not forget these intimations of Russian triumphalism. Those historians who have wondered why both men showed themselves so distrustful of Russian intentions so swiftly, could do worse than to take into account the fact that they were both intimates of Princess Lieven and had plenty of opportunity to observe her mood at this moment of Russian success.

Wellington's hopes rose briefly in the summer of 1830 when the Lievens were called back to St Petersburg. Indeed, for a brief moment, even Dorothea feared that she might be leaving England never to return. The hopes of her enemies were soon dashed. Heytesbury reported that Prince Lieven was being asked to take charge of foreign affairs only during a period of leave for Nesselrode, and that the Princess, having travelled as far as Warsaw, would be returning to Richmond immediately. The ambassador was right when he counselled Aberdeen that 'if you really wish the Princess to be definitively removed you must make up your mind *to speak out* . . . She will defeat any attack but a direct attack.' She would, he added for good measure, 'leave nothing undone to avoid coming to St Petersburg where she detests everybody and everybody detests her'. There was now nothing to be done, unless a direct demand for the recall of the Lievens was made; with the Prince in charge at the Foreign Ministry, Heytesbury could hardly indulge in elliptical conversation with Lieven about the shortcomings of the Russian representatives in London. All he could suggest to Aberdeen was a few well-placed articles in the press whose criticism might sting the Princess into wanting to quit England. In fact it was fate that came nearest to removing the Lievens. The Prince fell seriously ill in Warsaw on his way back to England, and Dorothea feared for his life. In the meantime, she was involved in an unpleasant accident when her carriage was overturned and her back was damaged. However, events across the Channel were about to bring a dramatic change in Princess Lieven's attitude towards the Duke of Wellington.

In July 1830 there was a revolution in Paris against the reactionary policies pursued by Charles X and the Duc de Polignac, with the King abdicating and being replaced by his cousin, the Duc d'Orléans. This was the first major challenge to the Vienna system, and both Wellington and Aberdeen considered whether they should invoke the Concert of Europe, before deciding against it. There were two good reasons for refraining from calling on other powers to intervene in France: in the first place, such interference might actually drive the revolution in a more extreme direction; in the second, it had to be admitted that Charles X had done much to provoke legitimate protests against his increasingly arbitrary rule. Another motive for non-intervention was one that could hardly be admitted to foreign governments; much though Wellington feared the forces of liberalism, he feared even more the possible effects of a Russian-led intervention in western Europe. The prospect of this last came a league nearer in late August with the second major challenge to the Vienna system – the outbreak of a separatist revolt in Brussels, demanding the dissolution of the union between Holland and Belgium. The powers agreed to Wellington's suggestion that since their ambassadors were already meeting in conference in London to discuss the settlement of the boundaries of Greece, the fate of Belgium should be added to their agenda.

The renewed spectre of revolution in France and western Europe was unwelcome to the Russians, and had its effect upon Princess Lieven's attitude towards British politics. Long and assiduous though her cultivation of Grey had been, Dorothea now had her doubts about whether a man with his very pronounced liberal sympathies would serve 'our [Russian] interests'. 'Notwithstanding my regard for Lord Grey,' she told her brother Alexander in September, 'I would much rather that he stood aloof, because with him would probably enter those whose ideas would not suit us in these critical times.' She had also come to accept that Wellington was likely to remain as Prime Minister under the new King. Dorothea had attended a dinner given by the Duke for the new King at Apsley House at which William had expressed his full confidence in his premier. When Dorothea attempted to get a private audience with William IV, he refused to see her, saying, according to Mrs Arbuthnot: 'She'll try to get about me & talk smoothly; but if she catches me I'll be damned.' In these circumstances her thoughts turned towards a Wellington administration diluted by the influx of her friends, Palmerston and Melbourne, with Grey and some of the more moderate Whigs coming in. Such a ministry would, she thought, 'be just what is needed to keep France in check, to uphold Conservative doctrines, and to get

English democrats to accept them willingly or of necessity. In such a Ministry we should count upon friends to Russia.'

There was a good deal of reactionary wishful thinking in such ministry-mongering. As Mrs Arbuthnot, whose understanding of these matters was greater than that of the Princess, put it: 'Grey is a man of violent temper, haughty, arrogant & overbearing . . . a Liberal in the fullest sense of the term. He would not, I am sure, go on a day amicably with the Duke.' Wellington himself saw the wisdom of trying to bring less intractable souls such as Palmerston into his net, and the Princess herself urged Lady Cowper to 'use your influence to prevent pride from spoiling the whole affair . . . because the Duke needs fresh support.' However, Palmerston, having resigned from Wellington's government nearly two years before with his friends, was unwilling to return without them, a price the Duke thought too high. Palmerston explained his reasons to the Princess in two long letters on 7 and 9 October. Given the differences between him and the Duke, it was essential, he said, that he should return to the Cabinet only fortified by others of a like mind who would either help him maintain his views, or at least be able to explain why he had ceded, should that be necessary. But this was clearly not meant to exclude further negotiations with Wellington when the latter might be more willing to yield on terms Palmerston could accept.

Ironically, the only one of his opponents whom the Duke had won over by the start of the parliamentary session was Princess Lieven. One of the reasons Palmerston and company had been reluctant to join Wellington was their conviction that the administration, weakened by the results of the summer election that had followed George IV's death, could not stand for long without them. On one side the Duke faced Grey and the Whigs, who were coming together to press the issue of parliamentary reform; on the other were the so-called Ultra Tories, led by the King's highly reactionary brother, the Duke of Cumberland, who wanted nothing more than to destroy an administration that had emancipated the Catholics. The skills the Duke had evinced on the battlefield were absent from the political arena. Deciding that it would rally his own troops and some of the Ultras, the Duke dug in with an uncompromising defence of the existing constitution. This was a disastrous move. The Ultras were not to be reconciled thus, and the Canningites now had to vote with the Whigs to retain their liberal credentials.

So it was that in a motion on the Civil List on 15 November, the government lost the confidence of the Commons. At midnight Lord Grey wrote to Princess Lieven with the news that there had been a majority against Wellington of twenty-nine: 'You desired me to send you anything *piquant*. What do you think of this?' The following day Grey was asked to form an administration. Six months earlier the Princess would have been unequivocally delighted; now she would see the truth of the maxim about being careful what you wish for in case it comes true.

Grey's advent to power should have been Princess Lieven's finest hour. Her closest political friends were now in office. She had cultivated Grey assiduously since the early 1820s, and her friendship with Palmerston, although of more recent vintage, had been a close one; both men wrote to her regularly. Her dearest female friend, Lady Cowper, had both her lover (Palmerston) and her brother (Melbourne) in the new administration, while other friends such as Lady Granville were sympathetic to the Whig government. Throughout the Wellington years, Dorothea had blatantly allied herself with his enemies and worked to bring together just such a coalition as Grey now endeavoured to construct. Indeed, in the very act of forming the administration, he sought advice from the Princess – although he surely knew her well enough to realize that he would get it in any event. She even claimed, to the disbelief of Sir Charles Webster, to have been instrumental in getting Palmerston into the Foreign Office. Yet, in spite of all of this, there are clear indications that the fulfilment of her earlier desires was not as welcome as might have been thought. One observer noted in November that: 'Mme De Lieven's joy [has been] dampened by instructions recently received from home; the Emperor, whom the revolutionary movements have made Ultra, has expressed great confidence in the late government, deprecating change, and especially one which might bring Lord Grey to power.' Dorothea found herself having to apologize for the new government – and tried hard to persuade her masters that it was not as bad as they feared.

'All that is happening on the Continent is lamentable,' Dorothea wrote to Alexander in early October, 'and, what is worse, offers no guarantee to the future.' Here was the rub from the point of view of a Russian ambassadress. Until July 1830 the wind seemed set fair for Russia. Her armies had secured huge triumphs over Persia and Turkey and had established Russia as the dominant power in the region between the Black Sea and the Persian Gulf, and her diplomats seemed to have reassured the chancelleries of Europe that this portended no ill for them. The Austrians may have had their doubts about Russian policy in Greece, but not even Metternich had been able to do anything to frustrate St Petersburg and, in general, he was bound to ally himself with the conservative diplomacy of Nicholas I. The same was true of Prussia and of the France of Charles X. Whatever fears the British entertained about Russia's intentions, even the great Duke of Wellington had been impotent in the face of her strength. In such circumstances it was safe for the ambassadress to flirt with Whiggery. Indeed, in so far as Wellington's fears of Russia might push him in the direction of trying to thwart Russian diplomacy, it was imperative that the Princess should build up a 'Russian party' from among the ranks of the opposition to frustrate him; that she had done to great effect. But with the return of the forces of revolution, new priorities came to the fore, and what was safe in calmer times might become dangerous in stormier ones. Hindsight showed how unrevolutionary the regime of Louis-Philippe in France was, but at the time no one could foretell what might happen, and for men and women raised in the shadow of the great revolution of 1789, nothing seemed impossible.

Dorothea Lieven had some inkling of all of this even before Grey was called to office. One reason why she advocated a Wellington administration with an admixture of Palmerston and company was that she feared Grey's liberal instincts. But she also knew that if what she called 'English Jacobinism' was to be 'kept down', then Grey's presence in an administration was essential. All she could do was to take refuge in the hope that the experience of office would effect a change in Grey's views as he came to realize the 'actual position of affairs ... its dangers, its difficulties and its responsibilities'. The vehemence with which Grey advocated parliamentary reform in the great debate on the subject that preceded the Duke's ejection from office, led Dorothea to describe his speech as 'detestable'. She sought to reassure her brother, and through him the Tsar, by stating that if Grey became Prime Minister, 'we shall have in his very monarchical, very aristocratic principles ample guarantee that revolution will never receive from him protection or support, and that the maintenance of peace and order will be the aim of his wishes and his efforts.' It was towards these ends that Dorothea sought to influence her admirer as he set about the difficult task of forming the first Whig ministry for twenty-five years.

14. 'The last day of our alliance?'

In 1823, when their relationship was still *en couleur de rose*, the Whigs looked at Dorothea Lieven askance 'because I have some influence over their leader'. Now that Grey was Prime Minister, Princess Lieven certainly expected to have some influence; but the question of what sort of influence is difficult to answer, not least because of the nature of the relationship between them. Their correspondence was copious and continuous, but it was not without asperity, even before he became Prime Minister. Once he was in 10 Downing Street, Grey became extremely sensitive to any suggestion that the contents of his correspondence with Dorothea might become known to others and when, as we shall see, he found out that a comment of his about the Polish revolt had leaked out, he was 'much vexed' and warned that 'if I have not a complete assurance that my name is not to be mentioned, my mouth must be completely shut as to everything but the mere gossip of the day.'

Dorothea took the warning, and for a while their correspondence continued as before. He is said to have written to her in the mornings and to have perfumed the envelopes with musk, and he referred to Dorothea as his 'Egeria'. That their relationship had been an intimate one is likely, and Grey certainly allowed her a great deal of latitude. Back in 1823 he told her that 'he would like to kill himself' because 'cleverness is beside the point when one is no longer young'; this was, as she remarked to Metternich, 'an original reason', and she wondered whether he had been 'seized by a romantic passion.' She agreed with Metternich that it was 'ambition' that kept Grey 'alive and struggling', and confided to him Emily Cowper's belief that he would never be a minister because he 'eats too many sweets', which impaired his digestion and made him 'bilious' and 'ill-tempered'. Notwithstanding this characteristic, and his occasional prickliness, Grey fascinated Dorothea enough for her to carry on a long correspondence with him, even when, as in the early 1820s, his chances of office appeared remote. When he finally attained office, she expected to be able to reap the dividends of her investment in his political stock. The first fruit of her influence was, she told her brother, the appointment of Palmerston to the Foreign Office, but she begged him to be very discreet about this since 'not a soul here has the slightest idea of the influence by which this has been brought about. I assure you I pass for being altogether ignorant of what is going on.'

Palmerston's appointment was certainly not an obvious one. The Foreign Office was one of the great prizes of government, and Palmerston was not even a Whig, so the question of how the most famous of Victorian Foreign Secretaries first got the job is one of some interest. In her diary, Princess Lieven takes the credit for suggesting the appointment to Grey. In his definitive first volume on Palmerston's foreign policy, Sir Charles Webster demurs, pointing out that the post was first offered to Lansdowne and then Holland before it ended up with Palmerston; while this spoils the details of Dorothea's fanciful version, it does not quite explain why Grey selected Palmerston, even as a third choice. Dorothea's account should not, however, be dismissed out of hand; if it does not contain the full story, it does tell us much about how she saw her role, and if we place it against a more probable version of the truth, it also reveals some of the reasons for her ultimate failure.

The first thing to note in the version recorded by Princess Lieven is its context, which is what gives it its air of veracity, however much some of the detail might be questioned. She describes how Grey 'came to consult me on whom to choose as Minister of Foreign Affairs' and how she 'refused to give an opinion'. In her account of events she came under pressure from two sources: on the one hand, 'the diplomats, alarmed at seeing affairs fall into the hands of the Whigs, urged me to discourage candidates too deeply dyed with that colour'; on the other, Emily Cowper and Palmerston himself 'came and urged me to press keenly on Lord Grey' the virtues of Palmerston as Foreign Secretary. There appears to be no reason to query any of this detail. Grey certainly 'consulted' her – which does not, of course, mean that he intended to take her advice, but his relationship with her was such that both of them expected her to proffer her views. An essential part of the flirtation between them had been Grey's role as the 'coming man' of power, and now that he was Prime Minister both of them moved up to a new level and shared the same excitement in Cabinet-making. Grey was also conscious of the likely reaction by foreign courts to the advent of a Whig government, and being no fool, he used the Princess to discover what was being said and by whom; what he did with that information was his own affair, but it was essential that a man so long out of office should have access to up-to-date information about foreign affairs, and until he had had the chance to read what his ambassadors were saying, the Princess was a valuable source of information.

Nor is anything more likely than that Emily Cowper and Palmerston were pressing his claims. The connection between Grey and Palmerston was not a close one. Although the two men shared many characteristics, not least in their philandering, there was a nearly thirty-year gap between them, and they moved in different circles. During the Wellington years the Princess had done her best to bring the two men together socially, and she and Emily Cowper were the two major links connecting Grey to Palmerston; without the 'female politicians' the two men would hardly have known each other. None of this means that the Princess was solely responsible for Palmerston's appointment, but Sir Charles Webster's instinctive distrust of her made him disregard the role that women played in early nineteenth-century politics.

There were two obvious candidates for the post of Foreign Secretary – if one excludes Grey himself – Lords Lansdowne and Holland. Both men were leading Whig grandees with a long interest in foreign affairs; but this just about exhausted their qualifications for the job. The Foreign Office was the most prestigious post after that of Prime Minister, but where the latter job was more or less what its occupant chose to make of it, the former carried quite literally a killing workload. Castlereagh's life had been shortened by the burdens laid upon him at the Foreign Office, as had Canning's.

The unwillingness of the aristocratic taxpayer to stump up more than a minimum amount of money kept government small, and nowhere was the effect more obvious than at the Foreign Office, where a staff of nineteen clerks and one private secretary was considered sufficient for the needs of a global empire. Moreover, the clerks were just what their name suggested, men who transcribed despatches to and from British embassies abroad; policy was made elsewhere. Constitutionally, foreign policy was the prerogative of the monarch; in practice the idleness of George IV and his brother made the King a cypher. In theory this elusive 'elsewhere' was the Cabinet, but a group of a dozen or so men, most of them with their own departmental business to look after, was not an effective body for making foreign policy; in practice the role of the Foreign Secretary was crucial, as was his relationship with the Prime Minister. The Foreign Secretary needed to be able to master a great deal of detailed information, which meant a tremendous amount of hard work for whoever held the post; neither Lansdowne nor Holland wanted to work that hard. Princess Lieven may well, as she claimed, have advised against Lansdowne because he wore 'the Whig Livery', but both she and Grey seriously considered him for the post. That he did not become Foreign Secretary owed everything to his own disinclination to shoulder the burden involved; he preferred to take the less onerous but still prestigious post of Lord President of the Council, from which gilded perch he could interfere in foreign affairs as much as he liked without having to master any detail; in practice this would limit the effectiveness of his interventions.

Similar considerations led Grey's other nominee, Lord Holland, to decline the post. Holland, the keeper of the Whig flame of his uncle, Charles James Fox, was much under the influence of his wife who held one of the great Whig salons at Holland House. Now beginning to age, he knew that he lacked the vigour necessary to deal with the amount of work that being Foreign Secretary would involve. He chose, instead, the sinecure post of Chancellor of the Duchy of Lancaster, which would give him the opportunity to intervene in foreign policy – and the leisure so to do. Both he and Lansdowne would have their turn when the time came to say something on foreign policy, but it did not need the wiles of Dorothea Lieven to deny them the Foreign Office, even if she thought otherwise.

In these circumstances it is not unlikely that Dorothea's claim to have brought Palmerston to the Foreign Office through her contact with Grey was essentially correct. The caveat 'essentially' is necessary because her version of events tells us more about how she thought her influence worked than about how it actually did. According to her account, having stymied Lansdowne because, like many Whigs, he would not 'reassure foreign courts' about the foreign policy of the new government, Grey asked her 'where can I find the man?' The notion of the rather haughty Grey playing such a role seems a trifle far-fetched, although that does not rule out the notion that he was indeed doing just that – role-playing. Certainly he and the Princess were in constant communication during the vital period when the heart of the government was being formed, and although no record exists of what was said, there was plenty of opportunity for much conversation.

There were at least two reasons, beyond the purely personal, why the Princess pressed Palmerston's claims to the Foreign Office. In the first place, as we have seen, after the revolutions of 1830, Dorothea had thought better of her feud with Wellington. It was now in Russia's interests that the Whiggish element in the new government should be diluted with a good admixture of Tories, and Dorothea's favourites were the ex-Canningites, who actually did rather well out of Grey. It was not simply Palmerston who received a rich reward from his adopted party, his fellow-Canningite, Melbourne, went to the Home Office, while the Ultra Tory Duke of Richmond went to the Post Office. Grey knew the weakness of his own position.

Because the Whigs had not held office for more than a generation, they were at best an unproven quantity when it came to running the country; office was certainly the perquisite of power, but while any idle fool could be Lord President or Chancellor of the Duchy (or Prime Minister, if it came to that), some jobs required efficiency and experience; few Whigs possessed the first quality and none the second – which was where Palmerston came in. Precisely because he was not a Whig, Palmerston had more years in office than the rest of the Whig Cabinet put together and multiplied by two; he was, if nothing else, a safe pair of hands. He, along with Melbourne and Richmond, would also bring parliamentary support to what was a weak government, at least until a general election could be held. If Grey listened to Princess Lieven, he did so for his own reasons. If Palmerston's appointment suited Dorothea's strategy of diluting the Whiggish nature of the new government, it suited her in another sense also – he was 'Russian'. As she recorded in her account: 'He had given us Russians pledges of goodwill.'

The quarrelsome Radical politician and journalist David Urquhart, who always accused Palmerston of being a Russian agent, would have found Dorothea's comment manna; but what did it mean? As we have seen, throughout the Wellington government Dorothea had kept in contact with Palmerston, who had been one of her most regular correspondents; in addition to this direct line of communication, she also had Emily Cowper as another link to him. As Palmerston sought to don the mantle of Canning, he closely identified himself with those who criticized Wellington and Aberdeen's eastern policy as being illiberal and ungenerous, especially on the question of the Greek frontiers. With her usual knack of confusing personal friendship and political principles, Dorothea imagined that Palmerston would be more favourable to Russian interests than those Whigs whom Grey might have preferred to him; nor was this quite as odd as it came to seem later. In the early winter of 1830 the greatest threat to European peace lay in a possible conjunction between the two revolutions of the summer, specifically in the new French government deciding to take advantage of events in Belgium to acquire territory and influence there. On that issue Palmerston, whose suspicions of France were uncharacteristic of Whiggery, was a better choice for the Foreign Office than the Francophile Holland. In describing the new Cabinet to her brother Alexander, Dorothea laid stress on the number of Canningites it possessed (four), and on its moderate nature, with Palmerston being described as 'perfect in every way'; this feeling would not persist.

It is worth emphasizing that Dorothea sought to wield influence not merely for her own gratification. However much her feud with Wellington took on a personal tone, it was occasioned not by personalities but by the perception that his government's policy over the Eastern Question was not in Russia's interests; the same was true, *mutatis mutandis*, with regard to Grey. Because historians have focused upon Grey's domestic policy, in particular the dramatic struggle for what became the first Reform Act, it is easy to neglect the anxiety occasioned abroad by his arrival in office. The Princess was not exaggerating when she cautioned Grey about the effect that his choice of Foreign Secretary would have on the other great powers. 'The change which has come over England,' she warned, 'will startle Europe – let Europe be reassured.' Ever since Waterloo, British foreign policy had been in Tory hands. It was true that under Canning there had been some resiling from the warm cooperation of Castlereagh's day, but the presence of that international statesman, Wellington, was sufficient guarantee that Britain would uphold the sanctity of the Vienna settlement. The Whigs, however, had been critical of the Vienna settlement, and since no one knew anything about them, their policy was unpredictable; this created great discomfort in Europe's chancelleries. As Heytesbury told Palmerston in one of his first despatches to him: 'I should be wanting in my duty if I omitted to mention to Your Lordship the unpleasant impression which the intelligence of the change of Ministry in England produced upon this Government.' The Russians, taking at face value the speeches made by the Whigs when in opposition, assumed that 'a system would be adopted diametrically opposed in every respect to that which has been pursued by the Duke . . . and that an intimate, an exclusive Alliance would be sought with France.'

This was where Dorothea's friendships gave Russian diplomacy an invaluable insight into the new British government. For example, when Grey made a speech in November 1830 expressing his sympathy for the Belgians, the Princess assured St Petersburg that far from heralding any radical change of policy, Grey was 'quite upset by this interpretation of his speech, and protested that his sole object had been to warn France against any deviation from the ways of moderation'. She was able to reassure Alexander (and through him Nesselrode and the Tsar) that Grey had said 'we shall have reason to be satisfied with him', and that his policy was 'to maintain peace'. When she quizzed him – 'and the observance of treaties?' – he 'smiled and asked me not to press him on any special point at the moment'. He did, however, promise 'to take cognisance of the state of affairs, and repeated to me his assurances that we should be satisfied'. Wellington's comment was also worth repeating to St Petersburg: 'As for foreign policy, my successors have only one course – to continue what I have begun. If they don't, there will be war.'

Wellington had good reason to anticipate problems. The revolt in Belgium, and the prospect of a revolutionary France seeking to profit from it, aroused in Russia all the instincts that had prompted the Holy Alliance. At the beginning of November Tsar Nicholas signalled a hardening of Russian policy by announcing that he had placed the army on a war footing. In order to counter the alarm this caused across Europe, Nesselrode sent a circular despatch to all Russia's ambassadors stressing that it was 'the policy of Russia to be strictly *conservative*, & to have no other object than the peace and tranquillity of Europe' by maintaining the 1815 settlement. This, Nesselrode asserted, required not only 'the most intimate union' but also 'a perfect *solidarité* of interests and actions, amongst all the members of the Quadruple Alliance'. To accept a derogation from the territorial settlement of Vienna *and* the right of the Belgians to revolt against their lawful sovereign was asking a great deal too much of the autocrat of all the Russias. Equally, to expect a revolutionary French government to stand by and see the Belgian revolt crushed with the assistance of Russia, was to ask too much of opinion in Paris.

The Polish revolt at the end of November marked, for a while, the end of the spectre of Russian military intervention, since her armies were needed elsewhere; but the fate of Belgium still remained to be decided and raised questions of enormous importance for the European powers. If the Russians, Prussians and Austrians were concerned with the questions of legitimacy and monarchical solidarity, and the French with taking advantage of the situation to secure the relaxation of the limits imposed on them in 1815, the British were most worried by this last point. No part of the Vienna settlement was of more concern to Britain than the union of Holland and Belgium. A cardinal nostrum of British diplomacy was to prevent 'an enemy possessing the long line of coast by which we had been hostilely confronted during the reign of Napoleon'. The ideal solution to the problem of the old Austrian Netherlands had been that proposed in 1815, but the way in which the Dutch had ruled the Belgian provinces had so goaded the Belgians that they had now risen in revolt; at the end of November they declared their desire for complete independence of the House of Nassau.

Although anathema in principle to the Russians, the Tsar was prepared to accept the idea of Belgian independence as the least worst alternative solution – especially when the French still appeared to have designs on the provinces. On 20 January 1831 the London Conference agreed to recognize 'the absolute and entire separation of Belgium and Holland as an irreversible fact', but this left many questions, including the boundaries of the new kingdom of Belgium and its ruler, undecided; the answer to these questions would determine the issue of war or peace in Europe.

Of the three possible candidates for the Belgian throne – Prince Leopold of Saxe-Coburg, the Duc de Nemours and the Prince of Orange – Grey and Palmerston preferred the first. He was the former husband of George IV's only child, Princess Charlotte, and could be expected to be amenable to advice from London. Nemours, who was the second son of the new French King,

Louis-Philippe, was *persona non grata*; while Palmerston doubted the capacity of the Prince of Orange. However, Princess Lieven managed to persuade her British admirers that they would be better off backing the Prince of Orange; what she did not tell them was that the Princess of Orange, who was the Tsar's sister, the Grand Duchess Anna, had entrusted her with half a million francs with which to back the Orangeist cause.

By supporting the Prince of Orange, the Russians hoped to ensure that Belgium would remain under the control of the House of Nassau – albeit in a different way from that envisaged in 1815. Dorothea brokered a meeting between Grey and the Prince at her house, and secured Britain's acceptance to the idea that he should be proposed as sovereign. Grey and Palmerston seem to have changed their minds about backing Leopold, at least in part, because of reports from Belgium that the cause of the Prince of Orange seemed a good deal more popular than had appeared to be the case a month earlier. Again, Dorothea does not appear to have told them that the disbursement of the monies she had been given by the Princess of Orange might have had something to do with this state of affairs.

In early January 1831 it was decided that the election of the Prince of Orange would provide the best solution to the Belgian problem, and he was asked to write to his father and to his supporters to do what was needful on his behalf. Talleyrand, the new French ambassador, complained bitterly about the influence the Princess had exercised in bringing about this state of affairs. When Palmerston put the idea to Talleyrand, suggesting that the King of Holland might want to give Luxemburg to his son as an incentive to the Belgians to accept him, the old diplomatist revealed something of the motives behind French policy when he suggested that 'Luxemburg might be given to France.' Palmerston may have been a diplomatic novice, but he knew what answer to give: 'such an arrangement appeared to me to be impossible, and that nobody could consent to it.' This showed Palmerston that France was 'unchanged in her system of encroachment' and made him adhere even closer to Russia; indeed, throughout the crisis, Dorothea's influence depended as much, if not more, on Palmerston's fears about France as it did on any of her own arguments.

However, keeping Britain aligned with Russia, which was the ultimate objective of Dorothea's diplomacy, was made no easier by the revolt in Poland. The Russians immediately set in train a campaign designed to crush the rebellion, but no measure was more likely to outrage liberal opinion in Britain and France. Nesselrode told Heytesbury that while he recognized that 'in England any interference with the public press was impossible', he hoped that British ministers would refrain from 'all allusion of a personal nature' if they had to speak on Poland, as well as saying nothing to encourage the rebels. Dorothea did her best. She told her brother Alexander that 'notwithstanding the indiscreet words he may have uttered before becoming Prime Minister', since he came into office Grey had 'been the most pronounced enemy of revolutions, revolutionists, and of disturbance in general wherever it shows itself'.

There was a good deal of wishful thinking in this, and it shows the extent to which Dorothea misread Grey – on this occasion with some serious consequences, when she gave wider circulation to one of his comments that she chose to misconstrue as an expression of hope that the rebellion would soon be put down. When Grey discovered this he was furious and threatened to cut off all confidential communication if he could not be sure that his remarks would remain secret. Her explanation, which was that she had simply been trying to reassure her government of Britain's good intentions, shows the extent to which she conceived it to be her duty at this point to put the best interpretation on everything that Grey said. 'Do you consider it,' she asked him incredulously, 'so little essential to your interests that goodwill and good faith should be felt towards you and your Government, rather than the mistrust and hatred which antagonistic doctrines must necessarily inspire?' That being said, she apologized for offending him and promised not to repeat the offence. In return, Grey and Palmerston did their best to avoid offending the Russians over an issue on which they were, as the Princess constantly pointed out, extremely sensitive, including declining a suggestion from the French that they should jointly offer to mediate between the Tsar and the Polish rebels.

For the moment, however, universal mistrust of the French did much of Princess Lieven's work for her. The very character of the new French ambassador did nothing to alleviate British and Russian suspicions of France. The decision to send the aged Talleyrand to London was a sign of the importance Louis-Philippe attached to Anglo-French relations, but the old man came with a sulphurous reputation. Mrs Arbuthnot, who liked him, penned one of the best descriptions of him at this time: 'He is still more ugly, really hardly human, as old as Methusalem, with a most enormous quantity of powdered hair hanging over his ears & tied in a tail behind.' The fact that Talleyrand's dinners at the French embassy were presided over by his niece, the Duchess of Dino, who was also his mistress, added to the air of scandal that surrounded this legendary figure from a bygone era. To Wellington's comment that he had always found Talleyrand a 'very straightforward man', Dorothea could only riposte that he had also thought Charles X's last Prime Minister, Polignac, 'a very clever man'. When asked by William IV for her opinion of 'old Talley', she replied pithily that 'a man who had spent seventy-five years in intriguing would not have forgotten the business in his seventy-sixth.'

If legend suggested that the new ambassador was a slippery customer, his words to Palmerston about Luxemburg were sufficient to bring to the surface the not very suppressed fear of France felt by men who had experienced the Napoleonic Wars. Dorothea certainly supported the interpretation that Palmerston put on Talleyrand's words: 'all the apparent *innocence* of M. de Talleyrand has no other end in view but to obtain Belgium as a bequest to France. This will be his last will and testament. He will restore what he once caused her to lose.' Still, as Dorothea reminded Grey, 'you have two honest men on your side – my Emperor and the King of Prussia.' She encouraged him to continue to support the candidature of the Prince of Orange, dismissing his fears about its chances: 'I cannot agree with you, and I suspect France is interfering and exerting influence in this matter. In the name of wonder, why should all the other Powers submit to her pleasure?' She also reported, in the most flattering terms, the appreciation of the Prince for the efforts Grey had already made on his behalf: 'he candidly owned to me that he was certain the Duke of Wellington would never have done for him the half of what you have already achieved.'

Keeping Britain and Russia together during the Belgian crisis was not an easy task, and for once Dorothea was able to act as oil to the wheels of diplomacy rather than as sand in the works. The Tsar accepted the idea of Belgian independence, but only on condition that the King of Holland did likewise, which, as Palmerston put it with his usual pungency, meant 'he might as well refuse it in plain terms' because the Dutch King would never accept it as long as he knew that 'by holding out, he prevents any of the Powers from ratifying'. Dorothea was able to secure agreement from St Petersburg to proceed towards a settlement of the crisis, although Palmerston, observing the final terms, wondered whether he had not 'given way too far to the Russians & Russian champions of the Interests of the Dutch King'.

Thus it was that on 20 January the London Conference agreed upon a protocol stating the *bases de séparation*, or terms on which Holland and Belgium would be divided: Holland's boundaries were fixed as those of 1790, while Belgium received the rest of the Kingdom of the Netherlands with the exception of Luxemburg, which remained in the possession of the Dutch King as part of the German Confederation; it was decided that Belgium should be a 'perpetually neutral state', guaranteed by the five great powers who renounced any intention to seek territorial advantage at its expense. This last point gave rise to a long discussion, since Talleyrand insisted that either Luxemburg should be included in the declaration of neutrality, or should that be impossible, that France should be awarded the frontier fortresses of Philippeville and Marienburg to make her feel more secure. The first of these was impossible, as Palmerston pointed out, since the powers could not dispose of the fate of a territory belonging to the King of Holland; as to the second demand, that amounted to 'plunder . . . for the benefit of one of our members'. However, as Palmerston told Granville with much satisfaction: 'At last we brought him to terms by the same means by which juries become unanimous – by starvation.' By ten o'clock the old Frenchman conceded the terms of *les bases*, and Palmerston could comment that if he complained that 'our confidence in him seems abated, you may say this was the natural consequence of our finding that he was aiming at obtaining for France territorial acquisitions, at the same time that France was crying out for non-intervention and peace'.

A week later, and without any protests from Talleyrand, a second protocol was signed, which sanctioned the previous one and dealt with other technical details such as the division of the public debt of the Kingdom of Holland (where the Belgians ended up having to take a larger share than the Dutch, which was to dog negotiations between the two main parties for years), and the terms of overseas trade between Belgium and Holland. From the British point of view the crucial issue was the status of the port of Antwerp, which the 1815 settlement had established as a purely commercial one; this was reaffirmed by the protocol of 27 January 1831. Equally crucial for the British was the renewal of the French declaration that they would 'neither consent to a union of Belgium with France, *nor accept the Crown even if offered to Nemours*'.

This last possibility, which Dorothea's scheme to make the Prince of Orange the Belgian monarch was designed to avoid, was still dear to the French. Talleyrand sounded Palmerston out on 1 February, only to be told that the British would look upon Nemours becoming King of Belgium 'as a union with France, and nothing else'. Palmerston warned him that France should 'consider *all* the consequences which such a departure from her engagements must necessarily expose her to'; and just in case the message was unclear, he added: 'I do not believe the bulk of the French nation wish for Belgium at the price of a general war.' This was a crucial moment, since French intrigues were about to produce a situation where Nemours would be offered the crown by the Belgians. On 2 February Palmerston demanded from the French a promise that Nemours would not accept the crown even if it were offered to him. 'We are reluctant,' he told Granville in Paris, 'to think of war, but if ever we are to make another effort this is a legitimate occasion.' On 4 February Granville reported that: 'Never was a change of tone, of temper, and of language, so rapid as that which took place yesterday.' The French Prime Minister, General Sébastiani, upon hearing of the British determination, told Granville that although Nemours had been offered the throne, Louis-Philippe would not let him accept it.

The road to resolving the Belgian crisis was a difficult one, and had the British and the Russians not cooperated so closely, it would have led nowhere. The advent of the Whig government had created a potentially fatal obstacle to such cooperation, and in overcoming it Princess Lieven played a notable role. The Tsar's insistence that the Belgian question should be decided 'in favour of the House of Nassau . . . [because] any other arrangement will ultimately be productive of the very evil which all parties so anxiously deprecate, namely a general war', was a potential source of conflict between the two powers. In securing Palmerston's support for the candidature of the Prince of Orange, the Princess brought the two countries as close together as it was possible to do. But the Russians realized that, paralysed as they were by the Polish revolt, and faced with such incontestable evidence of French ambitions, 'the means of successful opposition . . . are only to be found in intimate union & cordial cooperation with England.' The Russian mistrust of the Whigs made them want to stick as close to them as possible to ensure that they did not make concessions to the French. Princess Lieven's insight into Grey and Palmerston provided Nesselrode with the reassurance he needed that this policy was one worth persisting in. On the eve of the Whigs' accession to office Dorothea had written to her brother that she hoped 'we should not look upon their advent as the last day of our alliance.' She had been referring to her connections with Grey and Palmerston, but, as things had turned out, she might have been alluding to the wider question of Anglo-Russian cooperation. That it had not been 'the last day' owed much to her efforts – and to the fear aroused in St Petersburg and London by France.

15. 'He listens when I am speaking'

Writing in December 1830, Dorothea had told her brother Alexander that 'Europe just now presents a scene of incredible confusion'; within the year that confusion had increased exponentially. To the problems caused by events in France, Belgium and Poland were added the struggle for the Reform Bill in Britain, which occasioned much public disorder, and finally revolution in Portugal; and since both the Polish and Belgian questions dragged on through 1831, fresh crises simply added to the burden facing Europe's politicians. The Polish struggle continued because of the time it took the Russians to suppress the revolt. The Belgian issue carried on vexing Europe because of the difficulties of persuading the Belgians to agree to '*les bases*'. The need for Britain and Russia to cooperate therefore remained acute; but the potential obstacles to this were still as great as ever.

When Dorothea wrote: 'Dismiss from your mind the idea, if you ever had it, that Lord Grey is a Liberal', she was betraying the limits of her understanding of him. Her comment that over Belgium the Whigs would act wisely, 'with distrust in France and with confidence in us', was true on the first point but less so on the second. Her analysis of the European situation and of Grey's reaction to it was not without merit, but it lacked the subtlety needed to understand his real position. She saw what was difficult to miss, namely that the Whigs had a 'natural antipathy to Austria' and a 'decided aversion to Metternich', and she was quick to spot the distrust of French intentions that marked Palmerston's attitude; from this she deduced that Grey wanted 'a good understanding with all – but especially with Russia'. All of this was true – but only up to a point. It was not that Grey had 'confidence' in Russia, it was that he and Palmerston had none in the French, which was why both men steered British policy on the Belgian issue in the direction they did. But the conduct of the Russians in Poland perpetually threatened Anglo-Russian amity.

Technically the status of the Duchy of Warsaw was covered by the Vienna settlement, and the British press, which generally took a pro-Polish position, was quick to point out that this gave Britain a say in the future of Poland – something Dorothea persistently denied. Palmerston refused to accept this Russian line, arguing that under the Vienna settlement, which was part of the public law of Europe, Poland was 'attached to the Russian Empire by its constitution' and that the Russians had a duty to provide it with a 'distinct administration'. While pressing this line on Nesselrode through Heytesbury in St Petersburg, Grey, conscious of the 'course public opinion here is likely to take if the business is protracted', tried to convince Dorothea not only that 'there is a case against you on the treaty of Vienna', but of the need for the Russians to proceed carefully if relations between the two countries were not to be damaged.

Grey's prescience was shown by the British reaction to the attack on Poland made by the Russian army in February. As the troops advanced on Warsaw, the British press became progressively more hostile and abusive about the Tsar. With one article in the *Courier* in mind, Dorothea asked Grey whether he had ever seen 'anything more insulting and injurious than what is written here of a Sovereign and a Power in friendly alliance with England'. Given that the article in question said that it was 'written with authority', Dorothea inquired whether 'the authority which sometimes inspires its articles might equally forbid such articles as these?' Grey explained, as so many British statesmen have done to so many foreign diplomats, that 'we really have no power over that, or any other paper', but he might as well have saved his breath. The idea of a free press was so strange to the Russians that not even one who had lived in Britain for twenty years quite grasped what it meant.

Dorothea cut Grey the next time she saw him, and in response to his protest, she showed how much his accusations of breaches of confidence had hurt her. 'It is quite true that my feelings to you yesterday were not what they have been for many past years,' she told him, adding that he could hardly be surprised when she had heard reports that he had commented about the Russian attack on Warsaw: 'All is ended; and it is *most* unfortunate.' She could, she said, 'no longer recognise the friend, still less do I recognise the statesman'. She ended frostily: 'I do not know what to think, and probably I had better keep silence.' Grey stoutly denied the allegation. He wrote that while he had never denied that he felt compassion for the 'poor Poles', this had not 'influenced the conduct which my public duty prescribed to me'. He could be as petulant as his Egeria: 'I am not a little vexed at your so easily believing this absurd story, and at your being so ready to withdraw the kindness which I had hoped did not depend altogether on our political agreement.' This last comment said more about Grey's enormous vanity than it did anything else. Sensing she had gone too far, Dorothea appealed to his vanity by replying that although she believed the person from whom she had had the report 'as I believe in my own self', it 'now appears to me . . . that I believe in you more than in myself, since your note has obliterated all trace of the pain that I had at heart. See, my lord, the extent of your power over me.' But she 'took back nothing of what I said'. She regarded his note as a 'good and perfect reconciliation', adding that 'I should not have been so distressed yesterday, had I cared less about you.' Although the quarrel ended there, for the moment, it was an indication of the damage that the Polish issue could do to relations between Russia and the Whig government.

The fact was that the British were extremely exercised about Poland. Palmerston took his stand on the Vienna settlement because it was the only ground he had from which to try to prevent Russia taking action that would 'give her an inconvenient ascendancy over Austria and Prussia'. This he argued was bound to be the effect of allowing Russia to garrison Poland with her own troops rather than, as Vienna provided, with Polish levies. If such considerations had weighed in Castlereagh's mind, they had, Palmerston argued, 'acquired additional weight . . . in consequence of the increased security which Russia has acquired on her southern

& on her Asiatic frontiers by the success of her arms against the Turks and the Persians'. While wanting these arguments put to Nesselrode, Palmerston warned Heytesbury 'not to take any step on this business which could lead to any unfriendly discussions with the Russian Government' with whom the government was 'under present circumstances, more than ever desirous of keeping up the closest relations of friendship'.

Heytesbury told Palmerston that what he wanted was impossible. Even to raise the subject of Poland in the way he suggested would irritate the Russians to a degree that 'present circumstances' made undesirable. Palmerston, who thought it would be 'a lasting reproach to Europe if the triumph of Russian arms were to be followed by Muscovite severity, which friendly communications from Allied Courts might have prevented', relied upon Heytesbury's 'skill and tact' to 'convey our sentiments without giving any pretence for taking offence'. Heytesbury carried out his instructions with great delicacy, but without much hope. He warned Palmerston that even an autocrat such as Nicholas had to take account of the fact that 'there is a force of public opinion in this country when strongly excited, which cannot be braved, even by the Sovereign, with impunity.' The Russian people expected the Polish rebels to be punished, and if they were not, 'the cry of the nation may become too powerful for even the Sovereign to resist.' In any case, he added in a postscript, what Nesselrode resented far more than the British government's comments on Poland, was the fact that they were acting in concert with France on the issue. This was the nub of the matter. As Heytesbury (who was increasingly regarded by some of the Cabinet as 'apostolical') reminded Palmerston, whereas in 1815 Austria and Prussia had been willing to cooperate out of fear of Russia, 'France, not Russia is the bug-bear now' and 'to secure the support of Russia against France (that ambitious & restless Power, equally intriguing and encroaching under every form of Government) is the great object' of the other powers. Although he was specifically writing about Austria and Prussia, the ambassador might as well have been writing about Britain – at least until the Belgian issue was settled.

Palmerston told Heytesbury to remove from Nesselrode's mind the impression 'which seems to exist . . . that there is anything like a tendency in our Government to unite with France in a course of action unfriendly to Russia'. He cited his relationship of 'unreserved confidence' with the Lievens, adding that: 'the course of the Belgian negotiations . . . has been indeed calculated necessarily to throw England into intimate union with Russia' against France. What was not said here was pregnant with significance for the future of the Lieven embassy in London – namely that the 'intimate union' was necessary *only* while the future of Belgium was unresolved. Fortunately for Dorothea, if not for anyone else, the Belgian question dragged on through the whole of 1831 and into 1832.

The attempt to get the Prince of Orange accepted as a possible monarch had palpably failed by the spring of 1831. It left an embarrassing legacy for Princess Lieven. As bills began to be drawn on the money which the Princess of Orange had left in Dorothea's keeping, she demanded detailed accounts. Puzzled by this, Dorothea reminded her that the money had been remitted to her in order to help the cause of the House of Orange. Far from pacifying the Grand Duchess, this prompted her to write to her brother the Tsar accusing Dorothea of stealing half a million francs. Princess Lieven explained to Nesselrode what had happened, sending him the instructions she had received from the Grand Duchess. She was correspondingly relieved to hear from him that the Tsar's response had been to exclaim: 'My sister is mad!'

The length of time it took to resolve the Belgian problem is sufficient testimony to its intractable nature. Its central features remained unchanged by the events of 1831. On the one side was the Belgian National Convention which continued to accept those parts of '*les bases*' which suited it, and refused to recognize the rest. In this it was encouraged by the view that the French would prevent military intervention by the Holy Alliance powers. On the other side was the King of Holland, who until early 1832 remained of the opinion that the Belgians would end up back under his rule, either directly or through his son, the Prince of Orange. This view was strengthened by the Russian insistence that

'*les bases*' could come into operation only when he accepted the
independence of Belgium – which of course he was unlikely to
do as long as he thought he had Russian support in refusing to do.
However irritating Dutch stubbornness and Russian intransigence
were to Palmerston, they counted little in the balance against the
greater danger to be apprehended from an ambitious and restless
France. 'We should settle the matter in three weeks,' Palmerston
told Granville on 9 March, if the 'French Government would
make up their minds to act with good faith about Belgium . . . but
the men in power cannot make up their minds to be honest with
stoutness, or to play the rogue with boldness.' Because he was
willing to work with the Russians on this issue, this did not mean
that he was sympathetic to their point of view – and it was this
that Dorothea quite missed. Indeed, part of his impatience with
the French came from his fear of what might happen when the
Russians were no longer distracted by events in Poland. 'Might
they [the French] not be reminded that when the Russians have
reconquered Poland, which (were it not for the ill-concealed spirit
of aggrandizement of France) I should say I am *afraid* they will,
the tone of Russia about Belgium will be different from what it
has been.'

From Dorothea's point of view, despite the running sore of
Poland, her diplomacy was bearing fruit. Throughout the crisis in
Belgium, she praised Grey for the stout manner in which he
resisted all French pretensions. Conscious of Russia's inability to
intervene in the west because of Poland, the Russians looked to
the British to do what was necessary to keep the French at bay.
Whenever it looked as though they might be prepared to concede
a point to the French, Dorothea was vehement – and not very
subtle. Thus, when it was rumoured that the British might be
prepared to back the Prince of Naples rather than Leopold, she
expostulated: 'And is it England – who took the lead of the other
Powers in measures of precaution directed against France – who
is now going to support France?' Grey was content to act firmly
when it could be done. But he was too downy an old bird to be
caught by the Russian lime. He would act in Britain's interests,

and where they coincided with those of Russia, that was a good thing, but he would not be pushed into untenable positions – even by his Egeria. As he inquired pointedly: 'are you prepared to march 150,000 men to the Rhine without a subsidy?' They both knew the answer, but Dorothea was not deterred, and pushed the Dutch case strongly: 'To let the affair drag on seems an avowal of weakness quite unworthy of England. I reckon as much on your pride as on your wisdom. One must keep up one's dignity, in order to carry the point abroad, just as at home.' Privately (although given her propensity to gossip, the adjective must be used in a qualified way) she was 'greatly annoyed' by the 'pitiable cowardice of Lord Grey' and frustrated that 'our powerlessness for the moment' prevented Russia from taking a much tougher stand.

Grey, who was in the middle of the political crisis occasioned by his Reform Bill, was becoming weary of the whole Belgian affair. Dorothea thought that the reference to Belgium in the King's speech was 'most unseemly', since it talked about the 'right of the Belgian people to regulate their own internal affairs'. Grey told Dorothea that he was 'half inclined to withdraw altogether from the party, and leave you to settle all your Continental matters as you may'. Fearing that Grey intended to break up the conference and simply recognize Leopold of Saxe-Coburg as King of Belgium, the Princess sought out her old adversary, Wellington. She told him that this would make a breach between Britain and Russia through which the French might be able to make gains. Wellington made a speech in the Lords commending the government's Belgian policy thus far and urging a continuation of the London Conference. The Princess took Grey's continued commitment to the conference as a proof of her success. 'It will not be broken up and we shall keep England within bounds,' she wrote exultantly. She sent copies of Grey's letters to Nesselrode so that he would 'know Lord Grey – out of such details one can construct the whole. I am always on the best of terms with him . . . he listens when I am speaking.'

The result of this Anglo-Russian amity was that on 4 June the London Conference decided that Leopold should be King of

Belgium. On 27 June a new protocol was issued which gave Belgium more favourable boundaries and reduced the amount of the national debt she would have to pay. Such concessions disgusted Dorothea, who bitterly regretted Russia's inability to deal with the rebels as they deserved. Palmerston successfully used the possible threat of Russian involvement to persuade Leopold to accept the protocol of 27 June, while at the same time persuading the Russians to take a more moderate line by holding out the prospect of Britain having to work with France if the King of Holland proved obdurate.

Unfortunately, King William was obdurate. He refused to accept the new protocol and, on 2 August, his troops entered Belgium. The French responded by sending their army into Belgium, ostensibly to protect Leopold. Since Talleyrand had raised the idea of provoking a Dutch invasion as a 'pretext for marching foreign troops and introducing foreign armaments into the territories and ports of Belgium, and then dividing the Country among the powers', Palmerston naturally wondered whether this was the 'first step of the realization of this plot'. The fact that the French troops did not retire from Belgium once the Dutch had withdrawn their armies aroused all Palmerston's fears of France. On 11 August he told Granville to warn the French that: 'if this expectation should not be fulfilled, the French Government will be accused of bad faith in the whole transaction; and that . . . with the strongest desire to be friends with France and to preserve the peace of Europe, it is impossible to say what decisions we may be driven to take.' He warned him that the usual French defence of needing to satisfy their public opinion would not wash: 'they must remember that there is a public feeling in England as well.'

Palmerston's suspicions were confirmed when Talleyrand, in a rare unguarded moment, told the Prussian ambassador that the only permanent solution to the problem was 'partition'. If 'France, Prussia, and Holland united, the thing would be simple, and England must be contented with the making of Antwerp a free port'. Palmerston told Granville to warn the French of the dangers of pursuing this line. The whole issue of 'war or peace' hung on

the answer to the question: 'Will the French Government withdraw their troops . . . as soon as the Dutch have evacuated
Belgium?' When the French tried to attach conditions to any
agreement to withdraw their troops, Palmerston stepped up the
pressure, telling Granville on 17 August that: 'One thing is certain
– the French must go out of Belgium, or we have a general war,
and war in a given number of days.' This was music to Princess
Lieven's ears.

There were those, including the French, who wondered
whether Palmerston's tough line was not the result of his friendship
with the Princess. Talleyrand's illegitimate son, the Comte de
Flahaut, was unwise enough to complain to Grey (of all people)
about 'Russian petticoat influence'. It was easy enough to see why
such a suspicion should have arisen. Despite Palmerston's confident
comments to Granville about the state of opinion in England, it
was by no means certain that a majority of the Cabinet would have
supported his bellicose line. The Whig Cabinet was inclined to be
Francophile, and 'Belgian' simply on ideological grounds. Men
such as Holland, who had spent their lives mouthing platitudes
about 'the people' and 'revolution', would have welcomed the
partition of Belgium. Holland preached the need to understand
France and not to provoke a war by being too harsh. The Comte
de Flahaut was not slow to remind him that Palmerston had been
a Tory for most of his career, and again insinuated that Princess
Lieven seemed to have too great a say in his policy. Indeed,
although initially supporting Palmerston's high tone, Grey himself
came down in favour of a more moderate line, which consented
to discuss some of the French desiderata after they had agreed to
evacuate their troops. But although Grey had his way, and was
correct in thinking that the French would not try to push matters
too far, it proved a long and wearisome road towards anything like
a proper settlement of the Belgian question. This was at least in
part because the Russians continued to give their support to the
Dutch King.

For the moment, Palmerston continued to warn the French and
Belgians of the danger of Russian intervention (something that

became at least more probable after the suppression of the Polish revolt in the late summer); he also hinted to the Russians that too great an intractability on the part of the King of Holland might force England towards the French. On 14 October Palmerston persuaded the London Conference to modify *'les bases'*, replacing the eighteen articles with twenty-four, which were incorporated into a treaty on 15 November by which the great powers guaranteed that the settlement would be upheld. Although this treaty was slightly more favourable to the Dutch than its predecessor, both they and the Belgians initially rejected it; however, the latter, under pressure, finally agreed to it. The King of Holland, fortified still by Russian support, held out. As Palmerston put it to Heytesbury in exasperated tones on 16 January 1832 (so exasperated that, for once, he misdated the letter as '1831'): 'As long as the Emperor makes his Ratification depend upon the acceptance of the articles by the King of Holland, he might as well refuse it in plain terms.'

This was one of a number of signs of the change that was coming over Russian policy, and since it was to have a decisive effect on the career of Princess Lieven, it is worth describing it through the eyes of Heytesbury, who was one of the first observers to notice it. Writing on 17 December 1831, the ambassador warned: 'I see here so evident an approachment towards what is called the Old Russian Party, & old Russian Politics, that I cannot but point it out to your attention.' Alexander I, like Catherine before him, 'was enabled to impose silence upon his detractors & stifle the murmurs of the discontented at home' by 'the splendour of his European reputation & the respect and even national pride which that reputation engendered'. Nicholas I had followed the same course – until the French revolution of 1830 and the Belgian revolt. Before that date he had been treated as 'the Arbiter of the destinies of Europe', but since then: 'All his actions have been misconstrued, his power & influence have been denied & ridiculed, & his subjects have been incited to resistance & revolt, not secretly & insidiously, but openly & loudly, & as it were by a general Chorus from all the Presses & all the Tribunes of Europe.' This change did not go unnoticed: 'The Emperor saw that his position was altered, that his hold on Europe was gone – & that it was necessary for him to look for support elsewhere. Where was he to seek this but in his own People?' Heytesbury had noticed that Nicholas had 'turned away from his habitual advisers' to ask counsel of those he had formerly kept at a distance, and he feared that the harshness with which the Polish rebellion was being crushed was the first fruit of this change of orientation in Russian policy.

Those Nicholas was turning to were the 'Old Russians' who perpetually asked: 'Of what use to us are European connections?' They saw little purpose in interfering in 'affairs in which we have no immediate interest'. They looked to the West merely as a source of revolutionary contagion. They acknowledged that 'a general conflagration is preparing' but asked 'what will that signify to us?' Emboldened by the success against Napoleon in 1812, they could not believe that any foreign army would venture to attack Russia, and they took the view that 'the backwardness of our civilisation and the ignorance of our People secure us against the efforts of incendiaries.' From this 'Old Russian' perspective all that was needed was 'to keep well with our immediate neighbours' and to 'husband our resources & strengthen our means, whilst those of the rest of Europe are wasting'. Russian official policy would not change 'in an hour', and Heytesbury still hoped that something might happen to turn the Tsar back towards a more 'European' orientation, but the warning was there.

Had Palmerston but realized it, this was an immensely significant analysis of the changing situation. As we have seen, the arrival of the Lieven mission in London was part of the 'European' orientation of Russian policy, as indeed was the prominence in foreign affairs of the 'Baltic barons'. For all her insolence and arrogance towards Britain and the other great powers, indeed in these very qualities, Princess Lieven was part of the political elite that saw Russia as a European rather than an Asiatic power. She had been happy to see Russia gain a great reputation from her successful war against the Ottomans and thought that sufficient; she had not wanted to try to obtain vast grants of territory, seeing that this would have malign ramifications on Russia's place within the Concert of Europe. She, like the other 'Europeans', was happy that the other powers looked towards Russia to play an important role in the crises in Belgium and Portugal. When Grey and Palmerston were insufficiently attentive to Russian sensibilities over Poland, Dorothea tried to remind them of the need to be so in return for the advantages Britain gained from having Russia on her side.

For his part, although like Palmerston sympathetic to the Poles, Grey realized that Britain did gain weight in the Belgian crisis from being able to invoke the spectre of Russia before France's wilder flights of fantasy. So when the Princess asked him to alter the references to Poland in the King's speech to replace the phrase 'civil war' with 'civil struggle' in order to avoid giving the impression that the Poles were a separate nation 'at war' with Russia, he was happy enough to oblige by changing the second word to 'commotion'; there was no point in giving needless offence. But such gestures, while welcome, were no more than palliative in their effect. If one assumed that the Belgian question was the central issue in international politics, then Britain and Russia could be kept together, and however irritating the Russian encouragement of the Dutch King's intransigence, diplomatic contacts such as the Princess could be used to convince them of the damage that such a policy might inflict by giving opportunities to the French. Dorothea did make this assumption and was to carry on thinking that her job was to interpret the Whigs to Nesselrode and the Tsar and vice versa. If, however, the central issue in international politics became how to react to the wave of revolutions across Europe, Britain and Russia were unlikely to agree, and arguably the better they understood each other the more likely they were to disagree rather violently.

Grey's moderation over Poland in the King's speech hardly represented his or the government's real attitude towards Poland. Both he and Palmerston thought that the Russians were insufferably wrong-headed and were storing up trouble for themselves for the future. Towards the end of 1831 Palmerston made a renewed attempt through Heytesbury to impress his point of view on the Russians. It was a sign of the changing times that Nesselrode first received Heytesbury's recapitulation of Palmerston's familiar arguments with silence, and then 'he asked me, after a moment's pause, what advantage I proposed to myself – what advantage my Government proposed to itself – from a communication, of the inutility of which it must have been fully convinced by the previous explanations of Prince Lieven?' The more the British pressed their case, the more it irritated the Russians, who resented being preached at about Poland by a nation that suppressed Ireland at will. It was a dialogue of the deaf – and the question of whether interlocutors were necessary in such an exercise would soon be raised.

16. 'I am *Grey*'

Writing to Grey on 11 October 1831, Princess Lieven assured him that 'all will go well if England and Russia keep on good terms'; referring to rumours that she was beginning to show Tory predilections, she responded with a prettily turned compliment: 'I only display one colour – that is, yours. I am *Grey*.' She relied upon the British distrust of France to keep them in Russia's camp; but a combination of Palmerston's successes and the changing nature of Russian policy began to erode the Anglo-Russian alignment. Ironically, the very high tone that the Princess had so admired in Palmerston helped bring Britain and France closer, in so far as the French finally began to realize the limits of what the British would allow and observed them.

As it became clear that the prolongation of the Belgian crisis was not the result of French intrigues, Palmerston and Grey began to place the blame where it really belonged – on Russia's encouragement of Dutch obstinacy. In December, Grey's tone towards Dorothea started to change in proportion as he came to attribute the failure to make any breakthrough on Belgium to Russian influence. As the Dutch King continued to refuse to accept the treaty, Grey told the Princess: 'If he is encouraged to hold out, so much the worse for him, and for those who encourage him. I am told that you are of this number.' He hoped, he added, that this was not true, and professed himself unable to believe that it could be because: 'You have too much regard for me to do what would be distressing to me personally, and too much care for the interests of your country to force this Government into a close connection with France.' It was a clear enough indication of where Grey's policy was beginning to go, and the coolness between Britain and Russia that resulted was mirrored in his relations with Dorothea.

Several degrees of frost were added by Britain's response to the end of the Polish revolt.

As we have seen, Heytesbury was pressed in November and December to make representations to Russia about the importance Britain attached to Poland being granted a constitution. Russia's initial reaction convinced Grey that 'it is quite clear that Russia will overturn the constitution, and will reject all remonstrances', in which she would, he thought, be joined by Prussia and Austria – thus marking a drawing together of the old Holy Alliance powers. The question was: 'However much . . . we may be in the right . . . whether we are bound to take any measure, which we have no means that I can see of enforcing.' He allowed Palmerston to make the case once more, but doubted it 'doing much good' since he believed that 'the Emperor neither can nor dare do what we suggest.' Grey was right to think that 'everything we propose will be rejected.' He then proceeded to make a bad situation worse.

In his letter warning the Princess of the likely consequences of continuing to support the obstinacy of the King of Holland, Grey indicated that the leader of the Polish revolt, Prince Adam Czartoryski (the former adviser to Alexander I and the lover of his wife), was arriving in Britain. Dorothea reacted with a fury she did not bother to conceal. On the first point, she protested that: 'You invest me with an influence and an importance that is both curious and novel.' She professed to be unable to understand his reasoning: 'Why should the non-ratification of one of the four Powers throw you into the arms of France? Your inclination must indeed be great if so trifling an incident could entail so grave a decision.' Personal infidelity was one thing, its political equivalent quite another. She could not believe that England, the 'ancient and puissant upholder of order and tranquillity in Europe', would make 'common cause with a revolutionary Power'. She reminded Grey 'that France has ever been the enemy of England'; but 'truisms do not gain by mere repetition. My dear lord, do you really think I can believe you when you thus threaten me?' To believe what he said: 'I should have to forget that you were an Englishman, a clever man, and what I have always believed heretofore, a great statesman.' As for Czartoryski: 'The intention is certainly not flattering to me, but you have not made me angry my dear lord, for I have long ceased to be irritated on this subject.' Russia, she told him in peremptory manner, 'fears no one'. Grey attempted to turn aside her wrath by refusing to engage with her 'angry letter', adding that he was sure that 'upon reflection you would find that you had been unjust.' That he could entertain such an idea showed how little he understood her. Dorothea was about to lose her temper.

The great explosion was set off by a casual mention in the last paragraph of Grey's first letter of 1832 that Czartoryski had dined with him the previous day: 'I cannot express to you,' he said with the folly of a man inviting a mauling, 'how much I feel for him. This feeling you ought not to object to and I think you will not.' He went even further when he added: 'It is impossible that you should not have it yourself.' Quite what game Grey was playing it is difficult to know. The solipsistic nature of the English liberal mind is legendary, but even in the pure form embodied by Grey, it ought to have realized that the Russians were unlikely to share what he 'felt' for the man who had been responsible for the death of so many of their soldiers. Any such notion was banished upon receipt of Princess Lieven's letter, which must rank high among the most imperious ever received by a British Prime Minister from the wife of a foreign ambassador. She told him coldly that Prince Lieven would be making a formal representation on the matter to Palmerston, but that for her part she was horrified that his 'humane' commiseration with Czartoryski should have led him to let such a man dine at his table – a man whom the Russians regarded as 'a State criminal', who had been 'convicted of high treason against his Sovereign', who was, after all, Britain's ally. In letting his 'pity' for the Pole predominate, Grey had, she wrote icily: 'lost sight of this, namely, that a statesman is responsible to the public for his several acts' and that 'it is neither sympathy nor affection that ought to dictate his line of conduct.' He should have realized that Russia would take his action as an insult: 'When Lord Grey is Premier of England, Lord Grey as a private person ceases to exist. Your actions are now those of England.' She was, she added, 'more amazed than I can express that this view of the matter should not have represented itself to your mind'.

Grey received Lieven's formal protest through Palmerston on 4 January. He had never, he told the Foreign Secretary, 'read anything with greater astonishment. It is really too much for a Foreign Minister to interfere with respect to the private society which any member of the Government to which he is accredited, may think fit to cultivate.' Grey thought it unnecessary and unbecoming to offer an official explanation of his actions, but the fact that he went into some detail to explain himself to Palmerston is indication enough of an uneasy conscience. Here, at least, his correspondence with Dorothea offered an unofficial way out of the imbroglio. He would, he told her, be inclined not to receive such a protest from any other ambassador, nor would he reply to it: 'But to *you* I cannot write in such a harsh and peremptory tone.' After recapitulating the way in which Britain had not joined with those who wanted to make capital out of Russia's misfortunes, Grey explained that in receiving Czartoryski he had acted purely in a private capacity out of courteousness: 'And it is this,' he protested, 'that is magnified into a hostile proceeding, the first that Russia has received from England during the long course of nineteen years!'

Privately, Dorothea thought that 'all this fuss is the result of sheer stupidity and ignorance of good manners. The English learn Latin – but they don't learn the art of living.' In a telling example of what she considered 'good manners', Dorothea responded to Grey's olive branch by subjecting it to a withering examination. Proclaiming her desire to 'drop a disagreeable discussion', she could not do so, considering that 'in the present instance I am the party complaining and aggrieved'; however, in deference to her feelings for Grey, she would, she wrote, 'content myself with merely offering some brief observations on the subject of your last letter'. If nearly a dozen pages could be described as 'brief', then Grey should have counted himself lucky that she did not expatiate at length.

Dorothea's mode of argument was simple and, from one point

of view, effective; she repeated herself several times and with greater vehemence, as though under the impression that the duller wits of her interlocutor might, as by a process of osmosis, absorb the essence of her case. So here, she reiterated the case against receiving Czartoryski. She admitted that 'heretofore we have never had to complain of any want of consideration arising from unfriendly feeling on the part of the British Government', but made the point (in answer to Grey's insinuation) that while Wellington's government had been 'hostile' to Russia over the Turkish war, 'still he never showed any lack of courtesy towards our Emperor'. This led her to inquire why, since no discourtesy had been shown at a time when relations between Russia and Britain had been bad, 'should we meet with unfriendliness when the politics of the two nations are in perfect accord'. She bent as far as admitting that Grey's behaviour during the time of the Polish revolt had been impeccable: 'You know well how sincerely grateful I have been to you for all this, and it is precisely for this reason that my vexation has been the greater at seeing you depart from the judicious line of conduct you had hitherto adopted.' She finished by expressing her 'earnest hope that this disagreeable discussion may be finished'. The disadvantage of treating one's interlocutor in such a fashion is that, while it gets the point over, its impact is lessened in proportion to the irritation induced.

Grey kept his temper, but Dorothea's wish that she should have the last words on the subject was not granted. Writing, again at length, on 6 January 1832, Grey refuted her arguments with six well-honed ones of his own, the most telling of which was that it should be possible to 'reconcile personal regard with a dissent from personal conduct'. He asked whether she would prefer 'a hostile policy' accompanied by 'external regard, or a friendly policy, which has been uniform and faithful, with such a proceeding as you think it right to complain of'. He was, he told her, glad that she acknowledged that 'my conduct towards Russia has been uniform and friendly. This experience, and some knowledge of my character ought, I think, to have protected me against such a complaint as was made against me.' She was, she responded, 'not in the slightest degree convinced by any argument contained in your letter', and could, she wrote, have refuted them all had she cared; however, she preferred to adopt the advice of her old nurse: 'the least at fault should bring the quarrel to a close.' And there, for the moment, the squabble ended.

At one level what had happened was no more than a lovers' tiff translated into the world of diplomacy, but the gap it revealed was one that would swallow up the Lieven embassy. On the one side was Russia, a curious mixture of self-confidence and insecurity; the long period of dominance, success and admiration since 1815 suddenly succeeded by this time of revolution and military uncertainty. It had taken the Russians a great deal of effort to put down the Polish rebellion, and they were, as they knew, powerless to do anything about the threat of revolution elsewhere; nor could they expect any sympathy from those western powers in whose interests Russia had (as it was seen from St Petersburg) defeated and contained the French Revolution. On the other side was a Whig government which had been pulled into a 'Russian' policy on Belgium because of the anti-French instincts of Palmerston and Grey, but which was beginning to find its feet diplomatically, and whose instincts were to support liberalism everywhere – except in those places where it might give the French room for territorial aggrandizement. Even this last point was hardly universal in a Cabinet containing Francophiles such as Lord Holland.

As the Belgian negotiations slowed to a crawl at the end of 1831, Palmerston continued to hold out against the idea that the French should have any say in which of the Belgian frontier fortresses should be dismantled. These had been erected after Vienna as a means of defending the Low Countries from French invasion, and throughout the year the French had argued that they should be consulted if they were to be dismantled. This aroused all Palmerston's suspicions, and he consistently refused to let the French in on what was, he insisted, a negotiation between Britain, Holland and Belgium.

Lord Holland was not the only member of the Cabinet who found Palmerston's conduct, and the secrecy with which he concealed the negotiations from the French, deplorable. He had 'unconquerable repugnance' for the idea that Britain and France might end up at war over the question. Palmerston's response to Holland's protests was to make it plain that he would not 'truckle to France'. Holland's position was in the Whig tradition, Palmerston's was not. He was not slow to find an explanation for Palmerston's policy – namely 'his renewed intimacy with Lady Cowper and her incredible and unaccountable subservience to Mme de Lieven'. He hoped that the Russian refusal to ratify the November treaty might 'estrange Palmerston from Russian counsels, especially if it be true that Princess Lieven had intelligence of the refusal to ratify before her husband and was more rejoiced than chagrined at it'. Prince Lieven was, Holland wrote, 'a plain man' but the Princess was 'unquestionably more Antigallican than he and seems to have imbibed much of the Ultra spirit.'

It was Holland's last observation that pointed to the cause of the growing gap between the Princess and her British admirers. Dorothea had, indeed, imbibed the 'Ultra' view prevalent in St Petersburg. An autocrat to her soul, she detested the idea of 'revolution' and regarded the notion that 'the people' had any political rights with extreme distaste. The world was, from her point of view, a singularly well-ordered one, and her only desire was to preserve it. From that angle she was fortunate in being a Russian, and she took considerable pride in the role Russia played as the gendarme of Europe. Like all 'Ultras', she regarded France as the incarnation of all the evils of revolution, and it was with some dismay that she discerned a shift in British policy: 'France and England are coquetting together, and Lord Grey's surroundings are distinctly democratic. He is weak and easily led, so everything is not going on well.'

As Dorothea watched the crisis over the Reform Bill reach one of its peaks, with Grey threatening to ask the King to create enough Peers to pass it, she shuddered at the radical direction in which he appeared to be going. Her friends in the Cabinet were among the 'moderates', she told her brother Alexander, but she feared the influence of the 'extremists' – that is most of the Cabinet.

There was a correlation between the position taken up on reform and on the Belgian issue; the extremists 'are in favour of an alliance with France'. Her fear was that Grey was being 'led' by his son-in-law, the earl of Durham, or 'Radical Jack' as he was known. In fact, regardless of Durham's influence, Grey was beginning to lose patience with the Russians because of the part they were playing in encouraging the Dutch King's attitude of defiance. On 1 January Grey had written to his Lord Chancellor, Brougham, that the Russians were 'doing all they can to throw the whole Belgian affair into confusion. It is,' he commented acidly, 'to be regretted that we had no power of sending a fleet into the Baltic last summer to settle the matter of Poland.' Even making allowance for the irritation produced by Princess Lieven's lectures, such a tone hardly suggests that Grey's protestations of sincere friendship for Russia were an accurate reflection of the way his mind was moving.

The rumour that the Princess had known about the Tsar's refusal to ratify the treaty without the consent of the King of Holland was a half-truth, and Grey had been closer to the whole when he had suspected that she was among those who were happy that the King had refused to ratify it. This was because when the Tsar discovered what was in the treaty Lieven had put his name to he was furious, and all that the ambassador and Nesselrode could do was to cower before the storm and hope that it would pass over without doing them too much damage. Precisely because he still distrusted the French, Palmerston contained his own growing frustration with the Russians and agreed to postpone the ratification of the Belgian treaty until the end of January, as Lieven had requested; this was in order to give time for the Tsar's formal instructions to arrive. Lieven had actually asked for a delay of six weeks, but Palmerston feared that would 'have looked like giving up the Treaty altogether'.

Palmerston warned Heytesbury to tell Nesselrode that if the ratification had not taken place by 31 January, 'England and France will ratify without the other Three' and that this 'must be considered as an alliance defensive or offensive between France, England and Belgium to carry into effect the treaty of November against whoever may oppose it'. Palmerston was signalling his willingness to keep the Concert of Europe together, but not at any cost. If the Russians delayed any longer they would find they had conjured up exactly the diplomatic combination they feared most. Grey pressed Dorothea to secure a Russian ratification of the treaty, dangling before her the spectre of an Anglo–French alliance. She was alarmed enough to warn the Tsar, through her brother, that if Russia continued to take up the cause of the Dutch King 'we shall lose England, who, unwilling to remain without allies, will throw herself into the arms of France, and Europe will be handed over to the influence of these two Liberal Powers, and then – we shall see what we shall see.' Even before Palmerston's warning had been delivered, the Tsar had sent his special envoy, Count Orlov, on a mission to The Hague to discover how the Dutch King could be brought to agree to the treaty. Nesselrode told Heytesbury that he remained committed to that 'intimate union between England and Russia upon which the peace of the world so mainly depended'.

But for all Nesselrode's assurances that King William of Holland could no longer look to Russia for support, there was no movement from The Hague. However, although Britain and France ratified the treaty, Palmerston did not carry through his threat, and held back from executing the terms of the treaty while Orlov got on with his mission. Unfortunately for Palmerston's temper, Orlov moved exceedingly slowly and failed to work wonders, but his presence at The Hague at least averted an Anglo–French alliance – although there was much talk of it on the British side. When Heytesbury pressed Nesselrode in early February for an answer to the question of whether, in the event of Orlov's mission failing, 'you will not ratify the Belgian Treaty without the consent of the King of the Netherlands', the Russian did 'not deny that' and said that in that event 'a new era will then commence. "*Alors, nous verrons.*"' This, as Heytesbury complained, was 'no answer at all'. But the Russians, despite Dorothea's warnings, declined to believe that 'England would separate herself from her old Allies upon a question of mere form'.

It is an indication of how much Palmerston distrusted the French, and how much he was able to control the direction of British foreign policy that, despite the continuous delays from Orlov, he remained committed to working with the Russians to resolve the Belgian crisis. He authorized Heytesbury to tell Nesselrode that the French foreign minister, Casimir Périer, had been talking about the inevitability of an Anglo-French alliance if the three Eastern powers would not ratify the treaty. The Russians expressed their gratitude for this revelation, which Nesselrode took as 'a proof of the friendly feeling of the British Government', but he advised Heytesbury that the French ambassador in St Petersburg was always 'speaking of Russia as the natural ally of France'. As time wasted away, with both the Dutch and Belgians spending a fortune on their armies, and British trade through Antwerp being disrupted, Palmerston's frustration with his allies rose to new heights. 'It is,' he told Heytesbury on 15 March, 'now five months since the Treaty was signed . . . the true and only obstacle to a settlement is *Russia*.'

For a brief moment in early April, Palmerston's hopes rose as he heard that Metternich and the Prussians had agreed to ratify the treaty, but they sank back again on being told that the Prussian ratification depended upon that of Russia – which had still not been given. He was somewhat soothed by assurances from Orlov, to whom he had taken, that the Russian ratification would turn up within a couple of weeks, and that the delay had nothing to do with the hope that the Whigs might go out of office if their Reform Bill was defeated, 'but arises entirely out of the Emperor's personal feelings towards the King of the Netherlands'. But in the meantime, he told Granville, 'Metternich has made April fools of us.' However, he reflected, 'Metternich leads, & thinks, & acts, though generally upon mistaken Principles, still he is a man of talent and a leader.' It seemed somehow inevitable that when the Russian ratification of the treaty was finally given in late April, it should depend upon the Dutch King being satisfied on various details still in dispute.

What these later stages of the crisis demonstrated was the extent to which Austria and Prussia were prepared to follow Russia's lead. Although inclined to do so, Palmerston thought they were perhaps 'not wholly to blame for pursuing a course that has in it little of that high-minded sense of National Dignity which ought to belong to Rulers of First Rate European States'; he sensed that the 'circumstances of Europe may make them fancy that a close connection with Russia may be essential for their safety'. But in drawing the autocratic powers together against the threat of revolution, Russia had, in Palmerston's view, 'split up the Alliance' and 'suspended' if not destroyed the London Conference, while simultaneously running 'the risk of bringing on that very danger of war which she has professed to have been no less anxious than we are to avert'.

Palmerston began to suspect that the Russians were dragging their feet in the hope that the Reform Bill crisis would see the Whigs out of office soon. He was aware of connections between the Dutch and the opposition, and he and Grey knew that Aberdeen and Wellington were being primed with information designed to embarrass the government in the Commons, but by March he had become convinced that there was a direct link between the crisis over the Reform Bill and the Russians dragging their feet over Belgium: 'the fact is it is all a miserable intrigue between the D. of Wellington & Metternich, & the D. of Cumberland & the Prussian Princes.' He told Lady Cowper's brother, Frederick Lamb, the ambassador in Vienna, that 'I have long had an instinctive contempt of these arbitrary Cabinets, but it is only of late that I have learnt how just this sentiment has been.'

The fraying of the Anglo-Russian alliance was not all on one side. The Russians regarded the incessant hints about a possible Anglo-French alliance as an attempt to 'menace' them, and Nesselrode told Heytesbury in April that it was precisely the Emperor's displeasure at the 'peremptory tone' of the British that had made him hesitate again before consenting to ratify a treaty that he had always disliked. Heytesbury, whose despatches deserve a better fate than to languish unread in the archives, thought that half the difficulty was that 'there are here two different Powers almost always in separate action.' On one side was the 'headstrong spirit of the Emperor, carried away by first impressions, & acting upon opinions based upon some abstract principle of honour', which not infrequently led to 'decisions at variance with those which sound reason & good policy would suggest'. On the other side was 'the slower march of the Ministers, seeing things in a soberer point of view, and undermining & circumventing by insinuation & persuasion their Master's first hasty determination'.

An acute observer, Heytesbury warned of the 'expediency of soothing these people'. Tsar Nicholas was coming very close to saying that 'thrown off by Europe, he would also throw off Europe'; this would be to play into the hands of the 'Old Russian Party', which was constantly counselling him in just that direction. Heytesbury did not believe that such a state of affairs would be good for either Britain or Russia: 'we want Russia, not as a preponderating, but as a make-weight Power, & we could hardly afford that she should be thrown, or that she should throw herself, out of the scale.' Even Nesselrode, who rarely spoke outside his brief, had been bold enough to speak 'very confidentially' on the dangers of Russia retreating into isolation, mindful, of course, that 'a change of policy' would lead to a 'change of persons'.

For Dorothea, the personal *was* political, and so it was not surprising that her relationship with Grey declined as Anglo-Russian relations deteriorated. By May 1832, with the Reform Bill on the way to the statute book, it was clear that Grey and his administration would survive. She reflected gloomily to her brother Alexander that: 'It's a poor Government, but God knows if others would make a better, one must put up with what one cannot alter, and try to make the best of things until circumstances open up another course.' She knew her duty: 'I believe that to remain on good terms, with some reserve, with England, is the best way of keeping the rest of Europe in peace and in order. For this reason, until I receive notice, which I beseech you to communicate to me, I shall continue to cultivate Lord Grey, although he bores me not a little.' Realizing that she had seen very little of Grey during the spring and early summer, Dorothea attempted to revive their correspondence. On 1 May she wrote to him again: 'I am quite annoyed at seeing that you no longer think of me.' Writing infrequently had the advantage of concealing the extent to which relations were breaking down; more frequent communication would do the opposite.

Grey's inability or unwillingness to contrive a casual or private meeting irritated Dorothea, who was reduced to trying to persuade him in writing that the Russian terms for ratifying the Belgian treaty were better than he thought. She saw no reason why Russia's reservations should not be kept secret, and chided Grey for continuing to delay matters. His response was terse: 'Ask your own conscience to whose fault it is owing that this has not been done long ago.' When the final ratification took place on 4 May, the Princess wrote to congratulate Grey and Palmerston on their achievement: 'it restores Europe to its equilibrium. Let England and Russia only keep well together, and the peace of Europe will not be disturbed.' But as the state of her relationship with Grey revealed, the task of keeping the two countries together was a wearing one – and the ties that bound them were beginning to fray.

17. 'Palmerston is a mule'

In an attempt to persuade the Tsar to accept the need to use coercion against the Dutch if they continued to reject the Belgian treaty, Grey hit upon the bright idea of sending his son-in-law, the earl of Durham, on a special mission to St Petersburg. Heytesbury was tired, unwell and anxious to return home, so the notion seemed a good one. Durham himself was a considerable thorn in the side of his father-in-law. One of the richest men in the country, 'Radical Jack' Lambton fancied himself a champion of 'the people'; not, it might have been thought, the best qualification for an embassy to Russia. Princess Lieven, who was told about the idea only after Grey had already decided upon it, was diplomatically cautious in her response: 'Your letter gave me a surprise . . . They will wonder at it much in Russia.' In private, she confessed that: 'his mission torments me.' Durham was 'the haughtiest aristocrat', and was 'cordially and universally disliked'. King William IV had told her, with relief: 'Thank God, we've got rid of him for some months' – to which Dorothea had replied: 'That is all very well, Sire, but why should it be at our expense?' Dorothea advised her brother, Alexander, to play on Durham's very considerable vanity. A concerted attempt at St Petersburg to flatter him might pay enormous dividends: given the influence Durham had over Grey, if the Tsar could win him over 'he may, through Lord Durham, direct the policy of the English Cabinet.'

But even as Princess Lieven was looking to the politics of the personal to help restore Anglo-Russian relations, the harsh tones of the Commons burst in to help further sour them. Palmerston had successfully resisted an attempt in April 1832 to raise a debate on the issue of Poland, but in late June he was unable to repeat this feat. The Liberal side of the House was unrestrained – and very personal – in its abuse of Russia. Daniel O'Connell, the Irish

leader, called Nicholas 'a miscreant', while the Radical Joseph
Hume said that he was 'a monster in human shape'. The Princess
protested to Grey about such language, and about Palmerston's
'silence' in response. In a sarcastic aside to her brother, she wrote
of the 'sotte position de Palmerston' who, accused in public of
being a 'Russian tool', had said not a word in reply. In fact,
Palmerston had deprecated the language used by those MPs
who had criticized Nicholas I, but not in a manner that satisfied
Dorothea. She told Grey that she feared lest the report of the
debate should create difficulties in St Petersburg for Durham, and
wondered whether he could not say something in the Lords to
make amends for Palmerston's slowness. Grey did his best on
3 July, and the Princess expressed her thanks – and so Durham
went off to St Petersburg sure of a warm welcome.

Whatever doubts the Princess had about the wisdom of
Durham's mission, her tactic of urging that he should be accorded
every honour that flattery could devise paid dividends. Tiresome
though Durham could be, he had been devoted to his wife, Grey's
daughter, and her recent death had left both men bereft. Indeed,
part of Grey's motive in sending him to Russia seems to have been
to take his mind off his grief; it was wise counsel that Dorothea
gave to her masters in St Petersburg – and they heeded it well.
Those who had expected that the great radical and champion of
the Poles would strike at the heart of the tsarist autocracy found
themselves profoundly disappointed. Durham was fêted and flattered wherever he went, given unprecedented access to the Tsar,
and courted at every move. In return he peddled Palmerston's line
that in seeming to support liberal movements in Belgium, Portugal
and elsewhere, the British were simply encouraging them to look
to the more conservative British than to revolutionary France. And
he explained, yet again, why it was so important to solve the
Belgian crisis, and why it was impossible for the British to take the
line on Poland that the Russians might want.

Durham came back from Russia in October thoroughly im-
bued with the idea that what mattered in foreign policy was an
identity of interests, not of ideology. As Palmerston commented

to Granville drily: 'Between you and I, Durham was thoroughly bamboozled by the Emperor and Nesselrode.' Dorothea was delighted, telling Wellington that the Russians had bathed Durham in politeness, and he had responded by raising no difficult questions at all: 'et voilà son *importante* mission terminée.' She was profuse in her compliments to Grey, telling him that Nesselrode and company wanted to know, 'Is Lord Grey satisfied? For it is he whom we have always in mind in all we do to show consideration for his son-in-law and daughter.'

Basking in this praise and in the success of his initiative, Grey returned to his old theme of trying to remove one of the major obstacles in the way of good relations with Russia: 'if something could be done to mitigate the condition of the poor Poles, what satisfaction it would give to this country and to Europe.' It was an interesting commentary on Durham's mission that he had decided against raising the Polish issue. Dorothea responded to Grey's attempts to do so by diplomatically ignoring them; it was an issue that would always generate far more heat than light.

Despite the slightly dismissive tone of her comment to Wellington, Dorothea had great hopes of the Durham mission. On her advice, Nesselrode suggested to Durham that he should return to London via the other major courts of Europe, a suggestion which, naturally, she supported when offering Grey advice on the matter at the end of August: there would be everything to be gained 'both for the public and for his own advantage'. Grey favoured the idea, and thought it useful not only that Durham should meet men such as Metternich and be able to report back on his impressions of Vienna and Berlin, but also that 'he should have an opportunity of convincing them that this Whig Administration is no friend of agitators and revolutionaries.' The danger in this arrangement was spotted by the ambassador in Vienna, Emily Cowper's brother, Fred Lamb, who warned Palmerston against erecting a rival to himself: 'may it not be inconvenient to you to sit in a Cabinet with a man arriving with all the Sovereigns of Europe in his pocket?' It was likely, Lamb warned, that Durham's views would coincide with those of the continental powers: 'Now if you, not having the support of the reformers at home, lose that of the European Powers, and consequently that of the King, where will be your strength?'

Nor was it only to Lamb that this idea had occurred. Princess Lieven wrote to Nesselrode on 1 October telling him that she would use his letter of praise for Durham to good advantage against Palmerston. Grey and Palmerston 'detest each other', she told Nesselrode, and this should allow her to use Durham 'in every case in which Palmerston's actions do not suit us and he will always be on our side when it is a question of condemning the other's conduct'. Palmerston's feebleness over Poland had finally convinced Dorothea that although he was a '*bon enfant*', the 'inconvenience of his Liberal principles and obstinate character are very great and we would see him go without regret'. For all the passages of arms she had had with Grey, who was 'as Liberal and vain' as Palmerston, he was 'flexible and his opinion can be easily changed. Palmerston is a mule.'

The reasons for Dorothea's disenchantment with Palmerston were various, but added up to the fact that having once seemed very willing to seek and take her advice, he did so no longer. As the Belgian crisis entered a new phase, Palmerston seemed increasingly inclined to side with the French in insisting that the treaty should be imposed on Holland, by force if necessary. He told Dorothea in late September that he did not see the crisis in the pessimistic way that she did and thought that it could be brought to a close successfully. But he wondered why Russia, the power with the most interest in curbing France's pretensions, insisted on placing Belgium in a position where it would need French military help. There was no doubting from his tone that he would work with France if necessary, if only because it might be the only way of exercising any control over her. The difference between Britain and Russia was not, Palmerston told her, a great one: 'vous dîtes, restons unis, et moi, je dis, marchons ensemble' ['you say, stay united, I say let us move on together']. Dorothea was not convinced, and his willingness to ally with France confirmed her low opinion of her former protégé: 'Lord Palmerston

is a poor, small-minded creature, wounded in his vanity [by
the Durham mission], who wants a great warlike demonstration
behind which he hopes to conceal his blunders.' She hoped to be
able to use Durham to circumvent Palmerston's policy – and perhaps to replace him. Neumann, the Austrian ambassador, warned
Metternich that the Princess was spending a good deal of time
down in Brighton, trying to stir up the King against Palmerston as
part of her campaign to displace him.

Dorothea was, as we have seen, all too prone to personalize her
politics, but in taking up the cause of Durham as she did, she
had effectively declared war on Palmerston. She relied upon her
influence with Grey, and Grey's feelings for his son-in-law, to aid
her cause. But her irritation with Palmerston led her to make the
fatal mistake of underestimating him. Palmerston recognized the
dangers outlined by Fred Lamb, but told him that he was not afraid
of Durham: 'he has no influence in Cabinet except upon Grey . . .
But I am strong enough with Grey & with my other colleagues
not to fear Durham.' Indeed, he managed to deflect Durham from
the idea of going to Austria, and did everything he could to
neutralize him upon his return. If the Princess wished to play
at diplomatic hazard with Palmerston, he was well equipped to
respond.

Back in early 1831, Heytesbury had indicated his wish to retire
from his onerous duties in St Petersburg, and Palmerston had
suggested that Stratford Canning might be a suitable replacement.
There were strong personal and political grounds for making such
an appointment: in the first instance Palmerston owed a debt to
George Canning, and Stratford had been a member of that small
group of Canningites to which he had belonged in the period after
1827; secondly, as a senior diplomat with considerable knowledge
of the Eastern Question and of Greece in particular, he was eminently well qualified for the post, and might, Palmerston thought,
be preferable in the minds of the Russians to 'a Whig Peer of
highly radical notions'. Princess Lieven told Nesselrode on 19 April
1831 that, although Canning would be 'difficile et désagréable', he
would be less so under a minister as friendly as Palmerston. But as

her opinion of Palmerston changed, so did her views on the advisability of Stratford Canning. Nesselrode had been hostile to the idea at the time, and he pressed Dorothea to put pressure on Palmerston to abandon it, but she argued that she must not get into too close a relationship with Palmerston lest she arouse Grey's jealousy. Palmerston urged Heytesbury to stay on, but by June 1832 even the most earnest entreaties failed, and it was agreed that he should return to England. Durham's special mission averted, for the moment, the question of his successor. It was a sign of the success of Nesselrode's treatment of Durham that he was able to persuade him to prevent Canning being nominated as Heytesbury's successor. It was around this question that the duel would be fought.

Although the issue of the succession to the St Petersburg embassy would be the occasion for a pitched battle between Dorothea and Palmerston, it was not its prime cause. The Princess wanted to be rid of Palmerston because she had concluded from his conduct over the Belgian crisis that he was now an apostle of cooperation with France. Durham had not made much of a case in St Petersburg for persuading the Russians of the virtue of the British argument that the Dutch might need to be coerced into accepting the treaty of the previous November. Grey told the Princess that unless the Russians agreed to take a 'firm tone', the crisis would never be settled. She stoutly denied his allegations, protesting that 'it was not *we* who have spoilt matters by showing any partiality for Holland', but rather the 'disfavour shown by England'. Dorothea sought to poison the wells with Grey by telling him that: 'from all sides I hear how extraordinarily suspicious Lord Palmerston is of Russia, attributing to us all the blame for the resistance Holland is now making. Lord Durham,' she added pointedly, 'knows the Emperor's views . . . why do they not wait and hear him, and learn from him what are his impressions on Russian politics?' Whatever her role in getting Palmerston appointed, Princess Lieven was now trying to get him removed; but she overestimated her influence with Grey – this time fatally.

Grey had become convinced that the Russians were acting in

'bad faith' over the Belgian question. He told Palmerston on 1 July 1832 that 'as it is now clear that we can now expect no sincere and effective cooperation from them [the Russians], we must take measures in conjunction with France to bring this to a conclusion.' This hardly put Grey in the mood to listen to any representations from the Russians on the subject of Canning's possible appointment as ambassador. He urged Palmerston at the end of September to use 'very firm language' with St Petersburg, adding that 'the sooner Stratford Canning can go, the better.' On the other side, Durham weighed in, trying to persuade his father-in-law to withdraw Canning's name, as did Dorothea. Grey was puzzled, asking Palmerston: 'Do you know the cause of this opposition to which I do not feel at all inclined to give way?' On 22 October the British signed a treaty with the French providing for military cooperation against the Dutch if they did not withdraw all their troops from Belgium by 12 November. On 30 October the *London Gazette* carried the news that the King had approved the appointment of Sir Stratford Canning as British ambassador to St Petersburg.

Dorothea was furious at what she perceived as a direct insult. Writing to Nesselrode on 1 November, she was 'scandalised' at the 'impudence' of Palmerston in officially putting forward Canning's nomination. She forwarded him a letter which Durham had sent her in which he said that the first he had known of the appointment was from the newspapers; he had, he wrote, done his best to make the case against Canning. Nor was it only Durham who treated the matter as a personal insult – her own husband, she told Nesselrode, usually so phlegmatic, was furious. She urged Nesselrode to 'teach these islanders manners' by refusing to accept the nomination; after all Canning would never become a Cabinet minister, since he could hardly speak in the Commons. It was not in her nature to confine such emotions merely to paper, and even Grey, who had some considerable experience of her behaviour, wrote that he had never seen her 'so montée'; as it turned out, he had, as they say, seen nothing yet.

The duel between Palmerston and Princess Lieven was one between two ill-matched antagonists: the one was armoured with an unshakeable belief in his own will, and all the power of the British Foreign Office; the other, despite an equally unshakeable will, stood on less solid ground. Wellington had always hesitated to demand her removal, knowing, as he did, that she had powerful protectors at home. Palmerston cared nothing for this. The woman had put herself at his mercy, and like many of her sisters, Dorothea was to find it an uncomfortable place. Hearing from Grey and from Lady Cowper that Dorothea was telling all and sundry that he had promised that Canning would not be nominated, Palmerston wrote to her on 4 November to deny this. He told her bluntly that he knew that because of his attitude 'dans la position où se trouvent des Questions plus Importantes, vous soyez disposée à me chercher querelle' [on more important matters she was seeking a quarrel with him], but he relied upon her 'jugement éclairé' and 'esprit d'équité' to help her to realize, when the political waves subsided, that he was doing no more than his duty. If his last sentences were an attempt at an olive branch, Dorothea broke it and flung it back in his face. The 'political waves' to which he referred, she told him, were not of her making; she had not sought out a quarrel, she said, but had been offered one by his actions; as for the other matters he referred to, she left them, she said, to her husband.

Whatever emotions were prompted by the tone of Dorothea's letter, her last comment must have raised an eyebrow or two. With their knowledge of how the Princess had behaved during Wellington's premiership, neither Grey nor Palmerston was disposed to let her have her way on this question, although it is unlikely that, at this stage, they realized that she had gone so far as to tell Nesselrode to refuse the nomination. The fact that the Princess was up to her old trick of meddling in British politics by trying to replace Palmerston with Durham simply made the former more determined to carry his point. Palmerston was a man of imperious will, and he made it clear to St Petersburg that it should be understood that 'the King of England is the best judge of whom it may be for the good of his service to employ . . . and that we cannot allow any foreign authority to dictate to us on such matters or to *taboo* our best men *merely because* they are so.' He told Grey firmly that when Dorothea claimed to have had a promise from him not to nominate Canning, 'she exercises largely the privilege which belongs to her in her double capacity of a lady and a diplomatist, namely the privilege of fibbing.' He was sure, he told the Prime Minister, that there were 'more important matters' behind this: 'The Holy Alliance really want to ride us rather too hard; but the Russian branch of it, is so angry with us at present, for what we are doing about Belgium, that they are glad to fasten upon any collateral topic, and to vent upon it, the wrath which belongs chiefly to more important matters.'

Palmerston was correct to think that the British decision to work with the French to coerce the King of Holland had excited the wrath of the Russians, but he underestimated Dorothea's stubbornness by some degree. In December Prince Lieven let Grey know that the Tsar was prepared to offer Canning one of the chief Orders of the Russian Empire if the nomination were withdrawn. Grey told Palmerston that this hardly accorded with the Russian line that Canning was in some way personally objectionable to the Tsar, and that he was not inclined to give way: 'I should be very sorry indeed,' he added, 'if this silly quarrel were to end in their being recalled, but I don't see the possibility of yielding to such a proposal.'

It was not only Grey who had come to realize how serious the consequences of a continued impasse could be for the future of the Lieven embassy in London. In an attempt to heal the breach between her lover and her friend, Emily Cowper tried to bring them together at Panshanger in the New Year. The result was not good, as she told her brother Fred. Dorothea, although 'a dear good soul', was 'very like a Spoilt Child' and 'cannot bear contradictions and has not got temper to stand things turning out differently from her wishes', while Palmerston 'got piqued and angry and thwarted and then bad became worse'. Emily also tried to persuade Fred to exchange appointments with Canning, but this too was of no avail, since Metternich was determined not to receive the cousin of his old enemy. Thus, when Dorothea heard the news from Nesselrode at the end of January that on no account would the Tsar accept Canning as the British ambassador, the likely consequences were finally borne in on her.

At Emily's urging, Dorothea now tried a personal appeal. Starting out in a calmer style than usual, putting the arguments against Canning, she soon became more emotional: 'Toute ma dignité m'abandonne' ['All my dignity deserts me'], she admitted, when she thought of having to leave her life in London. That such an affliction should be visited on her by those she had considered her friends, not least Palmerston himself, was, she wrote, almost more than she could bear. Could he not, she asked, spare her such a fate, and allow her to continue to experience the happiness of the last twenty years? 'Remember, my lord, that you are about to destroy and overturn my whole existence.' He could judge her state of mind, she wrote piteously, from the fact that she was making such an entreaty, and she could not, she added, believe that he would inflict upon her the humiliation of showing her that she had appealed in vain. She relied, she concluded, upon his delicacy and honour not to reveal the secret of her letter, which was known only to one 'seule et unique person'.

No response appears to survive, although it is likely that Emily Cowper added her appeal to that of her friend. Dorothea was, characteristically, forgetting the extent to which she had been the author of her own fate by encouraging Nesselrode to refuse Canning's nomination; had Palmerston been aware of this fact, his sympathy would have been even more limited than it was for someone he knew wanted Durham to replace him at the Foreign Office. Whether because of the heart-rending tones of Dorothea's letter, or the entreaties of his lover, Palmerston tried to defuse the crisis by agreeing to Grey's suggestion that they might extend into an ambassadorial appointment the mission Canning was undertaking to Spain; but Canning would not accept it without a peerage, which Grey refused to give, and so the deadlock continued.

Cause and effect can often be difficult to separate. At one level, Lady Cowper's analysis of what was happening was accurate enough. Dorothea had tried to carry her point in her usual high-handed manner by going over Palmerston's head to Lord Grey, something for which he had decided to punish her. Dorothea, relying on the bonds of their intimacy, had appealed to Palmerston not to 'destroy' her happiness, and he had responded by trying to find a way around the Canning issue which did not involve a compromise of British honour. But there was another level at which Palmerston was correct in thinking that this was about 'more important issues'. To see the quarrel as a purely personal one would be to commit Dorothea's characteristic error of viewing the political through the personal – which is not to deny the personal element, but is to place it in its wider context.

The timing of the quarrel is significant. Those British politicians who were seen by Dorothea as being hostile to Russia usually found themselves the target of her venom; hence her initial hostility to George Canning, which changed overnight once it became clear that he was willing to work with Russia. The subsequent Russo-Turkish war had, however, seen the Russians make significant gains, and worried the British accordingly. During this period Dorothea had systematically done everything she could to undermine Wellington and Aberdeen, and her friendship with Grey and with Palmerston had led her to believe that their advent to power would be a boon for Russia. Once they had come to office, Dorothea did all in her power to excuse to Nesselrode any faults they might have, and emphasized how conservative Grey's policy really was. At the same time, she praised Grey when he acted as she wanted, criticized him when he did not, and generally acted as his window on Russian policy. Because the major crisis affecting Europe during this period concerned the future of Belgium, there was plenty of material for Dorothea to work with. However concerned Wellington and company had been over Russian gains in Asia Minor, the prospect of France making territorial acquisitions in the Low Countries was a much more potent threat, and to combat it Grey and Palmerston would have worked with the devil himself. The difficulties attendant upon Russian suspicions of the intentions of a Whig government had been smoothed over by the good work of both embassies; Dorothea's efforts had been paralleled by those of Lord Heytesbury in St Petersburg.

When he had been appointed in early 1828, Dorothea had commended him highly to her brother and to the Tsar: 'He is the most European Englishman of my acquaintance, the most straightforward diplomatist, and of all the Duke of Wellington's Ambassadors the one who holds the most enlightened opinions and the most conciliatory views.' Heytesbury's commentaries on events in Russia had borne out this high opinion, although it is likely that the Princess merely thought that a Tory would be favourably inclined towards Russia. As ambassador he had given both Aberdeen and Palmerston acute advice upon the changing mood within the Russian court, and as London's impatience over Russian policy on Belgium began to increase, he had used his personal influence at St Petersburg to inform Nesselrode of this, without further fraying the relationship between the two countries. It was precisely because Anglo-Russian relations were deteriorating that the question of his successor was so important; from this perspective, Stratford Canning was far from ideal. Stiff and angular, he possessed the self-righteous qualities of his great cousin without his charm and wit. As a former ambassador to the Porte, he was suspicious of Russian intentions, and neither personally nor politically was he liable to do anything to help Anglo-Russian relations as they entered their most difficult phase since 1830.

The Belgian crisis, which had brought Britain and Russia together, had now joined the list of issues which pushed them apart. Britain's decision to work with France to coerce the Dutch marked a clear breach with the line pursued until October 1832. Dorothea had invested a great deal in the policy of cooperation with the Whigs, and the revelation that Palmerston was not amenable to her influence induced a feeling of disappointment; which was where the earl of Durham came into play. The tactic of flattering Durham's vanity had worked well, and afforded a number of opportunities. He might, at worst, reinforce her influence with Grey, and at best he might provide an alternative Foreign Secretary to the disappointing Palmerston. It was at this point that Dorothea's understanding of the situation was at its most defective, and it was this which ultimately destroyed her career. It was simply a major error to suppose that the change in British policy was the result of Palmerston's failings, and it was to compound it several times to imagine that it might be altered by the appointment of a new Foreign Secretary. It was certainly reasonable to suppose that Stratford Canning would do nothing to improve relations between Britain and Russia; it was, however, difficult to see how any new ambassador could do this; nor was it easy to see how this might be done while the wife of the Russian ambassador was known to be conspiring against the British Foreign Secretary.

The brute fact was that two years after the revolution in France, the main fault-line in international politics had come to be between those who believed that the forces of revolution could be tamed and channelled by astute leadership, and those who thought that the only way to deal with them was to suppress them. This was at the heart of the growing differences over policy towards Belgium. At bottom, the Tsar did not want to see the King of Holland deprived of territory which was rightfully his; at this level the British fundamentally disagreed with his approach. They wanted a settlement of the problem, and since the restoration of the King of Holland was the least likely solution, it was not one that detained them too long. Fear of France made the British cooperate with the Russians for as long as possible, but in October 1832 Palmerston decided that the best way of holding the French was also the best way of solving the crisis – that was to work with Paris in coercing the Dutch King. This determined the Russians to end the policy of working with the London Conference, a line made all the easier by the fact that Austria and Prussia were already feeling aggrieved with Palmerston and the British for condemning their policy of suppressing the free and liberal press in the German Confederation. Add the long-running saga of Poland to this, and the fact that the Russians were supporting the forces of reaction in Portugal against those of the 'liberal' child-queen, Dona Maria, and one begins to get a measure of the gulf opening between London and St Petersburg.

Even before the great schism, the relations between Grey and Dorothea had been tense. In December 1832 Grey had occasion to chide her over Russia's interference in Portugal, and on account of the activities of the Russian ambassador in Paris, Pozzo di Borgo, who had been 'describing this administration as Jacobinical'. Her response had been barely civil: 'Really my dear lord, you only write to me now to pick quarrels with me, and at that price I would rather not have your letters.' She told him that if he had used his letter 'to prove your friendship for me, and to give me a little news, both my heart and my curiosity would have been satisfied'. Refusing, however, to imitate him, she said that 'for the future I shall have no opinions, since I see that unless mine agree with yours, you get angry. It is always so with politics; but as I have none I do not get angry.' That she could write, with a firm hand, that she had 'no politics', illustrates one of the reasons she aroused such exasperation in some quarters; had that been the case, she would have remained in London.

18. 'I thought myself clever at diplomacy'

At the turn of 1832 Dorothea had written to Grey in emollient fashion, wishing him the best for the coming year and, 'for myself, I hope that I may pass the year with you in England. The matter lies in your hands, and it seems to me that your friendship assures me it will turn out in accordance with my desires.' She got her year in London, but not even Grey's friendship could secure that 'matter' turned out as she desired.

Whether or not it was the result of her appeal to Palmerston in January, both he and Grey tried to find a way of dealing with the Canning business. In mid-February, when Grey suggested that they might extend his mission to Spain, he added that: 'I certainly feel no disposition to truckle to Russia tho', I confess, I should be sorry to see the Lievens removed.' But with Canning refusing to go to Madrid, the problem remained. In March 1833 Palmerston informed Prince Lieven that, having failed to find alternative employment for Canning, his nomination for St Petersburg was confirmed. Prince Lieven had said that he could not speak to Grey about the matter without making it into something like an official complaint; but Dorothea could – and did. She wrote to Grey immediately, asking him to 'remember your promise'. She relied, she said, upon his 'breathing no syllable about it to anyone' – not wanting to make it an official matter. 'I thought myself clever at diplomacy,' she told Grey, 'but I never am so with you, for I cannot get rid of my old habit of telling you all that is on my mind.' Grey advised her to let the matter 'rest as it is, though I am certain there must have been some misunderstanding'. It would be better, he wrote, 'if you could justly accuse yourself of being off your guard in any communication with me', adding that she could always rely on his discretion, even if it was not always reciprocated: 'it has more than once occurred to me to hear things repeated from others which you had told me under the strictest injunction of secrecy, and for these I cannot answer.' While on the subject of indiscreet language, Grey told her that where Palmerston was concerned, 'you ought not to be surprised if the violent, and as I believe, most unjust, things that are said against him, when repeated, should produce some impression.' This was good advice – which meant Dorothea let it pass unheeded.

Privately, Dorothea despaired of Grey's administration. She told her brother that 'it is a very poor concern; it has only one quality – stupidity.' She took some malicious pleasure from observing that 'everything here is going on wretchedly. Ineptitude and bad manners in foreign policy; radicalism at home and abroad; flirtations with France; suspicion, animosity, almost hatred of Russia – such is, roughly speaking, our daily bread.' None of this stopped her from wanting to have her bread and eat it, and she continued to act as though some providential act would keep her in London.

For a brief moment it seemed as though Dorothea had been able to work the miracle through her vast network of personal contacts with members of the government. On 14 June she reported to Nesselrode that she had seen Grey, Melbourne and Lord John Russell in an effort to stop the 'wicked determination' of Palmerston and Canning. They had given her the 'most positive and satisfactory promises and assurances'. In a postscript written at seven o'clock, she told him, triumphantly, that Grey had just left her, and had talked to Palmerston: 'tout est arrangé', she crowed, and there was 'no more any question of S. Canning'. In the meantime, Mr Bligh would remain as the British chargé while other arrangements were made. Grey, she said, was the very spirit of goodwill. Nesselrode, who had sent a letter to Grey saying that even Napoleon, at the height of his power, had not attempted to compel other nations to receive a particular ambassador, was greatly relieved at the good news he had had from the Princess – and to be relieved of Canning. The good news meant that she could return on leave to Russia in the summer in high spirits.

Dorothea had not been back to Russia for nearly a decade, and her visit seems to have been prompted, at least in part, by a desire to shore up her position in St Petersburg. Her reception by the Tsar was, she told Grey, overwhelming; he had been profuse in his 'marks of his confidence and his friendship'. She stuck to the Empress like a leech, and quickly involved herself in the hectic social life of the imperial court. But Dorothea's antennae were more attuned to London's politics than those of her own capital. She either did not notice the growing influence of the 'Old Russian Party', noted by Heytesbury, or she assumed that her own contacts at court would serve her well enough for her not to need to conciliate it. She certainly managed to irritate one of the leaders of this group, the man who had made such a good impact during his mission to The Hague, Count Orlov. Count Matuscewitz, who had been at the London embassy since 1829, was one of Orlov's confidants, and he was anxious to have Matuscewitz appointed there permanently, perhaps as a prelude to replacing Lieven himself; this Dorothea was able to prevent; it did her little good with Orlov.

All of these things were reported back to Palmerston by Bligh, who added that rumour had it that even Nesselrode was becoming irritated with her because of her habit of circumventing him by communicating directly with the Tsar through her brother, Alexander. Although no inkling of it occurs in her letters, it seems clear that Dorothea had as many enemies at home as she had in London – especially among those such as Orlov who wanted Russian diplomacy to turn away from the 'western' orientation which the Lievens so signally represented.

There were plenty of signs of the influence of Orlov and his friends, not least in Russia's policy towards the Ottoman Empire; as usual, these took the form of a more unilateral policy – which, as ever, aroused the suspicion of Palmerston. When Dorothea arrived back in England in August she found 'nothing new here – the same Ministers, the same stupidity and insolence, the same powerlessness'. 'Everybody,' she told Alexander, 'is furious at our Treaty with Turkey.' This did insufficient justice to Palmerston's capacity for fury.

The 'Treaty with Turkey' was the infamous Russo-Turkish

agreement of Unkiar Skelessi, which Palmerston later called his greatest diplomatic blunder. When the Sultan failed to give Mehmet Ali his reward for helping him against the Greeks, the Egyptian Pasha raised the standard of revolt. Ostensibly he wanted the Pashalik of Syria, but the British consul-general in Alexandria, Mr Barker, warned after the fall of Acre (in the Pashalik of Syria) in June 1832 that Mehmet 'has at length thrown off the veil . . . and publicly declared that his aim is to dethrone the Sultan . . . and to put the son of the Sultan in his place'. In December, at the battle of Konieh, Mehmet's son, Ibrahim, inflicted a crushing defeat on the Turkish army, capturing the Grand Vizier, Reschid Pasha, and opening the way to Constantinople. Grey, like many Whigs, thought the Ottoman regime effete to the point of exhaustion; Palmerston, although of a similar opinion, none the less took the view that it would not be in Britain's interests for Mehmet, who was backed by the French, to take control of Constantinople. In January 1833 Sultan Mahmoud issued a direct appeal to the British for urgent assistance.

Palmerston would have liked to have responded, but with the British fleet helping in the blockade of Holland and the Cabinet distracted by the Reform Bill crisis at home, there was neither the means nor the political will to intervene. Deserted by the British, he turned to the Russians, who obliged by sending troops to the Asiatic side of the Bosphorus. Attempts by Palmerston to put the Russian triumph into commission, so to speak, by persuading the other great powers to insist that Russia act as part of the Concert of Europe, foundered on the growing ideological divide between Britain and France, on the liberal side, and Austria and Prussia on the other one; the latter two preferred to keep in with the Tsar by acquiescing in his actions. In the meantime, the Russians capitalized on the Sultan's need for their help. Orlov went to Constantinople in May in order to begin negotiations for the Treaty of Unkiar Skelessi, which was signed on 8 July. This treaty provided for a defensive alliance between Turkey and Russia, with the latter promising military and naval assistance, while pledging to protect the complete independence of the Porte.

Palmerston regarded it as a major diplomatic defeat for Britain, and when the Tsar met Metternich and the Prussians at Munchengratz in September, he feared that he might be facing a plot to partition Turkey.

Part of Palmerston's fear stemmed from the secrecy with which both the Treaty of Unkiar Skelessi and the Munchengratz meeting were shrouded. Dorothea did not mention the treaty to Grey 'as [he] did not allude to it', nor did she tell him in advance of the Tsar's visit: 'We are not called upon to render an account to these people of all that we do, and also I shall not be sorry to see this bomb burst over them unawares.' As far as she was concerned, she told Alexander, she had kept silence over both these contentious issues 'out of respect for a husband's wishes'; she was sure, she wrote, that the Prince would want to deliver the news himself. 'Well! Let them digest our policy if they can; it will do their stomachs good, after all.' Dorothea's view that, when 'they knew the contents of the treaty they will be satisfied', showed how little she understood the gulf that was opening between her country and a liberal Britain. The meeting of the three Emperors was, in effect, the signal for a renewal of the old Holy Alliance, and after long discussions between the three courts, a treaty was signed in Berlin on 15 October which provided for the right of any sovereign who felt threatened to call any other power in to help him. It was a signal for the sort of intervention Metternich had favoured back in 1820 – and as such hardly likely to commend itself to Palmerston or the Whigs. The fact that he could get so little information about either the Treaty of Unkiar Skelessi, or what was happening as a result of the Munchengratz meeting, prompted Palmerston to make a formal protest at St Petersburg about the Turkish treaty; but he found Grey less than eager to do so.

Palmerston was not to be denied by the misgivings of a mere Prime Minister. On 8 October he told Grey that his attitude 'disturbs and embarrasses me greatly'. Pointedly, Palmerston commented that he could 'quite understand that Mme de Lieven should wish to persuade us not to do so, because not only as a general principle is it under present circumstances her great object as

Russian ambassadress to paralyse us', but also, since St Petersburg had been 'annoyed' at the British protest to the Sultan, 'it would be a great coup if the Lievens could persuade us not to present the protest at St Petersburgh [*sic*]'. To protest to Turkey, 'the weaker Power & the tool, and not dare even to whisper our dissatisfaction to Russia, the stronger Power, & the Plotter' would, Palmerston thought, be incompatible with 'our national honour'. 'We would lose caste in Europe, & Russia would henceforth treat England as a Power from whom no serious resistance need ever be apprehended.'

Grey did not see how not delivering the protest would have the effect Palmerston thought it would; indeed, he would not, he wrote on 9 October, have suggested withholding it had that been the case, but he did not feel strongly enough about it to persevere with his views if other ministers agreed with Palmerston. When Palmerston pushed his case, Grey conceded the point, although 'I still think you mistaken.' He had also noted the presence of Dorothea's name in Palmerston's letter, and commented on it: 'I am sorry you should have appeared to suppose that I have been in any degree influenced by Madame de Lieven on this or any other subject. I hoped you had known me better.' His sensitivities quivering, Grey added: 'It is rather unpleasant to me to answer a suspicion of this nature, but I can assure you that she only mentioned the expectation of a courier [from Nesselrode] as a reason for putting off her visit here, which is now given up altogether, nor had one word upon the Protests either in conversation or writing ever passed between us, nor on the affairs of Turkey generally.' The only conversation he had had, he protested, had been with Lieven himself, and he had circulated a copy of it.

Whatever Palmerston might have thought, Grey was speaking no more than the truth; there is no trace in his correspondence with Dorothea of any discussion of the Turkish question. Palmerston had his way, and the British protest was duly delivered. Nesselrode's reply made Dorothea laugh out loud – it refused to take the British note seriously, and claimed that Russia was doing no more than Britain had done. However, Palmerston's suspicions had clearly done their work since, as she told Nesselrode on 24 November, Grey refused to discuss the matter with her.

Count Esterhazy, the Austrian ambassador in London, reproached Dorothea with doing nothing to help defuse the situation – a charge that was well justified. He argued that the Russians should have explained to the British what had been agreed at Munchengratz; their failure to do so had, he thought, aroused great suspicion in Britain. Dorothea admitted, according to his account to Metternich, that a war with Russia would be very popular in Britain, and that the government would have no trouble getting a vote of credit for one. Esterhazy and Metternich eventually persuaded the Russians to offer some explanations to the British, and the crisis was defused, but Metternich was convinced that Princess Lieven had helped make matters worse by assuring Nesselrode that Durham and others would stop the protest; this was a little unfair. Dorothea's letters to Nesselrode, while full of criticism of Palmerston and Grey, never suggested that the protest would not be delivered; what she did was to report the Cabinet divisions on the subject and suggest that it might not be delivered – something which, had Grey had his way, would have been correct. Even at this stage of affairs, Dorothea still underestimated Palmerston's determination to make his will prevail.

The revival of the old Holy Alliance witnessed the drawing together of the 'Northern Courts' under Tsar Nicholas's leadership. In this sense it did not mark a retreat by Russia into isolation, but it did signal the determination of her supreme autocrat to suppress the forces of revolution wherever they showed themselves; this, in turn, marked another stage in the growth of the Anglo-Russian antagonism. Back in 1832, Metternich had suggested allowing the Spanish to intervene in Portugal to put an end to the simmering civil war there between the usurper, Dom Miguel (who was supported by the autocrats of Europe), and his brother, Dom Pedro (who was accounted a liberal because he had promulgated a constitution and was hated by the reactionaries). Palmerston had responded brusquely that 'the days of the Holy Alliance are gone, never to return and such propositions do not belong to the present time'; on both counts, it now seemed, he was incorrect. With the death of Ferdinand VII of Spain leading to a disputed succession there, in which the Ultra-Catholic Don Carlos looked to the Holy Alliance powers for succour, while the Queen-Regent, Maria Christina, looked for Western support for herself and her infant daughter, Isabella, by the end of 1833 it seemed as though Europe was drifting into two diplomatic camps; the division defined by ideology. None of this boded well for the future of Anglo-Russian relations – or the future of the Lieven embassy in London.

Grey's assurances of the summer notwithstanding, the question of Stratford Canning going to St Petersburg had not been dropped. Canning continued to demand a peerage as the price for standing down, and Grey, who was 'strangely averse' to increasing the peerage, even to reward his political friends, declined to do so on Canning's behalf; there remained only the hope that the collapse of Grey's government might transform the situation. Nor did this seem far-fetched, since throughout the autumn the government staggered from one crisis to another, with Grey increasingly complaining that, at seventy, he no longer had the energy to manage the premiership.

With blithe disregard for the way she had behaved when he had last been Prime Minister, the Princess thought her lot would be better if Wellington and the Tories came to power. She told Alexander that a visit to Wellington had caused 'no little annoyance to the Government', because the Duke had invited the Austrian, Dutch and French ambassadors to his house at the same time: 'it was not one Power, but Europe collectively which was conspiring with the leader of the Opposition.' The opportunity had been taken to complain to Wellington about the state of Anglo-Russian relations, while Dorothea discussed with him 'the best means to be adopted for enlightening public opinion and for counteracting the obvious ill-will of the ministerial papers'. She arranged to have an article placed in the *Quarterly Review*, which would put the Russian point of view. As an additional measure to undermine Palmerston, she told Talleyrand how much he was disliked by him. She dismissed fresh protestations of goodwill from Palmerston as nothing more than a welcome consequence of Russia's firm rebuff of the British protest.

Dorothea's hopes rose even further as the Cabinet divided bitterly on the question of whether or not British troops should intervene in Portugal to help the liberal side. Grey and Palmerston, who along with John Russell, Holland and the Chancellor, Lord Brougham, wished to do so, found themselves in a minority in Cabinet. Only with the greatest persuasion was Grey induced not to resign. Although ministers tried to claim there was no division in the Cabinet, the truth was obvious – and Dorothea exulted in it and in Grey's emollience across the range of issues that now divided the two countries. But the government did not (quite) collapse, and Palmerston made it plain that he expected the Russians to accept Stratford Canning as ambassador to St Petersburg. 'Palmerston,' she complained, 'will never be more than a schoolboy, and is not brilliant at that.'

The tensions of the early months of 1834 passed away without any war, as the Princess had thought they would, but Anglo-Russian relations remained extremely bad – and the Canning question continued unresolved. Dorothea, as was her wont, blamed Palmerston's ill will for much of the trouble, a view reinforced by Melbourne, who when asked what he put the problems down to said: 'l'affaire de Stratford Canning qui est resté dans l'estomac de Palmerston' ['the Stratford Canning business, which sticks in Palmerston's craw']. When she protested that this was to treat Palmerston as though he was the sole minister, Melbourne tried to convince her that it was Russia's immense military strength and menacing presence, everywhere from the Baltic to the Persian Gulf, that made her such a worry to the British. She dismissed this as 'une bêtise'. But such matters were soon to be of no great concern to her. At the beginning of May came the news that the Tsar was recalling Prince Lieven to St Petersburg to become governor to his children. Dorothea was so upset that for a few days she even stopped noticing what was happening in British politics – her 'nourishment for the last 22 years'. So the blow had fallen.

Princess Lieven was not the only one to be surprised at the outcome of the saga. Grey told her on 22 May 1834 that: 'Nothing could have come upon me more unexpectedly or more painfully.' He hoped that what he called this 'event' could still be averted: 'the idea of parting with a person whom I have known for so long, who has always been so kind to me, and for whom I bear so sincere an attachment, occasions a pang which I have not power sufficiently to express.' Dorothea, who was touched by his letter, responded: 'I have always known that by *you* my husband would have justice done him; that in politics you would always act so as to conciliate wherever possible; and that for me personally you felt much friendship. Would to Heaven it had been *you* alone who had to give effect to these sentiments!' She could, she wrote sadly, 'hardly write, I feel so sick at heart.'

For all her pride in Russia, its power and its glory, Dorothea was shattered at the thought of returning there. As she explained to her beloved Alexander: 'a complete change of career. Of moral and material habits and surroundings after twenty-four years is a serious epoch in one's life.' But with a flash of her old spirit, she added: 'It is said that one regrets ever one's prison after spending many years in it'; but it had been a gilded cage: 'I may well be permitted to regret a fine climate, a delightful social position, ways of comfort and luxury which I can find nowhere else, and many friends wholly independent of politics.' If Dorothea pretended to have mixed feelings about her recall, others were less reticent.

On 23 May her old enemy, *The Times*, published an article which the Duchess of Dino described as 'a national disgrace'. The newspaper's leader declared that 'we cannot say of Her Serene Highness that the *petit nez retroussé* has occasioned much mischief, whatever her organs of speech or her implements of writing may have done.' It went on in the same vein: 'There never figured on the Courtly stage, a female intriguer more restless, more arrogant, more mischievous, more (politically, and therefore we mean it not offensively) odious than this supercilious Ambassadress.' Such comments, at this moment of vulnerability, made Dorothea weep. She told the Duchess of Dino that she was sorry to think that these were the farewell words from a country that she was leaving with such regret. But she soon recovered her mood, and wondered whether she had not been a little harsh in her allocation of tickets for Almack's; the venom of the press was one thing, but more bitter still was the pity of those such as the Duchess of Dino. But Dorothea had not quite given up hope. As Grey's government was on its last legs, she speculated that 'the first act of the new Foreign Secretary would be to ask the Russian Government that M. de Lieven might not be removed'; the government survived long enough to see her out.

On the King's birthday, 28 May, it was the custom of the Foreign Secretary to throw a great diplomatic dinner to which all the foreign ambassadors were invited. Princess Lieven, determined to make a statement, turned up in the new national dress which St Petersburg had decreed should be adopted for state occasions. This was, the Duchess of Dino noticed, 'so noble, so rich and so graceful that it suits any woman, or rather it suits no woman ill'. The Princess's dress 'was particularly well planned and showed her off well, as the veil concealed the thinness of her neck'. The *placement* was less well planned from the point of view of the Foreign Secretary – Palmerston sat down with the Duchess of Dino on his left and Princess Lieven on his right: 'he was chilly on the right and breezy on the left, and obviously ill at ease.' Even less at ease than the Foreign Secretary was Lady Cowper, who found herself caught between her lover and her friend. Her attempts to explain the one to the other lacked her customary tact.

She had told Dorothea at the end of May: 'I assure you that Lord Palmerston regards you as an old and pleasant acquaintance whom he is very sorry to lose'; she added that he recognized Prince Lieven's 'excellent qualities' and knew that 'Russia could not be more worthily represented than by him. But you see that that is the very reason why England must profit by your departure.' Dorothea was 'no less struck by the sincerity of the avowal than annoyed by its implication.' The Duchess of Dino noted that it was so widely believed that Palmerston was responsible for the

Princess's recall that 'no one even pretends to conceal his conviction that this is the case, not even Lord Palmerston's colleagues in the Ministry.' As a result, he was invited to none of the many farewell dinners for the Princess – which was 'the more remarkable, as of course, Lady Cowper is always there'. Palmerston was much annoyed at this, not least at Grey's attitude, which was to blame him; he took his ill humour out on Emily.

Lady Cowper redeemed herself to some extent by joining in the great subscription organized by the Duchess of Sutherland to which all Dorothea's friends were asked to contribute ten guineas. As might have been predicted, even this act of kindness created its own problems. Some ladies thought that ten guineas was too much, others withdrew because their choice of present was not adopted. In all, thirty ladies contributed to a bracelet with a large pearl set into it. Even then, the trouble was not over, since it was necessary to agree upon an inscription. The Duchess of Dino noted that 'twenty different ways' of putting it were tried: 'poetry and allegory were suggested. Some wished for a play of words, suggesting that a pearl had been chosen because the Princess was a pearl among women.' Yet others thought that this was not 'sufficiently precise; they wanted some allusion to be made to the Princess's talent for affairs, a suggestion that was declared out of order'. In the end the Duchess proposed an inscription which was translated into English and engraved upon the bracelet: 'Testimony of regard, regret and affection presented to the Princess Lieven on her departure by some English ladies of her particular acquaintance (July 1834).'

On 10 July, in the midst of the round of farewell parties, Grey finally resigned as Prime Minister, to be replaced by Melbourne. However, since Palmerston stayed at the Foreign Office there was no need to cancel the subscription. Ironically, it was Palmerston himself who gave the final dinner for Dorothea. According to the Duchess of Dino, the Princess 'went against her will' and the other ladies went 'simply for her sake'; unsurprisingly it was 'a melancholy occasion'. A decade earlier it had been written that:

She is gone, as the *Herald* announces
To latitudes wilder and colder;
She is gone with her pearls and her flounces,
She is gone with the bows on her shoulder.

Now, she really had gone. There would never be another like her.

Conclusion: 'The sport of evil fortune'

An air of melancholy settled firmly upon Dorothea. She loved the idea of Russia more than its reality. 'Our existence is honourable and brilliant,' she wrote to Aberdeen in October 1834, 'but I would love it more if I were able to forget England, and if I did not live in a climate made for bears.' Although she was in a beautiful palace built in the style of Versailles, and although there were agreeable people to talk with, 'the circles of ideas and conversation are very different from those which have been my daily bread for twenty-five years.' 'It is,' she told Grey in early November, 'a sad life I live here. It is snowing, and I feel we are such a long way off one from the other.' A month later, she complained: 'I am vegetating in this most atrocious of climates.' As ever when she was bored, her health began to suffer, and throughout the winter she complained of pains in the chest and of incessant colds. But there was more to it, as she confessed to Grey: 'Ah, my lord, there is a longing in my heart which hurts me even more than the climate; how often do I not sigh for the life of the past! I am really in a pitiable condition. You would hardly recognise me if we met.'

The Tsar eventually agreed that she could 'go in search of the sunshine and warmth of the south', but she felt unable to travel by herself, and so stayed to endure the rigours of the Russian winter. The only item of news that cheered her up was that in the British general election of early 1835, Palmerston lost his seat in Hampshire: 'Lord Palmerston's discomfiture has amused me greatly,' she confessed to Grey. 'A great man greatly fallen!' But, as others would also discover, Palmerston was not easily discounted. He found another seat and resumed what would be a long career at the Foreign Office.

By this time, however, Dorothea had more pressing sorrows. In late February her son George, *l'enfant du Congrès*, fell sick with the scarlet fever and died a month later. She was devastated. Then, in April, her youngest son, Arthur, who had been recovering from the same illness, suffered a sudden relapse and died. In response to Lord Grey's condolences she replied simply: 'My dear friend, what can I write? I have no words left, and what can you say to comfort me? Was any bereavement more complete than mine?' Her anguish was such that both her husband and the Tsar decided that she must travel southwards in search of sunshine and forgetfulness. Prince Lieven accompanied her as far as their first diplomatic posting, Berlin; she never saw him again. Dorothea spent a dismal summer travelling around the German spa towns. Writing to Grey in July 1835, she told him that 'my plans are still vague; I long more than ever for England; but being in England I could not go to London, for in London I should have too many sad recollections, and too many social calls, to make it possible for me to venture there now.'

Dorothea travelled on to Paris, where she took rooms near the British embassy so that she could see her old friend Harriet Granville. She reported to her brother, the Duke of Devonshire, in September, that: 'I have twice tried to see Lieven; have had a most melancholy and affectionate note from her. She lives *chez elle*, drives all morning with a beautiful niece who lives with her, receives from eight till ten, *avide* for news. "*Causez*" ["Speak to me"] is her cry, and she writes to me, "*distrayez mon esprit*" ["distract me"].' Harriet found it 'a comfort in being of use to her' although she was 'very stout about not letting her be more *exigeante* than suits me'. It was not long before Dorothea's salon was attracting 'the pleasantest women in Paris' – and their menfolk. In early 1837 Harriet reported to her sister, Lady Carlisle, that Dorothea was 'in great beauty and high spirits. She always has an *entourage*.' But the Princess was unsure how long she would be allowed to sample the delights of Paris. As she told Grey in October 1836: 'My fate is very uncertain, for it is subject not only to my own caprices, but to the will of those in power in St Petersburg.'

In July 1837 Dorothea returned briefly to England, where she had an audience with the new young Queen, Victoria. It was all very different from the decadence of the court of George IV. The little Queen had, she told Aberdeen, 'aplomb, and a commanding air, with her childlike face and small stature'; there was, she thought, a reserve in their conversation; this may have been because the Queen's uncle, King Leopold of Belgium, had warned her to be on her guard against such a notorious intriguer. While there, Dorothea received orders from St Petersburg that she must return home.

As a Russian subject, she knew the rules; in exchange for the privileges they enjoyed, the Russian nobility were at the disposal of the Tsar, and now Nicholas had decided she should return. Acting upon the Tsar's command, Prince Lieven wrote to her, telling her that she must obey orders; she should meet him in Italy, from whence he would escort her back to their lives in Russia. Dorothea immediately fell ill and protested that she could not comply with his wishes. As so often in a crisis, she resorted to the state of her health as a reason for not doing something she had no desire to do at all. Although the Paris salon lacked the political importance that her activities in London had possessed, it did restore her to a world she found far more congenial than that of St Petersburg. She renewed her acquaintanceship with Talleyrand – 'to observe him is as good as comedy', she told Lady Cowper; and her rivalry with the Duchess of Dino once more flourished. French politicians flocked to her salon, and two in particular, Thiers, the Prime Minister, and his great rival, Guizot, attracted her attention. She found the latter an object of particular fascination.

A widower, a scholar and an orator, François Guizot was noted for the austerity of his character, and his opposition to the government. He 'came to my house every evening', she recorded in her notes. 'He took pleasure enough in hearing me chat about my old trade of diplomacy, and about England, a country for which he had great admiration.' On 15 February 1837, Guizot lost his eldest son, and Dorothea, 'having bought so dearly the right . . . to enter into your sorrows', wrote him a letter of condolence. 'When Heaven chastised me so severely,' she told him, 'I began to look for other unhappy people in the world. If your heart does the same, then let your thoughts dwell on me who am a hundred times more unhappy than you, as unhappy at the end of two years as I was at the beginning.' Guizot resigned from the French Cabinet soon afterwards, and Dorothea, admiring his explanation to the Chamber of Deputies, congratulated him on the success of his speech. As he later recorded in his memoir of Dorothea: 'thus began between her and myself a friendship, which became more serious and more intimate every day. Both of us had known great sadness in life and we had reached the age of disillusion ['*l'âge des méscomptes*']. The intimacy which sprang up between us was simple and natural, without any political thoughts.' In June 1837 she and Guizot became lovers. To leave this new love, and the life she had created for herself, was beyond Dorothea's will – or power.

Through the medium of the Russian ambassador, Count Orlov, Dorothea attempted to negotiate with her husband, and at first she thought matters could be arranged to her satisfaction. When she received a kind letter from him, outlining where they might meet and saying how much he wished to see her, Dorothea felt a little sad. As she told Guizot, had it arrived a month or so earlier, she would have welcomed it. While she did not enjoy her husband's company, and while her heart was not with him, he was 'un créature qui m'aime', and to whom she belonged and who thought about her. There were all those things that women valued so much, long intimacy and habit, but 'another life has begun for me, a life which cannot wipe out my sorrows, but which helps me forget them, and which makes me fail to understand, any longer, the old life I led for so long.' But Orlov's mission was a failure. He saw Prince Lieven in Marienbad and reported to Dorothea that he was 'in a great rage against Paris'. Conveying this unwelcome news to Lady Cowper, Dorothea did 'not know what will be the end of this horrible episode. One thing is certain, that I am not in a fit state to leave Paris. But the fact we never see each other gives a bad impression everywhere. What terrible political scandals it will create! But at least I shall be spared any private gossip.'

The Prince remained insistent that his wife should return, and perhaps stung by gossip about her and Guizot, wrote to her letters that she described as 'very cold'. He even forbade their son Paul, who was in the diplomatic service, to see Dorothea as long as she stayed in Paris. This hurt her greatly, and she admitted that were it not for Guizot she would follow the call of duty and be across the Rhine with her husband and two sons: 'I am suffering, it is true; but if it is for you, I would go to the ends of the earth, despite my health; I fear nothing.' Prince Lieven categorically insisted that she should tell him whether she was going to return; if she did not do so, he threatened, he would have to take very severe action. She told Guizot that now that his jealousy had been aroused, he would be 'terrible'. He evidently did not believe a word that her doctors wrote about her health.

It was now clear to Dorothea that her husband was acting under strict orders from the Tsar himself, and she tried to explain the situation to Guizot. 'In my country, Monsieur, I am a very great Lady, the first Lady by my rank and by my position at Court, and even more so because I am the only one who could be said to have lived on terms of familiarity with the Emperor and Empress. I belong to the Royal Family; see my social position at St Petersburg and see, also, why the anger of the Emperor is so great at seeing this country of revolutions honoured by my presence. Monsieur, do not laugh, however much I have need of laughter, this is very serious.'

In a further letter at the end of September 1837, Prince Lieven warned her again that he would have to take serious steps against her if she failed to return. He adjured her to consider her duties as a wife and mother, and to think about the future as much as she thought about her life in Paris. Dorothea was indignant: 'What is it he is wanting, a separation? Why? Because I am ill in Paris?' She complained to Grey that 'no one in Russia . . . will believe that I am really ill', although she was convinced that 'for me, to live at Petersburg is simply to go to my death: and however miserable one may be, one still clings to life.' Then, in October, the blow fell. The Prince wrote to say that he would have to cut off her allowance, and that if she tried to avoid him by not responding to his letter, he would do so within three weeks. Dorothea told

Guizot that she could feel only pity for a man who was capable of taking such action because ordered to by his Tsar.

Lady Cowper, who was always at her best in a crisis, did what she could to comfort and reassure her old friend. 'I am very unhappy at your sorrows, but am still in hopes – it seems to me impossible that M. de Lieven should act in such a manner. He thought he would frighten you by this threat, but when he sees he has not succeeded he will withdraw it – this is what I expect will happen.' But Emily Cowper's long experience of her husband's complaisance in her affair with Palmerston was no guide to how a Russian grandee under pressure from the Tsar would behave. Dorothea wondered whether her husband would come to Paris to get her, and was correspondingly horrified when, at eleven o'clock on 18 October, she was told that 'Prince Lieven' had arrived: 'My good angel protect me!' He did: it was her son, Prince Alexander, and not his father. From him she learned that her husband was not even reading the letters from the doctors, and that he had not told the Tsar that there were medical reasons why she was not leaving Paris. Dorothea hoped that Alexander would be able to persuade him otherwise; she was wrong. She wrote to her brother, Alexander, appealing for help against her cruel husband, but he responded frostily: 'You should not be surprised after so many years of superiority over him, that he should seek revenge.' Dorothea was indignant: 'This superiority – I did in fact exercise for many long years to his *own* use and service, and now he can no longer make use of it, he punishes me.'

In early 1838 the Prince finally cut off her allowance. Dorothea protested. 'My demands,' she told Lady Cowper, 'are extremely humble. If he deprives me of everything, I shall send my diamonds to England, where I think they will fetch a better price than they would here. I shall not feel any hurt to my pride. Dearest, one's heart can be very sore, and one's pride very high at the same time. My pride rises the more people try to humiliate me. But sometimes I cannot help laughing, and I ask myself, "What is the point of it all?"'

Increasingly, for Dorothea, the 'point' was Guizot. She felt that in him she had found a soulmate. When he asked her 'who had spirit in their heart', after long reflection she could recall no one but Guizot himself. When she had asked Metternich the same question many years before, he had 'sent me six pages of writing which bored me to death'. She asked Guizot to help her bear her griefs: 'do you not think everything is rather extreme with me? I do not know how to bear myself. You have already done much to make me worthy of you. You are wrong to tell me to stay as I am. Encourage me to become more moderate, less at the mercy of my impulses, to bear with greater calmness what Heaven sends me.' She could think things through, she told him, but no sooner had she composed herself than she dissolved into tears again. 'Help me, guide me. Organise me: yes, organise me.' She told him that she 'needed to be governed. Why do you not govern me?' She could be governed only by one she loved – and she loved him dearly. She was, she told him, 'far more unhappy than you. You have children to bring up; you have a country to serve; you have your public duties and brilliant career ahead of you; you have a *home*. What do I have? Think of all that I have lost. Think what remains to me, and do not be displeased if I show sadness, very great sadness at times. I am less sad when I am near you, I even forget my sorrows then. But when I come face to face with myself – no one but myself! Ah! That is terrible!'

Prince Lieven stopped writing to Dorothea. She told Lady Cowper in March 1838 that she had not heard from him for two months: 'and he will keep me completely in the air as to what I am to expect, or not to expect, from him. He is really treating me like a dog. Either I must think him mad, or else I must think the Emperor very cruel, if it is he who is intervening between a husband and wife. The whole thing is a mystery which I shall never fathom.' If there was a 'mystery', it should not have been beyond her wit to have fathomed it.

In May Prince Lieven broke his silence and told her that 'everything will be explained when we meet again.' He relented slightly about her allowance, and by June 1838 he was letting her have 4,000 francs a month. He wrote to her again in August, from Ems:

'You know my peculiar character so well, my dear, that you will understand my present position and the true reasons for my silence . . . It is a sad position in which we have been for a very long time. It has often been painful for me. I do not know what you think of it, or the influences to which you are subject . . . Is it together or separately that we are to live this last act of our lives?'

Seeing some sign of a thaw, Guizot suggested that the best thing would be for her to go to Baden to talk to her husband; this unleashed an emotional avalanche. 'You forget that officially I cannot move . . . and that if I left France I should not be allowed to return . . . you are bored with me and want to put me away. I am not what you thought I was at the beginning of our relationship and you scorn my character.' Guizot, who was badly hurt, told her: 'I love you with that love which dominates all things, is equal to all things, promises much, and always gives more than it promises . . . That is how I love you. And I see two things: one, that my love cannot do as much for you as I think it can; the other, that you are incapable of putting your faith in it. You are unhappy and you are unfair. You are all that I believed and still believe you to be.' Although she wondered why, and sometimes doubted it, she now recognized that Guizot did indeed love her.

'I will never,' Guizot told her in September 1838, 'be resigned to your moments of depression, those moods which make me doubt what I am to you, and what I may yet be. I do not want to rob anyone. I love all your feelings, and I love you for them. You do not know how much my affection for you is coloured by your state of mind.' He had been attracted to her, he told her, by her 'unforgetting heart, a heart in which the dead still live'. At the very outset of their relationship this attraction 'overcame the misgivings I had felt concerning you, either for my own part, or from what I had heard. Later it made me pardon things in you which hurt and wounded me . . . You must never, in any circumstances, for a single moment, have the faintest doubt of my constant and unwearying sympathy with your sorrow.' A few days later he told her: 'I love you; you do not know how much I love you.' In time she came to some appreciation of the affection and support he gave her.

Guizot needed every ounce of his 'unwearying sympathy' to help Dorothea cope with the next blow that fate, in the form of her husband, threw at her. She regularly corresponded with her sons, and, despite Prince Lieven's strictures, she managed to see something of Paul and Alexander; the same was not true of her second son, Constantine, who, having quarrelled with his father, had gone to live in America. In October 1838 one of her letters addressed to him was returned with the single word 'dead' written on the envelope. She learned that the Prince had been told the news in July 'and yet the father of this son – my husband – has left *me* in total ignorance of the event . . .' she told Grey. 'Ah. My dear lord, this is horrible, and my heart is in revolt at it! . . . Russia is indeed a horrible country when a man must thus abdicate all natural sentiments and shrink from fulfilling the most common and sacred duties of life.' For all her tendency to over-dramatize situations, it was hard not to sympathize with her howl of anguish: 'have you ever known any creature more persistently the sport of evil fortune than I am?'

Dorothea told Emily Cowper in November that her husband was 'so mean' about money that she had decided that she would have to sell her diamonds after all. Her one solace was that all her Parisian friends, especially Harriet Granville, 'have been wonderful to me'. She wrote to all their friends, telling any she thought might meet the Prince on his journey to Italy on holiday that they should show, by their attitude to him, what they thought of his behaviour. As Harriet told her brother, the Duke of Devonshire, it was essential that 'an impression in her favour' should be made upon Prince Lieven, 'who has behaved shamefully'.

Whether through the intervention of another, or simply guilt, the Prince finally wrote to Dorothea again in December 1838. He once more promised a full explanation of his behaviour when they met, and told her that he would live wherever her 'poor heart' and 'bodily ailments' could best get relief. She was not impressed by his letter, and asked Lady Cowper to write to him; it was too late. On 10 January 1839 Prince Lieven died. The news came as yet another blow to Dorothea, who told Lord Aberdeen: 'I have lost so much that I do not know how to cry.' She was glad that he had expressed repentance before he died, and she felt that his 'true feelings' had returned: 'I thank God his last thoughts towards me were tender ones. I mourn him with less bitterness, but I mourn him sincerely. We passed our lives together, I have only known life with him – married at fourteen, thirty-eight years together – the joys and the griefs of life, we shared them all. Today, everything is finished. There is nothing but desolation all around me.' To Grey she wrote: 'I live a very sad life now . . . I pass my days in solitude. I think of all that is passed – passed never to return – and I have no future to look forward to.'

Emily Cowper wrote to condole with her, adding that 'I forgot to include Lord Palmerston among those of your old friends who talk of you with affection – he has asked me several times to express to you his sympathy in your unhappiness.' However little she appreciated sympathy from that source, Dorothea wanted to keep on good terms with Palmerston in case she had to send her diamonds to him via Granville. With 40,000 francs owing to her from her husband's estate, she had hoped she might yet hang on to her gems, although the discovery that most of the money went to her children came as discouraging news. Harriet Granville told her brother, the Duke of Devonshire, that Dorothea 'feels – naturally deeply . . . and much more than those who do not see her in these moments, when all is laid open, would ever believe her to be capable of. Tenderness for whatever called for it in the past, forgetfulness of every cloud, on her knees with torrents of tears, hoping she had not often given pain, failed in kindness, indulgence. Then her own peculiarity of nature – no thought of *les apparences*, power of turning soon and eagerly to other objects of interest and curiosity. All this, the good and the weak side of which no person who knows her but little can measure.' In order to protect Dorothea in her great grief, the kindly Harriet let her lodge in the British embassy where 'nobody but myself should see it'.

Gradually, with Guizot's help, Dorothea picked up the threads of her life. When Prince Lieven's estate was settled, she had about £1,000 a year on which to live – which was quite sufficient in

Paris. Her anger at the cupidity of her sons was such that her niece, Marie von Benckendorff, the daughter of her brother Constantine, who had been with her throughout her stay in Paris, decided to leave. Emily Cowper's brother, Frederick, reported that: 'they tell me Madam de Lieven's niece could stand it no longer. They say she was *roide comme une planche* with her sons about money, who on their side behaved very ill. I try to keep liking her but I feel it a relief to you that She don't go to England.' Harriet Granville, however, thought that her old friend seemed a little happier: 'There is peace yet, even for her if she will but tread in its path. Is it not one of the most wonderful things belonging to this state of existence that she can still cling to and lean upon this, to her, miserable earth?' It was Guizot, rather than the 'miserable earth', to whom Dorothea clung; she now made her life in Paris.

Just as Dorothea settled there with Guizot, she heard from Emily Cowper that at long last, nineteen years after first becoming his lover, and two after the death of her husband, Lord Cowper, she had finally married Palmerston. Dorothea showed herself generous towards her old friend for the help she had given her, and although her head was 'full of conflicting emotions', she congratulated 'dear Emily'. Her words applied to herself as much as they did to the new Lady Palmerston: 'Dearest, you have done a very sensible thing. It is wise of you to look for happiness and comfort; a peaceful home; someone to care for you; support, constant companionship, and a common interest for the rest of your days. May God bless your marriage. You are happy, you have always been happy and always will. My *sisterly* heart rejoices with you in this happiness.' She even asked her to tell Palmerston that 'I remember the good times when we were intimate together. Ask him to give me his friendship again, and I promise to give him mine.' Like Emily, Dorothea settled for being 'sensible', but with one difference – she never married Guizot. When a friend inquired whether it was true, as she had heard, that she was going to marry him, Dorothea replied with a flash of her old self: 'Oh! My dear, can you really see me being announced as Madame Guizot!'

The Princess's new existence bore at least a passing resemblance to her old one. All the leading politicians and diplomats in Paris frequented her salon, and when Guizot was appointed ambassador to London in early 1840, she was able to use her old contacts to help smooth the way for him. Aberdeen told her that 'your friendship will be the means of making' Guizot's acquaintance 'this more easy'. Emily Palmerston was one of the first people Guizot saw in London, and she reported that he was 'the lion of my *soirée*'. Dorothea advised Guizot not to accept too many invitations, and then only from the right people – she, of course, would be the judge of that. His accounts of evenings spent with Lady Palmerston and the Duchess of Sutherland aroused Dorothea's jealousy, which may have been one of the reasons she decided to visit him in the summer. Lady Palmerston passed on a hint from the Russian ambassador, Count Brunow, that she should not do so; intelligent people, she told her old friend, must sometimes make sacrifices for the benefit of fools. Dorothea could not have disagreed more: 'There would be no point in having intelligence if one was obliged to obey the whims of fools . . . In my official capacity I was sometimes obliged to treat them with tact; my present complete independence allows me to ignore them, and I intend to do so . . . My political importance is over. I am enjoying the pleasures of my nullity.' In many ways, that was exactly what Dorothea did – for as long as she could. She enjoyed her brief stay in London in August, but she was not sorry when Guizot returned to Paris as foreign minister in October. There they remained until the revolution of 1848 forced them to flee to London.

Writing in her diary in 1840, Lady Palmerston noted: 'The end of life is so full of disappointment, sorrow and anxiety that it is quite refreshing to one's spirit to meet with those by whom one's early and happy days are remembered – and who can feel and share in one's old reminiscences and recollections.' The flight to England brought Dorothea up against those memories, especially since she found herself staying in Brighton, the scene of so much of her social life a quarter of a century before. Of her English friends, Grey had died three years earlier, and Wellington, while still alive, was now an aged and fragile figure. Harriet Granville had returned to London in 1845 after the death of her beloved Granville, but Emily Palmerston and her husband thrived mightily, with the latter, as Foreign Secretary, reflecting smugly on how much better things would have been for the Holy Alliance had its members not heeded his lectures on constitutionalism. To his satisfaction, among those washed up on the shores of England by the revolutions was old Metternich himself.

Emily travelled down to Brighton in January to see her old friend. She told Palmerston that: 'The Lieven was very kind and agreeable & very amiable in her inquiries after you. I thought her sincere.' For Dorothea, it was intriguing to see Metternich once more. She noted with some satisfaction that his third wife, Princess Melanie, was 'fat' and 'vulgar', although she had 'a pleasant manner'. Her judgement was equally hard upon the former object of her affections, the fallen Chancellor himself. Dorothea noticed now what she had once been blind to – that Metternich's 'serenity' amounted to 'smugness', and his conversation, larded as it was with interminable anecdotes and philosophizing, was both 'slow' and 'boring'.

Towards the end of 1849 Princess Lieven returned to Paris, where she continued to run her salon and to live with Guizot until 1854, when with the outbreak of the Crimean War she was obliged, as a Russian, to quit the French capital; not until 1856 was she able to slip back to her old life. She had lived long enough to see the unhappy denouement to the Anglo-Russian relationship she had spent so long trying to foster. Britain had, after all, sided with France, and not even a liberal one. Still, it mattered little to her now.

In January 1857 Dorothea Lieven came down with bronchitis, which quickly became pneumonia. She faced the inevitable with serenity. Guizot and her son Paul were with her when she received communion according to the Lutheran rite. Paul, touched by her courage, turned aside so she would not see his tears. 'He is kind hearted,' she told Guizot, 'I beg you to be his friend – always.' She survived one more night – to her surprise. Towards midday on 27 January she said to her doctor: 'If I do not die this time, it will be a shame. I am quite ready.' That evening, about ten o'clock, her condition worsened and she asked Guizot and Paul to leave her alone; she wanted to save them the distress of seeing her die. An hour after her death Paul handed Guizot a letter written by Dorothea the previous evening: 'I thank you for twenty years of affection and happiness. Do not forget me. Farewell, farewell. Do not refuse my carriage tonight.' In her will she left Guizot an annuity of 8,000 francs and a carriage – he must keep up standards. Her body was carried to the family home in Courland, where it was buried beside two of her sons, George and Arthur. Writing to Metternich just before Castlereagh's death, Dorothea had commented: 'I am a woman, and very much of a woman. I want things passionately and I believe them readily'; as epitaphs go, it suits her well enough.

Bibliography

1. *Manuscript sources*

British Library
Lieven Papers
ADD. MSS. 47236–435
A. Papers of Prince Lieven (ADD. MSS. 47236–340)
B. Papers of Princess Lieven (ADD. MSS. 47341–94)
C. Family Correspondence (ADD. MSS. 47395–420)
D. Estate Papers (ADD. MSS. 47421–32)
E. Miscellanea (ADD. MSS. 47433–5)

Aberdeen Papers	ADD. MSS. 43052–5
Heytesbury Papers	ADD. MSS. 41511–63
Lamb Papers	Correspondence between Frederick and Emily Lamb (ADD. MSS. 45550–52, 45911) Correspondence between Lord and Lady Palmerston (ADD. MSS. 45553–4) Correspondence between Princess Lieven and Lady Palmerston (ADD. MSS. 45555–6)

National Archives, Kew

Stratford Canning Papers	PRO 352
Granville Papers	PRO/30/17–29
Cowley Papers	FO 519

Public Record Office of Northern Ireland
Castlereagh Papers
Clanwilliam Papers

Hartley Library, University of Southampton
Wellington Papers
Palmerston Papers

Hatfield House
Diary of Lady Palmerston

2. Published primary sources

(Place of publication London, unless otherwise stated.)

A. Edited correspondence of Princess Lieven

J. Hanoteau, *Lettres du Prince de Metternich à la Comtesse de Lieven 1818–1819* (Paris, 1909)

E. Jones Parry, *The Correspondence of Lord Aberdeen and Princess Lieven, 1832–1854*, 2 vols. (1938–9)

G. Le Strange, *The Correspondence of the Princess Lieven with Earl Grey*, 3 vols. (1890)

J. Navile, *Lettres de François Guizot et de la Princesse de la Lieven*, 3 vols. (Paris, 1963)

P. Quennell, *The Private Letters of Princess Lieven to Prince Metternich 1820–1826* (1937)

L. G. Robinson, *Letters of Dorothea, Princess Lieven, During Her Residence in London, 1812–1834* (1902)

Lord Sudley, *The Lieven–Palmerston Correspondence, 1828–1856* (1943)

H. W. V. Temperley, *The Unpublished Diary and Political Sketches of Princess Lieven* (1925)

B. Other edited correspondence/diaries/memoirs

Lady Airlie, *Lady Palmerston and Her Times*, 2 vols. (1922)

A. Aspinall, *The Formation of Canning's Ministry* (1937)

F. Bamford and the Duke of Wellington, *The Journal of Mrs Arbuthnot*, 2 vols. (1950)

Duc de Broglie, *Memoirs of the Prince de Talleyrand*, 5 vols. (1891)

Vicomte de Chateaubriand, *Chateaubriand's Memoirs*, 6 vols. (1892)

Lady Granville, *Lord Granville Leveson Gower, Private Correspondence*, 2 vols. (1916)

The Earl of Ilchester, *The Journal of the Hon. Henry Edward Fox* (1923)

A. Kriegel, *The Holland House Diaries 1831–1840* (1977)

T. Lever, *The Letters of Lady Palmerston* (1957)

F. Leveson Gower, *Letters of Harriet, Countess Granville 1810–1845*, 2 vols. (1894)

Lord Londonderry, *The Correspondence, Despatches and Other Papers of Viscount Castlereagh*, vols. VII–X (1854)

A. de Nesselrode, *Lettres et Papiers du Chancelier Comte de Nesselrode*, vols. VII–VIII (Paris, c. 1908)

M. C. Nicoullard, *Memoirs of the Comtesse de Boigne*, 3 vols. (1907–8)

Princess Radziwill, *Memoirs of the Duchesse de Dino*, 3 vols. (1909)

H. Reeve, *The Greville Memoirs*, 8 vols. (1913 edn)

E. J. Stapleton, *Some Official Correspondence of George Canning*, 2 vols. (1887)

Virginia Surtees, *A Second Self: the Letters of Harriet Granville 1810–1845* (1990)

C. K. Webster, *British Diplomacy 1813–1815* (1921)

A. R. Wellesley (ed.), *Despatches, Correspondence and Memoranda*, vols. 1–8 (1867–80)

G. Wellesley (ed.), *Wellington and His Friends* (1965)

3. Biographies of Princess Lieven

M. Bingham, *Princess Lieven: Russian Intriguer* (1982)

E. Daudet, *Une Vie d'ambassadrice au siècle dernier* (Paris, 1903)

F. Guizot, *Mélanges biographiques et littéraires* (Paris, 1868)

H. M. Hyde, *Princess Lieven* (1938)

L. P. Stebbins, *London Ladies* (New York, 1966)

Lytton Strachey, *Portraits in Miniature* (1931)

P. Zamoyska, *Arch Intriguer, a Biography of Dorothea Lieven* (1957)

4. Other biographies

K. Bourne, *Palmerston: the Early Years* (1982)

Sir H. Bulwer-Lytton, *The Life of Lord Palmerston*, 3 vols. (1870)

M. E. Chamberlain, *Lord Aberdeen* (1983)

——, *Lord Palmerston* (1987)

P. K. Grimstead, *The Foreign Ministers of Alexander I* (Berkeley, 1969)

J. M. Hartley, *Alexander I* (1994)

H. M. Hyde, *The Strange Death of Lord Castlereagh* (1959)

R. E. McGrew, *Paul I* (Oxford, 1992)

L. Mitchell, *Lord Melbourne* (1997)

A. Palmer, *Metternich* (1972)

——, *Alexander I* (1974)

S. Lane Poole, *Stratford Canning*, 2 vols. (1888)

E. A. Smith, *Lord Grey 1764–1845* (Oxford, 1990)

A. G. Stapleton, *George Canning and His Times* (1859)

G. M. Trevelyan, *Lord Grey of the Reform Bill* (1920)

5. Studies of British and Russian foreign policy

M. S. Anderson, *The Eastern Question 1774–1923* (1966)

F. Bridge, 'Allied diplomacy in peacetime: the failure of the Congress "System" ', in A. Sked (ed.), *Europe's Balance of Power 1815–1848* (1979)

C. A. W. Crawley, *The Question of Greek Independence* (Cambridge, 1930)

S. R. Graubaud, 'Castlereagh and the peace of Europe', *Journal of British Studies*, 1963

H. N. Ingle, *Nesselrode and the Russian Rapprochement with Britain, 1836–1844* (Berkeley, 1976)

P. Jupp, *British Politics on the Eve of Reform* (1998)

H. A. Kissinger, *A World Restored* (1957)

A. J. Reinerman, 'Metternich, Italy, and the Congress of Verona, 1821–1822', *Historical Journal*, 1971

——, 'Metternich, Alexander I, and the Russian Challenge in Italy, 1815–1820', *Journal of Modern History*, 1974

F. S. Rodkey, 'Lord Palmerston and the rejuvenation of Turkey, 1830–41', *Transactions of the Royal Historical Society*, 1929

P. Schroeder, *The Transformation of European Politics 1763–1848* (1994)

H. Temperley, *The Foreign Policy of Canning* (1925)

M. Vereté, 'Palmerston and the Levant Crisis, 1832', *Journal of Modern History*, 1952

Sir A. W. Ward and C. P. Gooch (eds.), *The Cambridge History of British Foreign Policy*, vol. II (Cambridge, 1923)

C. K. Webster, *The Congress of Vienna 1814–1815* (1934 edn)

—, *The Foreign Policy of Palmerston*, 2 vols. (1951)

—, *The Foreign Policy of Castlereagh*, 2 vols. (1963 edn)

6. Miscellanea

Lady C. Lamb, *Glenarvon* (1816; New York, 1972 edn)

K. D. Reynolds, *Aristocratic Women and Political Society in Victorian Britain* (1998)

M. Villiers, *The Grand Whiggery* (1939)

Notes

Preface

p. xi 'two intelligent people': P. Quennell (ed.), *The Private Letters of Princess Lieven to Prince Metternich 1820–1826* (1937) [hereafter *Private Letters*], 1 March 1822, 158.

p. xi 'plebeian and has no manners': ibid., 7 January 1823, 219.

p. xi 'worth living for': The Marquess of Zetland (ed.), *The Letters of Disraeli to Lady Chesterfield and Lady Bradford*, vol. II (1929), to Lady Chesterfield, 20 June 1876, 55.

p. xi 'I suppose, a little increases': ibid., to Lady Bradford, 7 June 1876, 52–3.

p. xiii 'incorporated wife': K. D. Reynolds, *Aristocratic Women and Political Society in Victorian Britain* (1998).

p. xiv 'people have no idea to what an extent women influence the elections in England': *Private Letters*, 11 March 1820, 21.

p. xv 'an unscrupulous woman'; 'an unamiable trait': ibid., xv, xvi.

p. xv 'quite enough so to have lovers': H. Reeve (ed.), *The Greville Memoirs*, vol. VIII (1903 edn), 20 January 1857, 77.

p. xvi 'such charges to be unfounded': ibid., 28 January 1857, 83.

Chapter 1

p. 1 'saved Europe': J. M. Hartley, *Alexander I* (1994), 119.

p. 2 'unless I use the help of foreigners': P. K. Grimstead, *The Foreign Ministers of Alexander I* (Berkeley, 1969), 28.

p. 2 strong-minded women: Grand Duke Nicolas Mihailovich, *Russkie Portrety*, vol. 3.2 (St Petersburg, 1907), no. 104.

p. 3 '*Corpulente et majestueuse*': ibid.

p. 4 'little monster's face': M. Bingham, *Princess Lieven* (1982), 6.

p. 5 'I thought of nothing else': *Private Letters*, 25 October 1820, 86.

p. 5 'love affairs of little girls were treated with military strictness': ibid.

p. 5 'head of dark chestnut curls': P. Zamoyska, *Arch Intriguer* (1957), 13.

p. 6 'ugly stench of scandal clinging to him': R. E. McGrew, *Paul I* (Oxford, 1992), 160.

p. 6 'what I enjoy': British Library Papers of Princess Lieven, ADD. MSS. 47395 [hereafter BL, Lieven MSS.], 'Dasha' to Count Lieven, *c.* 1799.

p. 7 'she is only marrying you to get away from the convent': BL, Lieven MSS., Count Lieven to Mlle Benckendorff, n.d. 1799.

p. 7 'you pardon me and that you still love me': ibid., 'Dasha' to Count Lieven, *c.* 1799.

p. 8 'and I thought about everything, except I was taking a husband': *Private Letters*, 24 February 1820, 15.

p. 8 'the object of universal terror and hatred throughout his Empire': H. W. V. Temperley, *The Unpublished Diary and Political Sketches of Princess Lieven* (1925) [hereafter *Diary*], 245.

p. 9 he sat high in the favour of the new Tsar, Alexander I: ibid., 245–67.

p. 10 Dorothea had loved him, he added, gallantly, that he understood why: J. Hanoteau, *Lettres du Prince de Metternich à la Comtesse de Lieven 1818–1819* (Paris, 1909) [hereafter *Lettres Metternich*], 252–3.

p. 10 'he was always that to me, and worthy of confidence': *Diary*, 23–8.

p. 11 'the Society here is deadly': H. M. Hyde, *Princess Lieven* (1938), 65.

p. 12 Dorothea Lieven was young, tall, skinny and flat-chested: L. P. Stebbins, *London Ladies*. (New York, 1966), 134–5.

p. 12 however aristocratic their background and exquisite their manners: H. Reeve (ed.), *The Greville Memoirs*, vol. I (1913 edn), 3 February 1819, 15–16.

p. 13 'never would I wish to die in this country': L. G. Robinson (ed.), *Letters of Dorothea, Princess Lieven, During Her Residence in London, 1812–1834* [hereafter *London Letters*] (1902), to Alexander, 6 April 1813, 2–3 [henceforth the letters should be assumed to be to Alexander unless stated otherwise].

p. 13 'and I cannot believe any ardent feelings under it': Virginia Surtees (ed.), *A Second Self: the Letters of Harriet Granville 1810–1845* (1990), 8 October 1815, 89.

p. 14 'ribbons to the whole family': *Private Letters*, 20 March 1820, 22–3.

p. 14 'what else she did is shrouded in obscurity': ibid., 11 March 1820, 20–21.

p. 15 'beautiful thing its Constitution is!': ibid., 20 March 1820, 23.

p. 16 she 'quite liked Prime Ministers': ibid., 2 June 1820, 37.

p. 16 'our house is large enough to lodge a number of guests': *London Letters*, 6, 18 October 1813, 7.

p. 16 'Lieven continues to succeed as well as his wife continues to fail': Hyde, *Lieven*, 73.

p. 17 'we must naturally desire most to promote': Lord Londonderry (ed.), *The Correspondence, Despatches and Other Papers of Viscount Castlereagh*, vol. VIII (1854) [hereafter *CC* followed by volume number], Castlereagh to Cathcart, 15 January 1813, 304.

p. 17 Castlereagh was convinced that he could bring Prussia and Austria into line to form one final great coalition against Bonaparte: ibid., 301–5.

p. 17 Count Lieven was warning that she might be driven from the war: Public Record Office, Northern Ireland [hereafter PRONI], Castlereagh MSS. D/3030/3451, Castlereagh to Cathcart, 10 April 1813.

Chapter 2

p. 18 'very kind to her and give her all sorts of information and advice about England': PRONI, Castlereagh MSS. D/3030/T2/MC 3/392, Castlereagh to Lady Castlereagh, 12 March 1814.

p. 18 'I shall not become Mme Clarence': H. M. Hyde, *Princess Lieven* (1938), 81–5 for the visit of the Grand Duchess.

pp. 19–20 'even the Opposition'; 'Your Prince is ill-bred'; 'knew what to do'; 'This is intolerable': ibid.

p. 21 'the deliverance of Europe from ruin': J. M. Hartley, *Alexander I* (1994), 117.

p. 21 'That's what the man's like': Hyde, *Lieven*, 87–8.

p. 22 improper to show a foreign monarch a mad king: ibid., 89.

pp. 23–4 Duke of Clarence's advances to Dorothea: *Diary*, 34–8.

p. 25 Duke of Devonshire's aversion to Dorothea: Virginia Surtees (ed.), *A Second Self: the Letters of Harriet Granville 1810–1845* (1990), to Lady Morpeth, 14 July 1815, 69.

p. 25 Harry-O: descriptions from A. Foreman, *Georgiana* (2001), 319, and M. Villiers, *The Grand Whiggery* (1939), 193

p. 26 she dreaded 'tiffs': Surtees, *A Second Self*, 4 October 1815, 88.

p. 26 'My women are good humoured and bear with her I think almost better than I do': ibid., 6 October 1815, 88–9.

p. 26 how peevish and sullen Dorothea had been: ibid., 10 October 1815, 89.

p. 26 'her very cross dry way and his perpetual titter': ibid., 89.

p. 26 'a mixture of the strangest impudence and most artful contrivance': ibid., 21 October 1815, 90.

p. 27 'It is a bad concern but with thousands of excuses – and very unhappy': ibid., 25 October 1815, 90.

p. 27 'as Madame de Lieven is agreeable, you *must* like her': F. Leveson Gower (ed.), *Letters of Harriet Countess Granville 1810–1845*, vol. I (1894) [hereafter *Granville Corr.* followed by volume number], to Lady Morpeth, June 1817, 117–18.

p. 27 'keep off bores, because she has the courage to *écraser* them': *Granville Corr.* II, to Lady Carlisle, January 1837, 221.

p. 27 'How much better the world would be if people were kinder': *Private Letters*, 1 March 1820, 17.

p. 28 Dorothea and Lord Gower: Surtees, *A Second Self*, 8 February 1816, 97.

p. 28 'How well you look dear': *Granville Corr.* II, to the Duke of Devonshire, 8 December 1828, 38.

p. 28 a woman who had a 'bust like a skeleton's': *Lettres Metternich*, Introduction, xlvi.

p. 28 Lady Bessborough on Dorothea: Lady Granville (ed.), *Lord Granville Leveson Gower, Private Correspondence*, vol. II (1916), Lady Bessborough to Lord Granville, September 1813, 479.

p. 28 'these are things which are *not* said': Earl of Ilchester (ed.), *The Journal of the Hon. Henry Edward Fox* (1923), 96.

p. 29 'l'ensemble est fin et spirituel': *Lettres Metternich*, Introduction, xlv.

p. 29 'independent of her body': *Granville Corr.* II, to Lady Carlisle, January 1837, 221.

p. 29 'her economy of clean linen': Hyde, *Lieven*, 76.

p. 29 'she was never of remarkable beauty, but she produced all the effect of being so': *Diary*, 42, quoting Ralph Sneyd, who knew her in old age.

p. 29 'Madame de Lieven was for a whole week invariably gay and brilliantly agreeable': *Granville Corr.* I, to Lady Harrowby, 19 January 1822, 221.

p. 29 Dorothea on Princess Esterhazy: *Private Letters*, 19 March 1820; 10 February 1821; 15 March 1822, 22, 113, 164.

p. 30 Comtesse de Boigne on Dorothea and Esterhazy; M. C. Nicoullard (ed.), *Memoirs of the Comtesse de Boigne*, vol. II (1907) [hereafter *Boigne Memoirs* II], 137.

p. 30 'One sees Lieven crunching the meek Apponyi's bones': *Granville Corr.* I, to Lady Carlisle, 23 November 1827, 437–8.

p. 30 'they have husbands, and I confess myself baffled': *Private Letters*, 2 August 1820, 57.

p. 30 'Englishmen cannot resist hairy arms', which no doubt explained everything: ibid., 2 July 1822, 84–5.

p. 30 'she is so clever and agreeable': T. Lever (ed.), *The Letters of Lady Palmerston* (1957), 27 March 1821, 76.

p. 31 they might take their pleasures where they found them: M. Villiers, *The Grand Whiggery* (1939), 192.

p. 31 'but not chaste, not chaste': L. Mitchell, *Lord Melbourne* (1997), 5.

p. 31 Lady Melbourne and Byron: Villiers, *Grand Whiggery*, 192.

p. 31 Emily Cowper: ibid., 244.

p. 31 'charming, subtle, amusing and kind': *Private Letters*, 5 April 1823, 253

p. 31 'Those were good days': Lady Airlie, *Lady Palmerston and Her Times*, vol. II (1922), Dorothea to Emily, 12 August 1841, 67–8.

p. 32 'I think it hard to exclude a person from a ball where six hundred people go if they really are received everywhere': ibid., vol. I, 41–2.

p. 32 improper that a man and woman should be so intimately connected in public: *London Letters*, footnote 1, 26.

p. 32 Byron on the waltz: P. Zamoyska, *Arch Intriguer* (1957), 47.

p. 33 'different from what you knew it': *London Letters*, 9 January 1816, 22.

p. 33 'a great change has taken place': *Granville Corr.* I, to Lady Morpeth, 1816, 86; Surtees, *A Second Self* dates it 14 or 15 February 1816, 97.

p. 33 'I was never so comfortably bored and I can conceive the connoisseurs thinking it a sort of little Paradise': Surtees, *A Second Self*, 19 February 1816, 98.

p. 33 'his wife, who *affected* to be very attached and submissive towards him': *Boigne Memoirs* II, 138.

p. 33 'I live like the rest of my fellow-creatures': *London Letters*, 1, 13 February 1816, 24–5.

p. 34 'my soirees and those of Lady Jersey are the most agreeable and the most brilliant': ibid., 16, 28 May 1816, 25–6.

Chapter 3

p. 35 'enjoyed an undisputed importance and political influence of a wholly personal character': *Boigne Memoirs* II, 136.

p. 35 'much feared but little loved': ibid., 138.

p. 35 'as much noise as a regular John Bull': *London Letters*, 30 October 1816, 28.

p. 35 'whirling our English beauties round the circle to a quicker movement than they had previously learned to practice': ibid., 1, 13 December, 30–32.

p. 35 Duke of Wellington, whom she pronounced 'very agreeable': ibid., 1 July 1817, 33.

p. 35 'rumours concerning her personal conduct': *Boigne Memoirs* II, 138.

p. 35 The number of her putative lovers: H. Reeve (ed.), *The Greville Memoirs*, VIII (1903 edn), 28 January 1857, 77–8.

p. 36 'the sentiment which she had imbibed, appeared in their eyes assumed and unnatural': Lady Caroline Lamb, *Glenarvon*, vol. I (1816), 151–2.

p. 36 'amused himself with instructing me in things I need never have heard or known': Lady Caroline Lamb, *Glenarvon* (New York, 1972 edn), Introduction, vii.

p. 37 'a profound knowledge of the human heart often leaves them unable to decide': *Lettres Metternich*, 30 January 1819, 166.

p. 37 'I prefer any other form of suffering': *Private Letters*, 3 April 1821, 128.

p. 37 'it would be stupid to die of boredom': ibid., 25 May 1823, 266.

p. 37 'my madness ebbed as the water advanced': ibid., 14 March 1822, 162–3 (she writes 'the third canto', but there are no references to drowning there).

p. 39 'considerable talents, without common sense to guide them': PRONI, Castlereagh MSS. D3030/5075, Clancarty to Castlereagh, Frankfurt, 4 October 1814.

p. 39 'a prettier little Congress, it will not cause me any unpleasantness': A. Palmer, *Metternich* (1972), 176.

p. 39 'his face expressed both benevolence and the most delicate gentleness': H. M. Hyde, *Princess Lieven* (1938), 101.

p. 40 no beautiful Russian princesses when he arrived at Aix: *Lettres Metternich*, lxii.

p. 40 Madame de Catalani, who, in Dorothea's opinion, could not sing a note in key: National Archives [hereafter NA], Granville MSS. PRO 30/29/17/4/PT. 3, to Lady Granville, 11 October 1818.

p. 40 'renewed my *tendresse*': *London Letters*, 3, 15 January 1819, 37; *Diary*, 23.

p. 40 the paucity of pretty women: NA, Granville MSS. PRO 30/29/17/4/PT. 3, to Lady Granville, 13 October 1818.

p. 40 'pretty woman who wants everything but love': *Lettres Metternich*, 1 December 1818, 45.

p. 41 there was more to this than she revealed to Harriet Granville: NA, Granville MSS. PRO 30/29/17/4/PT. 3, to Lady Granville, 22 October 1818.

p. 41 'I never realised he could be so useful – more useful on top of his rock than he ever was on his throne': *Lettres Metternich*, 24 March 1820, lxiii–iv.

p. 41 He knew, at that moment, that he had misjudged her: ibid., 28 November 1818, 27.

p. 41 'we stayed the night at Spa and in the morning we amused ourselves by driving around the neighbourhood': Madeline Bingham, *Princess Lieven* (1982), 91–2.

p. 42 'I could love you more than I have ever loved before?': *Lettres Metternich*, 28 January 1818, 28–30.

p. 43 'Vow to keep a beautiful memory and do not have any regrets': ibid., n.d., 1.

p. 43 'In fact I believe this, as one believes in something one does not understand': ibid., 15 November 1818, 3–4.

p. 44 be in his thoughts when he awoke: ibid., midnight, 4–5.

p. 44 her passion for Count Elmpt: *Private Letters*, 25 October 1820, 85–6.

p. 44 with others around he had dared not say what he felt: *Lettres Metternich*, midnight, 17–18 November 1818, 7–8.

p. 44 asked her not to forget him and their time in Aix: ibid., midnight, 18–19 November 1818, 9–13.

p. 45 How many friends, he wondered, would give her such advice: ibid., 18 November 1818, 14–15.

p. 45 'be my friend for ever – for life': ibid., n.d. but *c.* 26–27 November 1818, 22.

p. 45 'that nothing my friends say can diminish my pain': ibid., 28 November 1818, 11 p.m., 33–5.

p. 45 'what a moment!': ibid., 29 November 1818, 11 p.m., 35–6.

p. 46 'I shall always retain a pleasant remembrance': *London Letters*, 3, 15 January 1819, 37.

p. 46 'the great misfortune of our position is that we have so little contact': *Lettres Metternich*, 18 December 1818, 67.

p. 46 No transfer for Count Lieven: *London Letters*, 2, 14 May 1819, 39–40.

p. 46 'For a woman love is everything, for a man it is just part of his life': *Lettres Metternich*, 3 January 1819, 104.

p. 46 'what young woman has not?': ibid., 30 January 1819, 166.

p. 47 'because loving is beyond the will of the individual': ibid., 14 December 1818, 61.

p. 48 'But it is certain that I could not do otherwise': ibid., 2 February 1819, 173–8.

p. 49 He had not been in England since he was eighteen, in 1794: ibid., 3 February 1819, 178–80.

p. 49 'I already love your little daughter – but never as much as her mother': ibid., 25 February 1819, 217–21.

p. 50 'My Clement, have you ever time for dreams?': ibid., Dorothea to Metternich, 3 September 1819, 316.

p. 50 'she had never had a happier confinement than this one': BL, Lieven MSS., ADD. MSS. 47410, Lieven to Karl Lieven, October 1819.

Chapter 4

p. 51 'My dear, you love me well, for you now love that Austria which you used not to love': *Lettres Metternich*, 4 February 1819, 180.

p. 51 'the Emperor of Russia is desirous of ending matters as he began, by dictating his will as the sovereign law of all Europe': PRONI, Castlereagh MSS. D/3030/4567, Clancarty (Vienna) to Castlereagh, 26 May 1815.

p. 52 'a stable international system': H. A. Kissinger, *A World Restored* (New York, 1957), 111.

p. 52 'strove for a balance of forces which would not place too great a premium on self-restraint': ibid.

p. 52 'clear that his mind was affected': PRONI, Castlereagh MSS. D/3030/4716, Castlereagh to Liverpool, 28 September 1815.

p. 52 'must have an immediate influence on the council of princes and guide all their steps': J. M. Hartley, *Alexander I* (1994), 133–4.

p. 53 'might save him and the rest of the world much trouble, so long as it should last': PRONI, Castlereagh MSS. D/3030/4716, Castlereagh to Liverpool, 28 September 1815.

p. 53 'to maintain the true spirit of the alliance, the Peace of Europe & the settlement we have concluded': PRONI, Castlereagh MSS. D/3030/4783, Castlereagh to Cathcart, 23 December 1815.

p. 53 trying to persuade the British that they ought to be wary of Russian ambitions and do more to counter them: Kissinger, *World Restored* 216–18.

p. 54 turned aside Alexander with the excuse that the Holy Alliance provided for all that was necessary: C. K. Webster, *The Foreign Policy of Castlereagh*, vol. II (1963 edn), 142–65; Kissinger, *World Restored* 225–6.

p. 54 'in that case London would see me infrequently': *Lettres Metternich*, 29 January 1819, 164–5.

p. 54 'He is sulking now, and his sulks will strain their relations': *Private Letters*, 29 January 1820, 7.

p. 54 'every question could be reduced to one of personalities': *Boigne Memoirs* II, 138.

p. 54 'I like you to realise sometimes that I am stupider than you': *Private Letters*, 26 April 1823, 259.

p. 55 'whatever you may say, great intelligence is not really my strong point': ibid., 14 February 1820, 12.

p. 55 'I am sometimes witty, sometimes stupid, and strong and weak and a number of dissimilar things, it must be very entertaining': ibid., 1 March 1822, 158.

p. 55 'He continually hesitates to form any': ibid., 1 July 1820, 46.

p. 55 'since we have enough intelligence for this kind of amusement, let us go on': ibid., 5 April 1820, 27.

p. 56 Count Karl Nesselrode . . . suggesting that she might like to keep up an occasional correspondence with him: BL, Lieven MSS., ADD. MSS. 47355, from Nesselrode, 20 June 1819.

p. 56 Nesselrode became State Secretary for Foreign Affairs in 1814: P. K. Grimstead, *The Foreign Ministers of Alexander I* (Berkeley, 1969), 196; see also H. N. Ingle, *Nesselrode and the Russian Rapprochement with Britain, 1836–1844*, (Berkeley, 1976).

p. 56 'the Emperor's *Secretary*': *CC*, vol. IX, Walpole to Castlereagh, 9 August 1814, 83.

p. 56 'the person who may happen to fall in most with his views': C. K. Webster, *British Diplomacy 1813–1815* (1921), 5 November 1815, 222.

p. 56 'I am not in a position to say anything': BL, Lieven MSS., ADD. MSS. 47251, Nesselrode to Count Lieven, *c.* 1813.

p. 56–7 Nesselrode favoured a cautious, conservative policy, and in this he and Metternich were natural allies: Grimstead, *Foreign Ministers*, 201–2.

p. 57 'the dynastic and territorial integrity of the great powers': ibid., 270.

p. 58 the King was most unhappy, not least with Castlereagh: *Private*

Letters, 9 February 1820, 12; F. Bamford and the Duke of Wellington (eds.), *The Journal of Mrs Arbuthnot*, vol. I (1950) [hereafter *Arbuthnot Journal* followed by volume number], 12–15 February 1820, 2–3.

p. 58 he would be willing to come to England in person to dissuade the King from taking such a step: ibid., 13 February 1820, 3.

p. 58 who would have the honour of cutting Castlereagh's throat: *Private Letters*, 25 February 1820, 15–17.

p. 59 'everybody knows that he is always followed': ibid., 1 March 1820, 17–18.

p. 59 Dorothea was convinced that it would not be long before there was a new government: ibid., 26 April 1820, 31–2.

p. 59 'defeated by a woman': ibid., 6 June 1820, 39–40.

p. 59 Canning's resignation: ibid., 9 June 1820, 40.

p. 60 Dorothea remained doubtful of their capacity to do it: ibid., 15 June 1820, 42–3.

p. 60 Wellington on Spain: A. R. Wellesley (ed.), *Despatches, Correspondence and Memoranda*, vol. I (1858) [hereafter *WDCM* and volume number], Wellington memorandum, 16 April 1820, 116–21.

pp. 60–61 Castlereagh's State Paper: Sir A. W. Ward and C. P. Gooch (eds.), *The Cambridge History of British Foreign Policy*, vol. II (Cambridge, 1923), Castlereagh's Confidential State Paper of 5 May 1820, 623–33.

p. 61 'The British Cabinet wish, as the Duke of Wellington has often said to me, that the Alliance sleeps': Webster, *Foreign Policy of Castlereagh* II, 242.

p. 61 'wise constitutional regime': A. Palmer, *Metternich* (1972), 191–3.

p. 62 'I firmly believe; but the seed he has sown is still sprouting': *Private Letters*, 20 July 1820, 53.

p. 62 Austria 'must come out of it with clean hands': ibid., 21 July 1820, 53.

p. 62 Britain would support Austrian action – although, of course, she could take none herself: Webster, *Foreign Policy of Castlereagh* II, 261–3.

p. 62 Alexander's demands at Troppau: ibid., 265–6.

p. 63 'his unruffled appearance has overawed the mob': *Private Letters*, 12 August 1820, 59.

p. 63 Castlereagh sleeping at the FO: ibid., 19 August 1820, 62.

p. 63 'the sentiments which are to be found on either side of the House of Commons': Webster, *Foreign Policy of Castlereagh* II, Castlereagh to Sir Charles Stewart, 21 September 1821, 272.

p. 64 '*outrée* with England for refusing to take a part in this new dish of Continental troubles': *Granville Corr.* I, to Lady G. Morpeth, 6 October 1820, 183.

p. 64 'if the King were to sanction them he would be on the road to abdication': Webster, *Foreign Policy of Castlereagh* II, 302.

p. 64 'Europe's safety anchor. Why change it now?': BL, Lieven MSS., ADD. MSS. 47246, Lieven to Nesselrode, 8 December 1820.

Chapter 5

p. 65 Castlereagh and the alliance: BL, Lieven MSS., ADD. MSS. 47246, Lieven to Nesselrode, 21 December 1820.

p. 65 'an odd option for them to make in the present state of Europe': C. K. Webster, *The Foreign Policy of Castlereagh*, vol. II (1963 edn), 305–6.

p. 66 Britain was not in any way associated with the actions of the other powers: ibid., 314–23.

p. 66 'that Command and Influence which makes other men willing instruments': PRONI, Castlereagh MSS. D/3030/6186, Sir Robert Peel to Lord Londonderry, 23 July 1839.

p. 67 'and he never leaves me': *Private Letters*, 28 March 1822, 166.

p. 67 'his inclinations urged him towards friendship with Austria': ibid., 14 August 1822, 193.

p. 67 this offered the chance for her to see Metternich again: ibid., 5 April 1821, 129.

p. 67 'I found myself isolated, lost and very sad': NA, Granville MSS. PRO/29/17/4/PT3, to Lady Granville, 3 June 1821.

p. 67 'I forget that differences of character and disposition now and then cause me unpleasant moments': *Private Letters*, 3 June 1821, 135.

p. 67 'all your intelligence to arranging where to sleep and where to dine': ibid., 6 June 1821, 136.

p. 67 'ah mon dieu que c'est bête d'avoir de l'Esprit': NA, Granville MSS. PRO/29/17/4/PT3, to Lady Granville, 7 June 1821.

p. 68 'and I am wasting away through boredom': ibid., 13 June 1821.

pp. 68–9 she would be criticized and her motives would be suspect: ibid., 7 July 1821.

p. 69 'your skin as soft as satin, whilst the warmth is delicious': ibid., 29 August 1821.

p. 69 he would not be able to get there until after his wife: *Diary*, 54; *Lettres Metternich*, 320–22.

p. 69 'I have never in all my life heard so many pretty things said about me': A. Palmer, *Metternich* (1972), 207.

p. 70 'certain that if we give the slightest occasion we shall be dismissed the same day': Duke of Wellington (ed.), *Wellington and His Friends* (1965), from Wellington, 10 June 1821, 295.

p. 70 'if the King is mad, his Ministers are very feeble': *Private Letters*, 25 June 1821, 138.

p. 70 'much less to a woman whose only notoriety arose from so shameful a cause': *Arbuthnot Journal* I, 10 October 1820, 43.

p. 70 'our political standpoint would certainly gain by England's taking a more vigorous grasp in the world's affairs': H. M. Hyde, *Princess Lieven* (1938), 130.

p. 70 it was likely to bring Canning to the Foreign Office: *Arbuthnot Journal* I, 17 March 1821, 83.

p. 70 'he had never been of the use to us which, from his great talents, he ought to have been': ibid., 5 December 1820, 56.

p. 71 'that is never forgiven in England': *Private Letters*, 3 October 1820, 77.

p. 71 'who must be treated all the better for that very reason': ibid., 28 March 1822, 166.

p. 72 'to accommodate the interests and *amour propre* of the two sides': BL, Lieven MSS., ADD. MSS. 47246, Lieven to Nesselrode, 9 December 1821. Castlereagh had become the 2nd Marquess of Londonderry upon the death of his father on 8 April 1821.

p. 72 'their agreement is so important in the present state of Europe, that this circumstance alone ought to outweigh all other considerations': Webster, *Foreign Policy of Castlereagh* II, 371.

p. 72 he ought to have known, since his wife was the most active agent in maintaining it: BL, Lieven MSS., ADD. MSS. 47246, Lieven to Nesselrode, 21 December 1820.

p. 72 Castlereagh 'gave a loud Ha, ha': *Private Letters*, 30 November 1821, 142–3.

p. 72 the King monopolized Dorothea for most of the evening: ibid., 9 December 1821, 143–4.

p. 73 we should even lack evidence that the two of them were lovers, although everyone assumed they were: ibid., Introduction, ix–xiv; *Lettres Metternich*, i–vii, for the details.

p. 73 Castlereagh was, in Harriet Arbuthnot's words, 'a great flirt & very fond of ladies': *Arbuthnot Journal* I, 29 August 1822, 178.

p. 73 he occasionally resorted to prostitutes for relaxation from his labours: H. M. Hyde, *The Strange Death of Lord Castlereagh* (1959), 184.

p. 73 'would assist the game of the revolutionists in Europe, to whom, and to whom alone the late events are to be attributed': Webster, *Foreign Policy of Castlereagh* II, 373.

p. 74 'at the hazard of all the destructive confusion and disunion which such an attempt may lead to, not only within Turkey, but in Europe': ibid., Castlereagh to the Tsar, 28 October 1821, 376–7.

p. 74 'the advantage of being able to prove to Russia how far one can go with England when one understands how to speak her language': ibid., 381.

p. 74 Capodistrias, who had edited the final declaration in which the powers pledged themselves to combat the forces of revolution: P. K. Grimstead, *The Foreign Ministers of Alexander*, vol. I (Berkeley, 1969), 277–8.

p. 75 'which he thinks I prefer. I let him do it, for it is all to the good': *Private Letters*, 25 January 1822, 148–9.

p. 75 'Devil take me, I think I must have got into bad company': ibid., 26 January 1822, 150.

p. 75 'may kindle a flame which all our efforts may perhaps hereafter be insufficient to extinguish': Webster, *Foreign Policy of Castlereagh* II, 387–8.

p. 75 to exert a pacifying influence upon the Tsar: University of Southampton, Hartley Library, Papers of the Duke of Wellington, WP1/698/3, Londonderry to Bagot, 19 January 1822; WP1/700/10, copies of despatches from St Petersburg, 18 February 1822; WP1/704/4, Lieven to Londonderry, 17 March 1822.

p. 76 'he must trust me, and he is right': *Private Letters*, 23 February 1822, 157–8.

p. 76 it would be better if more senior and skilled negotiators were entrusted with the task: ibid., 4 March 1822, 159–60.

p. 77 'Is it really possible to be in love with a woman who accepts diamonds and pearls?': ibid., 23 December 1821, 145.

p. 77 she lamented to Metternich in January 1822: ibid., 31 January 1822, 151.

p. 77 'She is the most changeable person in the world': ibid., 27 April 1822, 167.

p. 77 'than getting round a woman's vanity, when one can appeal neither to her reason nor her decent feelings': ibid., 21 May 1822, 171–2.

p. 78 'Either I am mad or he is!': ibid., 2 June 1822, 173–4; Hyde, *Lieven*, 138–9.

p. 78 'he had never seen a man in such a state': *Private Letters*, 2 June 1822, 175.

p. 78 'he will soon come to his senses': ibid., 10 June 1822, 178–9.

p. 79 Castlereagh was much more like his old self: ibid., 17 June 1822, 179–80.

p. 79 'I will stand alone and the struggle will be unequal': PRONI, Castlereagh MSS. D/3044/F/18, Metternich to Londonderry, 6 June 1822.

p. 79 'we must all run at your bidding': *Private Letters*, 17 June 1822, 189.

p. 79 'they all look as though they were on the point of committing suicide': ibid., 22 June 1822, 181.

p. 79 'how sad you must be': ibid., 13, 14 August 1822, 191–3.

Chapter 6

p. 80 'His colleagues are not at all like that': *Private Letters*, 9 September 1822, 205.

p. 81 'Canning could talk French and nobody else could, therefore he must be Foreign Secretary': E. J. Stapleton (ed.), *Some Official Correspondence of George Canning*, vol. I (1887) [hereafter *Canning Corr.* I or II], 22.

p. 81 'he will receive the most important post in the Government': *Private Letters*, 10 September 1822, 206.

p. 81 ' "Admit the rogue" ': ibid., 13 September 1822, 206–7.

p. 81 'the rogue' was admitted: *Canning Corr.* I, 16–18.

p. 82 'he still thought he might be made a useful person': *Arbuthnot Journal* I, 16 September 1822, 192.

p. 82 'no stability in his principles': *Private Letters*, 21 August 1822, 199.

p. 82 'resume the liberty of action which suited the temperament of his nation': *Diary*, 83.

p. 83 the Grand Alliance which was the object of Canning's aversion: H. Temperley, *The Foreign Policy of Canning* (1925), 43–9.

p. 83 'therefore require the interference of the Alliance': *CC* XIII, Bathurst to Castlereagh, 20 October 1818, 56–7.

p. 83 no British representation at Verona: *Canning Corr.* I, 43–4; Temperley, *Canning*, 48.

p. 84 'I must find some way of distracting myself': *Private Letters*, 29 August 1822, 202.

p. 84 a 'boring life' indeed: NA, Granville MSS. PRO/29/17/4/Pt 3, Dorothea to Lady Granville, 4 October 1822.

p. 84 the Tsar 'disapproved' of it: BL, Lieven MSS., ADD. MSS. 47415, Dorothea to Alexander, 1 December 1822.

p. 85 only the first category who stayed with Dorothea and Metternich until the early hours of the morning: NA, Granville MSS. PRO/29/17/4/Pt 3, Dorothea to Lady Granville, 9 November 1822.

p. 85 'the sole representative of my species': BL, Lieven MSS, ADD. MSS. 47415, Dorothea to Alexander, 23 October 1822.

p. 85 '*effiloquer la soie*' [silken dalliance]: Vicomte de Chateaubriand, *Chateaubriand's Memoirs*, vol. VI (1892), 72.

p. 86 'you have so much chance of finding what you need': *Private Letters*, 29 April 1822, 168.

p. 86 'hunchback without the hump': ibid., 8 May 1822, 168–9.

p. 86 'A clever man who does that must be a fool': ibid., 3 July 1822, 186.

p. 86 'that I would sigh also if that would give him pleasure, but it would not, in any way': NA, Granville MSS. PRO/29/17/4/Pt 3, Dorothea to Lady Granville, 9 November 1822.

p. 86 'His Majesty will not be a party': *WDCM* I, Canning to Wellington, 27 September 1822, 304.

p. 87 an unpleasant shock to Metternich when Wellington broke the news on 30 October: ibid., Wellington memorandum, 31 October 1822, 505.

p. 87 'England separated herself from the allies during the affair of Naples very unnecessarily': ibid., Wellington to Canning, 5 November 1822, 492–507.

p. 87 ten years, she reminded him, was 'a long time': *London Letters*, 7 December 1823, 60.

p. 88 the influence she could try to exercise: *Private Letters*, 6 January 1823, 217.

p. 88 other ways of regarding the events at Verona: Temperley, *Canning*, 74.

p. 90 'he is real gold, the purest and most precious': *Private Letters*, 7, 8 January 1823, 218–20.

p. 90 'there is no longer very great unity' between him and Canning: ibid., 17 January 1823, 225.

p. 91 Canning's 'insatiable ambition': ibid., 26 January 1823, 226–30.

p. 92 'I shan't take him': ibid., 9 January 1823, 221.

p. 92 'I believe he can be managed': ibid., 11 January 1823, 222–3.

p. 92 'I have not a very clear idea of you myself': ibid., 21 January 1823, 226.

p. 92 Canning's 'plebeian' manner: ibid., 31 January 1823, 231–3.

p. 93 'nobody tells me the truth these days': ibid., 3 February 1823, 234–5.

p. 93 'she is too fond of her husband and her husband is too fond of Mr Canning': ibid., 19 March 1823, 244.

p. 93 'The best is bad; but the worst would be hateful, and there is nothing in between': ibid., 5 March 1823, 241–2.

Chapter 7

p. 94 'we do not know him well enough': *Private Letters*, 28 January 1823, 228.

p. 95 'Listen to the opinions of the whole of England, and you will see if we can do anything to help people with such ideas': ibid., 31 January 1823, 232.

p. 95 'I cannot think Mr Canning will go on long': *Arbuthnot Journal* I, 29 January 1823, 208.

p. 95 'a most erroneous conclusion': *The Times*, 12 February 1823.

p. 96 'abhorrence than he did': H. Temperley, *The Foreign Policy of Canning* (1925), 86.

p. 97 'I had taken what the King said in the right spirit and for what it was worth': *Private Letters*, 28 March 1823, 245.

p. 98 no British politician had a foot in as many camps as the Russian ambassadress: ibid., 16 April 1823, 254–5.

p. 98 'My Ministers want to start a revolution in England': ibid., 20 April 1823, 256–7.

p. 98 'the majority of the two Houses': ibid., 15 March 1823, 243.

p. 99 'If the wind is in the east, I am ill-natured and cross': ibid., 9 May 1823, 261.

p. 99 'it was my foreign accent that amused them': ibid., 3 April 1823, 250–51.

p. 100 'imagine me in the middle of all of this?': ibid., 7 April 1823, 253–4.

p. 100 'I am stupider than you', she told Metternich during this period: ibid., 26 April 1823, 259.

p. 100 'I change with the wind': ibid., 9 May 1923, 261.

p. 101 'only sick and sad-hearted': ibid., 6 August 1823, 66–7.

p. 101 'I remembered Verona': ibid., 14 August 1823, 280–81.

p. 102 the promise from Metternich that he would meet her there: NA, Granville MSS. PRO 30/29/17/4/PT 1, Countess Lieven to Lady Granville, 23 October 1823.

p. 102 'I am not Metternich's mistress and never shall be': *Arbuthnot Journal* I, 6 June 1823, 319–20.

p. 102 'The motion was passed unanimously': *Private Letters*, 5 July 1823, 272.

p. 102 'you have never done me the honour of treating me as a pretty woman': ibid., 1 March 1823, 240.

p. 103 a 'furious letter' from Grey about Wellington's conduct at Verona and the government's foreign policy: ibid., 1 February 1823, 234.

p. 103 him to give her the credit for the 'moderation' he had shown in the debates over Spain: ibid., 26 April 1823, 259.

p. 103 'Lord Grey,' she informed Metternich on 9 May, 'is very attentive to me': ibid., 9 May 1823, 261.

p. 103 'That is what comes of letting oneself be ruled by Lord Grey': ibid., 13 May 1823, 262.

p. 103 'I found out how much I was formed to love and esteem you?': G. Le Strange, *The Correspondence of the Princess Lieven with Earl Grey*, vol. I (1890) [hereafter *Grey–Lieven* followed by volume number] from Grey, 5 January 1826, 20.

p. 103 he 'almost certainly at some time in the later 1820s became her lover': E. A. Smith, *Lord Grey 1764–1845* (Oxford, 1990), 281.

p. 104 'I am too bored and cross and ill to take trouble over anything': *Private Letters*, 5 July 1823, 272–3.

p. 104 'I have never heard of sentimental knees before': ibid., 5 October 1823, 292.

p. 104 'treat me as I deserve': ibid., 14 October 1823, 294.

p. 104 'leaves my mind utterly vacant': ibid., 20 October 1823, 294–5.

p. 105 'go back to our habits of five years past – weekly letters. Will that suit you?': ibid., 31 October 1823, 297.

p. 105 'Indeed, I am only staying as a matter of form': ibid., 4 November 1823, 287.

p. 105 'You are hurting me; while I am only sparing you boredom': ibid., 28 November 1823, 301.

p. 105 'at no age should a woman dispense with reserve about her relations with a man': ibid., 25 January 1824, 306–7.

p. 105 'It is very bad policy not to write to me': ibid., 12 February 1824, 308.

p. 105 'You can see that you will not be able to overthrow Mr Canning': ibid., 14 March 1824, 312.

p. 106 'he might pay too dearly for it': H. M. Hyde, *Princess Lieven* (1938), 124–6.

Chapter 8

p. 107 'very much surprised by the changes I should find' now that she was back: *Private Letters*, 17 June 1824, 317.

p. 107 opposition to Canning: *Arbuthnot Journal* I, 3, 20, 28 February 1824, 284, 287–9, 3 February 1824; *Private Letters*, 17 June 1824, 317.

p. 107 'the damnedest fellow in the world & that he could not bear him': *Arbuthnot Journal* I, 29 April 1824, 305–9.

p. 107 'as if I would sit at the table with such a pair of damned cannibals': ibid., 6 June 1824, 319.

p. 108 trying to find the rising sun so they could genuflect in its direction: ibid., 7, 11 April, 10 June 1824, 299–300, 321.

p. 108 'Duke of Portland had no more idea of speaking than I have; and yet he was head of the administration': *Private Letters*, 17 June 1824, 317–19.

p. 109 'to gratify his own spleen': *Arbuthnot Journal* I, 16 July 1824, 328.

p. 110 'to change the politics of this Government by changing *me*': NA, Granville MSS. PRO 30/29/8/7, Canning to Granville, 11 March 1825.

p. 111 showed who Canning believed his enemies were: *Arbuthnot Journal* I, 16 October 1824, full texts, 342–51.

p. 111 she it was who had stirred him up to oppose it: *Private Letters*, 8 October 1824, 331–2.

p. 111 'things cannot go on like this': ibid., 2 November 1824, 336.

p. 111 'Wellington cannot fairly be called a member of the "Coterie", though he occasionally attended their meetings': *Diary*, 243.

p. 112 Wellington was 'the only check we have on Mr Canning's follies': *Private Letters*, 8 October 1823, 334.

p. 112 'Heaven preserve you from the knees of the King and the Duke of York, especially in 25 degrees of heat': ibid., 2, 13 September 1824, 329, 331.

p. 114 a 'complete revolution in the political system of Europe': ibid., 24 November 1824, 338.

p. 115 '& we may have, for anything he knows to the contrary, all Europe against us!': *Arbuthnot Journal* I, 4 December 1824, 359–60.

p. 115 Wellington offered to resign over the issue: *WDCM* II, Liverpool to Wellington, 5 December 1824, Wellington's reply, 354–8, 364–6.

p. 115 he saw no way open other than resignation: *Private Letters*, 4 December 1824, 338–9.

p. 116 'Now we have one who is a master of both arts, & we know nothing & are consulted about nothing': *Arbuthnot Journal* I, 10 December 1824, 364–6.

p. 116 'therefore the best thing to do was to yield but to watch Mr Canning narrowly and keep him as straight as possible': ibid., 18 December 1824, 368.

p. 116 'So the outcome of all these Cabinet meetings is that they have ended as [Canning] wished them to end. What weakness!': *Private Letters*, 20 December 1824, 341.

p. 116 'will he say and do when he receives Pozzo's account of the South American treaties? Will he publish a manifesto?': NA, Granville MSS. PRO 30/29/8/6, Canning to Granville, 17 January 1825.

p. 117 'had now reached a definite separation from the Neo-Holy Alliance over Greece, as over everything else, and isolation is dangerous in diplomacy': *Diary*, 335.

p. 117 'high and mighty': H. Temperley, *The Foreign Policy of Canning* (1925), 152–3.

p. 118 'to teach the Holy Alliance': NA, Granville MSS. PRO 30/29/8/7, Canning to Granville, 4 March 1825.

p. 118 'I know nothing of the present temper of the English nation': ibid., 11 March 1825.

p. 118 Canning resented Metternich's tendency to attribute his own motives to Canning: NA, Stratford Canning MSS. FO 352/10/A, G. Canning to S. Canning, 13 March 1825.

p. 119 'such a system had all English opinion against it': *Private Letters*, 4 February 1825, 343–4.

p. 119 'But he is one of those men who always kill any conversation. You have continually to begin again; and I get bored': ibid., 18 June 1824, 319–20.

p. 119 'The truth is that there is a sort of attraction about the people one hates': ibid., 20 July 1824, 321–2.

pp. 119–20 Metternich had put off his journey to Paris because of him: ibid., 6 March 1825, 344.

p. 120 'we must put up with this plague until he takes it into his head to break his own neck': ibid., 10 March 1825, 345.

p. 120 how the press were commenting on his visit to Paris, which he thought would have a good effect politically: ibid., 22 March, 2 April 1825, 347, 349.

p. 120 'Metternich . . . is quite incorrigible': NA, Granville MSS. PRO 30/29/8/7, Canning to Granville, 1 April 1825.

p. 120 'may let the House of Commons, & the Publick into the secret': ibid., 4 April 1825.

p. 120 visits by Dorothea and Esterhazy to the 'Cottage': ibid., 19 April 1825.

p. 120 to make overtures of peace: ibid., Joan Canning to Granville, 29 April 1825.

Chapter 9

p. 121 Stratford Canning, who was on a special mission to St Petersburg, and who wrote that he had been met with great coolness: NA, Stratford Canning MSS. FO 352/10/A, S. Canning to G. Canning, 16 February 1825.

p. 121 'we shall again be on terms of good understanding with Russia': ibid., G. Canning to S. Canning, 23 February 1825.

p. 121 'a second dissent & separation like that of Verona would have made us supremely ridiculous': ibid., 13 March 1825.

p. 121 'quite strong enough to hold if it is not strained too hard': ibid., 23 February 1825.

p. 121 'Canning has become friendly, at least to my husband': *Private Letters*, 8 April 1825, 349.

p. 122 'rendering us the mark of their common attack – a clever scheme!': NA, Granville MSS. PRO 30/29/8/7, Canning to Granville, 12 April 1825.

p. 123 Russia's willingness to at least leave open the option of talking separately to the British: NA, Stratford Canning MSS. FO 352/10/A, S. Canning to G. Canning, 5 March 1825.

p. 123 the British still wished to avoid the use of force: ibid., 31 March 1825.

p. 123 the Tsar did not forgive his old ally: *Diary*, 85.

p. 123 'tell the Emperor the truth, if he did me the honour to speak to me of his affairs': ibid., 86.

p. 124 'in order to wait a long time': ibid.

p. 125 'it only remains to make a tyrant of him': ibid., 93.

p. 125 'I do not know why, but this embarrassment gave me courage': ibid., 88–91 for this and the account of the meeting with Alexander.

p. 126 an attempted coup, one of whose leaders was Lebzeltern's brother-in-law, Count Trubetzkoi: ibid., 90–91.

p. 127 'Canning is a Jacobin': *London Letters*, 27 April 1823, 64.

p. 127 'was the enemy of Prince Metternich': *Diary*, 92.

pp. 127–9 Final conversation with Nesselrode: ibid., 97–9.

p. 129 'try to make your peace': *Private Letters*, 2 September 1825, 353.

pp. 129–30 'The Emperor took me for a man; he treated me as one as regards confidences, and as a woman as regards attentions and consideration': ibid., 2 October 1825, 354.

p. 130 'It is impossible for ill humour to be expressed more strongly than in the tenour [*sic*] of these two documents': *Canning Corr.* I, Canning memorandum, 25 October 1825, 313–15.

p. 130 'I have understood the sense of the "living despatch" that you have sent me': *Diary*, 107, Lieven to Nesselrode, 30 October 1825.

p. 130 'without the certainty of being betrayed': *Canning Corr.* I, Canning to Liverpool, 25 October 1825, 317.

p. 130 '*If* we act we must finish what is to be done': NA, Granville MSS. PRO/30/29/8/9, Canning to Granville, 31 October 1825.

p. 131 'liberty to protest against the Emperor of Russia's march to Constantinople in a representative capacity as well as in his personal one'; – something the French could not do: ibid., 8 November 1825.

p. 131 it was clear that he would have to go: NA, Foreign Office Correspondence, Russia, FO 181/65, Canning to Strangford, 12 October 1825.

p. 131 'This event echoed through Europe like a thunderclap': *Diary*, 109.

p. 132 'I believe I should have done good': *Private Letters*, 6 January 1826, 356.

p. 132 Lebzeltern was 'compelled to withdraw himself from Society' and to ask to be recalled to Vienna: NA, Cowley MSS. FO 519/41, Sir H. Wellesley to Canning, 31 January 1826.

p. 132 'a revival of a policy more conformable to his view': *Diary*, 110.

p. 133 'the only agent by whom I could suppress & extinguish Strangford': NA, Granville MSS. PRO/30/29/8/9, Canning to Granville, 13 January 1826.

p. 133 Canning's confidence in his own ability to conjure up a solution remained strong: *WDCM* III, Canning to Wellington, 10 February 1826, 85–93.

p. 133 'I don't think I can prevent it': *Arbuthnot Journal* II, footnote 2, 7.

p. 133 'compromise him [the Duke] and mock him at the same time – a double pleasure': *Diary*, 111.

p. 133 Nesselrode's possible removal: *WDCM* III, Wellington to Canning, 19 February 1826, 136.

p. 133 whether or not the Lievens would be removed: *Private Letters*, 10 March 1826, 360–61.

p. 134 'You cannot say more than is true, of our desire to keep him here': *WDCM* III, Canning to Wellington, 10 February 1826, 96–7.

p. 134 Lieven who 'could not be replaced here with advantage': ibid., 4 March 1826, 146–7.

p. 135 'were too prudent to laugh': *Diary*, 113.

Chapter 10

p. 136 'This is not a threat; I would rather kill myself': *Private Letters*, 16 May 1826, 368–9.

p. 138 She made her excuses and left: ibid., 14 May 1826, 367–8.

p. 138 'a scene that was sufficiently ridiculous at his age': ibid., 14 June 1826, 370–71.

p. 138 'thousands of opportunities for showing his Minister a politeness which is not due to his rank in society': ibid., 26 April, 14 June 1826, 366, 371.

p. 138 'In everything he will always get what he wants': ibid., 4 June 1826, 370.

p. 139 'She quite pursued him about the room, to the great amusement of the whole party': *Arbuthnot Journal* II, 22 June 1826, 31.

p. 139 passing messages on to Canning from her own government and reporting back on his responses: NA, Granville MSS. PRO 30/24/8/ 10, Canning to Granville, 22 June 1826.

p. 139 'We are the only persons,' Dorothea proudly boasted to Lord Grey, 'on whom this title has been conferred': *Grey–Lieven* I, to Grey, 22 September 1826, 27.

p. 139 'he has covered himself with ridicule': *Private Letters*, 14 January 1826, 358.

p. 140 there was general approbation for her put-down: *Arbuthnot Journal* II, 9 November 1826, 53–4.

p. 140 whether it might be possible to move him to Paris: NA, Granville MSS. PRO 30/24/8/10, Canning to Granville, 22 June 1826.

p. 140 'I have become sensible': *Arbuthnot Journal* II, 17 June 1826, 37.

p. 140 losing his last insight into the heart of Russian policy: NA, Cowley MSS. FO 519/41, Wellesley to Canning, 31 January 1826.

p. 141 'In truth it is the only thing that makes me laugh at this moment': NA, Howard de Walden MSS. FO 360/5, Dorothea Lieven to Count Lieven, 14 July 1826.

p. 141 'I do not understand it in the least': *Private Letters*, 14 June 1826, 372–3.

p. 141 'this little bit of the future aged 7': ibid., 8 August 1826, 373.

p. 141 'truth will emerge more clearly from this exchange of letters than from any memoir which may be published': ibid., 9 November 1826, 374–5.

p. 142 'If you meet your like, show him to me. Good-bye': ibid., 22 November 1826, 376.

p. 142 'Chevalier of the Holy Alliance had ended by concluding a *mésalliance*': H. M. Hyde, *Princess Lieven* (1938), 168.

p. 142 'prevent the separation of the Continental Powers upon great political questions': NA, Cowley MSS. FO 519/41, Wellesley to Canning, 29 April 1826.

p. 142 'by whomsoever attacked': H. Temperley, *The Foreign Policy of Canning* (1925), 380–81.

p. 143 'the most satisfactory announcement of the intention of the French Government to withdraw its army from Spain': NA, Granville MSS. PRO 30/24/8/11, Canning to Granville, 14 December 1826.

p. 143 'mon mari me battra' ['my husband will beat me']: A. G. Stapleton, *George Canning and His Times* (1859), 547.

p. 143 'to satisfy their pride and their insatiable rapacity': Temperley, *Canning*, 384.

p. 144 'the most abominable ever heard': *Arbuthnot Journal* II, 15 December 1826, 64.

p. 144 'we pass in Europe for a Jacobin club': *Canning Corr.* II, Wellington to Bathurst, 170.

p. 144 'so abominably false I hate the Duke to talk to her': *Arbuthnot Journal* II, 11 February 1827, 78.

p. 144 'necessary to tranquillise the apprehension of Europe': NA, Cowley MSS. FO 519/14, Wellesley to Canning, 29 April 1826.

p. 144 'it would be rash to reveal it': *WDCM* III, Nesselrode to Wellington, 25 June 1826, 333–5.

p. 145 Canning had talked of the independence of the Greek state as a given fact – which in his view it was most certainly not: Hartley Library, University of Southampton, Wellington MSS. WP1/861/30, Wellington to Bathurst, 7 September 1826.

p. 145 an informal agreement between Canning and the Russians: Wellington MSS. WP1/862/5, Bathurst to Wellington, 5 September 1826.

p. 145 'We may do what we please about it': Wellington MSS. WP1/862/9, Bathurst to Wellington, 10 September 1826.

p. 146 they actually wished to provoke a war with the Turks: NA, Cowley MSS. FO 519/41, Wellesley to Canning, 3 November 1826.

p. 146 Canning's invincible self-belief: C. A. W. Crawley, *The Question of Greek Independence* (Cambridge, 1930), 52–4.

p. 146 'your refusal to go to war cannot be too peremptory': *WDCM* III, Wellington to Canning, 8 November 1826, 446.

p. 146 'we are prepared in this case to pursue with Russia alone this work of conciliation and peace': ibid., Canning to Lieven, 20 November 1826, 460.

p. 146 his anxiety to include France before moving forward: BL, Lieven MSS., ADD. MSS. 47247, Lieven to Nesselrode, 27 November 1826.

p. 147 'Mr Canning's perpetual notes': *Arbuthnot Journal* II, 15 December 1826, 65.

p. 147 'mean & revolting trickery': ibid., 16 December 1826, 68.

p. 147 the only member of the Cabinet who was actually aware of what Canning was doing: Crawley, *Greek Question*, 70.

p. 148 'a laudable endeavour to drive these miscreants out of Europe': *Grey–Lieven* I, from Grey, 12 November 1826, 31.

p. 148 hopeless to expect him to play his old role: *Arbuthnot Journal* II, 20 February, 5 March 1827, 81, 85.

p. 148 he was not inclined to be led by the son of one: A. Aspinall (ed.), *The Formation of Canning's Ministry* (1937), xlix.

p. 148 'or what is required by the interests of his country': *Grey–Lieven* I, from Grey, 27 January 1827, 35.

p. 148 hardly surprising that he did not want Canning to be Prime Minister: ibid., 14 March 1827, 36.

p. 148 moderate Lord Lansdowne with a view to making him Prime Minister: *Private Letters*, 14 May 1826, 366–7.

p. 149 Canning was a 'charlatan parvenu' under whom no gentleman should consent to serve: Aspinall, *Canning's Ministry*, Londonderry to Wellington, 12 April 1827, 66.

p. 149 a better way with the King: *Diary*, 116.

p. 149 'Then it is really very difficult for he wants to be it': ibid., 122.

p. 149 'all the talent and incontestable superiority of Canning were insufficient to conceal the inferiority of his origins': ibid., 123.

Chapter 11

p. 152 'her husband was a marvel, but she much preferred that he should not be called upon to prove it': *Diary*, 125.

p. 152 'this title then was more than equal to a radical today': ibid., 126.

p. 152 'which makes them irreconcilable': ibid., 126–7.

p. 152 Granville would be going to the Foreign Office: *Grey–Lieven* I, from Grey, 23 April 1827, 42–3.

p. 153 it was not until 6 July 1827 that it was finally signed: H. Temperley, *The Foreign Policy of Canning* (1925), Appendix VIII for the full texts.

p. 153 'But I must take a few days' rest . . . for I am quite knocked up': NA, Granville MSS. PRO 30/29/8/12, Canning to Granville, 13 July 1827.

p. 153 'in the premature extinction of great talents in the very moment of their successful ambition': *Grey–Lieven* I, from Grey, 21 August 1827, 52.

p. 153 'I assert we ought to love Canning': *London Letters*, 27 January, 8 February 1837, 90–91.

p. 154 'so long as one attains one's object': ibid., 1, 13 July 1827, 103.

p. 154 'everybody who is not Metternich is in despair': ibid., 29 July, 10 August 1827, 104.

p. 154 The 'Apostolics', she told Grey, 'will sing a paean of victory': *Grey–Lieven* I, to Grey, 7 August 1827, 49.

p. 154 it was, she averred with startlingly inaccurate complacency, 'of no consequence': *London Letters*, 8, 20 October 1827, 107–9.

p. 155 'who allow themselves to be duped by Russia': ibid., 14 November 1827, 110–12.

p. 155 he could find no justification for what had happened: *Grey–Lieven* I, from Grey, 16 November 1827, 70–72.

p. 155 could only say 'rejoice': ibid., to Grey, 19 November 1827, 72–4.

p. 155 She was sure that if war came, the British would join it: *London Letters*, 14 November 1827, 110–12.

p. 156 'his nerves will no longer stand the strain': ibid., 5, 17 December 1827, 114–15.

p. 157 was anxious to cooperate with Russia: Sir H. Bulwer-Lytton, *The Life of Lord Palmerston*, vol. I (1870), Palmerston to William Temple, 27 November 1827, 203–5.

p. 157 increased the gulf between her and her old admirer: *Arbuthnot Journal* II, 2 December 1827, 149.

p. 157 'a chord you can always touch with effect, and therefore there is no ground for apprehension': *London Letters*, 5, 17 December 1827, 114–15.

p. 157 'only too happy if I could be assured that it existed in anything approaching the same degree' on her side: *Grey–Lieven* I, from Grey, 30 November 1827, 77–80.

p. 157 to revenge himself on Britain and Russia for daring to act without him: ibid., to Grey, 1, 3, 8 December 1827, 80–85.

pp. 157–8 demanding reparation for Navarino was likely to bring one about all the same: ibid., 8 December 1827, 87–8.

p. 158 'Let us, however,' she concluded, 'leave all this for our *tête-à-têtes*': ibid., 13 December 1827, 90–91.

p. 158 'go home and *take care of himself*; and keep himself quiet': Bulwer-Lytton, *Palmerston* I, 211–12.

p. 159 'the idea of being treated with such contempt': *Arbuthnot Journal* II, 19 January 1828, 165.

p. 159 'making Russia tremble, at which I simply shrug my shoulders': *London Letters*, 8, 20 February 1828, 122–4.

p. 159 'It is curious enough that the loves and intrigues of *une femme galante* shd have such influence over the affairs of Europe': *Arbuthnot Journal* II, 19 January 1828, 165.

p. 160 'had assented to a continuance of the system of free trade and of Canning's foreign policy': *London Letters*, 117.

p. 160 only Holland defended it: *Hansard*, 3rd series, vol. xviii, col. 9, foll.

p. 160 'penetrate even to Constantinople, there to dictate peace under the walls of the Seraglio': *WDCM* IV, 230–50.

p. 160 but also on her frontiers: ibid., Wellington to Dudley, 5 March 1828, 297–8.

p. 161 The result was further negotiations with Lieven and the French: Bulwer-Lytton, *Palmerston* I, Palmerston's Journal, 9 March 1828, 229–31.

p. 161 her impatience with Wellington grew apace: *London Letters*, 16, 28 March 1828, 126–7.

p. 161 'neither considers her as a friend nor as a politician, & that she cannot brook': *Arbuthnot Journal* II, 6 March 1828, 168.

p. 161 that he 'came to the conferences predetermined to say nothing & to settle nothing': ibid., 15 March 1828, 169.

p. 161 Canningites wanting cooperation with Russia: C. W. Crawley, *The Question of Greek Independence* (Cambridge, 1930), 104.

p. 162 who 'both hate Madame de Lieven', were influencing him: Bulwer-Lytton, *Palmerston* I, Palmerston's Journal, 4 April 1828, 249.

p. 162 the British should 'trust' Nicholas and act with Russia: *London Letters*, 7, 19 May 1828, 132.

p. 162 'he will give way rather than give up his place': ibid., 7, 19 May 1828, 132–3.

p. 163 they now had the 'Austrian' Wellington: Bulwer-Lytton, *Palmerston* I, Palmerston Journal, 8 June 1828, 283–4.

Chapter 12

p. 164 Dorothea's objections to Wellington: *London Letters*, 5, 17 January, 8, 20 February 1828, 120, 122.

p. 164 'Mme De Lieven and Lady Cowper are very personally bitter and angry with the Duke?': *Granville Letters* II, 8 February 1828, 10.

p. 164 took her attempts at friendship at their true value – which was nothing: *Diary*, 133.

p. 166 a Tsar like Nicholas I – 'firm and haughty': *London Letters*, 5, 17 January 1828, 120.

p. 166 'Eastern Question has never been clearly explained' to them: ibid., 8, 20 February 1828, 122.

p. 166 'Mr Canning's friends have joined Mr Canning's enemies': NA, Granville MSS. PRO 30/29/17/5, Devonshire to Lady Granville, 18 January 1828, fo. 20.

p. 166 her 'cold-heartedness & ingratitude': *Arbuthnot Journal* II, 22 March 1828, 174.

p. 167 Dorothea 'disgusted all parties by her uncalled for interference in our internal affairs', she was not wide of the mark: ibid., 6 March 1828, 168.

p. 167 Palmerston and Grey both paid her court and thanked her for her help: BL, Lieven MSS., ADD. MSS. 47366, Correspondence with Palmerston, 1828; Hartley Library, University of Southampton, Broadland MSS., Palmerston Papers, GC/LI/24/1–27 for Palmerston's letters to her 1828 to 1830.

p. 167 she even had its Prime Minister: Grey himself: *Grey–Lieven* I, to Grey, 8 October 1828, 160.

p. 168 in a 'sort of neuter position': ibid., 1 February 1829, 235.

p. 169 Wellington's government was 'contemptible and cannot last', she told Alexander in late February: *London Letters*, 16, 28 March 1828, 125.

p. 169 It was only 'there for want of a better': ibid., 16, 28 February 1828, 124.

p. 169 that Palmerston was 'our Minister': ibid., 7, 19 May 1828, 132.

p. 170 'I feel again and again that in your eyes I have the defect of not being an Englishwoman': *Grey–Lieven* I, 29 January 1828, 231.

p. 170 'I still regard you too much as my friend to be vexed with you': ibid., 17 December 1828, 206.

p. 170 they both needed to be in London at such a critical moment: *London Letters*, 16, 28 March 1828, 127.

p. 171 threatening to leave him unless his behaviour improved: P. Zamoyska, *Arch Intriguer, a Biography of Dorothea Lieven* (1957), 125–6.

p. 171 'he was driven on by his wife': *Arbuthnot Journal* II, 19 February 1828, 164.

p. 171 'I am always glad to see you, but I am very sorry to see you Minister for Foreign Affairs because I consider you Austrian and an enemy to Russia': Sir H. Bulwer-Lytton, *The Life of Lord Palmerston*, vol. I (1870), 238.

p. 171 her later comment to him when she accused him in so many words of lying: *Grey–Lieven* I, 16 October 1828, 329.

p. 171 'a wretched Minister!': H. M. Hyde, *Princess Lieven* (1938), 182.

p. 171 'excite my curiosity and interest to the utmost': *Grey–Lieven* I, 8 October 1828, 160.

p. 172 'some of his former coquetries': *London Letters*, 10, 22 August 1828, 149.

p. 172 expressing sympathy for Russia's losses in the Turkish campaign and offering his advice: ibid., 13, 25 October 1828, 157.

p. 172 'His change of language can only be deceit': ibid., 13, 25 October 1828, 158.

p. 173 preferred to suffer their machinations a little longer rather than take them as seriously as they took themselves: BL, Heytesbury, ADD. MSS. 41558, Wellington to Heytesbury, 8 April 1829.

p. 173 'he is no more than an Irish adventurer': PRONI, Clanwilliam MSS. D/3044/F/4, diary, 19 September 1830, 188.

p. 173 'la tête plus forte en politique de ce pays ci': *WDCM* VI, Aberdeen to Wellington, 21 July 1829, 34–5.

p. 173 Aberdeen, who was rather more susceptible to the charms of the Princess than Wellington: Lord Sudley, *The Lieven–Palmerston Correspondence, 1828–1856* (1943) [hereafter *Lieven–Palmerston*], from Lieven, 27 November 1828, 7.

p. 173 'at the bottom of every intrigue': *WDCM* VI, 54.

p. 173 'Lord Grey entertains some old opposition opinions of Mr Fox's that the Turks ought to be driven out of Europe': ibid., Wellington to Aberdeen, 29 July 1829, 58.

p. 173–4 'we cannot consider their presence in England as likely to contribute to the good understanding of the two governments': BL, Heytesbury, ADD. MSS. 41558, Aberdeen to Heytesbury, 22 August 1829.

p. 174 'appears vitally to affect the interests, the strength, the dignity, the present safety, & future independence of the Ottoman Empire': BL, Heytesbury, ADD. MSS. 41559, Aberdeen to Heytesbury, 31 October 1829.

p. 174 'with all the caution and explanations which may be necessary to prevent it producing an unpleasant effect': ibid., 7 November 1829.

p. 175 'engaged in every intrigue which can possibly be set on foot to shake the King's Ministers': ibid., 22 December 1829, fo. 98 r.

p. 175 not going to demand their recall only because 'this would do more harm than good': Zamoyska, *Arch Intriguer*, 138.

p. 175 Wellington was their chief target and that 'their language regarding me is different': BL, Heytesbury, ADD. MSS. 41559, Aberdeen to Heytesbury, 22 December 1829, fos. 98–101.

p. 175 Wellington was 'the most obstinate mule I have ever known': *London Letters*, 16, 28 November 1828, 163–4.

p. 176 she took additional pleasure in Russia's successes because they would embarrass him: H. Reeve, *The Greville Memoirs*, vol. I (1908 edn) [hereafter *Greville Diary* and volume number], 323–4.

p. 176 'her insolence is beyond all bearing': *Arbuthnot Journal* II, 3 November 1829, 312–13.

p. 176 'English Minister should have exposed himself to a rebuke at once so severe and so just': *Grey–Lieven* I, 20 October 1829, 335.

p. 176 'their removal from this country would unquestionably be a great advantage under present circumstances': BL, Heytesbury, ADD. MSS. 41559, Aberdeen to Heytesbury, 22 December 1829, fo. 99.

p. 177 his words would be 'repeated *verbatim* to the Emperor': ibid., Heytesbury to Aberdeen, 25 January 1830, fo. 186v.

p. 177 'that it is impossible to be too cautious with foreigners of any nation': ibid., Aberdeen to Heytesbury, 12 March 1830, fo. 174.

p. 177 the most probable source of the Lievens' knowledge of Aberdeen's letter was easily identified: ibid., Heytesbury to Aberdeen, 16 April 1830, fo. 202.

p. 177 'of the attempt to get you removed': *Grey–Lieven* I, 23 June 1830, 416.

p. 178 'If this should happen all our friends will be in power': *London Letters*, 16, 28 May 1830, 221.

Chapter 13

p. 179 'the sole cause of the coolness which exists between the two governments at the moment': *WDCM* VI, letter 24 August 1829, 99.

p. 179 'I don't believe one word of the desire for peace of a young Emperor at the head of a million men, who has never drawn his sword': ibid., letter 21 August 1829, 99.

p. 180 taking too much territory from the Ottoman Empire would precipitate its decline: NA, Stratford Canning MSS. FO 352/20 part 2, Aberdeen to S. Canning, 11 and 20 September 1828.

p. 180 'We have at least shown that we do not seek to destroy this Empire': *Grey–Lieven* I, 12 October 1829, 324.

p. 180 so small in size as to be in effect a Turkish appendage: *WDCM* VI, to Aberdeen, 25 August 1829, 105–6.

p. 180 'the Emperor of Russia has behaved precisely like a second

Bonaparte' summed up their response: *Arbuthnot Journal* II, 15 October 1829, 309.

p. 181 how Britain regarded the peace treaty: BL, Heytesbury, ADD. MSS. 41559, Aberdeen to Heytesbury, 31 October 1829; see also *WDCM* VI, Ellenborough to Wellington, 15 October 1829, 227–31, and also 211–19 for further views in the same vein; what follows is based on these three sources.

p. 181 without reducing the Ottoman Porte to a degree of weakness which would deprive it of the character of an independent state': BL, Heytesbury, ADD. MSS. 41559, Aberdeen to Heytesbury, 31 October 1829.

p. 183 to devote a larger portion of her forces and of her revenue to intervention in the affairs of Europe: Hartley Library, University of Southampton, Wellington MSS. WP/1051/8, Ellenborough's letter, 15 October 1829, fo. 7.

p. 183 'rely upon it that the object of Prince Lieven is not to keep this country on good terms with the Emperor excepting by the humiliation of this country': *WDCM* VI, Wellington to Aberdeen, 24 August 1829, 102–5.

p. 183 was impeding the achievement of a good understanding between Russia and Britain: ibid., Wellington to Aberdeen, 4 and 5 September 1829, 129–38.

p. 183 'They have misrepresented to their Court all that we have done, and particularly that I have done': ibid., Wellington to Heytesbury, 8 September 1829, 145–6.

p. 183 'throws obstacles and difficulties in the way of the business with which you are entrusted': *Grey–Lieven* I, from Grey, 7 December 1829, 378.

p. 184 said much about the fascination she had for him: ibid., to Grey, 16 October 1829, 329.

p. 184 'and for what purpose but to expose himself?': ibid., from Grey, 20 October 1829, 336.

p. 185 'he is a little caught': *Arbuthnot Journal* II, 12 November 1829, 315.

p. 185 'Of which Government are you speaking – of ours, or of the French?': *Grey–Lieven* I, to Grey, 25 November 1829, 362.

p. 185 'You surely must have fascinated Aberdeen to make him talk in such a manner': ibid., from Grey, 10 December 1829, 385.

p. 185 things continued to deteriorate: *Arbuthnot Journal* II, 16 December 1829, 321.

p. 185 Harriet Granville refusing to bow to him, and saying that she was amused to see how it put him out of countenance: ibid., 16 February 1830, 336.

p. 185 fell some way short of dealing with the problem: ibid., 22 February 1830, 339.

p. 185 include Huskisson, Lord Melbourne and Lord Holland: *Grey–Lieven* I, from Grey, 20 October 1829, 337.

p. 186 Russia 'must adopt a firm attitude and enforce it by polite but cold language': *London Letters*, 22 January, 3 February 1830, 209.

p. 186 'it lay with us to destroy it had we so chosen': *Grey–Lieven* I, to Grey, 22 October 1829, 338.

p. 187 Dorothea feared that she might be leaving England never to return: *Grey–Lieven* II, to Grey, 11 June 1830, 4.

p. 187 'where she detests everybody and everybody detests her': BL, Heytesbury, ADD. MSS. 41560, Heytesbury to Aberdeen, 10 July 1830.

p. 187 a few well-placed articles in the press whose criticism might sting the Princess into wanting to quit England: ibid., 21 July 1830.

p. 187 her carriage was overturned and her back was damaged: *London Letters*, 1, 13, 14, 26 August 1830, 232–3; *Grey–Lieven* II, to Grey 20, 29 July 1830, 26, 27–8.

p. 188 Charles X had done much to provoke legitimate protests against his increasingly arbitrary rule: BL, Aberdeen MSS., ADD. MSS. 43059, Wellington to Aberdeen, 14 August 1830.

p. 188 'those whose ideas would not suit us in these critical times': *London Letters*, 8, 20 September 1830, 242.

p. 188 'if she catches me I'll be damned': *Arbuthnot Journal* II, 28 July 1830, 376.

p. 189 'In such a Ministry we should count upon friends to Russia': *London Letters*, 8, 20 September 1830, 242.

p. 189 'He would not, I am sure, go on a day amicably with the Duke': *Arbuthnot Journal* II, 3 May 1830, 354.

p. 189 Wellington himself saw the wisdom of trying to bring less intractable souls such as Palmerston into his net: ibid., 26 September 1830, 389.

p. 189 'the Duke needs fresh support': *Lieven–Palmerston*, 4 October 1830, 19.

p. 189 a price the Duke thought too high: *Arbuthnot Journal* II, 2 October 1830, 390.

p. 189 the latter might be more willing to yield on terms Palmerston could accept: BL, Lieven MSS., ADD. MSS. 47366, from Palmerston, 7 October 1830, fos. 37–40; from Palmerston, 9 October 1830, fos. 40–46. See also Sir H. Bulwer-Lytton, *The Life of Lord Palmerston*, vol. I (1870), 381–2; *London Letters*, 25 October, 6 November 1830, 261–2.

p. 190 'What do you think of this?': *Grey–Lieven* II, from Grey, 15 November 1830, 119.

p. 190 instrumental in getting Palmerston into the Foreign Office: C. K. Webster, *The Foreign Policy of Palmerston*, vol. I (1951), 21.

p. 191 'especially one which might bring Lord Grey to power': PRONI, Clanwilliam MSS. D/3044/F/4, Diary, 22 November 1830.

p. 191 'offers no guarantee to the future': *London Letters*, 25 September, 2 October 1830, 252.

p. 192 'its dangers, its difficulties and its responsibilities': ibid., 8, 20 September 1830, 242.

p. 192 led Dorothea to describe his speech as 'detestable': ibid., 25 October, 6 November 1830, 267.

p. 192 'maintenance of peace and order will be the aim of his wishes and his efforts': ibid., 4, 16 November 1830, 272.

Chapter 14

p. 193 'because I have some influence over their leader': *Private Letters*, to Metternich, 5 July 1823, 272.

p. 193 'the mere gossip of the day': *Grey–Lieven* II, 5 January 1831, 132.

p. 193 'seized by a romantic passion': *Private Letters*, to Metternich, 23 June 1823, 271.

p. 193 'bilious' and 'ill-tempered': ibid., 29 August 1823, 284.

p. 194 'I pass for being altogether ignorant of what is going on': *London Letters*, November 1830, 410.

p. 194 much some of the detail might be questioned: *Diary*, 165–6.

p. 197 it did not need the wiles of Dorothea Lieven to deny them the Foreign Office, even if she thought otherwise: *London Letters*, 8, 20 November, 275.

p. 197 Grey asked her 'where can I find the man?': *Diary*, 167.

p. 197 was plenty of opportunity for much conversation: *Grey–Lieven* II, 17, 20 November 1830, 122–3.

p. 198 'He had given us Russians pledges of goodwill': *Diary*, 166.

p. 199 Palmerston being described as 'perfect in every way': *London Letters*, 8, 20 November 1830, 276.

p. 199 'will startle Europe – let Europe be reassured': ibid., 10, 22 November 1830, 280–81.

p. 199 'an intimate, an exclusive Alliance would be sought with France': BL, Heytesbury, ADD. MSS. 41560, Heytesbury to Palmerston, 19 December 1831.

p. 200 'his sole object had been to warn France against any deviation from the ways of moderation': *London Letters*, 11, 23 November 1830, 282.

p. 200 'his assurances that we should be satisfied': ibid., November 1830, 410.

p. 200 'If they don't, there will be war': ibid., 10, 20 November 1830, 277.

p. 200 'a perfect *solidarité* of interests and actions, amongst all the members of the Quadruple Alliance': BL, Heytesbury, ADD. MSS. 41560, Heytesbury to Aberdeen, 17 November 1830.

p. 201 'an enemy possessing the long line of coast by which we had been hostilely confronted during the reign of Napoleon': Sir H. Bulwer-Lytton, *The Life of Lord Palmerston*, vol. II (1870), 2.

p. 201 when the French still appeared to have designs on the provinces: BL, Heytesbury, ADD. MSS. 41560, Heytesbury to Palmerston, 16 December 1830.

p. 202 entrusted her with half a million francs with which to back the Orangeist cause: *Diary*, 177; *London Letters*, 25 October, 3 November 1830, 266.

p. 202 'such an arrangement appeared to me to be impossible, and that nobody could consent to it': Bulwer-Lytton, *Palmerston* II, Palmerston to Granville, 7 January 1831, 23.

p. 203 if they had to speak on Poland, as well as saying nothing to encourage the rebels: BL, Heytesbury, ADD. MSS. 41560, Heytesbury to Palmerston, 16 December 1830.

p. 203 Grey had 'been the most pronounced enemy of revolutions, revolutionists, and of disturbance in general wherever it shows itself': *London Letters*, 9, 13 December 1830, 285.

p. 203 threatened to cut off all confidential communication if he could not be sure that his remarks would remain secret: *Grey–Lieven* II, from Grey, 5 January 1831, 131–2.

p. 203 promised not to repeat the offence: ibid., to Grey, 6 January 1831, 132–3.

pp. 203–4 a suggestion from the French that they should jointly offer to mediate between the Tsar and the Polish rebels: BL, Heytesbury, ADD. MSS. 41560, from Palmerston, 31 December 1830.

p. 204 'a most enormous quantity of powdered hair hanging over his ears & tied in a tail behind': *Arbuthnot Journal* II, 25 October 1830, 393.

p. 204 Polignac, 'a very clever man': *Grey–Lieven* II, to Grey, 1 October 1830, 99.

p. 204 'a man who had spent seventy-five years in intriguing would not have forgotten the business in his seventy-sixth': *London Letters*, 2, 14 October 1830, 258.

p. 204 'you have two honest men on your side – my Emperor and the King of Prussia': *Grey–Lieven* II, to Grey, 18 January 1831, 137.

p. 205 'Duke of Wellington would never have done for him the half of what you have already achieved': ibid., 21 January 1831, 139–40.

p. 205 'given way too far to the Russians & Russian champions of the Interests of the Dutch King': BL, Heytesbury, ADD. MSS. 41563, from Palmerston, 16 January 1831.

p. 206 'France was crying out for non-intervention and peace': Bulwer-Lytton, *Palmerston* II, to Granville, 21 January 1831, 30–31.

p. 206 'neither consent to a union of Belgium with France, *nor accept the Crown even if offered to Nemours*': ibid., 27 January 1831, 31–5.

p. 206 'I do not believe the bulk of the French nation wish for Belgium at the price of a general war': ibid., 1 February 1831, 35–6.

p. 207 'to think of war, but if ever we are to make another effort this is a legitimate occasion': ibid., 2 February 1831, 36–7.

p. 207 Louis-Philippe would not let him accept it: ibid., from Granville, 4 February 1831, 38.

p. 207 'ultimately be productive of the very evil which all parties so anxiously deprecate, namely a general war': BL, Heytesbury, ADD. MSS. 41561, to Palmerston, 31 January 1831.

p. 207 'are only to be found in intimate union & cordial cooperation with England': ibid., 8 February 1831.

p. 207 'we should not look upon their advent as the last day of our alliance': *London Letters*, 25 October, 6 November 1830, 266.

Chapter 15

p. 208 'Europe just now presents a scene of incredible confusion': *London Letters*, 9, 13 December 1830, 285.

p. 208 the limits of her understanding of him: ibid., 286.

p. 208 'a good understanding with all – but especially with Russia': ibid., 10, 22 December 1830, 287.

p. 209 something Dorothea persistently denied: *Grey–Lieven* II, to Grey, 21 January 1831, 141.

p. 209 the Russians had a duty to provide it with a 'distinct administration': BL, Heytesbury, ADD. MSS. 41561, Palmerston to Heytesbury, 21 March 1831.

p. 209 carefully if relations between the two countries were not to be damaged: *Grey–Lieven* II, from Grey, 24 January 1831, 144.

p. 209 'the authority which sometimes inspires its articles might equally forbid such articles as these?': ibid., to Grey, 8 March 1831, 182.

p. 209 but he might as well have saved his breath: ibid., from Grey, 8 March 1831, 182–3.

p. 210 'I do not know what to think, and probably I had better keep silence': ibid., to Grey, 11 March 1831, 184–5.

p. 210 'I had hoped did not depend altogether on our political agreement': ibid., from Grey, 12 March 1831.

p. 210 'I should not have been so distressed yesterday, had I cared less about you': ibid., to Grey, 12 March 1831, 185–6.

p. 211 'more than ever desirous of keeping up the closest relations of friendship': BL, Heytesbury, ADD. MSS. 41561, Palmerston to Heytesbury, 21 March 1831.

p. 211 'convey our sentiments without giving any pretence for taking offence': ibid., Palmerston to Heytesbury, 22 March 1831.

p. 211 the fact that they were acting in concert with France on the issue: ibid., Heytesbury to Palmerston, 13 April 1831.

p. 211 Heytesbury (who was increasingly regarded by some of the Cabinet as 'apostolical'): ibid., Palmerston to Heytesbury, 19 April 1831 ('apostolical' was Whig code for devotees of the Holy Alliance).

p. 211 at least until the Belgian issue was settled: ibid., Heytesbury to Palmerston, 30 April 1831.

p. 212 'necessarily to throw England into intimate union with Russia' against France: ibid., Palmerston to Heytesbury, 9 May 1831.

p. 212 'My sister is mad!': *Diary*, 178.

p. 213 'the tone of Russia about Belgium will be different from what it has been': Sir H. Bulwer-Lytton, *The Life of Lord Palmerston*, vol. II (1870), to Granville, 9 March 1831, 49.

p. 213 'who is now going to support France?': *Grey–Lieven* II, to Grey, 11 February 1831, 164.

p. 214 'are you prepared to march 150,000 men to the Rhine without a subsidy?': ibid., from Grey, 12 February 1831, 165.

p. 214 'One must keep up one's dignity, in order to carry the point abroad, just as at home': ibid., to Grey, 10 June 1831, 237.

p. 214 'our powerlessness for the moment' prevented Russia from taking a much tougher stand: *London Letters*, 24 June 1831, 303.

p. 214 the 'right of the Belgian people to regulate their own internal affairs': ibid.

p. 214 'leave you to settle all your Continental matters as you may': *Grey–Lieven* II, from Grey, 3 June 1831, 230.

p. 214 'he listens when I am speaking': *London Letters*, 24 June 1831; see also *WDCM* VII, Wellington to Aberdeen, 5 June 1831, 461.

p. 215 'then dividing the Country among the powers': A. Kriegel, *The Holland House Diaries 1831–1840* (1977), 6 August 1831, 25–6.

p. 215 the 'first step of the realization of this plot': Bulwer-Lytton, *Palmerston* II, to Granville, 5 August 1831, 97.

p. 215 'they must remember that there is a public feeling in England as well': ibid., 11 August 1831, 100.

p. 215 'England must be contented with the making of Antwerp a free port': ibid., 12 August 1831, 102.

p. 216 'Will the French Government withdraw their troops . . . as soon as the Dutch have evacuated Belgium?': Bulwer-Lytton, *Palmerston* II, to Granville, 13 August 1831, 105.

p. 216 'One thing is certain – the French must go out of Belgium, or we have a general war, and war in a given number of days': ibid., 17 August 1831, 109.

p. 216 music to Princess Lieven's ears: *Grey–Lieven* II, 25 August 1831, 268.

p. 216 'Russian petticoat influence': K. Bourne, *Palmerston: the Early Years*, vol. I (1982), 341.

p. 216 after they had agreed to evacuate their troops: ibid.

p. 217 'As long as the Emperor makes his Ratification depend upon the acceptance of the articles by the King of Holland, he might as well refuse it in plain terms': BL, Heytesbury, ADD. MSS. 41563, to Heytesbury, 16 January 1831 [*sic* for 1832].

p. 218 Heytesbury still hoped that something might happen to turn the Tsar back towards a more 'European' orientation, but the warning was there: BL, Heytesbury, ADD. MSS. 41562, from Heytesbury, 17 December 1831.

p. 219 there was no point in giving needless offence: *London Letters*, enclosure dated 18 June, to Grey, 306–7.

p. 219 a renewed attempt through Heytesbury to impress his point of view on the Russians: BL, Heytesbury, ADD. MSS. 41562, to Heytesbury, 23 November 1831.

p. 220 'fully convinced by the previous explanations of Prince Lieven?': ibid., from Heytesbury, 18 December 1831.

Chapter 16

p. 221 'I only display one colour – that is, yours. I am *Grey*': *Grey–Lieven* II, to Grey, 11 October 1831, 289.

p. 221 'care for the interests of your country to force this Government into a close connection with France': ibid., from Grey, 14 December 1831, 304.

p. 222 'whether we are bound to take any measure, which we have no means that I can see of enforcing': Hartley Library, University of Southampton, Palmerston MSS. BP/GC/GR 2060, Grey to Palmerston, 12 November 1831.

p. 222 'everything we propose will be rejected': Hartley Library, University of Southampton, Palmerston MSS. BP/GC/GR/2061, Grey to Palmerston, 16 November 1831.

p. 223 Russia, she told him in peremptory manner, 'fears no one': *Grey–Lieven* II, to Grey, 15 December 1831, 306–7.

p. 223 'upon reflection you would find that you had been unjust': ibid., from Grey, 19 December 1831, 308.

p. 223 'It is impossible that you should not have it yourself': ibid., from Grey, 1 January 1832, 310.

pp. 223–4 'more amazed than I can express that this view of the matter should not have represented itself to your mind': ibid., to Grey, 2 January 1832, 311–12.

p. 224 indication enough of an uneasy conscience: Hartley Library, University of Southampton, Palmerston MSS. BP/GC/GR/2071, Grey to Palmerston, 4 January 1832.

p. 224 'the first that Russia has received from England during the long course of nineteen years!': *Grey–Lieven* II, from Grey, 4 January 1832, 312–15.

p. 224 'The English learn Latin – but they don't learn the art of living': *London Letters*, 24 December 1831, 5 January 1832, 321.

p. 225 'earnest hope that this disagreeable discussion may be finished': *Grey–Lieven* II, to Grey, 5 January 1832, 316–19.

p. 225 'I think, to have protected me against such a complaint as was made against me': ibid., from Grey, 6 January 1832, 319–20.

p. 226 And there, for the moment, the squabble ended: ibid., to Grey, 7, 11 January 1832, 322–3.

p. 227 the Princess was 'unquestionably more Antigallican than he and seems to have imbibed much of the Ultra spirit': A. Kriegel, *The Holland House Diaries 1831–1840*, 2 vols. (1977), 27 December 1831, 101–2.

p. 227 'He is weak and easily led, so everything is not going on well': *London Letters*, 24 December 1831, 5 January 1832, 321.

p. 228 Grey was being 'led' by his son-in-law, the earl of Durham, or 'Radical Jack' as he was known: ibid., 9 January 1832, 322–3.

p. 228 'no power of sending a fleet into the Baltic last summer to settle the matter of Poland': G. M. Trevelyan, *Lord Grey of the Reform Bill* (1920), 355.

p. 228 all that the ambassador and Nesselrode could do was to cower before the storm and hope that it would pass over without doing them too much damage: A. de Nesselrode, *Lettres et Papiers du Chancelier Comte de Nesselrode*, vol. VII (Paris, *c.* 1908), 216–20.

pp. 228–9 'to carry into effect the treaty of November against whoever may oppose it': BL, Heytesbury, ADD. MSS. 41563, Palmerston to Heytesbury, 16 January 1831 [*sic* for 1832].

p. 229 dangling before her the spectre of an Anglo-French alliance: *Grey–Lieven* II, from Grey, 31 January 1832, 329.

p. 229 'we shall see what we shall see': *London Letters*, 18, 30 January 1832, 324.

p. 229 'intimate union between England and Russia upon which the peace of the world so mainly depended': BL, Heytesbury, ADD. MSS. 41563, Heytesbury to Palmerston, 4 February 1832.

p. 229 there was much talk of it on the British side: C. K. Webster, *The Foreign Policy of Palmerston*, vol. I (1951), 151–2; K. Bourne, *Palmerston: the Early Years* (1982), 344–5.

p. 229 'England would separate herself from her old Allies upon a question of mere form': BL, Heytesbury, ADD. MSS. 41563, Heytesbury to Palmerston, 9 February 1832.

p. 230 Casimir Périer, had been talking about the inevitability of an Anglo-French alliance if the three Eastern powers would not ratify the treaty: ibid., Palmerston to Heytesbury, 16 January 1831 [*sic* for 1832].

p. 230 'speaking of Russia as the natural ally of France': ibid., Heytesbury to Palmerston, 7 February 1831.

p. 230 'the true and only obstacle to a settlement is *Russia*': ibid., Palmerston to Heytesbury, 15 March 1832.

p. 230 'Metternich leads, & thinks, & acts, though generally upon mistaken Principles, still he is a man of talent and a leader': NA, Granville MSS. PRO 30/29/14/6, Palmerston to Granville, 6 April 1832.

p. 230 it should depend upon the Dutch King being satisfied on various details still in dispute: BL, Heytesbury, ADD. MSS. 41563, Heytesbury to Palmerston, 15 April 1832.

p. 231 'which she has professed to have been no less anxious than we are to avert': ibid., Palmerston to Heytesbury, 15 March 1832.

p. 231 'a miserable intrigue between the D. of Wellington & Metternich, & the D. of Cumberland & the Prussian Princes': Bourne, *Palmerston* I, 351–2.

p. 231 'an instinctive contempt of these arbitrary Cabinets, but it is only of late that I have learnt how just this sentiment has been': ibid., 352.

p. 232 'a change of policy' would lead to a 'change of persons': BL, Heytesbury, ADD. MSS. 41563, Heytesbury to Palmerston, 15 April 1832.

p. 232 'I shall continue to cultivate Lord Grey, although he bores me not a little': *London Letters*, 3 May 1832, 327.

p. 233 'I am quite annoyed at seeing that you no longer think of me': *Grey–Lieven* II, to Grey, 1 May 1832, 338.

p. 233 chided Grey for continuing to delay matters: ibid., to Grey, 4 May 1832, 340–41.

p. 233 'Ask your own conscience to whose fault it is owing that this has not been done long ago': ibid., from Grey, 4 May 1832, 343–4.

p. 233 'Let England and Russia only keep well together, and the peace of Europe will not be disturbed': ibid., to Grey, 5 May 1832, 344–5.

Chapter 17

p. 234 'They will wonder at it much in Russia': *Grey–Lieven* II, 27 June 1832, 358.

p. 234 'he may, through Lord Durham, direct the policy of the English Cabinet': *London Letters*, 17, 29 June 1832, 328.

p. 235 Palmerston's 'silence' in response: *Grey–Lieven* II, 29 June 1832, 359.

p. 235 accused in public of being a 'Russian tool', had said not a word in reply: BL, Lieven MSS., ADD. MSS. 47415, to Alexander, 29 June 1832, not in *London Letters*.

p. 235 whether he could not say something in the Lords to make amends for Palmerston's slowness: *Grey–Lieven* II, to Grey, 29 June 1832, 359.

p. 235 every honour that flattery could devise paid dividends: BL, Lieven MSS., ADD. MSS. 47415, to Alexander, 29 June 1832, not in *London Letters*.

p. 236 'Durham was thoroughly bamboozled by the Emperor and Nesselrode': NA, Granville MSS., PRO/30/29/14/6, Palmerston to Granville, 23 November 1832.

p. 236 'et voilà son *importante* mission terminée': *WCDM* VII, Princess Lieven to Wellington, 17 August 1832, 403.

p. 236 'show consideration for his son-in-law and daughter': *Grey–Lieven* II, to Grey, 6 August 1832, 374–5.

p. 236 'what satisfaction it would give to this country and to Europe': ibid., from Grey, 9 August 1832, 376.

p. 236 he should return to London via the other major courts of Europe: BL, Lieven MSS., ADD. MSS. 47355, Princess Lieven to Nesselrode, August 1832.

p. 236 'both for the public and for his own advantage': *Grey–Lieven* II, to Grey, 28 August 1832, 383.

p. 236 'no friend of agitators and revolutionaries': ibid., from Grey, 2 September 1832, 386–8.

p. 237 'where will be your strength?': BL, Lamb MSS., ADD. MSS. 45567, Fred Lamb to Palmerston, 12 September 1832.

p. 237 'Palmerston is a mule': BL, Lieven MSS., ADD. MSS. 47355, Princess Lieven to Nesselrode, 1 October 1832.

p. 237 exercising any control over her: BL, Lieven MSS., ADD. MSS. 47366, Palmerston to Princess Lieven, 28 September 1832.

p. 237 ['you say, stay united, I say let us move on together']: ibid., 28 October 1832.

p. 238 'he hopes to conceal his blunders': *London Letters*, 6, 18 October 1832, 331.

p. 238 as part of her campaign to displace him: C. K. Webster, *The Foreign Policy of Palmerston*, vol. I (1951), 197–8.

p. 238 'a Whig Peer of highly radical notions': ibid., 321 for all of this.

p. 238 a minister as friendly as Palmerston: BL, Lieven MSS., ADD. MSS. 47355, Princess Lieven to Nesselrode, 19 April 1831.

p. 239 lest she arouse Grey's jealousy: ibid., 19 April, 25 May 1831.

p. 239 Palmerston/Heytesbury correspondence, January to June 1832, *passim*.

p. 239 the crisis would never be settled: *Grey–Lieven* II, from Grey, 2 September 1832, 387.

p. 239 the 'disfavour shown by England': ibid., to Grey, 6 September 1832.

p. 239 'what are his impressions on Russian politics?': ibid., to Grey, 1 October 1832, 402.

p. 240 'must take measures in conjunction with France to bring this to a conclusion': Hartley Library, University of Southampton, Palmerston MSS. BP/GC/GR/2126, Grey to Palmerston, 1 July 1832.

p. 240 'the sooner Stratford Canning can go, the better': ibid., BP/GC/GR/2150, Grey to Palmerston, 29 September 1832.

p. 240 'Do you know the cause of this opposition to which I do not feel at all inclined to give way?': Webster, *Palmerston* I, Grey to Palmerston, 26 October 1832, 323.

p. 240 the appointment of Sir Stratford Canning as British ambassador to St Petersburg: ibid.

p. 240 since he could hardly speak in the Commons: BL, Lieven MSS., ADD. MSS. 47356B, Princess Lieven to Nesselrode, 1, 5 November 1832.

p. 240 he had never seen her 'so montée': Hartley Library, University of Southampton, Palmerston MSS. BP/GC/GR/2184, Grey to Palmerston, 2 November 1832.

p. 241 he had promised that Canning would not be nominated: ibid.

p. 241 he was doing no more than his duty: BL, Lieven MSS., ADD. MSS. 47366, Palmerston to Princess Lieven, 4 November 1832.

p. 241 she left them, she said, to her husband: ibid., Princess Lieven to Palmerston, n.d. but 5 November 1832, according to Southampton, Palmerston MSS. GC/LI/34.

p. 242 'to *taboo* our best men *merely because* they are so': K. Bourne, *Palmerston: the Early Years* (1982), 361.

p. 242 'wrath which belongs chiefly to more important matters': ibid., 362.

p. 242 'I don't see the possibility of yielding to such a proposal': Webster, *Palmerston* I, Grey to Palmerston, 29 December 1832, 325.

p. 242 Palmerston 'got piqued and angry and thwarted and then bad became worse': BL, Lamb MSS., ADD. MSS. 45551, Lady Cowper to Fred Lamb, 14 January 1833.

p. 243 finally borne in on her: BL, Lieven MSS., ADD. MSS. 47356B, Nesselrode to Princess Lieven, 14 January 1833.

p. 243 which was known only to one '*seule* et unique person': Hartley Library, University of Southampton, Palmerston MSS. GC/LI/36, Lieven to Palmerston, 26 January 1833.

p. 243 so the deadlock continued: S. Lane Poole, *Stratford Canning*, vol. II (1888), 30.

p. 245 'the one who holds the most enlightened opinions and the most conciliatory views': *London Letters*, 6, 18 June 1828, 134.

p. 247 'as I have none I do not get angry': *Grey–Lieven* II, from Grey and to Grey, 4, 5 December 1832, 423–4.

Chapter 18

p. 248 'your friendship assures me it will turn out in accordance with my desires': *Grey–Lieven* II, to Grey, 31 December 1832, 432.

p. 248 'I should be sorry to see the Lievens removed': Hartley Library,

University of Southampton, Palmerston MSS. GC/GR/2209, Grey to Palmerston, 17 February 1833.

p. 248 'telling you all that is on my mind': *Grey–Lieven* II, to Grey, 10 March 1832, 446.

p. 249 'should produce some impression': ibid., from Grey, 10 March 1832, 446–7.

p. 249 'our daily bread': *London Letters*, 17, 29 March 1833, 336.

p. 249 'the very spirit of goodwill: BL, Lieven MSS., ADD. MSS. 47356B, Princess Lieven to Nesselrode, 2, 14 June 1833; as usual, translations are the author's own.

p. 249 to be relieved of Canning: BL, Lieven MSS., ADD. MSS. 47253, Nesselrode to Prince Lieven, 20 June, 23 July 1833.

p. 250 'marks of his confidence and his friendship': *Grey–Lieven* II, to Grey, 16 July 1933, 454.

p. 250 directly with the Tsar through her brother, Alexander: C. K. Webster, *The Foreign Policy of Palmerston*, vol. I (1951), 329–32.

p. 250 'furious at our Treaty with Turkey': *London Letters*, 10, 22 August 1833, 340–41.

p. 251 'his aim is to dethrone the Sultan . . . and to put the son of the Sultan in his place': NA, FO/214, Barker to Palmerston, 12 August 1832.

p. 251 take control of Constantinople: F. S. Rodkey, 'Lord Palmerston and the rejuvenation of Turkey, 1830–41' in *Transactions of the Royal Historical Society*, 1929; M. Vereté, 'Palmerston and the Levant Crisis, 1832' in *Journal of Modern History*, 1952, for Palmerston's views.

p. 252 'it will do their stomachs good, after all': *London Letters*, 10, 22 August 1833, 341–2.

p. 252 but he found Grey less than eager to do so: Hartley Library, University of Southampton, Palmerston MSS. GC/GR/2257, Grey to Palmerston, 5 October 1833.

p. 253 'no serious resistance need ever be apprehended': ibid. GC/GR/2378, Palmerston to Grey, 8 October 1833.

p. 253 if other ministers agreed with Palmerston: ibid. GC/GR/2260, Grey to Palmerston, 9 October 1833.

p. 253 he had circulated a copy of it: ibid. GC/GR/2261, Grey to Palmerston, 10 October 1833.

p. 254 Grey refused to discuss the matter with her: BL, Lieven MSS.,

ADD. MSS. 47356B, Princess Lieven to Nesselrode, 12, 24 November 1833.

p. 254 Durham and others would stop the protest: Webster, *Palmerston* I, 316–17.

p. 254 had Grey had his way, would have been correct: BL, Lieven MSS., ADD. MSS. 47356B, Princess Lieven to Nesselrode, 1833 for the evidence.

p. 255 it now seemed, he was incorrect: Webster, *Palmerston* I, 246.

p. 255 declined to do so on Canning's behalf: A. Kriegel, *The Holland House Diaries 1831–1840* (1977), 30 August 1833, 244.

p. 255 if Wellington and the Tories came to power: BL, Lieven MSS., ADD. MSS. 47356B, Princess Lieven to Nesselrode, 11, 24 November 1833.

p. 256 Russia's firm rebuff of the British protest: *London Letters*, 13, 25 December 1833, 359–60; BL, Lieven MSS., ADD. MSS. 47356B, Princess Lieven to Nesselrode, 14, 26 December 1833.

p. 256 Grey's emollience across the range of issues that now divided the two countries: *London Letters*, 12, 24 January 1834, 364–6; BL, Lieven MSS., ADD. MSS. 47356B, Princess Lieven to Nesselrode, 5, 17 January 1834.

p. 256 Canning as ambassador to St Petersburg: BL, Lieven MSS., ADD. MSS. 47356B, Princess Lieven to Nesselrode, 21 January 1834.

p. 256 'is not brilliant at that': *London Letters*, 28 January, 6 February 1834, 369.

p. 256 She dismissed this as 'une bêtise': BL, Lieven MSS., ADD. MSS. 47356B, Princess Lieven to Nesselrode, 16 March 1834.

p. 256 her 'nourishment for the last 22 years': ibid., 24 April, 6 May 1834; also see *London Letters*, 29 April, 11 May 1834, 375–6.

p. 257 'I have not power sufficiently to express': *Grey–Lieven* II, from Grey, 22 May 1834, 498–9.

p. 257 'I feel so sick at heart': ibid., to Grey, 23 May 1834, 499.

p. 257 'many friends wholly independent of politics': *London Letters*, 29 April, 11 May 1834.

p. 257 Duchess of Dino described as 'a national disgrace': Princess Radziwill, *Memoirs of the Duchesse de Dino*, vol. I (1909), 62.

p. 257 'this supercilious Ambassadress': *The Times*, 23 May 1834.

p. 258 a little harsh in her allocation of tickets for Almack's: Radziwill, *Memoirs* I, 24 May 1834, 62.

p. 258 'he was chilly on the right and breezy on the left, and obviously ill at ease': ibid., 29 May 1834, 67.

p. 258 'no less struck by the sincerity of the avowal than annoyed by its implication': ibid., 1 June 1834, 70.

p. 259 took his ill humour out on Emily: ibid., 19 June 1834, 94.

p. 259 'on her departure by some English ladies of her particular acquaintance (July 1834)': ibid., 18 June 1834, 93.

p. 259 'a melancholy occasion': ibid., 1 August 1834, 145.

p. 260 She is gone with the bows on her shoulder: H. M. Hyde, *Princess Lieven* (1938), 153.

Conclusion

p. 261 'very different from those which have been my daily bread for twenty-five years': E. Jones Parry (ed.), *The Correspondence of Lord Aberdeen and Princess Lieven, 1832–1854*, 2 vols. (1938–9) [hereafter *Aberdeen–Lieven* and volume number], 11, 23 October 1834, 19.

p. 261 'I feel we are such a long way off one from the other': *Grey–Lieven* III, to Grey, 8 November 1834, 46.

p. 261 'I am vegetating in this most atrocious of climates': ibid., 2 December 1834, 54.

p. 261 the rigours of the Russian winter: ibid., 4 January 1835, 70.

p. 261 'A great man greatly fallen!': ibid., 7 February 1835, 84.

p. 262 'Was any bereavement more complete than mine?': ibid., 22 April 1835, 106.

p. 262 'possible for me to venture there now': ibid., 30 July 1835, 139.

p. 262 'letting her be more *exigeante* than suits me': *Granville Corr.* II, Lady Granville to Devonshire, 28 September 1835, 196–7.

p. 262 'She always has an *entourage*': ibid., Lady Granville to Lady Carlisle, January 1837, 221.

p. 262 'the will of those in power in St Petersburg': *Grey–Lieven* III, to Grey, 8 October 1836, 212.

p. 263 a reserve in their conversation: *Aberdeen–Lieven* I, to Aberdeen, 30 July 1837, 72.

p. 263 on her guard against such a notorious intriguer: *Diary*, 195.

p. 263 rivalry with the Duchess of Dino once more flourished: *Lieven–Palmerston*, 14 March 1836, 120–21.

p. 263 'a country for which he had great admiration': *Diary*, 197.

p. 264 'as unhappy at the end of two years as I was at the beginning': J. Navile (ed.), *Lettres de François Guizot et de la Princesse de la Lieven*, 3 vols. (Paris, 1963) [hereafter *Guizot–Lieven* and volume number], to Guizot, 16 February 1837, 2–3.

p. 264 'without any political thoughts': F. Guizot, *Mélanges biographiques et littéraires* (Paris, 1868), 211.

p. 264 she and Guizot became lovers: *Guizot–Lieven* I, to Guizot, 24 June 1839, 245.

p. 264 matters could be arranged to her satisfaction: ibid., four o'clock, 23 July 1837, 47–8.

p. 264 'the old life I led for so long': ibid., 25 July 1837, 49.

p. 264 'I shall be spared any private gossip': *Lieven–Palmerston*, to Lady Cowper, 4 September 1837, 136.

p. 265 'very cold': *Guizot–Lieven* I, to Guizot, 28 August 1837, 89.

p. 265 'I fear nothing': ibid., 30 August 1837, 90.

p. 265 a word that her doctors wrote about her health: ibid., 24 September 1837, 119.

p. 265 'I have need of laughter, this is very serious': ibid., 25 September 1837, 121.

p. 265 'Because I am ill in Paris?': ibid., 27 September 1837, 125.

p. 265 'one still clings to life': *Grey–Lieven* III, to Grey, 8 November 1837, 248.

p. 266 ordered to by his Tsar: *Guizot–Lieven I*, to Guizot, 1 October 1837, 132.

p. 266 'this is what I expect will happen': *Lieven–Palmerston*, from Lady Cowper, 13 November 1831, 139.

p. 266 Prince Alexander, and not his father: *Guizot–Lieven* I, to Guizot, 19 October 1837, 143–4.

p. 266 persuade him otherwise: ibid., 20 October 1837, 145.

p. 266 'he should seek revenge': BL, Lieven MSS., ADD. MSS. 47415, Alexander von Benckendorff to Dorothea, 1837.

p. 266 'he punishes me': BL, Lieven MSS., ADD. MSS. 47416, draft of letter from Dorothea, 1837.

p. 266 '"What is the point of it all?"': *Lieven–Palmerston*, to Lady Cowper, 17 February 1838, 145–6.

p. 267 'bored me to death': *Guizot–Lieven* I, to Guizot, 31 August 1837, 92.

p. 267 'yes, organise me': ibid., 14 September 1837, 97.

p. 267 she loved him dearly: ibid., 22 July 1838, 172.

p. 267 'Ah! That is terrible!': ibid., 26 April 1838, 182.

p. 267 'I shall never fathom': *Lieven–Palmerston*, to Lady Cowper, 23 March 1838, 147.

p. 267 'when we meet again': BL, Lieven MSS., ADD. MSS. 47406, from Prince Lieven, May 1838.

p. 267 4,000 francs a month: *Guizot–Lieven* I, to Guizot, 28 June 1838, 158.

p. 268 'Is it together or separately that we are to live this last act of our lives?': BL, Lieven MSS., ADD. MSS. 47406, from Prince Lieven, August 1838.

p. 268 'you scorn my character': *Guizot–Lieven* I, to Guizot, 5 September 1838, 188–9.

p. 268 'still believe you to be': ibid., from Guizot, 7 September 1838, 190–91.

p. 268 'sympathy with your sorrow': ibid., 10 September 1838, 193–4.

p. 268 'how much I love you': ibid., 18 September 1838, 202–3.

p. 269 'the sport of evil fortune than I am?': *Grey–Lieven* III, to Grey, 13 November 1838, 282–4.

p. 269 what they thought of his behaviour: *Lieven–Palmerston*, to Lady Cowper, 14 November 1838, 157–9.

p. 269 'who has behaved shamefully': *Granville Corr.* II, Lady Granville to Devonshire, 18 November 1838, 274.

p. 269 could best get relief: BL, Lieven MSS., ADD. MSS. 47406, Prince to Princess Lieven, December 1838.

p. 269 asked Lady Cowper to write to him: *Lieven–Palmerston*, to Lady Cowper, 16 December 1838, 161.

p. 270 'desolation all around me': *Aberdeen–Lieven* I, to Aberdeen, 23 February 1839, 122–4.

p. 270 'no future to look forward to': *Grey–Lieven* III, to Grey, 18 February 1839, 292–3.

p. 270 'sympathy in your unhappiness': *Lieven–Palmerston*, from Lady Cowper, 16 December 1838, 161–2.

p. 270 diamonds to him via Granville: ibid., to Lady Cowper, 26 April 1839, 166–7.

p. 270 discouraging news: ibid., 27 July, 1, 18 August 1839, 167–9.

p. 270 'nobody but myself should see it': *Granville Corr.* II, Lady Granville to Devonshire, 11 January 1839, 279.

pp. 270–71 sufficient in Paris: *Grey–Lieven* III, to Lord Grey, 23 May 1839, 301.

p. 271 'She don't go to England': Lady Airlie, *Lady Palmerston and Her Times*, vol. II (1922), from Frederick Lamb, 17 June 1839, 20.

p. 271 'miserable earth?': *Granville Corr.* II, Lady Granville to Lady Carlisle, 23 July 1839, 292.

p. 271 'I promise to give him mine': *Lieven–Palmerston*, to Lady Cowper, 23 December 1839, 177.

p. 271 'announced as Madame Guizot!: Lytton Strachey, *Portraits in Miniature* (1931), Madame de Lieven, 138.

p. 272 'this more easy': *Aberdeen–Lieven* I, 10 February 1840, 132–3.

p. 272 Guizot saw in London: *Guizot–Lieven* II, from Guizot, 28 February 1840, 3.

p. 272 'the lion of my *soirée*': *Lieven–Palmerston*, from Lady Cowper, February 1840, 183.

p. 272 the judge of that: *Guizot–Lieven* II, to Guizot, 15 March 1840, 28–9.

p. 272 Dorothea's jealousy: ibid., 15, 17 March 1840, 28–30.

p. 272 'the pleasures of my nullity': *Lieven–Palmerston*, 7 May 1840, 186–7.

p. 272 'one's old reminiscences and recollections': Hatfield House, Diary of Lady Palmerston, 28 February 1840.

p. 273 lectures on constitutionalism: BL, Lamb MSS., ADD. MSS. 45554, Emily to Palmerston, 4, 5 October 1849.

p. 273 'I thought her sincere': *ibid.*, 24 January 1849.

p. 273 'slow' and 'boring': *Lettres Metternich*, 381.

p. 274 buried beside two of her sons, George and Arthur: H. M. Hyde, *Princess Lieven* (1938), 272–4.

p. 274 'I believe them readily': *Private Letters*, 17 June 1822, 179.

Index

(DL = Dorothea Lieven)